Performance Management

PH SERIES IN HUMAN RESOURCES MANAGEMENT

Performance Management

PH SERIES IN HUMAN RESOURCES MANAGEMENT

HARI DAS • ST. MARY'S UNIVERSITY

ANDREW TEMPLER, SERIES EDITOR • UNIVERSITY OF WINDSOR

Prentice Hall

Toronto

National Library of Canada Cataloguing in Publication

Das, Hari, 1948-
 Performance management / Hari Das.

(PH series in human resources management)
Includes index.
ISBN 0-13-041379-8

1. Performance—Management. 2. Employees—Rating of. I. Title. II. Series.

HF5549.5.P35D38 2003   658.3'14   C2002-904604-1

0-13-041379-8

Vice President, Editorial Director: Michael J. Young
Acquisitions Editor: James Bosma
Executive Marketing Manager: Cas Shields
Associate Editor: Angela Kurmey
Production Editor: Mary Ann McCutcheon
Copy Editor: Jennifer Therriault
Production Coordinator: Janette Lush
Page Layout: Phyllis Seto
Art Director: Julia Hall
Cover and Interior Design: Amy Harnden
Cover Image: PhotoDisc

1 2 3 4 5   07 06 05 04 03

Printed and bound in Canada.

Dedicated to:

Great teachers like Peter Frost, Vance Mitchell, Walter Nord, Ken MacCrimmon and Merle Ace, who inspired me toward high performance

Stimulating students like A.R. Elangovan, Don Bell, Mary Harriman, Chuck Bridges and Mary Mahoney, who continuously sought high performance from me

Inspiring professional colleagues like Hermann Schwind, Viswanath Baba, Albert Mills, Colin Dodds and Craig Pinder, who set high standards of performance for me, and

Mallika and Nitya who, in their loving way, continuously comforted, cajoled and at times coaxed me into high performance when I was least able to perform.

This book is for you.

Brief Contents

Contents

FOREWORD

HRM in a New Economy

Most readers will remember the newspaper headlines proclaiming September 11, 2001 as "the day the world changed." Whether this will prove true or not remains to be seen, but a more certain change in the world of work in Canada has been occurring with much less fanfare. This is the new economic reality in which knowledge-based businesses are replacing the commodity and manufacturing engines of the past. In what *The Economist* terms "a survey of the near future," Peter Drucker, the management guru, argues that, where we have been used to measuring our success through making things, the basis for success in the next society is knowledge—what we know and how we use it.[1]

We are on the threshold of change at least as radical as the Industrial Revolution. At the beginning of the twenty-first century, with respect to knowledge management, we are as advanced as industrial management was at the beginning of the twentieth century. Changing demographics and the growth in knowledge-work mean that the assumptions still held by many HRM professionals about the nature of the workforce no longer hold true. In the near future, most workers will no longer be full-time employees and knowledge-workers will dominate the total workforce. Stability, growth, monopolistic markets, and predictable technology characterized yesterday's reality. The next society will be a knowledge-society characterized by "borderlessness," increased opportunity, and instability.

As the importance of knowledge and its application to organizational innovations increase, HRM professionals are in a position, as never before, to play a vital role in the effectiveness of organizations. The problem is the gap between promise and delivery.

Where is HRM today? Most of what constitutes the field of HRM is based on thinking developed through industrial management in the past decades and most HRM texts reflect this traditional world. It is not surprising that recent studies indicate most HRM practitioners do not consult academic research and are frustrated at the lack of application and current relevance of what they do take the time to read. A hopeful sign is that the importance of HRM knowledge is increasingly recognized by tomorrow's generation. In a recent survey of HRPAO members, almost three-quarters of HRM professionals with less than 12 years experience reported that specialist education had played a highly significant role in their career progression.[2]

The development of the HRM field is also demonstrated in the growth of a national Certified Human Resources Professional (CHRP) designation across Canada, characterized by a mix of HRM knowledge and applied professional competencies. Students of HRM seeking the knowledge and application base necessary for achieving this designation and success in the profession will find the new Prentice Hall Series in Human Resources Management an essential element of this goal.

The Prentice Hall HRM Series

The Prentice Hall HRM series is designed for today's HRM students, instructors, and professionals who need access to HRM knowledge reflecting current realities (rather

---

[1] P.F. Drucker, "The Next Society, Special Survey," *The Economist*, 3 November 2001, 1-20.

[2] A.J. Templer and M. Belcourt. *HRPAO Professional Standards Education Survey*. Toronto: HRPAO, 2001.

than yesterday's traditions) in a usable and applied format that considers the time pressures within which they must succeed. Some of the key characteristics of the series are:

- Emphasis on the practical
- Ease of use and flexibility
- Applicability to daily HRM situations
- Guidelines for fostering leadership and strategic vision
- Guidelines for evaluating an organization's effectiveness
- Focus on innovations in HRM

The series intends to match all the key knowledge requirements of professional certification, but with an eye to the evolving nature of these requirements and the changed nature of HRM contribution in a knowledge economy. As such, I am pleased to announce our first text in the series, *Performance Management*, which clearly addresses the fundamental human contribution to organization performance.

Performance Management

Performance Management, by Hari Das, recognizes that effective HRM cannot begin from a traditional overview of "personnel department" activities, but from a comprehensive rethink of the role HRM professionals perform by facilitating employee performance. As the author points out, performance management is an ongoing process that attempts to match employee contributions with organizational goals and strategies. While recognizing the importance of work standards and the need for corrective actions, the focus is organizational success and an efficient integration of all organizational systems.

The text is organized around an integrating model of performance management encompassing five major HRM contribution dimensions: performance planning, performance facilitation, performance assessment, performance improvement, and performance system enhancement. In keeping with the goals of the series, *Performance Management* brings the best of knowledge and practical learning to the student and instructor. Much of the strategic application draws upon the author's excellent base in organization theory, while a real strength of the text is in its features and usable end-of-chapter material. The use of current cases, critical thinking questions, and web research will aid professionals and students alike.

Dr. Andrew Templer
Odette School of Business Administration
University of Windsor
2002

PREFACE

We are at the threshold of a major revolution in the way humans live and work, making it a very exciting era. Consider the following facts:

- The information contained in hundreds of thousands of pages can be stored on a small diskette and we can access it whenever and wherever we choose.
- We can travel to any part of the world in mere hours rather than the months or years it took in the not-too-distant past.
- Travel to outer space and living under the sea is no longer just a fantasy. Indeed, in the near future, they may become routine events.
- The cost of decoding a human gene is just a few hundred dollars today—it used to cost millions of dollars, even in the recent past.
- Massive amounts of information can be transmitted worldwide in a fraction of a minute by simply clicking a mouse.
- Billions of dollars of capital move across national borders each hour—something unthinkable to our ancestors.
- Whether you live in downtown New York City, a remote village in Africa, or a small island in the South Pacific, you can tune in to your favourite music or news program at your convenience.

These developments have changed the way we think, work, and live. Already, a large number of people don't have to travel to their workplaces to perform their duties—a major shift from the lifestyle we inherited from the industrial revolution of the eighteenth century. Many organizations have made their employees part owners, violating traditional assumptions of the employer-employee relationship. The more knowledgeable workers of today also do not want to be led by others. In many settings, they can and want to design, execute, and evaluate plans themselves. Hence, traditional notions of leader-follower relations have become irrelevant in today's work settings. Today, an organization's competition does not emerge from next door, from an adjacent province, or even from within the country. The competitor for a Canadian shoe or garment manufacturer, for example, may live in a small town in Korea or a village in India. Sometimes, we cannot even identify competitors in time to take actions.

This means that, to succeed, today's organization has to be agile—thinking, performing and changing continuously. To survive, it must meet the ever-changing needs of the market and constituents. To prosper, today's organization must be:

- Focused—knowing its strengths and market requirements well and responding to them;
- Fastidious—aiming for perfection and precision, continuously improving quality;
- Flexible—always changing its practices to meet emerging challenges and priorities; and
- Fast—responding in time and more quickly than the competition to the market needs.

Continuously monitoring and upgrading performance is critical whether the organization is profit seeking, private, non-profit, or governmental. Lethargy and inefficiency guarantee failure and possible extinction.

Performance Management is written to help you improve your own performance as well as that of your organization and workforce. While this book is primarily written for students in universities and colleges who pursue business studies, any manager, owner, or employee of any type of organization will find something inside that will help to improve individual employee or larger organizational performance. The following characteristics of the book help to achieve this improvement:

- A practical approach to defining, measuring, and improving performance. All major relevant theories are discussed from a practitioner's viewpoint rather than that of an armchair theorist.
- An abundance of case studies from real organizations and incidents based on real life events. The book examines how organizations responded to various situations—both successful and, at times, unsuccessful.
- A large number of forms and "how to" lists aid in the implementation of the various approaches discussed.
- Many figures and diagrams make it easy to understand the linkages among various concepts and procedures.
- A discussion of the latest concepts, including six sigma, ISO standards, and on-line performance monitoring techniques.
- Presentation of ethical issues critical for successful and long-term performance enhancement.

For the Student

This book is written with your needs in mind. Whether you are a novice in the area of performance management or coming to this field with experience and prior studies in the area of human resource management, you are likely to find several items here that will challenge and develop your thinking further. In particular, the following features are intended to make the learning process not only easier, but also interesting and exciting:

- A thought provoking opening quote in each chapter introduces you to the topic and stimulates your interest in the material.
- The learning objectives in each chapter inform you of the learning outcomes you can expect.
- All chapters begin with an example from a real organization relevant to the topics discussed in the chapter. Many incidents based on real organizations are also provided to help you recognize the importance of the subject matter discussed in the chapter.
- An easy-to-read, jargon-free language is used.
- Over fifty real life examples are used to illustrate the various concepts. In addition, dozens of incidents based on real life events are included to help you relate the material to real life situations.
- All key terms are bolded the first time they appear in the chapter, their definitions are produced in the margins for easy reference and retrieval, and a list, with page references, is provided within the end-of-chapter material.
- Over fifty figures are used to illustrate relevant ideas and concepts.
- A self-test in each chapter helps you relate important concepts to your personal life.
- Focus on Ethics and Focus on Small Business boxes in each chapter help you relate the material to other settings and reflect on important matters.
- Critical thinking questions challenge you to expand on what you have learned by discussing broader, real life relationships.
- A case incident at the end of each chapter helps you relate the chapter material to the solving of a practical problem.

- Each chapter contains several website links, shown in the margins, which help you conduct further research.

For the Instructor

Performance Management includes a variety of features to help instructors prepare and present the material.

- A PowerPoint® presentation is available to help you present the chapter material in class.
- Discussion Questions at the end of each chapter help you test the students' understanding of the chapter material and suggest topics for class or group discussions.
- The latest information on important concepts like Canadian competitiveness, the global trade challenge, and diversity management are covered, helping to make the material relevant in today's world.
- A Web Research question at the end of each chapter helps you assign outside class projects that can add value and currency to class discussions.
- The Case Incidents at the end of each chapter provide material for lively class discussions while the Cases help you test the students' ability to synthesize and integrate the material learned.
- Focus on Small Business boxes (one per chapter) help you relate the chapter material to the needs of small businesses.
- Focus on Ethics boxes (one per chapter) provide material for lively class discussions on a number of important topics.
- The easy-to-read and understand language used in the text, combined with the large number of real life examples, facilitate student comprehension and heighten student interest to conduct further research.
- A comprehensive Instructor's Manual, containing answers to Discussion Questions and multiple-choice questions, accompanies the text.

For the Practitioner and Trainer

Whether you are using this book for personal development or to train or advise others, you will find several features of this book attractive.

- More than fifty real life examples and incidents help you relate performance management concepts to practical work settings.
- The Implications for Practice section at the end of each chapter helps you apply key concepts to real life settings.
- Sample forms included in the text help you readily collect and store performance-related information.
- The Focus on Small Business box in each chapter helps you recognize the unique challenges of owner-operated and small units.
- A "how to" approach is stressed, making it easier to apply the various concepts.
- The text helps you implement new procedures that result in immediate improvements. Ideas like training evaluation techniques, quality control, and employee counselling emphasize the generation of practical results.

ACKNOWLEDGEMENTS

The writing of any book requires the cooperation and support of many persons. *Performance Management* is no exception to this. I am deeply indebted to a number of reviewers who commented on the manuscript and provided valuable and constructive suggestions. The book is stronger because of the comments coming from:

Debby Cleveland, BCIT

Jane Guzar, Mohawk College

Suzanne Kavanagh, George Brown College

Dr. Beverly Linnell, SAIT

David McPherson, Humber College

Shirley Richards, Humber College

Bob Russell, Assiniboine College

Dr. Andrew Templer, University of Windsor

Verlie Thomas, Mount Royal College

Diane White, CHRP Seneca College

I am also thankful to a number of my professional colleagues who helped me in producing and improving the manuscripts. Particularly noteworthy here are Shripad Pendse and Hermann Schwind of Saint Mary's. A number of my students were "guinea pigs" for class testing of cases and incidents included in the text. I would like to thank all of them for their patience and helpful suggestions in improving the material.

A very special thank you goes to the editorial staff of Pearson Education Canada. Developmental Editor Susanne Marshall, who shepherded the text from beginning to end, was a strong believer in the book and made several constructive suggestions which enhanced its quality. I am also thankful to James Bosma, Acquisitions Editor, and Mary Ann McCutcheon, Production Editor. Finally, I would like to mention my special thanks to Mike Ryan, former Executive Acquisitions Editor at Pearson, who initiated the project. But for Mike's persistent efforts, this book would have never emerged.

Last but not least, I want to express my gratitude to my wife Mallika and daughter Nitya. During the preparation of the manuscript, Mallika not only took care of my home duties but also actively critiqued several parts of the book, especially a number of cases and incidents. I often had to resort to the help of my daughter Nitya to supply me with the right word for the occasion. Her comments often helped think of patterns that I could not have conceived myself.

Hari Das

Hari Das received his M.Sc and Ph.D in business management from University of British Columbia, specializing in organizational behaviour and change. Before entering academia, he trained as an accountant and management consultant. He is a qualified accountant and an associate member of the Institute of Cost and Works Accountants of India, Calcutta.

Dr. Das is currently Professor at Saint Mary's University, where he teaches international management, performance management, human resources management and research methodology at the graduate and doctoral levels. In the past, Dr. Das served as the director of the MBA program and the chair of the Department of Management and has received a teaching excellence award for his work in Saint Mary's EMBA Program.

Dr. Das has written over 100 papers in areas such as organizational control, power, organizational change, training and development, and research methodology, with a number of his papers winning best paper awards at conferences. He wrote *Organizational Theory with Canadian Applications*, the first Canadian text in the area of organizational theory. His co-authored work, *Canadian Human Resource Management*, is a market leader in its field. It is used in over 70 colleges and universities in Canada and has sold over 150 000 copies. His book *Strategic Organizational Design for Canadian Firms in a Global Economy* examined the challenge of preparing Canadian firms to face today's global economy.

Dr. Das has served as consultant to a variety of private and public organizations. In addition to being a member of the Academy of Management and the Administrative Sciences Association of Canada, he has served as an academic reviewer for a number of journals and research agencies such as Shastri Indo-Canadian Institute and Social Sciences and Humanities Research Council.

Dr. Das can be reached at the following address: hari.das@stmarys.ca.

PART 1

PERFORMANCE MANAGEMENT FRAMEWORK

Performance management helps an organization define and achieve long-term and short-term goals vital to its success. Performance management has assumed a critical role today because of the economic, technological, legal, social, and cultural challenges faced by work organizations. Part 1 explores some of these challenges and outlines a performance management model upon which the rest of the book builds.

1 IMPORTANCE OF PERFORMANCE MANAGEMENT

More and more organizations are viewing the development of a performance management system as beneficial.[1]

Dana Robinson and James Robinson

CHAPTER OBJECTIVES

After studying this chapter, you should be able to:

- Define performance management

- Discuss the environmental trends that make performance management critical today

- List the steps used to implement a performance management system

- Outline the considerations when establishing a performance management department

Why did Eaton's, once dominant in the Canadian retail industry, declare bankruptcy? How did Laidlaw, a darling of many Canadian investors until mid 1990s, lose over 90% of its market value in less than seven months and face bankruptcy in 2001? Why is Pan Am, a major world airline fifty years ago, just a memory today? How did Enron, the U.S. energy giant, expand into one of the largest organizations in the world only to declare bankruptcy later? How did Microsoft achieve global domination in technology in less than fifty years? What makes Bombardier and Royal Bank of Canada consistently profitable while other firms in similar industries have not faired as well? How did Japanese car makers like Toyota and Honda become household names in North America yet the much bigger General Motors and Ford found it hard to crack the Japanese market?

There are no simple answers. No single factor can explain the success or failure of organizations. It has been suggested that a key factor differentiates the not-so-successful firms from the successful ones: a failure to reflect.[2] Many firms are so caught up in carrying out their day-to-day work that they rarely, if ever, stop to think objectively about themselves and their businesses. The link between organizational goals, strategies, and employee performance becomes tenuous and the organization's goals become socially irrelevant or unattainable. When a firm's competitors are offering more innovative and value-adding alternatives, the not-so-successful firm fails to re-evaluate its mission. A successful firm asks probing questions to change basic assumptions, refresh strategies, and enhance performance goals, thereby reinventing to keep up with the competitors. The resulting downward spiral brings in lower organizational resources that, in turn, lower capabilities and overall performance.

While the above argument provides an important insight, it should be noted that organizational success is often influenced by external, uncontrollable factors. Global and domestic competition, rapid changes in technology, and the growing diversity of the workforce are just a few factors that continuously pose challenges to organizations and question the continued relevance of their strategies. The organization may become unsuccessful over time unless there is a correct fit between the environment and the organization's strategies and systems.[3] Errors happen. Policies become outdated. These factors may cause a downward spiral of organizational performance and success.

Today, a continuous review and planning of organizational, departmental, and individual performance within the context of larger environments is vital for organizational success. This book is about performance—here, we learn to define, measure, reward, and improve performance to achieve organizational, employee, and societal needs. This chapter provides an overview of a performance management model that is detailed in the following eight chapters. Before we go any further we need to define performance management and its underlying philosophy.

Meaning of Performance Management

Performance management is an ongoing process that articulates organizational vision and objectives, identifies and installs organizational and individual performance standards in light of these objectives, and takes corrective action to ensure accomplishment of these standards using systems and procedures that are well-integrated with organizational culture and practices. The definition of performance management underscores several important dimensions of the process.

Ongoing Process

A sound performance management system is a planned, ongoing process, not an isolated or one-time exercise. It is an integral part of an organization's overall plan to compete and succeed in the market place. Organizations with performance management systems have clear plans, objectives, targets, and standards of performance. They also strive to improve performance through a variety of activities including continuous process improvement and total quality management.

Focus on Organizational Vision and Objectives

Performance management is an ongoing process to attain and enhance organizational success. It contributes to the achievement of organizational objectives and is

---

Performance management is an ongoing process that identifies organizational vision and objectives, installs organizational and individual performance standards, and ensures these standards using systems and procedures that are well-integrated with organizational culture and practices.

closely related to organizational strategy. The performance management system and the larger human resource practices are driven by an overall organizational philosophy to take timely corrective actions. The performance management system also provides the necessary information on employee performance. Consider the case of SaskTel.

> Avoiding layoffs is part of the managerial philosophy that Regina based SaskTel practices. SaskTel, Saskatchewan's Crown-owned telephone company, chosen as one of the best employers in Canada in 2001, has been around since 1908, and has never laid off an employee. By diversifying its services, SaskTel has been able to retain most of its business and employees. In return, the firm enjoys one of the most loyal workforces and is the employer of choice for most local residents. As one employee put it, "If you told your mother you'd turned down a job at SaskTel, she'd shoot you."[4]

IMPORTANCE OF PERFORMANCE STANDARDS

Instead of vague and unattainable performance standards, good performance management systems focus on specific, time-bound, and realistic performance goals that are accepted by employees. In organizations like Federal Express, the standards only provide minimum acceptable performance levels.

> According to Jon Slangerup, a past Vice President of Federal Express, "the issue is not that employees are not getting their work done. It's a matter of discretionary effort-having employees do things above and beyond the call of duty every single day. To me, that is the difference between a great company and a good one."[5]

FOCUS ON PERFORMANCE IMPROVEMENT

Performance related information must be collected, analyzed, and communicated to all concerned on a timely basis in order to improve organizational effectiveness. When performance is below standard, factors inhibiting high performance are identified and separated for review and modification. In the case of employees who perform at or above standards, the review process should reinforce performance and attempt to improve it. Superior performance should be related, whenever feasible, to the career and self-development of the employee concerned. In general, organizations with superior performance management systems focus on improving future performance rather than dwelling on past mistakes. Maritime Life Assurance is a good example of a company that fosters a climate of continued performance improvement.

> Maritime Life Assurance Company, of Halifax, is a progressive employer in the country. The company provides each of its 1900 employees with a Career Investment Account; an annual stipend that employees can use to purchase career development materials ranging from business journals to home Internet accounts. Employees can also use the funds to pay tuition for university courses. The focus of Maritime Life is on upgrading employee skills so that they are able to anticipate and meet emerging challenges and take on higher responsibilities.[6]

INTEGRATED SYSTEMS

The various procedures and systems employed in performance monitoring and enhancement should be well integrated. To maintain high performance levels, four activities are needed: performance planning, support for high performance, performance review, and performance development (Figure 1-1). Performance planning involves the identification of clear performance expectations that are understood by the employees. Fostering high performance is attempted through job design, improved working conditions, and reward systems. The performance review system ensures that performance deficiencies are identified on a timely basis and that employees who perform at or above expectations are recognized on a consistent basis. Performance development is attempted through a variety of training and coaching techniques and other employee development and organizational improvement programs.

Each of the components mentioned in Figure 1-1 should be consistent in scope and demands on the others.

> Training can provide new skills to employees, helping them to perform at higher levels. However, after training, employees need to be adequately rewarded for their efforts and offered an opportunity to use their new skills and competencies. Supervisors and the organization's reward system should encourage the use of newly learned skills to achieve higher performance.

Just as the individual performance management components should be consistent with the others, the entire performance management system should be consistent with the overall organizational character and culture. This point is elaborated in a later section of this chapter.

In summary, performance management aims to improve the productive contribution of individuals, teams, and departments while trying to attain organizational and individual employee objectives. Performance management is critical today for many reasons. The more important factors are detailed below.

CHALLENGES FACING CANADIAN ORGANIZATIONS

While Canadian organizations face a number of challenges today, five environmental trends that make performance management systems critical are discussed on the next page (Figure 1-2).

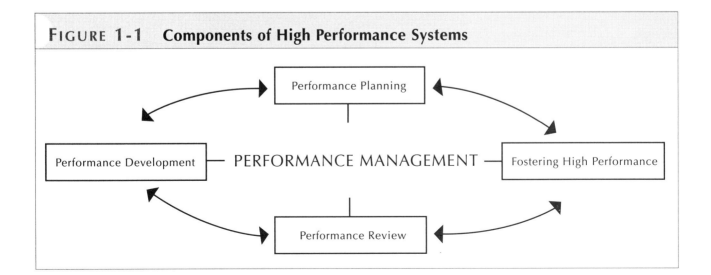

FIGURE 1-1   Components of High Performance Systems

Performance Planning

Performance Development — PERFORMANCE MANAGEMENT — Fostering High Performance

Performance Review

FIGURE 1-2   **Environmental Trends that Make It Critical to Have Performance Management**

Trend 1: Globalization and push for productivity improvement

Trend 2: Increasing importance of human capital

Trend 3: Increasing computerization and automation

Trend 4: Increasing workforce diversity

Trend 5: Increasing legal requirements

TREND 1: GLOBALIZATION AND THE PUSH FOR PRODUCTIVITY IMPROVEMENT

International trade has always been critical to Canada's prosperity and growth. Canada ranks high among exporting nations: With more than 200 trading partners, we export much more than either the U.S. or Japan on a per capita basis.[7]

> Canada's $418 billion worth of exports amounts to more than 40% of our gross domestic product (GDP). Our imports of $363 billion work out to approximately 35% of GDP. This means that more than ever before, Canadian economic prosperity is linked to global trade.[8] For example, Nortel played an important part in upgrading both Mexico's and China's telephone systems. Canadian banks like Royal Bank, TD Canada Trust, and CIBC have operations in most industrialized nations. Bombardier was involved in refurbishing Mexico's transportation system.

Expanding globalization has been a mixed blessing, however. As customers are exposed to many products and services, their expectations for better quality, service, and value increase. These higher expectations have to be met by improved performance to maintain customer satisfaction.[9] Further, the emergence of several low-cost trading nations with vast resources of highly skilled, cheap labour such as Thailand, China, and India, has caused Canada to lose its market shares in traditional strongholds such as pulp and paper, cotton yarn, and steel manufacturing. Unless we are able to add value to our products or reduce the costs of production, many firms may not be able to survive in the new market place.

The focus on improved productivity, necessitated by global competition, requires major changes in the way Canadian employers look at and manage their workforces. **Productivity**, the ratio of an organization's outputs (goods and services) to its inputs (people, capital, materials, and energy), increases as an organization finds new ways to use fewer resources to produce its output. In a business environment, productivity improvement is essential for long-run success. Through gains in productivity, managers can reduce costs, save scarce resources, and enhance profits.

> While Canadian productivity has been on the increase, our record is nowhere as impressive as that of our largest trading partner, the United States. Canadian productivity grew at a cumulative rate of 4.2% from 1996 to 1999; the comparable figure for the U.S. was 11.5%.[10]

According to a report released in August 2001 by Canadian Manufacturers and Exporters, Canada is last among the Group of Seven (G7) industrialized countries in terms of competitiveness.

> According to the study Canada's competitiveness earned 62 points out of a possible 100, compared to 94 for the U.S. (first place). Japan was second with 82 points, while the

Websites for productivity measurement:
www.policyalternatives.ca/ publications/articles/ article202.html

www3.sympatico.ca/dylan. reid/productivity.htm

Productivity is the ratio of an organization's outputs (goods and services) to its inputs (people, capital, materials, and energy).

European members of the G7 ranked in the 70s. Canada was last for the second year in a row; ten points behind sixth place France.[11]

In 1990, Canada ranked third among advanced economies in gross domestic product per capita, but by 1999 had fallen to fifth place. If Canada had retained its third place, the income for the average Canadian family of four would have been $10 000 higher in 1999 with an extra $500 a month in after-tax purchasing power.[12]

Another study estimates that if the gap in overall productivity growth between the U.S. and Canada persists, Canadian living standards would fall from 61% of U.S. levels in 1999 to 52% in 2010.[13] In recent years, Canadian managers and policy makers have recognized the urgency of improving Canadian productivity. The introduction of performance management systems and practices discussed in this text has both direct and indirect effects on productivity. Directly, operations become better and more efficient while indirectly, the introduction of these systems improves the quality of work life for employees.

Trend 2: Importance of Human Capital

Natural, financial, and technical resources alone do not provide competitive advantage to a business in today's knowledge-based economy. These traditional factors are widely available to all competitors in an industry. Further, having more money and advanced technology does not by default increase productivity. It is the ability of people to effectively and creatively use these resources, through their knowledge and skills, that generates value.[14]

Today's workforce can be divided into two main categories: information and non-information workers. Information workers may be either data or knowledge workers. Data occupations involve manipulation of symbolic information and knowledge occupations involve the development of ideas or expert opinions. Thus, data workers (i.e., most clerical occupations) use, transmit, or manipulate knowledge; knowledge workers (e.g., scientists, engineers, management consultants) produce it.[15] Non-information workers are those employed in the manufacturing and service sectors (e.g., machine operators and assemblers, security guards, babysitters).

Knowledge workers have been the fastest growing type of workers in the Canadian labour force in the last two decades or so.[16] The demand for knowledge workers is expected to be even higher in the foreseeable future.

> While total employment was growing at an average rate of 2.1% per year in the past two decades, the employment of knowledge workers grew at a rate of 5.2% per year. This is twice the pace of service workers, the second fastest-growing group of workers over that period. Today, information workers constitute over 54 % of the labour force. The proportion of labour force employed in blue-collar and unskilled jobs simultaneously reflects a decrease. In the foreseeable future, the demand for knowledge workers is likely to grow even faster than ever before.[17]

The ability of organizations to find, keep, and continually retrain highly skilled workers might spell success in the coming years. However, Canada's record in meeting this challenge has been less than enviable.

> Approximately 22% of Canadians 16 years of age or older (approximately 5 million people) fall in the lowest level of literacy, meaning they have difficulty with printed materials and most likely have problems reading.[18] Another 24 to 26% of Canadians fall in the second lowest level of literacy and can deal only with material that is simple and clearly laid out and where tasks involved are not too complex. About 30% of young Canadians drop out of school before they graduate. It is estimated that there are currently over 8 million Canadians without a basic school certificate or diploma.[19]

Low literary and numerical skills not only reduce the overall productivity levels in our industries, but may also be a major contributor to safety violations and accidents. Lack of these basic skills has also slowed down our ability to innovate and upgrade production processes.

> Canada is steadily losing its ability to innovate and create wealth compared with other rich countries, according to a study done by Massachusetts Institute of Technology in 1999. In the study, which ranked the 16 leading members of the Organization for Economic Cooperation and Development, Canada had slipped to ninth spot from sixth over the past decade. The study predicted that, unless Canada changes its course soon, the country will continue to lose ground. The report predicts that Canada will be tenth until 2005.[20]

Regardless of the industry—hi-tech, manufacturing, service, primary, or extractive—human capital is the key to success. Today, work is information based and becoming more of a mental activity.[21] Today's employee should be highly skilled and an active partner in all of a firm's effort. To effectively contribute in today's work environments, employees must have thinking, communication, learning, personal management skills (e.g., ability to accept responsibility, adaptability to new challenges), and teamwork skills (e.g., ability to work with others, ability to lead a team).[22] Labour is no longer a cost, but a form of capital on which the success and survival of a business depends.

Unfortunately, developing human capital takes years of effort, often at the national level. Individual firms may have to invest significant resources and time into changing organizational systems (e.g., recruiting, training) and culture. Since most employees do not work in isolation, training employees in group dynamics is of considerable importance. Some of the more progressive employers have recognized this challenge and have taken proactive actions to enhance employee skills.

> One manufacturer of conveyor belts for vegetable harvesters, located in P.E.I., converts its lunchrooms and offices into classrooms two evenings each week for employees and family members to update their math, reading, and writing skills. The project had a very positive impact on worker behaviour and attitude and the company was nominated for a national award for excellence in workplace literacy.[23]

TREND 3: INCREASING COMPUTERIZATION AND AUTOMATION

As in most developed countries, computers have become an integral part of Canadian life, changing the way we work and play.

> Currently, half of Canadian households have at least one person with regular access to the Internet. Over 40% of Canadian adults have access to the Internet, making us one of the most wired nations in the world.[24]

Part of the appeal of computers is that they make it possible to process large amounts of data and provide the information to managers. At the click of a mouse, a manager located in Guelph can compare the performance, pay, absenteeism, and safety records of its hourly and salaried workforce in Victoria and Halifax. The same manager can transfer large data files to India or Brazil in seconds. Often, decisions that took weeks in the past can now be made in minutes giving the information the important property of timeliness. In several instances, computers permit employees to **telecommute**—or work without ever leaving their homes by using the Internet, fax, phone, and other communication devices. Such telecommuting has been found to cut

Telecommuting is working from home using the Internet, fax, phone, and other communication devices.

employee stress and boost worker productivity in several instances, while at the same time reducing the costs of operations.[25]

> AT&T in the U.S. introduced telecommuting in selected departments and found that, in 80% of the cases, the change led to improved worker productivity and overall efficiency of departments.[26] A survey of 100 senior executives in Canada indicated that 57% felt that telecommuters were equal to or had greater productivity than the regular workforce.[27]

Computerization has accelerated the trend towards automation of many routine, repetitive, menial, and unsafe jobs. Automation increases predictability in operations and improves consistency in product quality. However, to reap the full benefits, computerization and automation should permit easy and effective meshing of existing and new technologies. Newer employee relations practices, especially in performance planning, training, and compensation are also needed. Well-planned performance management systems help achieve effective human-machine interfaces and ensure the best results from technological changes.

Website for the use of computers in productivity: *www.csls.ca/new/revpaper. html*

TREND 4: INCREASING WORKFORCE DIVERSITY

Over the years, the labour force participation rates for women, visible minorities, and other protected groups have been steadily increasing.

Website for labour market information: *www11.hrdc-drhc.gc.ca*

> Compared with several other industrialized nations, the participation rate of Canadian women in the labour force is high. It is estimated that by year 2005, 85% of Canadian women aged 25 to 54 will enter the labour force. More women have been leaving traditional, non-professional occupations (e.g., clerical) to work in management, law, engineering, and medicine.[28]

The co-existence of anglophones and francophones as well as dozens of other national, racial, and ethnic groups, each with its unique cultural and social background, makes Canadian society a cultural mosaic.[29] "Business immigrants" often act as engines of economic growth in this country, while immigrants from places like Hong Kong, Vietnam, India, Brazil, Uganda, Sri Lanka, and the Philippines have added to the cultural diversity and richness of this country. Indeed, in recent years, the face of the Canadian population has been undergoing a major change.

> Currently, only 47% of the total number of immigrants originates from Britain or other European countries.[30] Today, almost 5 million Canadians are referred to as allophones, which literally means, "other speaking." That is a 15% increase over 1991, and Chinese has surpassed Italian as the most common non-official language.[31]

The demographic profiles of workers have been changing, resulting in an aging workforce.

> For the first time in its history, Canada is facing a population decline. The first census figures of the new millennium, released in March 2002 by Statistics Canada, showed that the country's population reached just over 30 million in 2001. To keep the population at current levels, Canada will require more immigrants. The fertility rate (i.e., the average number of children a woman will have over her life time) is just 1.5 children, well below the rate of 2.1 children needed to sustain the population.[32] By 2010, the 65 and over age group will form approximately 14% of Canadian population. The average age of the population will approach 41 years in Canada while countries like India and Mexico have much younger workforces (average age will be under 30 years).[33]

Even within the same society, individuals show marked differences in attitudes and behaviours depending on their age. "Boomers" (born from 1940 to 1960) are significantly different in their values and behaviours than "X-ers" (born from 1960 to 1980).

> Some writers claim that X-ers think of work as a job while boomers are in the middle of careers. X-ers are unfazed by power and authority; boomers are impressed and attracted by it. X-ers see scarcity; boomers see abundance. X-ers mistrust most business practices; boomers instituted many of them and defend them. X-ers are self-reliant; boomers are team-oriented.[34]

To meet the needs of the new workforce, radical alteration in work practices and systems may be required. Increasing entry of women and educated young people in the workplace has necessitated fundamental changes in leadership styles and communication practices. The arrival of an ethnically diverse workforce has resulted in fundamental changes in work-related attitudes[35] including the notions of fairness, employment equity, and social welfare. Canadian national character, which in the past was referred to as a "conservative syndrome"[36] (reflecting Canadians' tendency to be guided by tradition and to focus on maintenance of order and predictability), has changed in recent years, focusing on aggressive entry into foreign markets, hi-tech industries, and reduced government programs. Effective performance management systems enable organizations to tap the skills of the new workforce segments and provide friendly workplaces where differences are recognized and valued. Effective diversity management not only helps improve our innovation and productivity records, but also enhances the quality and standard of life for all Canadians.

Websites for demographics and diversity management information:
www.statcan.ca
www.diversitymatters.ca
www.gendertraining.com

TREND 5: EVER INCREASING LEGAL REQUIREMENTS

Today's manager must abide by an increasing array of federal and provincial laws and city and municipal regulations. The most familiar ones are the Canadian Charter of Rights and Freedoms, Canadian Human Rights Act, Canada Labour Code, Hazardous Products Act, Canada Labour Safety Code, Canada Pension Plan, Minimum Wages Acts, and Workers' Compensation Acts. However, a large number of acts, regulations, and court decisions constrain the activities of employers and managers.

Website for Ontario safety and compensation requirements:
www.gov.on.ca/LAB/ohs/ohse.htm

> The law requires that applicant characteristics such as gender, race, and physical characteristics (e.g., height) cannot be used for the selection of employees unless the employer can prove that these characteristics are performance related. Even where a particular attribute (e.g., a certain height) or behaviour (e.g., working on a specific day of the week) is job relevant, past court decisions put the onus on the employer to show that, even with reasonable accommodation, persons who score low on that attribute or behaviour cannot perform satisfactorily.

Therefore, employee performance needs to be clearly defined and accurately measured. Failure to do so will not only reduce overall performance but also expose firms to possible lawsuits from job applicants who believe that they have been discriminated against. On the other hand, performance-based job descriptions may provide clearer guidelines for selecting employees for various positions.[37]

Website for performance criteria and selection:
www.employers.gc.ca

In the context of managing employees, once again, there are current legal requirements that make old practices such as "dismissal at will" unlawful.

> The owner of a small business terminated a supervisor in charge of 18 employees. The supervisor had been employed in the firm for over 20 years. The owner claimed that the supervisor's performance had gradually deteriorated, although he did not produce any evidence supporting this claim. In an out-of-court settlement, the owner had to pay over $100 000 to the supervisor for wrongful dismissal.

Even experienced human resource managers find some of the situations, such as determining what constitutes unfair dismissal, need outside legal expertise. Today, a manager has to produce documentary evidence showing poor performance and a record of due process—the existence of a set of rules and procedures for disciplinary action that have been well communicated to the offender and followed diligently—before terminating an employee. The offender also needs to have an opportunity to respond to the charges and improve performance.

In summary, a fundamental shift is underway in how and where the world's work gets done, with potentially serious consequences for Canadian managers. Today's "global village", rapidly changing technology, diverse workforce, and ever-tightening legal requirements necessitate that innovative, value-adding solutions be found consistently and on a timely basis. How a sound performance management system contributes to this goal is discussed in the remainder of this book. To thoroughly grasp this concept, it is important to examine the steps in performance management, which are outlined in the following section.

STEPS IN PERFORMANCE MANAGEMENT

Websites for performance management:
www.hr-guide.com
www.work911.com

Effective performance management systems aim to attain both organizational and individual employee objectives. Historically, the focus of performance management systems has been only on improving employee performance. Performance management was looked at as a slightly enlarged version of traditional performance appraisal function. A popular human resource management text defined it as "the process of collecting, analyzing, evaluating and communicating information relative to individual's job behaviour and results."[38] Several others have also focused on individual employee performance.[39] Further, the focus has been on monitoring performance, with little or no attention to performance improvement. In contrast to the outcomes of simple performance appraisal procedures, a well-planned performance management system results in a number of beneficial outcomes (Figure 1-3). It can also improve the overall quality of life, thus achieving broader social objectives.

FIGURE 1-3   Benefits of a Performance Management System

Individual Employee Level

- Clarity of performance standards
- Improved awareness of performance-reward linkages
- More focused career development
- Greater autonomy and better quality of work life
- Improved job satisfaction from valid performance feedback
- Clearer understanding of competencies needed for career growth

Organizational Level

- Higher employee productivity and efficiency
- Improved creativity
- Timely compliance with legal requirements
- Better alignment of performance goals with organizational strategy
- Better integration among various HR systems, procedures, and decisions
- Reduced employee turnover and absenteeism

This text adopts a broader definition of performance management including performance improvement at macro- and micro-organizational and individual levels. In today's turbulent environment, focus of performance at organizational, departmental (or sub-system), and individual employee levels has become necessary for organizational success. This means that any performance management system must focus on corporate, subsystem or operating, and individual level objectives and facilitate the achievement of these objectives (Figure 1-4). In the absence of consistency among the three level objectives, the corporate plans are unlikely to be translated into individual and team actions on a timely basis. The goals at these three levels also have to be related to and consistent with the goals of the larger, surrounding society.

> For the fifth year in a row, Royal Bank of Canada was named as the top Canadian corporation in the category of social responsibility. Even at the individual level, employee behaviours reflect this commitment. Many bank employees actively volunteer in a variety of social organizations and the Bank donates to or otherwise supports a variety of organizations engaged in health care, amateur athletics, community arts, multicultural activities and community development activities. This facilitates the achievement of larger organizational goals and raises the bank's stature and reputation in the community.[40]

Improving organizational and individual employee productivity has become so important that all but the smallest firms have some formal systems and procedures to plan, monitor, and improve performance.[41]

> In a major bank, performance standards and expectations are conveyed to the staff at the beginning of each financial year. What constitutes success and how it is measured are discussed and agreed upon at this time. During quarterly performance reviews, actual performance is compared to these standards and expectations. Wherever feasible, work outcomes (including employee behaviours) and facts are used to assess performance, which is then rated on the predetermined criteria. The results are discussed in a two-way problem-solving meeting at which time future actions such as training and education are also discussed. Basic career counselling is also offered at this point along with information on change in organizational direction or priorities for the future. The human resource department offers detailed career counselling or refers employees to outside counsellors where necessary.

While performance management systems show considerable variation across organizations, most carry out several common activities reflected in the above bank example. The five steps in implementing an objective-driven performance management system are shown in Figure 1-5 and are briefly discussed below.

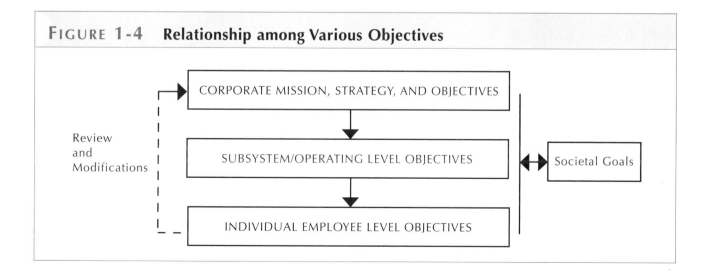

FIGURE 1-4   **Relationship among Various Objectives**

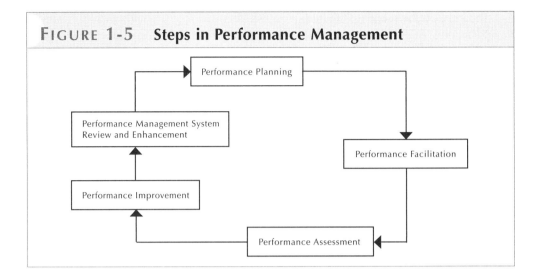

FIGURE 1-5   **Steps in Performance Management**

Focus on Small Business

Performance Management Spells Success

The Canadian economy thrives on small businesses. While large multinationals like IBM, Coca-Cola, Royal Bank, Bombardier, and Four Seasons Hotels tower over us, a large segment of Canadians work for small businesses and own "mom and pop" stores. Many of you may have worked for such a business and it is quite possible that one day you may decide to start one. What makes performance management important for small businesses?

The answer is simple. The success and very survival of small firms—even to a greater degree than large conglomerates—depends on the calibre and attitudes of the people they employ. The limited resources available to them, the often small market base, and the inability to buy and continuously upgrade technology all contribute to make small businesses more vulnerable to their environments than large firms, which have abundance of resources at their disposal. In the case of a small business, a few minor mistakes, the loss of a few customers, or a few inefficient systems or procedures may result in the total paralysis or death of the organization. Maintaining high levels of performance is the key to success. The way the owners and employees react to emerging challenges ensures continued survival while the innovativeness shown by its members will define how much and at what speed the firm will grow and prosper.

Performance management helps the small business manager position human resources as a major strategic advantage and overcome challenges by skilful use of employee talents. A small business has virtually no control over the industry structure and even less control over factors like resources.[42] Because of this, the entrepreneur must not only be competent and driven, but should be able to inspire and motivate employees to follow a plan of action and improve on it. Performance management, by focusing on

performance at all levels—organization, system, and individual—prepares small firms to improve customer relations and other constituents.

Zenon Environmental Inc., which began operations with less than 15 employees in Burlington, Ontario in the 1980s, is a good example of how a firm that capitalizes on the quality and calibre of its human resources grows.[43] The firm, which had developed a new membrane technology to purify and recycle water, began its operations in a 5400 m^2 building. It occupied less than a quarter of the space and rented space out to other firms to raise cash. Zenon kept some room for staff to practice putting or to shoot baskets. From the beginning, owner Andrew Benedek wanted to offer a comfortable workplace where his employees could take occasional breaks and have some fun. Zenon's performance management program actively promotes discussion between employees and managers throughout the year. Formal, biannual evaluations focus not only on employee performance but also on employee satisfaction. From the beginning, Benedek encouraged his staff to express their views on corporate issues through a "Zenon Parliament". Zenon, which now boasts of a workforce of 600 employees and is rated as one of the best employers in the country, continues to emphasize an egalitarian culture where employees work in open workstations and everyone flies economy class. Employees find Zenon a challenging place to work—several of them carry cell-phones 24 hours a day—however, they do not mind the extra hours as they feel as part of a worthwhile cause.

For more details, visit Zenon's website:
www.zenonenv.com

1. PERFORMANCE PLANNING

Performance planning should attempt to integrate individual, team, and departmental performance with corporate objectives and strategies. It starts with a clear definition of what the organization is attempting to do, how it plans to get there, and the time frame in which it has to work. Even organizations with similar goals show remarkable differences in their approaches to achieving the goals. There are at least three generic strategies that a firm may pursue: cost leadership, differentiation, and focus[44] (Figure 1-6).

An organization that pursues a **cost leadership strategy** attempts to gain a competitive advantage through lower costs. It aggressively seeks efficiencies in production and uses tight controls (especially in managing costs) to gain an advantage over competitors.

> Several products such as ABC (detergent), Timex (watches), and BIC (pens) compete on the basis of cost and attempt to remain the low-cost alternative in their field. Several retailers like Wal-Mart and Zellers attempt to compete on the basis of low prices.

Product differentiation strategy focuses on creating a distinctive or unique product that is unsurpassed in quality, innovative design, or other feature. This may be accomplished through product design, unique technology, or even through carefully planned advertising and promotion. The firm that employs this strategy may be able to charge a premium price for its product.

> Nikon (cameras) and Calvin Klein (fashion apparel) employ a differentiation strategy.

Under a **focus strategy**, a firm concentrates on a segment of the market and attempts to satisfy it with a very low-priced or a highly distinctive product. Within this specific market or target customer group, a focused firm may compete on the basis of either differentiation or cost leadership. The target market in this instance is usually set apart either by geography or by specialized needs.

Cost leadership strategy focuses on gaining competitive advantages through lower costs.

Product differentiation strategy focuses on creating a distinct or unique product that is unsurpassed in quality, design, or other key feature.

Focus strategy is a method organizations use to concentrate on and satisfy a segment of the market with a very low-priced or highly distinctive product.

FIGURE 1-6 Performance Requirements under Different Competitive Strategies[45]

	STRATEGY		
	Cost Leadership	**Focus**	**Differentiation**
Desired behaviours on the part of job incumbent	Predictable, repetitive	Predictable, repetitive	Creative, innovative
Skill application by employees	Narrow	Moderate	Broad
Emphasis on employee flexibility	Low	Moderate	High
Concern for quantity of production	High	Moderate	Moderate
Primary focus of employee performance appraisal procedures	Control	Mostly control; Some development	Employee development

An automobile manufacturer may sell large station wagons in North America and smaller cars in less developed countries where consumers have lower disposable income.

Given the firm's size, competitive advantages, objectives, and constraints each strategic option has to be examined for its viability. Unsuitable strategic options have to be dropped from consideration. Those that appear viable have to be scrutinized in detail for their advantages and weaknesses before being accepted for implementation. Questions to ask at this time include:

- Are the assumptions realistic?

- Do we have the competencies and resources to make this strategy viable?

- Is this strategy consistent internally? Do various elements of the strategy "hang together"?

- What are the risks? Can we afford them?

- What actions have to be taken to make the strategy viable? Are these feasible?

As Figure 1-6 shows, the overall strategy determines performance requirements. Chapter 2 elaborates on how individual and departmental performance are linked to the overall strategy. To effectively motivate, specific, challenging, and time-bound goals that measure critical dimensions of performance have to be set. Performance standards or criteria should be specific yet cover all major output requirements of the position. A definition of performance that is too narrow can create problems.

In the sales division of a large department store, a new pay incentive plan was introduced to reward employees on the basis of individual sales volume. The result was increased competition among the employees, neglect of the organization's long-term goals, and general confusion. There was considerable "sales grabbing" and "tying up the trade", as well as a general disregard of unmeasured functions such as stock work and merchandise display.

Website for human resources information and management systems:
www.hronline.com

A job analysis (discussed in Chapter 3) enables human resource managers to collect important information about jobs and establish performance standards. Performance standards formulated in consultation with employees generally produce better outcomes. These standards should be frequently reviewed to ensure relevance as changes occur.

2. PERFORMANCE FACILITATION

Hiring the right person for a job reduces errors, training time, and employee frustration. Employees who find they cannot perform well become frustrated and quit or engage in dysfunctional behaviours. Even the most competent hire will not perform well unless the internal reward systems and work climate are motivating. Establishing performance-reward linkage is, thus, a critical aspect of performance management. The recipient must value the rewards. Unless the employee perceives the rewards as fair and equitable, motivation may decline. Reward system properties are discussed further in Chapter 4.

The rewards provided to an employee may be extrinsic (e.g., a salary raise) or intrinsic (e.g., autonomy). Increasingly, workplace autonomy and employee involvement in decision-making have been found to positively impact performance. Chapter 5 discusses the more popular forms of employee involvement.

3. PERFORMANCE ASSESSMENT

Performance appraisals not only provide feedback to employees but also are critical for identifying training needs and compensating employees. In measuring performance, all critical dimensions of job performance must be measured validly and frequently. Impossible or unreasonable goals and standards may result in reporting of invalid information or other unethical behaviour as the following example illustrates.

> The international division of a large eyeglass dealer was accused of inflating revenues through faked sales of sunglasses. These glasses were later sold at cut-rate prices to dealers. Contact lens managers in the same firm, under pressure to beat sales targets and earn sales dependent commissions, were alleged to have shipped products that doctors never ordered.[46]

Valid and measurable standards facilitate delegation and control. Under **management by exception**, all requisite actions of individual managers and departments are determined in advance through plans and rules. Only when deviation between standards and actuals occurs are higher levels of management consulted for resolution. As long as the exceptions do not overload the management hierarchy, this approach is viable and can free valuable managerial time from routine activities. Exceptions of both kinds (cases of not meeting the standard and cases of exceeding the standard) are considered, permitting management to be aware of both problem areas and potential opportunities.

In **Management by exception** all requisite actions of individual managers and departments are determined in advance through plans and rules. Only when deviation between standards and actuals occurs are higher levels of management consulted for resolution.

Most organizations use a variety of devices to measure employee performance including budgets, variance reports, performance appraisal reports, personnel policies, and audits. Different firms may carry out performance appraisals on an annual, biannual, quarterly, or even a more frequent basis. The tools used reflect considerable variation across organizations and range from simple ratings to complex, multi-assessor assessment centre techniques. Several of these issues are discussed in Chapter 6.

4. PERFORMANCE IMPROVEMENT

When performance is below standard, there are two major options available to an organization: it can change the standards or it can improve performance. Strategies for adjusting standards include revising output goals, revising timelines, and allocating more resources. If the standards have been realistically set, revising the goals downward is not an option. Employees may have to receive training to achieve better results. A variety of training programs are discussed in Chapter 7.

In several instances, employees may require counselling to identify new work behaviours and routines. In the case of employees who already meet or exceed standards, counselling becomes even more important to encourage them to set higher goals. Without frequent feedback, employees cannot judge whether their actions are consistent with organizational priorities and in line with benchmarks. Without support from supervisors, employees may be averse to taking innovative and entrepreneurial actions. Chapter 8 looks at key issues in the counselling of employees and details the three steps that underlie all performance improvement attempts, namely:

- Assessing the magnitude of performance deficiency,

- Identifying reasons for the deficiency, and

- Removing obstacles to high performance.

5. PERFORMANCE MANAGEMENT SYSTEM REVIEW AND ENHANCEMENT

Like all other systems, performance management systems require continuous review and change. Every change in corporate goals or strategies requires modifications in operational priorities while changes in technology or workforce characteristics necessitate new ways of working. This means that a performance management system should evolve in response to emerging priorities.

> A predicted shortage of medical technologists motivated Reynolds to start an in-house development program to help six lab assistants become licensed medical technologists. After 15 months, they finished the program and passed the provincial certification test. The program was a success since the shortage was worse than predicted. Eight more lab assistants were recruited for the second program.

Website for articles on performance management: *www.shrm.org*

The aim was to achieve the organizational objective of finding qualified medical technologists. The strategy employed was an in-house development program. The fact that all six technologists passed the provincial certification test provided feedback that the strategy was a success. It enabled the performance management system to add real value to the organization and contribute to its success in a tangible way. Chapter 9 details various approaches to assess and revitalize the performance management system on a continuing basis.

THE ORGANIZATION OF PERFORMANCE MANAGEMENT FUNCTION

The responsibility for performance management rests with each manager. If a manager does not accept this responsibility, performance improvement may not occur at all or may occur very slowly. When a manager finds that planning and monitoring performance seriously disrupts other responsibilities, some of these activities may be reassigned to a specialist or a department. Such delegation does not absolve the manager of accountability for outcomes or productivity improvement of employees.

> Many managers may require a specialist in the performance management department to counsel a poorly performing employee. However, the manager will still be held responsible for the poor performance of the employee.

A separate performance management department or section usually emerges only when an organization becomes so large that performance planning and improvement activities would become overly time consuming to line managers. In other words, a separate performance management department may be created when the expected benefits of such a department exceed the costs. Until that point, managers handle performance management activities themselves or delegate them. A past survey found no consistent definition of performance management among responding organizations-most of which claimed to practice it. Only about 3% of the organizations had formal performance management departments.[47]

Performance management systems that integrate individual, unit, and organizational performance and continuously improve them are becoming more and more common. Sometimes, however, only some of the features of an integrated performance management system (Figure 1-7) may be seen. While performance management is closely related to strategic and human resource management, it also requires a deep

---

FIGURE 1-7 **Key Attributes of Organizations with Performance Management Systems**

Organizations that have an integrated performance management system are likely to implement several of the following activities. An organization's unique circumstances may necessitate more or less focus on certain activities.

- A clear mission statement understood by all employees
- Continuous communication of organizational priorities, business plans, and progress
- Presence of systems focusing on quality improvement
- Clear linkage between performance and rewards
- Focus on performance of members at all levels (including the CEO)
- Existence of clear, continuously-reviewed, performance standards
- Presence of systems (e.g., coaching, training) to foster high performance
- Emphasis on fostering good employee relations

---

commitment to continuous improvement and an integrated effort to improve performance. Such a philosophy is yet to emerge in many Canadian organizations that have well entrenched, but loosely connected human resource management procedures.

When a performance management unit emerges, it is typically small and forms part of the larger human resource department. Figure 1-8 illustrates the common placement of a performance management unit in the early stages.

As demands on performance analysts grow, a larger performance management section, or even a department, may become necessary. Many of the performance management functions assume greater importance and complexity. New demands are placed on the department and jobs in the department become more specialized. Consequently, the department or section may become organized into highly specialized subunits. Figure 1-9 demonstrates this increased specialization by outlining the functions of those reporting to the person in charge of performance improvement.

DEPARTMENTAL COMPONENTS

The subdepartments of a large performance management department approximately correspond with the activities already mentioned. For each major activity, a subde-

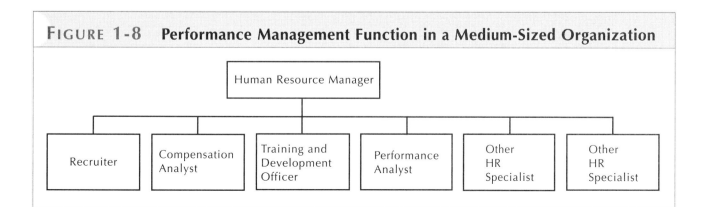

FIGURE 1-8 **Performance Management Function in a Medium-Sized Organization**

FIGURE 1-9   **Performance Management Department in a Large Firm**

partment may be established or a specialist identified to provide the needed service, as shown in Figure 1-9. While individual subunit responsibilities show considerable variation across firms, sample activities carried out by each subunit in Figure 1-9 are listed below:

Performance and Human Resources Planning:

(Key responsibilities: Plan performance goals and human resource requirements)

*   Match performance goals to organizational mission, objectives and strategies,

*   Conduct job/task analysis to clarify responsibilities,

*   Benchmark and improve performance standards, skills, and competencies,

*   Recommend improvements to raise productivity, quality, and stakeholder satisfaction, and

*   Carry out human resource planning and succession planning.

Work and Compensation planning:

(Key responsibilities: Identify and implement job and reward-related changes to facilitate high performance)

*   Link rewards to performance and re-design reward system to improve motivational properties,

*   Design jobs to enhance employee performance, and

*   Improve of productivity and performance quality on a continuous basis.

Performance Assessment:

(Key responsibilities: Ensure systematic and valid assessment of performance that provides timely feedback to all concerned)

- Review and modify performance assessment tools, procedures, and systems,

- Assist and train line managers to validly assess performance of employees and work teams, and

- Store, analyze, and predict performance levels of individuals and teams.

Training, Development, and Counselling:

(Key responsibilities: Identify and execute actions that improve future employee, team, and departmental performance)

- Identify training needs,

- Design, deliver, and evaluate training and employee development programs,

- Prepare trainers where applicable,

- Counsel employees and train supervisors to counsel,

- Implement progressive disciplinary procedures for marginal performers, and

- Create and maintain a culture of continuous learning.

Performance Research and Consulting:

(Key responsibilities: Act as an internal consultant and change agent to improve individual, systemic, and organizational performance)

- Measure the impact of organizational and systemic changes on performance,

- Work with managers, employees, and teams to improve performance and quality,

- Facilitate organizational change and learning, and

- Eliminate all systemic obstacles to performance excellence.

Activities not identified in Figure 1-9 are shared among different sections. For example, "communication" may be divided among all subdepartments with Performance Facilitation and Performance Consulting and Research doing the bulk of the activity. Similarly, "leadership development" or "organizational culture change" may be divided between Performance Improvement and Performance Research subunits.

THE SERVICE ROLE OF THE PERFORMANCE MANAGEMENT DEPARTMENT

Performance management departments are service departments. The role of these departments is to assist other departments and the larger organization. Managers in the performance management department do not have authority to order other managers in other departments to accept their ideas. Instead, the department has **staff authority**, which is the authority to advise, not direct, managers in other departments. In contrast, **line authority**, possessed by managers of operating departments, allows managers to make decisions about production, performance, and people. It is the operating managers who normally are responsible for job assignments, promotions, and other employee-related decisions. Performance improvement specialists advise line managers, who are ultimately responsible for employee performance.

In highly technical or extremely routine situations, the performance analyst may be given functional authority. **Functional authority** gives the manager or the department the right to make decisions typically made by line managers or top management. For example, some of the decisions about performance assessment pro-

Staff authority is the authority to advise, not direct, managers in other departments.

Line authority allows managers of operating departments to make decisions about production, performance, and people.

Functional authority gives a functionary, most often a staff person, or a department the right to make decisions usually made by line managers or top management.

cedures and tools are technically complex while uniform procedures to deal with poor performers may be necessary to maintain equity. In these instances, the top manager may give the performance management department the functional authority to decide the procedures or tools to use. If each department manager made separate decisions about performance assessment procedures or the disciplinary and counselling system, there might be excessive costs and inequities. Whatever the authority granted, performance analysts and counsellors need to possess a number of competencies to be effective.[48] Some of these are outlined in Figure 1-10.

Website for human resource management: competencies
www.chrpcanada.com

PERFORMANCE MANAGEMENT FUNCTION AND THE ORGANIZATIONAL CHARACTER

Organizational character refers to an organization's history, culture, philosophy, and unique methodology.

Every organization has a unique history and way of doing business. **Organizational character** refers to the sum of an organization's history, culture, philosophy, and unique methodology. To be effective, performance management department must recognize the organizational character of the organization as well as the constraints imposed by it. Four factors related to an organization's character deserve special attention.

Strategic posture Is the organization a leader or follower in the marketplace? Is the organization a defender[50]—a conservative business unit that prefers to maintain a secure position with established products or in relatively stable service areas instead of expanding into unchartered territories? Or, is it a prospector that emphasizes growth, entrepreneurship, and an eagerness to be first in a new market or selling a new product? Defender organizations are more likely to focus on control, emphasize predictability in operations, and foster long-term employee attachment to the firm. In contrast, prospector organizations focus on creating flexible, decentralized structures that encourage creativity and reward risk-taking. The role of the performance management department in this instance is more developmental and experimental in nature than in the former instance.

Degree of Competition Does the organization face fierce or moderate competition? Organizations facing fierce competition are likely to demand more from their performance management departments than those facing moderate degree of

---

FIGURE 1-10   Skills and Competencies of Performance Analysts

To be effective, a performance analyst needs to possess several skills and competencies. Key attributes are listed below:[49]

- Business mastery: A sound knowledge of the business of the firm and the ability to incorporate financial realities into their analyses and decisions.

- Expertise in human resource management: State-of-the-art knowledge in all areas of human resource management, with particular emphasis on performance appraisal, training, compensation planning, and organizational development.

- Negotiation and change management skills: Problem solving, negotiation, and critical thinking skills.

- Personal credibility: Trustworthiness, high ethical standards, and social responsiveness.

- Interpersonal skills: To play multiple roles such as a friend to the employee, a catalyst for change, and a monitor of excellence, an analyst needs listening skills, ability to communicate in a supportive manner, and a high degree of empathy.

SELF-TEST:

How Good Are Your Communication Skills?

One key attribute of successful performance analysts is their ability to effectively communicate with others. Use this self-test to identify your own communication style. Indicate whether you *strongly agree* (SA), *agree* (A), *neither agree nor disagree* (NN), *disagree* (D), or *strongly disagree* (SD) with each of the following statements. Do not omit any statement.

1. When I am in conversation with others, I tend to describe situations neutrally without labelling them as good or bad.

2. I am often critical of others' actions.

3. I have excellent relationships with people who think and behave very differently from me.

4. Had I chosen it as a career, I would have made an excellent judge.

5. I generally tend to explain situations to others without labelling them as desirable or undesirable.

6. Most of today's problems are due to people not recognizing events and behaviours as good or bad, instead classifying everything as in between.

7. I tend to describe situations so well that I sometimes feel I would have made a good newspaper reporter.

8. I tend to steer conversations to topics that I like.

9. Most people who know me would say that I am very empathetic.

10. Most people who know me would say that I can clearly distinguish right from wrong.

Scoring

For numbers 1, 3, 5, 7, and 9, assign a score of 5, 4, 3, 2, and 1 respectively for SA, A, NN, D and SD. For numbers 2, 4, 6, 8, and 10, assign a score of 1, 2, 3, 4, and 5 for SA, A, NN, D and SD. Add up your total score. It may range from 10 to 50.

Interpretation

Good communication has a number of dimensions. This exercise measures only one dimension, namely, your overall tendency to be evaluative or descriptive when dealing with others. Past research findings indicate that individuals who are descriptive are likely to create a nonthreatening atmosphere when communicating, tend to be non-judgmental, and accept others and events as they appear without categorizing them as good or bad and desirable or undesirable. A score of 38 or above suggests that you have acquired much of this important skill. With conscious effort, most individuals can improve their ability to view others as they are and recognize their true potential. Remember, there are other dimensions to communication. We will look at some of them in the following chapters.

competition. A business facing fierce competition values every cost advantage. Even minor product differentiation can spell the difference between success and failure in such a setting. Activities such as job analysis and training are likely to assume greater importance in such a setting.

Technology Improving predictability of operations has great importance in organizations using routine technology. In contrast, firms using non-routine technology may place greater value on employee creativity and innovation.

> Large steel factories and lumber mills use fairly routine production processes. Providing explicit job descriptions, job-specific training, and focusing on performance monitoring may be given greater emphasis in such settings. In contrast, advertising firms and software developers who use non-routine technology may focus on practices that foster creativity, innovation, and entrepreneurship.

Managerial philosophy Organizations characterized by top-down decision-making and strong organizational hierarchy demand different performance management procedures than those that have a more democratic work climate where employees actively participate in various decisions. Vancouver-based Sierra Systems Group Inc. is an example of an organization that shuns hierarchy.

> Sierra Systems Group Inc., established in 1966, may be Canada's oldest information technology consulting firm and is one of its most successful with almost 900 employees worldwide and annual sales exceeding $120 million. Founder Grant Gisel is President and when Sierra went public in 1998, the firm created the positions of Chief Executive Officer, Chief Financial Officer, and vice presidents to satisfy securities regulators. Beyond these, there are only three job categories in the firm: partners who manage the

Focus on Ethics:

What Is a "Right" Behaviour?

Ethics are moral principles that guide human behaviours and are often based on a society's cultural values, norms, customs, and beliefs. There are widely varying standards of behaviour across different cultures and even within the same society there can be varying ethical standards among individuals and groups, making judgements of "right" and "wrong" extremely difficult. There are different guidelines of "good" behaviour to address this variability.

1. **Universalist Approach**: There are moral standards that are universally applicable. In other words, regardless of the society or place, a bad act (such as killing or stealing) is bad. There are no exceptions to moral "rights" and "wrongs".

2. **Exceptionist Approach**: This approach suggests that morals are only guidelines. While they are to be followed on most occasions, an individual may have to make exceptions when situations justify them.

3. **Situational Approach**: What is good or bad depends on the situation or culture surrounding the actor. While telling the truth is desirable in some societies, there are cultures that do not give the same importance to truth. Similarly, while killing is bad, there may be situations that justify this act. It all depends on the specific situation at hand.

4. **Individual Subjectivist Approach**: There are no absolute rights or wrongs, no good or bad in any social situation. The individual decision-maker facing a situation should determine what is right and wrong considering all aspects of the situation. Moral decisions are based on personal values and preferences.

Performance management, which involves managing performance of humans and systems in dynamic environments, is full of situations with hard choices between good and bad, right and wrong, desirable and undesirable. The ethics feature in each chapter introduces you to some of the ethical challenges faced by managers and analysts. Once you have identified your responses, compare your answers

to those of your friends or family members. Find out why each person made the choices they did. Try to categorize the responses in one of the four categories listed above. Which approach seems to be used by most of your friends and acquaintances?

Consider the following two situations and decide how you will respond to each one. Record your answers on a separate sheet and compare them with those of your friends and acquaintances.

1. Late one evening, on your way home, you stop at a public telephone booth to escape from strong wind and rain. There, next to the phone, you find an envelope containing $70, a couple of business cards (one of a lawyer and one a chiropractor). You notice that the address of the owner is on the envelope. You recognize that the address is in an expensive neighbourhood where extremely rich people—many of them millionaires—live. The residential area is about 20 km from the phone booth. You also know that there are no buses to that area. Since you do not have a car or cannot get a ride, you will need to catch a taxi to reach the area. A taxi ride (one-way) will cost $18 and you are not sure if the owner will be there. Do you return the entire envelope to the owner, return only the business cards (by mail), or keep the entire envelope using the rule "finders' keepers" and assuming that the rich owner probably will not miss it?

2. While roaming through the street market in a foreign country, you see a powerful laptop computer with several features for $175. Most of the laptops you had looked at in regular shops in this country were priced anywhere from $600 to $1800. You have been desperately looking for a laptop for the past two weeks. A local acquaintance whom you met at the office told you that stolen products were often sold at marked discounts at this particular market. You have $850 dollars with you, but if you can save some money on this deal, you could use it for a much-desired mini-vacation. What do you do?

branches across the country; principals who are in charge of projects; and the consultants who work under them. Sierra Systems is a flat organization and the principle extends to more than just the job titles. All employees are expected to take courses regularly to upgrade their skills. Everyone participates in the profit sharing plan and is encouraged to suggest both changes and methods to achieve the changes.[51]

Reward systems that recognize hierarchy, status, and role differences may be more visible in the top-down kind of organizations. In contrast, reward systems in flatter organizations may focus on empowering employees, creating flexible structures and creating an organization-wide perspective. Because performance management is the management of people, the function should be carried out not only professionally but also humanely.[52] Improving productive contribution of the people to help the firm grow and prosper is a major aim of performance management but this cannot be done without improving the overall quality of work life—indeed, quality of life—of the workers involved.

THE FRAMEWORK USED IN THIS BOOK

This text is divided into six parts. Part 1 introduces the performance management model upon which the rest of the book builds.

Part 1: Performance Management Framework, which contains this chapter, offers an integrative model of performance management with five major components discussed in the following chapters.

Part 2: Performance Planning is covered in two chapters. Chapter 2 links an organization's mission, strategy, and corporate goals to performance goals. Chapter 3 discusses how these performance goals are operationally defined and translated into performance standards.

Part 3: Performance Facilitation is discussed in two chapters. Chapter 4 details the links between rewards and performance, focusing primarily on the extrinsic rewards. Chapter 5 focuses on designing jobs that provide intrinsic rewards to employees in order to enhance employee involvement and performance.

Part 4: Performance Assessment looks at the various strategies, tools, and systems for evaluating individual member and team performance. Chapter 6 discusses individual and team performance appraisal tools and the challenges facing the assessors.

Part 5: Performance Improvement discusses two important systems used in today's organizations for improving individual and group performance. Chapter 7 looks at various training methods that enhance performance and Chapter 8 looks at major employee counselling principles and systems.

Part 6: Performance Management System Review and Enhancement is discussed in the final chapter. Chapter 9 looks at the important task of reviewing and enhancing the performance management department's effectiveness.

Implications for Practice

1. Performance management systems are critical for organizational success today because of global competition, push for productivity, demand for knowledge workers, and rapidly changing workforce demographics.

2. To be effective, a performance management system should be an ongoing process that is value adding and integrated with other organizational systems. It should aim to achieve organizational, employee, and larger societal goals.

3. Performance management systems should plan, facilitate, assess, and improve performance.

Changes in corporate goals, strategies, technology, and workforce necessitate changes in performance management goals and procedures. This means that the performance management system should always be evolving.

4. Good performance management systems should not only control, but also provide freedom to job incumbents. In the absence of freedom to experiment (and even err), creativity and productivity may suffer.

5. The responsibility for performance management should rest with each manager.

6. Performance management departments should recognize that they are service departments with staff authority. Even where functional authority is granted, the primary goal should be to facilitate superior performance.

7. To be successful, performance analysts should possess a number of competencies including business mastery, expertise on human resource techniques, organizational change agent expertise, and personal credibility.

8. To be useful, performance management departments should recognize and adapt to the culture and character of their firm.

Key Terms for Review

Cost leadership strategy, p. 13

Focus strategy, p. 13

Functional authority, p. 19

Line authority, p. 19

Management by exception, p. 15

Organizational character, p. 20

Performance management, p. 2

Product differentiation strategy, p. 13

Productivity, p. 5

Staff authority, p. 19

Telecommuting, p. 7

Discussion Questions

1. What does performance management mean? How is it different from strategic management? From human resource management?

2. During a job interview the interviewer asks why performance management is important today. What facts and arguments will you use to justify the performance management function within an organization?

3. What are the steps in performance management? Select two organizations in a familiar industry. If you were to introduce performance management systems to these organizations, how would the introductions differ?

4. What is organizational character? Why should a performance analyst or counsellor be concerned about it? Describe the salient character dimensions of an organization that you are familiar with and discuss how these impact performance management in the firm.

Critical Thinking Questions

1. You are the person in charge of all employee related matters (e.g., compensation, recruitment of temporary workers) in a small business that employs twenty people. Recently, the owner asked the advisability of implementing a performance management system in the organization. What is your response? Why?

2. The dean of your college or university has invited you to serve on a committee that is responsible for improving faculty members' performance. You are asked to provide your thoughts on this project. What steps do you recommend?

3. Until last month, John Kinnock was a very successful supervisor in a plant employing 40 tailors and seamstresses to produce mass merchandise like shirts and jeans. Customer ratings of the products were always very high and the employees had a great deal of respect for John. Recently, he took a higher paying job in a fashion boutique that employs only seven, but has almost the same total revenue as his past employer. What in John's leadership style may require modification? Why?

4. The owners of a self-serve coffee and donut shop near a city shopping mall decided to close the facility and open a new shop in downtown core after years of mediocre profits. The new shop will sell only gourmet coffee and high-priced pastries and provides a sit-down service facility. What operational procedures will need to change for the new shop to be successful?

Web Research

Visit the web sites of three major firms in an industry of your choice. Collect the relevant information on their philosophy, operations, and employment policies. Are there any differences? If so, are these differences attributable simply to size or profitability or are there differences in their organizational character?

CASE INCIDENT

Ontario Electronics Company Limited: Performance of Plant B

Ontario Electronics Company Limited (OECL) is a manufacturer of electronic, communication, aerospace, and audio equipment. The company currently employs over 500 workers, many of whom are professionals. The company's head office and major plant are located near Scarborough, Ontario, and it has plants and sales offices in four other Canadian provinces and in major U.S. cities. The company has fared well financially in the recent past but the top management is somewhat unhappy with the productivity levels seen in certain plants. The management was particularly displeased with employee performance in Plant B. The management has decided to focus on this plant to improve work procedures and productivity.

Brenda Cole, recently hired as the Performance Analyst, reviewed the records and studied the situation for over one month. She also surveyed a representative sample of all workers in Plant B. A brief summary of Cole's findings were:

1. Of the 80 performance appraisal records examined, 72 showed little change from the previous year. Poor performers rated poor year in and year out.

2. Approximately 50% of the employees whom Cole informally interviewed complained about the lack of advancement opportunities. Most openings were filled from the outside and the workers were not told upfront that there was no room for promotion from within.

3. Nearly 75% of the appraisals were not initialled by the employee even though company policy required employees to do so after they had discussed their review with the rater.

4. Of the 25% employees who initialled the evaluations, over 60% commented that the performance standards were unfair.

5. An exit survey of 14 employees who had resigned recently was conducted. Ten of the 14 suggested that performance feedback was too infrequent.

Questions

1. *What is the central problem with the performance management process in the Plant B?*

2. *What other problems may exist in Plant B?*

3. *What changes can Cole make to improve performance?*

CASE

Pay and Save Groceries: Change in Strategy[1]

Pay and Save Groceries (PSG) is a regional grocery chain with 45 supermarkets in Eastern Canada. The firm, which began as a mom-and-pop store in Halifax 25 years ago, grew into its present size primarily because of the energy and vision of its founder, Jack Libbey. Libbey, his wife Janet and his three sons, Don, George, and David, continue to play key roles in the firm, although some functions such as human resources, finance, and legal relations are left to staff specialists. Jack Libbey is the CEO of the organization. Don, the eldest son, is in charge of marketing. George, the middle son, is responsible for purchasing and supplies. David, the youngest, manages the company's finances although the day-to-day financial decisions are left with Jeff Cameron, a chartered accountant. Peter Demick, the firm's solicitor, provided all necessary legal advice to the Libbeys on matters related to their family and business. Jane Werther heads the human resource department although, once again, no major decision can be made without approval from the Libbey family. An approximate organizational chart is given in Figure A.

The firm currently employs 480 full-time employees and a large number of part-time cashiers and other workers. The exact number of part-time employees fluctuates seasonally but ranges from 2300 to 2500.

Pay and Save's present size of operations may mislead a casual observer about its past. For the first five years of its operation, it struggled to survive. Nothing seemed to work. Trading stamps, free delivery at home, periodic sales, and contests all failed to draw customers. About 20 years ago, Jack hit on an alternative strategy. He analyzed the firm's revenues for the previous eight months and felt that if PSG were to reduce its prices substantially on all its items and improve operating efficiency, its overall revenues will rise. This required more investments so stock was peddled at $10 a share to any takers and many bought at $7 or $8. Jack reduced prices on virtually all nine hundred items sold by the company.

The results impressed even Jack who had anticipated a modest, though steady, improvement in overall sales. In reality, sales jumped over 50% in just four months. In the remaining eight months of the year, sales increased even more—by a whopping 70%. The management of the firm recognized that they had found the winning formula. The firm became a resolute cost cutter and the slogan, "Lowest

(continued)

FIGURE A   An Approximate Organization Chart of Pay and Save Groceries

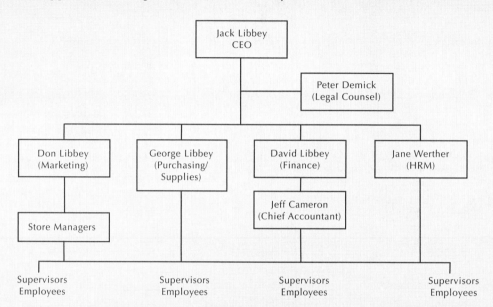

Price in the City" was promoted everywhere. Over the next ten years, sales and net income grew at more than 31% on average each year. PSG increased the variety of products in its stores. The management did everything under its control to keep costs down-whether purchasing materials from the lowest cost producer, keeping the low levels of inventory to reduce interest costs, wastage and spoilage, and getting the most out of its workforce. Jack was obsessed with "effective scheduling" of all activities. His system mandated the work each department and person should do in 40 hours, based on anticipated sales and the number of items sold each month. If store sales were down, a manager was expected to accomplish the same tasks and provide the same level of service with fewer employees—forcing employees to work beyond normal hours. Baggers often packed with both hands at the same time (the system was later changed in favour of self-packing by customers—a strategy that reduced the cost of operations even more) and supervisors worked unpaid overtime almost every day to meet the

week's work quota. Jack worked hard as well—he worked in the aisles or at a cash register during his random inspection tours. He was often said to state his goal of "making sure that there is an hour's worth of work for an hour's worth of labour". The firm's "lowest price in town" policy required that store employees perform multiple tasks to exacting time standards. Based on past experience, the company had clear time standards for unloading trucks, trimming produce for display, and boxing fruits.

The efforts paid off handsomely in the next few years. The firm's stock jumped from its initial $10 to $48 after splitting four times. With additional resources at its command, PSG expanded operations to more centres and regions in Atlantic Canada. Figure B summarizes some of the financial statistics pertaining to Pay and Save's operations in the past five years.

Today, PSG stores range from no-frills box stores to trendy food villages and 24-hour superstores in several cities including Halifax, Saint John, Fredericton,

FIGURE B   Summary Financial Statistics for Pay and Save Groceries

	Last Year	Three years prior	Five years prior
	(12 months)	*(12 months)*	*(12 months)*
Total revenue ($)	2 492 290	1 557 681	742 378
Earnings before interest and tax ($)	30 375	24 300	17 090
Profit or loss ($)	6 200	6 075	6 718
Total assets ($)	1 295 467	719 704	192 632
Dividends per share	0.27	0.35	0.40
Return on common equity	6.3	15.20	n/a
Employees			
Full-time	480	320	200
Part-time	2 770	870	450

(continued)

Charlottetown, and Moncton. PSG has also made a limited entry into Quebec and Ontario through the acquisition and conversion of six local grocery stores. PSG found that the Ontario and Quebec markets were harder to capture because of the large, established chains like Loblaws. PSG's stringent cost control strategies dictated that most stores were smaller (typically 3700 m^2) than those of its competitors (4650 m^2 to 6500 m^2), relatively limited product selection, and fewer employees.

Despite the growth, Jack Libbey attempted to maintain an informal atmosphere. He knew many employees by name and was against formality and paperwork. He often pointed out that decision situations are all different; therefore, installing standard procedures to cover all situations was futile. For example, the firm had neither job descriptions for most positions nor any "organized" approach to employee planning, performance appraisal, and discipline. The store managers and work supervisors had a fair amount of discretion in routine decision making; all major decisions involving more than $3000 in new outlays had to be approved by top management.

The salaries for new and part-time employees at Pay and Save are 3 to 4% above minimum wage. Although this is lower than that offered by the competition, Pay and Save employees who stay with the firm for three years or more often earn equal to or better than what they could have made elsewhere. While Pay and Save is not unionized at present, a national and a regional union have been making attempts to organize the employees. There are indications that these efforts are beginning to pay off. Recently, PSG management raised some employee benefits. Today, the firm offers free Christmas turkeys to all employees who are heads of households. There also provide additional leave for workers with young children (called "parenting days").

Jane Werther joined Pay and Save eight months ago. Almost all her professional life she lived in Western Canada and joined PSG to return to her roots in Nova Scotia. Jane has a Bachelor of Commerce degree from Saint Mary's University and was on the Dean's List. Since graduating and while employed in Vancouver, she has attended a number of human resource workshops. Her Calgary job, which lasted about seventeen months, required that she spend a fair amount of time travelling, another motivator for a move to the Atlantic region where she expects to spend most of her time in the head office in Halifax.

While she was excited about her new position, she also believed that her new job offered considerable challenges and operational difficulties. In both of her previous positions, she was given considerable freedom to experiment and expand HR activities as she saw fit as long budgetary constraints were met. The situation with PSG is somewhat different from this. Here, practically every new initiative needs approval by the Libbey family—something that has been an irritant to Jane on more than one occasion. Also,

past employers gave the human resource department a more prominent role in defining the organization's success. Compared to other companies, many systems and procedures in PSG seemed primitive. Still, Werther believed she could make a significant contribution to the firm. To start, she renamed the "personnel department" the "human resources department" to reflect the department's importance. To date, the employees and the management have reacted favourably to her initiatives.

Recently, Save More, a no-frills supermarket chain with extensive operations in Western and Central Canada, entered the Atlantic market. Compared to PSG, Save More possesses vastly superior resources and cost advantages because of its "self-serve" and "bulk-purchase" strategies. In the five stores it opened in Halifax, Saint John, and Moncton, it has been able to offer produce and goods at prices 15% to 20% cheaper than at PSG. Already, this has hurt PSG's sales; some PSG stores have lost as much as 15% to 25% of sales. Other, larger national grocery chains have also moved into Atlantic Canada. These competitors have resources to build or purchase in prime locations and offer full services and have fine-tuned their market analysis to such an extent that they offer a product mix catered to the specific needs of each neighbourhood and demographic group. Worried by the new threat and unable to match Save More's prices, the Pay and Save management reviewed the firm's past performance and likely future prospects and decided that a major re-definition of the organizational strategy was imperative.

The management team is meeting this week to: (a) Define the elements of the firm's new strategy; (b) Identify the necessary changes in internal systems and procedures to make the strategic change a success; and (c) Outline an action plan to implement the new strategy. Werther knows this will be the first major test for her expertise. She will not only be asked to contribute to the identification of a new, viable strategy, but also to provide factual arguments and rationale for her recommendations. Though not formally trained in business management, Jack Libbey is a shrewd businessman who gets to the bottom of issues and evaluates alternatives systematically. It will be a challenge to impress him with her ideas. But, Werther also knows that, if her recommendations are successful, her status and credibility will rise dramatically.

Questions

1. *What internal and external factors need to be considered when formulating a new strategy?*

2. *What are the implications of the changes for the firm and its employees?*

---

[1] This case was written by Dr. Hari Das of Saint Mary's University, Halifax. All rights reserved by the author.

PART 2

PERFORMANCE PLANNING

Performance planning, a primary step in performance management, integrates individual, team, and departmental performance with corporate mission and strategies. Chapter 2 examines how organizational mission, goals, and strategies are translated into performance goals. Chapter 3 discusses how these performance goals are operationally defined and translated into performance standards that drive departmental, team, and member actions.

2 ORGANIZATIONAL MISSION, STRATEGY, AND GOALS

The forces of change are demanding that organizations transform themselves if they are to survive. To be truly successful in the new world, organizations must be able to create value for all of their key constituencies.[1]

John Donovan, Richard Tully, and Brent Wortman

CHAPTER OBJECTIVES

After studying this chapter, you should be able to:

- Discuss the relationship among organizational mission, goals, and performance objectives

- Detail how organizational strategies are translated into performance standards

- Explain the steps in benchmarking performance

Into the early 1990s, Intrawest Real Estate Limited was a mainly urban real estate company that prospered by constructing the right buildings at the right locations in Vancouver and Seattle. Beginning in the mid 1990s, however, Intrawest changed its strategy dramatically and bought the near bankrupt Mont Tremblant, Canada's oldest ski resort. The company paid $38.7 million for the property and spent another $52 million upgrading and refurbishing the resort, including $10.4 million on one of the most elaborate snowmaking systems in North America. Intrawest built the resort from the ground up-a strategy that it continued later in Keystone, Colorado; Squaw Valley, California; and Snowshoe Mountain, West Virginia. The company knows that the population is aging and may not always favour strenuous sports like downhill skiing. To appeal to a wider market in all seasons, every company resort has championship golf courses and activities that appeal to children and other age groups. The result is that in early 2001, Intrawest had over $1 billion in assets. The company's stock price has outperformed the Toronto Real Estate Index by 700% since it went public in 1990.[2]

Intrawest's strategy is to buy depressed real estate at bargain prices, increase its value by developing a world-class resort, and sell or manage the developed land at a considerable profit. While the strategy is financially risky, the decision is based on methodical research and relentless number crunching, not on sudden inspiration. The operational goals of the firm are integrally related to the overall strategy of the company-to make bold, risky decisions that will help the organization offer high value services while mitigating the risk by appealing to wide audiences and offering a variety of choices to clients.

Intrawest illustrates how a match among mission, strategy, and operational goals is critical for success and even survival. This chapter introduces you to performance planning (Figure 2-1), a method that attempts to link organizational mission, strategy, and operational goals to performance goals. We first have to identify organizational mission and its relationship to organizational goals.

IDENTIFYING ORGANIZATIONAL MISSION

The starting point in performance planning is the identification of organizational mission and goals. An organization's mission is a vision of what the future course should be. A **mission statement** specifies the activities the organization intends to pursue and the course it has charted for the future.[3] It is a concise statement of who a company is, what it does, and where it is headed. Mission statements give an organization its own special identity, character, and path of development. Questions that help to identify an organization's mission include:

A **mission statement** is a clear statement defining an organization's character, operations, and future goals.

- What will performance be like in three to five years if we stay on the present track? If work is improved? Where should the business be in five years?

- Who is the customer? What represents value to the customer? Is the customer changing?

- In what direction should the company head to be a strong performer in five to ten years? From what areas should the company retreat?

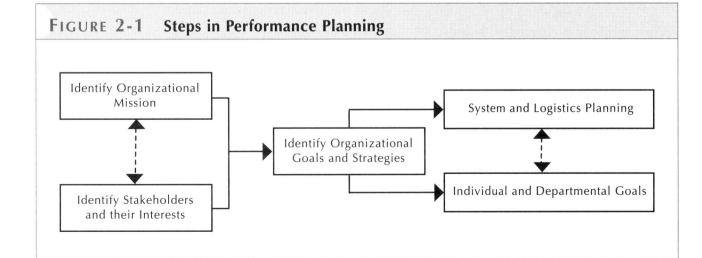

FIGURE 2-1   Steps in Performance Planning

• What product and market changes will help the company move from its present situation to where it wants to be?

Answering the above questions requires a clear definition of the domain within which the organization plans to operate. **Domain** refers to the industry or industries in which a firm decides to operate and compete. The way an organization defines its domain has very significant implications for its strategy and structure and is tied to its basic mission.

> Railway companies that define their competition as other railway companies have an entirely different domain perspective than railway companies that consider their competition other transportation businesses, therefore, competing not only with other railroads, but also with all other modes of transportation.

Accurate assessment of the organization's existing and future competition is a must for continued survival. Figure 2-2 illustrates a template that can be used for assessing competitors. As the figure shows, competitive analysis should not only look at the number of competitors and their actions but also their relative strengths. A weak competitor can harm a rival's chances only slightly while a strong competitor can reduce the rival's survival chances dramatically. Several sources that provide valuable information on competitors are listed in Figure 2-3. An analysis of competition should include a look at competitors' objectives, growth patterns, profitability trends, cost structures, and competitive strengths.

Competitive analysis combined with a careful examination of the various product-market options available to an organization is critical for defining the domain. Organizations may have identical domain goals, yet differ widely on their goals related to market niche and products sold. Figure 2-4 shows some of the options available to a computer manufacturer. The firm may define its position in the market as a vendor of high-priced computers used primarily by professionals in offices. Another firm may elect to focus on lower-priced, household computers and may concentrate on specific geographical areas.

Good strategies require a clear notion of the domain. If the domain is not carefully defined, even successful firms might not recognize potential challenges and opportunities. An organization's mission is also shaped by the firm's history. Every organization has a history of goals, achievements, and policies. Over time, previous

Domain refers to the industry or industries in which a firm operates and competes.

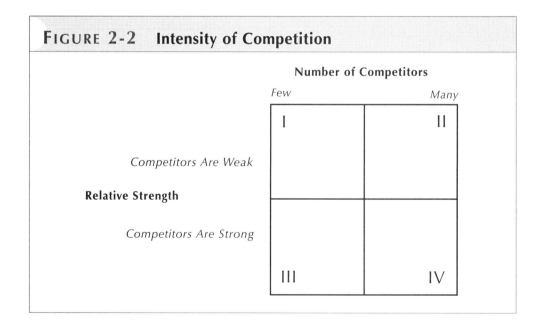

FIGURE 2-2   Intensity of Competition

FIGURE 2-3 **Sources of Information about Competitors**

1. **Information provided by competitors:**
   - advertisements
   - promotional material
   - speeches by the president and other managers
   - classified advertisements
   - patents and patent applications
   - annual reports
   - prospectuses
   - press releases

2. **Information available from other sources:**
   - case studies
   - books
   - consumer reports and evaluations
   - records of legal decisions involving the firm
   - industry studies
   - journals, research monographs
   - credit ratings

3. **Information that can be generated by original research:**
   - competitive shopping studies
   - close examination of competitor's product
   - survey of experts in the field
   - survey of customers
   - survey of suppliers
   - survey of former employees (subject to ethical guidelines)

---

missions may be forgotten or may be irrelevant to present environmental challenges. Unless a firm continuously monitors environments and changes its strategy (and even mission), its effectiveness may be questionable.

Coca-Cola is a good example of a firm that had to dramatically change its past approach. Although a successful marketer in terms of innovation, Coca-Cola had the reputation of the soft drink industry's plodding old giant. The New Coke fiasco of the 1980s left the company unwilling to respond to changing market interest in teas, juices, and flavoured waters. The company was late entering the Indian market of over 500 million thirsty people whom Pepsi targeted much earlier and in Britain, Coca-Cola ignored attacks by private label soft drink companies until they had siphoned off a sizeable portion of the market. All of this changed in the mid 1990s. New management brought a

---

FIGURE 2-4 **Product-Market Options for a Computer Manufacturer**

Price	Low	Medium	High
Customer	Households	Small businesses	Large businesses
Product features	Minimal	Moderate	Many
After sales service	At point of sale	Regional/National Centres	International Centres
Geographical area	Provinces	Canada	World

fresh vision and began aggressively expanding its markets and operations. In just seven months, the company opened plants in Romania, Norway, Fiji, and India. Several more plants were slated for other countries, including China, Hungary, and Thailand. In Japan, Coca-Cola's launch time for new products was cut from 90 to 30 days and the company now releases as many as 50 beverages a year. At the same time, recognizing growing concern in North America of childhood obesity (in part, related to large consumption of soft drinks), it reduced promotion of Coke in schools. Now, Coke vending machines in schools also dispense milk, orange juice, and even water-under the Coca-Cola brand name, of course.[4]

IDENTIFYING STAKEHOLDERS AND THEIR INTERESTS

Stakeholders are groups of people, including investors, managers, employees, creditors, suppliers, unions, government, environmental protection agencies, the general public, and even competitors, who have legitimate claims to an organization and its operations.

Almost all modern organizations have multiple **stakeholders** or groups of people who have legitimate claims on the organization or have a stake in its operations. These people include investors, managers, employees, creditors, suppliers, unions, government, environmental protection agencies and watchdogs, the general public and, at times, competitors. Figure 2-5 illustrates the several stakeholders of a modern organization.

Three stakeholders are particularly critical and are usually referred to as the primary stakeholders: customers, shareholders, and employees. The customers expect products and services of adequate safety and value from an organization. In return, they continue to support the continued operation and growth of the firm. Similarly,

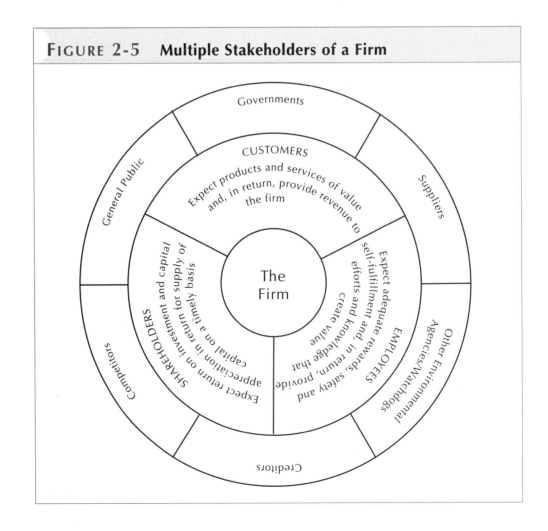

FIGURE 2-5   Multiple Stakeholders of a Firm

investors (typically, shareholders) expect not only capital protection and appreciation, but also adequate returns for their investment on an on-going basis. The employees, who produce the firm's goods and services that create value expect, in return, to be treated fairly with adequate pay, meaningful jobs, pleasant and safe working conditions, and possibility of career and individual growth.

To survive and prosper, an organization must create value for all its stakeholders, especially primary stakeholders. However the needs of the various stakeholders are qualitatively different-at times even contradictory.

> The personal goal of an employee to spend time with his or her family directly conflicts with an organization's goal to increase production through mandatory overtime work. The shareholders' goal of getting high returns often directly conflicts with the environmentalists' demand for tighter emission controls.

This creates an interesting situation: Focusing on the needs of a single stakeholder may prove to be a grave mistake as long-term value may not be created. Different stakeholders may have varying priorities in the short run. Given this, what should an organization do? Five approaches have been useful in managing conflicting priorities and are discussed below.

BARGAINING

Bargaining is a process where stakeholders and their supporting coalitions achieve part of their objectives through discussion and negotiations. Continuous bargaining among various coalitions helps determine an agenda that is most satisfactory (or least unsatisfactory) to all.

Bargaining is a process whereby stakeholders and supporting coalitions achieve a portion of their objectives through discussions and negotiations.

> Shareholders attempt to maximize their returns and investment security, while employees may bargain for better working conditions and employment security.

While bargaining is a popular approach, it often produces less than optimal solutions. The power held by different interest groups may severely constrain organizational actions. For example, a strong labour union may prevent any layoffs even when it is good for the long-term health of the company. Bargaining is often time consuming and can generate adverse feelings between bargaining parties (e.g., during a major labour strike). Further, an organization may be able to attract contributions from its stakeholders only as long as it can provide inducements. In other words, any coalition that believes its contributions to the organization are higher than the inducements it receives will withdraw its support and, in extreme cases, may leave the organization.

SATISFICING

Satisficing, a Scottish word for satisfying first used by Nobel laureate Herbert A. Simon, is a process designed to focus on the satisfactory realization of several goals simultaneously rather than on the maximum attainment of any one goal.[5] Thus, an organization may not maximize its profits, employee satisfaction, or product quality if these goals conflict, but may have satisfactory levels of performance in all goals.[6] While this is a practical and feasible solution, it often results in less than optimal solutions and generates decisions that may be mutually inconsistent, especially when the decisions to be made are complex or when individuals make decisions without consultation.

Satisficing is a process designed to achieve satisfactory realization of several goals simultaneously.

PRIORITIZING

Prioritizing involves ranking goals to indicate their relative importance.

Prioritizing involves assigning a rank to various goals in order to indicate their relative importance. Ranking goals often enables decision makers to make difficult choices among conflicting goals. Giving priority to one goal, such as increasing market share, does not mean that other goals are ignored; other goals (e.g., managerial development) continue to exist but are given lower priority at least temporarily. To ensure allocation of sufficient importance to all goals, an organization may have to reprioritize its goals frequently-a task that may cause confusion and or may not happen. In organizations characterized by high member turnover and loosely defined authority patterns, the frequent reprioritizing may also create member uncertainty.

SEQUENTIAL ATTENTION

Sequential attention is a process in which certain goals are systematically attended to before others.

At times, organizations may give **sequential attention** to various goals, whereby some goals are systematically attended to before turning attention to others. This approach enables an organization to attain satisfactory levels of performance on one goal before attempting to achieve another.[7] Consider how one organization handled conflicting goals between two departments.

> The marketing department of Canada Perfumes wanted to enter the lucrative market of Southeast Asia and capture a 25% market share before competition arrived. At the same time, the research and development department of the company had a major breakthrough, which, if given more money to develop, could have increased the total sales of the company significantly after 18 months. Limited funds meant that the firm could pursue only one of the above goals at a time. After considerable discussion, it was decided that the firm would spend the money needed to enter the Asian market immediately. Once the company had achieved the targeted market share there and sales revenues from Asia started flowing in, these revenues would be channelled to the development of new product. This solution meant that the firm would not lose out on a major marketing opportunity but would also maintain and improve its position in existing markets through product development.

Sequential attention strategy assumes that an organization can place decisions in a temporal sequence and attend to one at a time. This may not be practical in many instances. Opportunities may be lost while the firm waits to achieve another goal.

BALANCED SCORECARD APPROACH

A **balanced scorecard** is a system that outlines financial, customer-related, employee-related, and internal process goals and assesses the accomplishment of these goals.

More recently, several organizations have introduced a **balanced scorecard** to reflect the importance of multiple stakeholders in the firm. A balanced scorecard includes financial, customer-related, employee-related, and internal process-related goals of a firm along with a set of measures for assessing their accomplishment. The balanced scorecard approach allows managers to look at a business from multiple perspectives thus minimizing the risk of overlooking an important stakeholder or activity. Typically, four perspectives are considered:[8]

- How do our customers see us? (*Market focus*)
- How do our owners and shareholders see our performance? (*Financial focus*)
- How can we continue to improve work process and create value? (*Process focus*)
- In what must we excel to achieve our mission and goals? (*Internal and strategic focus*)

Website for a firm specializing in balanced scorecard approach:
http://balancedscorecard.com

Focus on Ethics:

What Is a Firm's Social Responsibility?

Is a business's primary responsibility to maximize profits? Or, does a firm have a social responsibility? If yes, to what extent should it be involved in activities that detract from profit-making?

Milton Friedman, a Nobel Prize winning economist, strongly endorses an efficiency perspective that states that a business's only purpose is to maximize wealth for its shareholders. According to Friedman, a corporate executive is an employee of the business owners in a free enterprise, private property system. The executive therefore must conduct business to comply with the stakeholders wishes and this usually means making as much money as possible while conforming to basic societal rules-both legal and ethical.[9] From this perspective, a firm does not serve its owners by subscribing to social causes and charities; it is up to the shareowners to decide how they want to spend their wealth. The executive's role is to simply act as an agent of the owners and manage the business effectively and efficiently in order to produce maximum wealth. Proponents of this school of thought believe that social responsibility is to be addressed by the government, not business. Individuals (as in the case of shareholders) can spend their wealth as they see fit; however, spending corporate resources on social causes only detracts the firm from its primary purpose. For instance, donations to a local ethnic organization should be avoided unless these donations, in turn, create a loyal customer group or result in tangible benefits for the firm.

The social responsibility perspective, on the other hand, emphasizes that managers (and businesses) have multiple roles to play and multiple stakeholders. Stakeholders are all those who have a stake in or claim on the firm[10] (e.g., suppliers, employees, members of local community) and they, indeed, grant the firm legitimacy and right to exist. While this approach has found favour with many, there are several challenges and issues to be resolved here. Who exactly is a stakeholder? Is an unborn baby a stakeholder? What about an unborn bird or bear? What happens when one stakeholder's interests conflict with another's? Are managers trained to identify and evaluate socially beneficial actions? Wouldn't the overall social cause be better served if governments or other professionals dealt with social priorities and causes?

Consider the following situations. Respond to each and then find out how your classmates or friends responded to them. Which of the two positions described above are reflected in people's responses? Which ethical position (see Chapter 1, page 22) seems to be latent here?

1. Your employer, who owns 12 boutique and clothing shops, has sent you to a developing country to purchase jeans and other apparel worth $500 000. Your firm's sales this year have been much higher than expected and your inventories are fast depleting. On arrival at the new supplier's place, you are very impressed with the quality of the merchandise and the low prices. You realize that the supplier in this country has several buyers abroad. It is not easy to get supplies-especially, high-quality merchandise-on short notice. You express a desire to tour the supplier's facilities. The manager was reluctant at first, but finally agreed after much pressure. When you visit the factory-in fact, a shack where an adult can hardly stand-you find dozens of children aged 8 to 13 working from 15 to 18 hours per day stitching the clothes. You learn that they are paid less than $0.50 for each day's work. You have heard about child labour, but this is the first time you have witnessed it and it upsets you to see the working conditions.

2. Your firm produces Dichlorodiphenyltrichloroethane (DDT), a powerful insecticide banned in most of the Western world but still used in several developing countries. DDT, first used in 1942, became an immediate success because there was nothing like it for killing certain insects (e.g., spruce budworm, mosquito, beetle, and body louse). Research indicates that DDT may cause cancer in humans. Evidence emerging from studies on animals suggests this as well. Some affected animals lived thousands of kilometres away from the nearest fields or towns where DDT was sprayed. Polar bears in the Arctic, penguins in the Antarctic, and plankton in the oceans showed traces of DDT. On the positive side, this pesticide that contaminates the food chain also controls the mosquito that carries malaria when it is sprayed on the interior walls of houses in the tropics. Today, malaria kills as many as 2.5 million people a year in tropical, developing countries. It is not an exaggeration to say that DDT is looked at as a killer in the rich, developed countries of the West but is considered a saviour in sub-Saharan Africa and parts of Asia. Your firm, which produces a number of chemical products and has annual earnings of $300 million, can make about $15 million a year by continuing to sell DDT in these developing countries. If your firm discontinues manufacturing DDT and replaces it with an alternate, safer chemical expected to achieve the same results, a new investment of $200 million will be required initially. It will take at least 18 months before the company will reach break-even sales in this case.

Balanced scorecard has been said to avoid the trap of over-emphasizing financial measures (such as return on investment), to the exclusion of non-financial measures. A firm's financial statements only indicate whether its strategy is working, but not why. By measuring other dimensions such as customer value and the firm's distinctive competencies, a more balanced and in-depth view of a firm's operations may emerge. A balanced scorecard approach also minimizes role ambiguity on the part of managers since they are aware of corporate goals and measures used to assess them. This guards against sub-optimization in decision-making. By forcing decision makers to consider all operational measures together, the balanced scorecard helps them assess whether improvement in one area was achieved at the expense of another important stakeholder.

> In one organization, a dividend increase was at the expense of investments into long-term value creation and product development. Review sessions forming part of the firm's balanced scorecard approach drew the decision makers' attention to this fact and facilitated necessary corrective actions.

The balanced scorecard approach is likely found useful in large firms where timely communication of organizational priorities to lower levels often poses challenges. It has been claimed to reduce information overload by limiting the number of measures used.

Figure 2-6 shows the application of balanced scorecard in one engineering company that focuses on four areas: financial, market, employees, and internal process. The associated questions it asks to translate its vision into specific goals are also shown. Today, a number of firms apply the balanced scorecard approach while setting goals.

Website for information on balanced scorecard implementation: *www.bsconline@bscol.com*

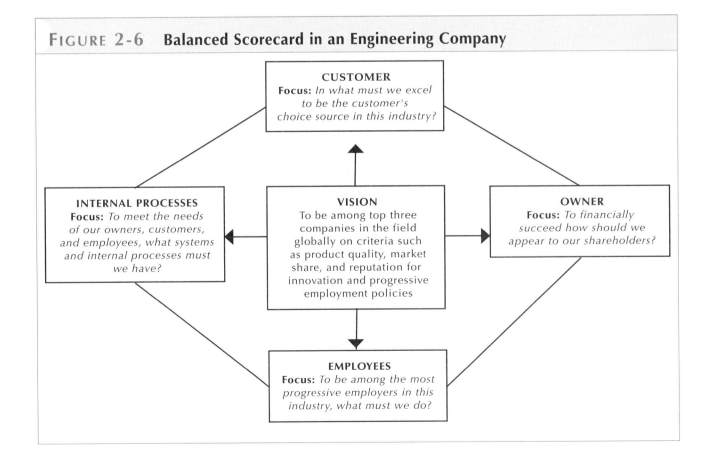

FIGURE 2-6   Balanced Scorecard in an Engineering Company

CUSTOMER
Focus: *In what must we excel to be the customer's choice source in this industry?*

INTERNAL PROCESSES
Focus: *To meet the needs of our owners, customers, and employees, what systems and internal processes must we have?*

VISION
To be among top three companies in the field globally on criteria such as product quality, market share, and reputation for innovation and progressive employment policies

OWNER
Focus: *To financially succeed how should we appear to our shareholders?*

EMPLOYEES
Focus: *To be among the most progressive employers in this industry, what must we do?*

Nova Scotia Power Inc. (NSPI) introduced the balanced scorecard approach in 1996 with very positive outcomes. NSPI reports that overall customer satisfaction in 1998 was 20% higher than in 1997 and at its highest since 1991. The total number of power interruptions decreased to record lows in 1998, accidents in 1998 were 25% fewer than in 1997, and the number of employees who "felt a greater sense of being valued" more than doubled in 1998 over 1997. Several firms like Apple Computer, Advanced Micro Devices, and FMC Corporation of the U.S. have reported beneficial outcomes from the balanced scorecard approach.[11]

Balanced scorecard, while useful in a number of settings, is no panacea for all the challenges in goal setting. The scorecard is based on the principle that "what gets measured gets done." By this very philosophy, a scorecard is biased in favour of quantifiable measures over qualitative measures (e.g., corporate culture, customer loyalty) that may not be accurately measurable using numbers alone. If not carefully monitored, goals requiring longer time horizons for accurate measures (e.g., employee development) may be passed in favour of short-term goals and targets. Finally, the trade-offs among the various priorities should still occur through bargaining, sequential attention, or prioritizing. In this sense, scorecard is a facilitating tool rather than a unique approach to choosing among conflicting goals and stakeholder interests.

IDENTIFYING ORGANIZATIONAL GOALS AND STRATEGIES

Almost all organizations have multiple goals-goals that are designed to meet the needs of different stakeholders. Further, even those organizations that operate in the same domain may show remarkable differences in their strategies and goals.

> Compare the goals and strategies of two successful hockey teams: one team may have set its current year's goal as winning the Stanley Cup, while another may have decided to treat this as a rebuilding year. A rebuilding team seeks to develop and give experience to rookies, often sacrificing winning in the process and will trade proven veterans who are nearing retirement for high-potential new players. The focus here is on the future.

> Federal Express, IBM, McDonalds, and Disney are all examples of organizations that have inculcated in their employees the importance of customer service. Some of these organizations value customer service to such an extent that it is no longer a mere goal, but rather part of their basic business philosophy.

Clear goals provide standards for evaluating the performances of an organization and its employees. Criteria such as profits, sales volume, percentage of market share, and number of customer complaints all provide measurable goals against which actual performance can be evaluated. When employee rewards are tied to organizational goals such as productivity and profits, employee motivation also increases as shown in the case of Dofasco.

> Dofasco, one of the largest steel manufacturers in Canada, has always emphasized good employee relations as a goal. Since 1938, when it introduced its profit-sharing plan, Dofasco has maintained economic efficiency in a highly competitive industry. Part of this is attributable to high employee motivation and a healthy cooperative relationship between labour and management.[12]

Website for articles on performance goals: *http://humanresources.about. com*

Organizational goals are closely related to strategies. A strategy can be compared to a "game plan" in football or soccer. Before a team enters the field, the coach looks at the team's strengths and weaknesses and those of its competitors. He or she carefully studies both teams' successes, failures, and performance on the field. The

SELF-TEST:

How Balanced Is Your Present Life?

This test will help you gain insight into your present life by simulating a balanced scorecard approach. Indicate whether you *agree* (A) or *disagree* (D) with each of the following statements. If you cannot make up your mind, indicate *undecided* (UD). If a question is not relevant (for instance, if you are not currently employed some of the questions may not apply), indicate *not applicable* (NA).

1. My workload as a student often prevents me from spending enough time with my family.

2. There are several occasions when I spend so much time with my friends that it adversely affects my job performance.

3. Frequently, my family responsibilities prevent me from spending adequate time on my studies.

4. I work so many hours at my job that I hardly see my family.

5. Frequently, my job requires me to miss or perform poorly on course assignments.

6. Frequently, my friends expect me to spend time with them even when they know that I have to complete course assignments.

7. My family roles do not give me any time to have fun with my friends.

8. Now that I am a student, I hardly socialize with my friends.

9. My employer expects me to work so long that I hardly get to see my friends.

10. On days when course assignments are due or I have to write exams, I can hardly focus on my job.

11. My friends make me spend time with them that I should have spent with my family.

12. Frequently, my family responsibilities do not permit me to be at work when my employer wants.

Scoring

Create four categories: *school* (S), *employer* (E), *family* (FY), and *friends* (FR). These are your "constituents". Depending on your current lifestyle you may have four or fewer constituents. For example, students who are not currently employed have three or fewer constituents. Ignore all questions that you marked NA.

For items 1, 8, and 10, assign a score of 2 for A and 1 for UD in category S. For items 4, 5 and 9, assign a score of 2 for A and 1 for UD in category E. For items 3, 7 and 12, assign a score of 2 for A and 1 for UD in category FY. For items 2, 6 and 11, assign a score of 2 for A and 1 for UD in category FR. For items 1, 4, and 11, assign a score of 2 for D in category FY. For items 7, 8 and 9, assign a score of 2 for D in category FR. For items 2, 10, and 12 assign a score of 2 for D in category E. For items 3, 5 and 6, assign a score of 2 for D in category S.

Interpretation

This exercise may help you understand the trade-offs you make among the four constituents in your life: your family, your friends, your employer, and your instructors. Ideally, your scores in the four categories should be equal. A highly skewed distribution indicates a pre-occupation with one constituent, perhaps requiring refocus.

In business, one firm may attempt to maximize its immediate profits and cash flows, while another may be willing to forgo short-term profits for a greater market share in the future. Even similar organizations can differ in the relative importance they assign to specific goals while different organizations may have vastly differing priorities. Figure 2-7 shows some of the popular goals seen in Canadian organizations along with their meanings and sample measures. Apart from formal goals, most organizations also have unwritten, informal goals which direct member behaviours and are related to a firm's overall mission.

FIGURE 2-7   Popular Organizational Goals

Goals	Meaning	Sample measure
1. Profitability	Revenue remaining after all costs and obligations are met	Return on investment
2. Growth	Increase in such variables as plant capacity, workforce size, and market share	Growth in workforce size
3. Innovation	Introduction of new products, processes, or ways of looking at phenomena with significant practical implications	Number of new patents
4. Productivity improvement	Ratio of organization's outputs (goods and services) to inputs (people, capital, materials, resources, and energy)	Labour productivity indices
5. Employee satisfaction	Extent to which an organization meets the needs of its employees	Attitudinal survey measures
6. Employee development	Improving the present and future competencies and skills of employees	Number and quality of training and development programs
7. Social responsibility	Extent to which an organization meets societal concerns and contributes to the society	Contributions to social projects

objective is to win the game with minimal risk and injuries to the players and the coach may not use all the team's best players if it is not warranted: they may be kept in reserve for future games or to maintain an element of surprise. Also, the game plan itself might be modified to recognize new realities, for example, the opponent comes out playing more aggressively than in the past.

A strategy is much more than a game plan, however. A game plan covers only one game and one opponent, while a strategy deals with a wealth of basic issues such as technological advancements, changes in customer preferences, and new government regulations. A strategy is oriented toward many elements of a firm's environment such as competitors, government, and employees. A **strategy,** then, is a comprehensive and integrated plan with relatively long-term implications designed to achieve the basic mission and objectives of an organization. Examples of strategies include decisions to compete in specific product market segments, to be a low cost producer, to diversify, to expand, or to close down specific operations.

Identification of organizational strategy is a complex task requiring a careful analysis of external environments and organizational capabilities. The process involved is very elaborate and outside the scope of this chapter. However, all strategies should complement and enhance an organization's competitive advantage. Some organizations have a competitive advantage in marketing while the strengths of others lie in innovation, product development, and financial management.

> Labatt's strength lies in its marketing skills and product reputation. Nortel achieved past success because of its technology, aggressive marketing, and efficient production, Inco's success has been attributed to quality, proprietary mineral holdings, and access to cheap electricity.

Gaining competitive advantage largely depends on two things: providing more value to suppliers and competitors and maintaining uniqueness.[13]

A **strategy** is a comprehensive and integrated plan with relatively long-term implications designed to achieve the basic mission and objectives of an organization.

Website for strategy, corporate mission, and goals:
www4.hr.com/hrcom/index. cfm/74/WeeklyMag/ weeklymagarchview.cfm

Focus on Small Business:

Assessing the Business Environment to Formulate Goals

As pointed out in Chapter 1, small businesses are more vulnerable to external threats and uncertainties. Good management and high calibre employees are vital for success of all firms, small or large. Yet, the unique characteristics of small businesses-often, limited capital, severe limitations on other factors of production, and constraints on access to markets and technology-make good management and a competent workforce even more critical for their success. Many small businesses operate in highly uncertain and competitive industries making performance management extremely important.

Consider a small business with which you are familiar. Now, rate it on the following ten questions using a scale of *strongly agree* (SA), *agree* (A), *uncertain* (U), *disagree* (D) or *strongly disagree* (SD).

1. It requires relatively little know-how to enter the industry in which this firm operates.

2. The start-up costs for entering the industry in which this firm operates are relatively low.

3. There are a number of established firms in this industry.

4. The products offered by firms operating in this industry are homogenous.

5. It is not risky and is relatively inexpensive to enter this industry.

6. No single firm or manufacturer in this industry holds 50% or more of the market share.

7. The technology employed by firms operating in this industry is fast changing.

8. The firms operating in this industry must continuously improve work processes to maintain competitiveness.

9. This industry is characterized by a high degree of change.

10. The labour costs in this industry are high.

11. The managerial expertise needed to succeed in this industry is very high.

12. The customer preferences in this industry are rapidly changing.

For all statements, assign a value of 5, 4, 3, 2, and 1 for SA, A, U, D and SD respectively. Add up your scores for questions 1-6 and 7-12 separately. Call them Score C and Score U.

This exercise examines two key dimensions of the environments within which a business operates: competitive intensity (Score C) and environmental uncertainty (Score U). The higher the score, the greater the competitive intensity and environmental uncertainty.

Competitive intensity refers to the extent of competition in the industry. When the costs to enter the industry are low and products are relatively homogenous, many competitors are likely to be present (as opposed to an industry where a single firm holds key patents). The firm also faces higher competition when there are large numbers of established firms in the industry (e.g., soft drink industry).

Environmental uncertainty is high when the costs associated with a mistake are high, when there are no clear criteria available for making decisions, and when the associated costs and benefits of various alternatives are not easily determined. In situations characterized by rapidly changing technology, high labour costs, and high dynamism in the environments, a firm faces considerable uncertainty.

While performance management is important in all firms, some activities assume greater importance in firms facing both high uncertainty and competitive intensity. A clear definition of organizational mission and strategies and the identification of innovative solutions and responses become critical in organizations facing rapid environmental change and intense competitive pressures. In more stable environments, the focus may be on improving the consistency of employee behaviour and systems and reducing errors or deviations. If innovation, out-of-the-box thinking, continuous learning, and change are encouraged in businesses facing unstable environments, quality control, consistency, and efficiency seem to be guiding principles for those operating in stable environments.

Now consider another business that operates in an industry different from the one you already selected. Do your conclusions support the above analysis?

PROVIDING MORE VALUE

Competitive advantage is achieved only if customers perceive that they receive value from their transactions. A product or service may be the best in the world, but if customers do not gain a perceived value from it, the business will have no competitive advantage.

A restaurant owner in Regina may go to Scotland to hire and bring the world's best haggis chef to Canada. While the entrepreneur might serve the best haggis in Saskatchewan, the firm will not have gained an advantage if no one comes to the restaurant.[14]

Many organizations take their industry conditions as given and set strategies accordingly. However, "value innovators" break the conventional parameters of strategic thinking and create their own. They think in terms of the total solution the consumers seek when buying a product or service and overcome existing obstacles in new and innovative ways.[15] These firms look for big ideas that help make quantum leaps in value offered.

For years, the major U.S. television networks used the same format for news programming. All had newscasts at the same time slots and competed on their analysis of events, professionalism, and reputation of anchors. In 1980, CNN came out with an idea that made a quantum leap in value. It introduced the real-time news from around the world 24 hours a day. Not only did it emerge as the leader of global news broadcasting, it was able to produce 24 hours of real-time news for one-fifth the cost of one hour of popular network news.[16]

Maintaining Uniqueness

Competitive advantage is also dependent on the uniqueness of a firm's product. If the firm offers a product its competitors cannot make, competitive advantage is high. The uniqueness may emerge from product features, the mode of delivery, or the after-sales service offered for example.

The uniqueness may be real or perceived. Most blind taste tests indicate that consumers cannot perceive any significant difference in the taste of popular cola drinks. However, major cola manufacturers have been successful in creating uniqueness for their products in the minds of the consumers by associating them with specific contexts (e.g., action, adventure, romance) or customer groups (e.g., young, attractive, sporty).

Gaining competitive advantage often involves considerable time and resource commitment. A future perspective may be necessary to give the firm a strong position in the marketplace. Rather than simply asking, "Which customers are you serving today?" or "Who are your competitors today?", successful organizations focus on their future customers, competitors, and competitive advantage. Rather than simply improving their present market shares, these market leaders redefine products and services to maximize their "opportunity shares"; they understand that the future should not be viewed through the narrow aperture of existing, already served markets.[17] In other words, they recognize that the future may not simply be an extension of the past. Some successful organizations are engaged in continually reinventing their future.

Identifying Individual and Departmental Goals

Once the broad organizational goals and strategies are identified, they need to be translated into everyday performance goals for individuals and departments.[18]

The mission of an Ontario school to encourage the education, development, and mental growth of the students by instilling a love of learning and intellectual curiosity has to be translated to day-to-day operational goals. Some of the latter goals may be to improve the student-teacher ratio, to provide more individual attention to the students, to reduce total operating costs, and to upgrade computer facilities within two years.

Figure 2-8 shows how the vision of the engineering company discussed in Figure 2-6 is translated into operative goals in the four areas. For example, customer satisfaction measures, overall sales volume (and market share), and percentage repeat purchases reflect its success in providing value to customers. To be useful, the vision and strategies should be translated in terms of factors that really matter to the stakeholder group concerned. The three goals used in Figure 2-8 under "customer" reflect the customer's concerns of delivery time, quality, performance, and service and are closely related to the firm's ability to meet these.

To provide direction, goals should not only delineate desired outcomes but should also be well understood by all organizational members. This means that the strategy and goals should be communicated up and down the organization and linked to departmental, team, and individual goals and action plans. The process has five major steps that are discussed below.

DETERMINE OUTPUT REQUIREMENTS FOR THE POSITION OR DEPARTMENT

The key performance outcomes associated with various departments, teams, and individuals that support the organizational goals have to be identified. A thorough review of the position involves asking several questions including:

- What are this position's unique contributions?

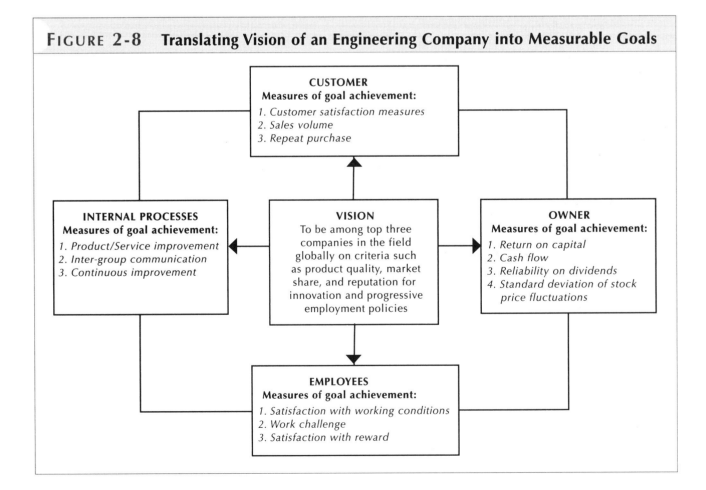

FIGURE 2-8   Translating Vision of an Engineering Company into Measurable Goals

CUSTOMER
Measures of goal achievement:
1. Customer satisfaction measures
2. Sales volume
3. Repeat purchase

INTERNAL PROCESSES
Measures of goal achievement:
1. Product/Service improvement
2. Inter-group communication
3. Continuous improvement

VISION
To be among top three companies in the field globally on criteria such as product quality, market share, and reputation for innovation and progressive employment policies

OWNER
Measures of goal achievement:
1. Return on capital
2. Cash flow
3. Reliability on dividends
4. Standard deviation of stock price fluctuations

EMPLOYEES
Measures of goal achievement:
1. Satisfaction with working conditions
2. Work challenge
3. Satisfaction with reward

- Why is this position needed? What would change if the position were eliminated?
- How does the employee spend his or her time?

> The output requirements for a sales manager in the case of the engineering company discussed in Figures 2-6 and 2-8 would include sales levels, sales policies, sales costs, line profitability, and customer satisfaction. These denote the major output requirements of the position.

Each one of the above areas can be further broken up to get clearer focus.

> For example, "line profitability" for the above sales manager may be broken up into specific measures such as gross profit, net profit, and profit by product line.

Such clear specifications not only ensure better communication across various departments and levels but also help identify any inconsistencies in goals.

IDENTIFY PERFORMANCE STANDARDS

Next, the long-range and short-range goals and performance standards have to be identified for all departments and key positions. For any given position, there may be from one to over ten objectives, although four to six objectives are typical. To be useful, such goals should be specific, measurable, cost-bound, time-bound, and realistic.[19] Figure 2-9 outlines the characteristics of well-formulated goals and standards. These objectives should focus on outcomes rather than on intentions or inputs.

> "Maintaining machines", "spending time and money in training subordinates", "educating farmers" and "attending to parishioners' needs" are poor objectives as they refer to efforts or inputs. The associated outcomes are "machine availability", "subordinate effectiveness", "high crop yield", and "development and maintenance of Christian values".

Figure 2-10 provides examples of poorly and well-formulated objectives. Performance standards should be determined after a careful consideration of the firm's objectives and resources. More recently, progressive organizations have used benchmarking to identify performance standards. Benchmarking is discussed in greater detail later in this chapter.

HORIZONTAL AND VERTICAL LINKING OF OBJECTIVES

Goals have to be linked horizontally across various departments and job positions to ensure coordination. All objectives should also link vertically across various management levels to ensure consistency and a concerted effort to achieve them.

FIGURE 2-9   Attributes of Well-Formulated Goals and Performance Standards

The acronym **START** can summarize the key features of well-formulated goals and performance standards. They are:

Specific–define the outcomes or expectations in clear outcome or behavioural terms.

Tangible and measurable–they can be measured unambiguously. Two persons independently measuring the performance are likely to come to similar conclusions.

Acceptable–the goals and performance standards have been understood and accepted by the employee and cover all major dimensions of performance.

Realistic–the standards are realistic considering the resources and skills of the employee.

Time bound–there are clear timelines attached to the accomplishment of the goal.

FIGURE 2-10   Poor Objectives and Their Reformulation

Poorly-Formulated Objectives	Reformulated Objectives
To improve our profitability	To attain a 14% return on investment and an 18% return on equity by 31 December 2005.
To be a socially responsive company	To hire and train 100 hard-core unemployed persons between the ages of 18 and 40 from surrounding communities by 30 June 2005. The trained persons should be able to operate a lathe with a waste rate of less than 2%. The cost of the program should not exceed $75 000.
To conduct market research on Product X	To complete market research on Product X by 1 June 2005 at a cost not exceeding $14 000, which will bring information on items 1, 2, 3, and 4 about Product X.

At Canadian Electronic and Computer Manufacturers Ltd., the new sales goal was 200 000 personal computers in 2002-2003. This meant that the four geographical divisions of Western, Prairie, Central, and Eastern Canada had to achieve sales of 70 000, 10 000, 90 000 and 30 000 units respectively. Based on this goal, each regional office, sales office, and sales manager in the company calculated its sales goals for the next year and for various months. The company also made sure that the needs of the production, materials, human resource, and finance divisions were met. Revised procedures and systems were initiated where necessary in order to meet the goals.

Collecting employee feedback enables the organization to check whether employees understand and accept organizational and performance goals. Figure 2-11 is a sample questionnaire that provides some general insights on employee beliefs in this context. In larger organizations employing hundreds of employees, careful questionnaire design and sampling are vital to generate valid information. Chapter 9 discusses employee surveys in greater detail.

SYSTEMS AND LOGISTICS PLANNING

It is not merely enough to have clear and challenging goals. The internal systems, resource allocation, and other tactical plans must support and reinforce the accomplishment of the goals. This requires, among other things:

- A clear understanding of task interdependencies. Unless the interdependencies among various tasks and job positions are understood, plans cannot be effectively executed. A variety of tools such as observation, job and task analysis, examination of equipment blue prints, and use of engineering plans aid this process. These are discussed in greater detail in Chapter 3.

- Budgeting and logistics planning. Allocating scarce resources (including time) to competing priorities must be done in a way to facilitate goal accomplishment.

- Continuous improvement and change management programs. Almost all modern organizations are continually looking for ways to improve operations. However, haphazardly planned change programs do not achieve strategic goals. The firm's training and development and change programs should reinforce and facilitate the accomplishment of overall corporate strategy and goals.

FIGURE 2-11   A Simple Survey to Gauge Employee Beliefs about Organizational Mission and Goals

Please indicate your responses to each question by checking the appropriate box strongly agree (SA), agree (A), neither agree nor disagree (NAD), disagree (D), or strongly disagree (SD).

	SA	A	NAD	D	SD
1. I am informed in a timely fashion of the changes in my organization's priorities.	❏	❏	❏	❏	❏
2. I have a good understanding of our mission.	❏	❏	❏	❏	❏
3. I understand the major issues facing my employer.	❏	❏	❏	❏	❏
4. The top management frequently communicates their vision to all levels.	❏	❏	❏	❏	❏
5. Often, I feel excluded from the decision-making process.	❏	❏	❏	❏	❏
6. I have a good understanding of my performance targets.	❏	❏	❏	❏	❏
7. The goals of various departments are inconsistent.	❏	❏	❏	❏	❏
8. My performance goals are clearly measurable.	❏	❏	❏	❏	❏
9. In general, this organization knows where it is going.	❏	❏	❏	❏	❏
10. There is very little employee input sought by management when setting organizational goals.	❏	❏	❏	❏	❏

Scoring: For all statements except 5, 7, and 10, assign scores of 5, 4, 3, 2, and 1 for SA, A, NAD, D, and SD. For items 5, 7, and 10, assign scores of 1, 2, 3, 4, and 5 for SA, A, NAD, D, and SD. Add up the scores. The scores may range from 10 to 50. A high score indicates that the mission and goals are clearly communicated to the respondent.

- Human resource management systems. The firm's human resource (HR) management systems and practices must support and enhance its corporate strategy. Key HR activities such as selection of employees, compensation planning, performance appraisal, and counselling must be in line with corporate objectives and strategies.

Website of the International Association of HR Information Management:
www.ihrim.org

Website for human resource audit:
www.shrm.org

> For the Ontario school mentioned earlier, one operational goal pertains to control of costs, specifically, in the maintenance department. In 2002, the principal decided that the costs of all routine maintenance (such as painting and repair costs) should not exceed 6% of the school's total budget expenditure. The school also decided to hire two part-time instructors in history and mathematics to reduce class sizes. This required changes in the hiring and compensation systems since qualified instructors could not be locally found and had to be attracted from elsewhere.

Sometimes, even major structural changes may have to be done to facilitate goal accomplishment. As an organization grows in size and complexity or changes its goals and product-market focus, new organizational forms become imperative for success. The appropriate choice depends on a variety of organizational and industry-related characteristics.

> The type of organizational structure that suits a small brewery in British Columbia marketing its products only within the province is unlikely to be suitable for a large brewery that produces many brands and sells them nationally. The structure appropriate to a multi-product and multi-technology organization with brewing as one of its businesses is likely to be very different again.

Structural dimensions such as degree of centralization and specialization have to be examined for their appropriateness with the firm's goals, strategies, and environments. Figure 2-12 shows key structural dimensions that need to be assessed in this context. The appropriateness of any single structure depends on a variety of factors including organizational philosophy and culture, technology employed, environmental dynamism, organizational strategy, and member characteristics.

Finally, goals, strategies, and internal systems should be periodically reviewed for their continued relevance in the present and future environment. When a firm's strategies no longer fit its needs, they have to be altered.

> Once a leader among North American department stores, Sears lost ground to competitors like Wal-Mart and Home Depot. Sears simply lost sight of its customers. "We didn't know who we wanted to serve," noted Sears' CEO. "That was a huge hole in our strategy." A major strategy overhaul led to the disposal of non-retail assets and a renewed focus on Sears' core business. Sears renovated outdated stores, upgraded women's apparel, and launched a new advertising campaign. The company found high brand loyalty to its hardware lines and increased its focus on hardware and home renovation, capitalizing on brand name products such as Craftsman, Kenmore, and DieHard. It planned to make these products available to consumers through numerous small stores, a change from its previous strategy of a few large stores.[20]

Goals and performance standards are often reviewed in light of industry trends. Many organizations have found benchmarking a useful approach for reviewing performance standards. The process of benchmarking is discussed in the next section.

BENCHMARKING PERFORMANCE

Benchmarking is the process of identifying and incorporating industry practices that are most likely to create breakthrough improvement in processes, products, services, designs, and equipment in order to generate value for stakeholders and to improve real performance.

Benchmarking involves the identification and incorporation of the most successful practices, either internal or external, in an industry to achieve breakthrough improvement in processes, products, services, designs, and equipment. The goal is to generate

---

FIGURE 2-12   Sample Structural Dimensions

Standardization
The extent to which similar work activities are performed in a uniform manner. In organizations like McDonald's, work content is described in detail and standardization is very high.

Specialization
The degree to which organizational tasks are subdivided into separate jobs. If specialization is extensive, each employee will perform only a narrow range of tasks as in the case of a traditional assembly line job.

Formalization
The amount of written documentation in organizations. Documentation includes procedures, job descriptions, policies, and regulations for members. In some instances, it also indicates the limits of power held by job incumbents (e.g., budget approval powers). There are some organizations like hospitals and financial institutions where documentation is considered highly important while in some smaller, owner-operated firms, formalization may be virtually absent.

Span of Control
The number of subordinates reporting to a single supervisor. Many management practitioners suggest that a span larger than six or seven individuals becomes less effective although in practice wide variations of span are common.

Hierarchy of Authority
Denotes who reports to whom and the span of control for each manager.

Centralization
Refers to the hierarchical level that has authority to make a decision. When all critical decisions are made at top levels, the organization is centralized.

value for stakeholders and improve real performance. In the past, benchmarking was synonymous with copying the best; more recently, it means integrating ideas from several sources to develop a new process or product that outperforms any one of the benchmarking partner's items.[21] It also involves creating better solutions based upon a firm and expanding knowledge base. In the past, benchmarking was primarily aimed at improving organizational processes. Today, it is employed to improve products and service delivery and to meet the needs of a firm's constituents. Some consider benchmarking the best tool for measuring and enhancing competitiveness.[22]

> The procedures employed by a department that has a reputation for outstanding value creation and superior performance may be used as benchmarks by other departments within the same firm.

BENCHMARKING APPROACHES

Benchmarking aims to improve, among other things, a firm's products, service, or manufacturing process (Figure 2-13). Whatever the focus, the objective is the same: identifying the best possible ways of designing products, delivering services, etc. Depending on the benchmarking objective, differing methods are employed to identify "the best" in each area. Four popular approaches are discussed below.

Competitive Product Benchmarking Laboratory analysis is used to understand competitors' product design concepts and manufacturing processes. The best value ideas are copied without violating patent or other intellectual property rights. It is not simply the product design and quality that is examined at this time, but a host of other features including:

- Product performance—how reliably, safely and effectively does the product perform?

- Product features—what attributes (e.g., ease of storage, colour) do competing products offer? What are some product features that don't add value? How does the design compare with others on factors such as ease of manufacture, ease of storage, and ease of operation?

- Cost—how does the competition's cost compare? Cost includes not simply the price, but also operating and repair costs. For example, an inexpensive car may not be most economical if it has an above average repair incidence.

- After sales service—how does after sales service and warranty compare with industry standards? With industry leaders?

FIGURE 2-13   Benchmarking Focus

- Manufacturing processes
- Products
- Services
- Designs
- Equipment
- Business systems

- Product recognition—Do customers immediately think of our products when asked to name key players in the industry? How effective are current advertising and promotion?

Information collected from the analysis above is used to modify design, manufacture, or delivery processes that add real value to the product. Creating value in today's virtual value chain involves five activities: gathering, organizing, selecting, synthesizing, and distributing information.[23] Often, information can be turned into new spin-off products. By shifting the focus from physical market place to multidimensional market space, new products, services, and combinations can be profitably introduced.

> The Globe and Mail is a newspaper that has capitalized on the value adding properties of information. Drawing from and building on the information used to report news, globeandmail.com provides breaking news as it happens; www.globeandmail.com/business provides breaking business news; www.globeandmail.com/campus provides news and information for students; www.globetechnology.com provides information on emerging technology; www.globeinvestor.com provides information on stocks; and www.ROBTv.com allows the viewers to watch news on their personal computers.

Comparative Service Benchmarking Competitive shopping is used in comparative service benchmarking to understand competitor's service processes and to emulate and improve on the best practices. The focus is to determine the best value future solutions rather than to simply implement the best practices seen elsewhere.

Simulation Modeling Simulation modeling involves the use of statistical, computerized, or other decision making tools to combine and analyze the best-value combinations for a firm and its customers in design and delivery of products or services. A variety of time, space, and cost simulations are currently available-all defining outcomes associated with various patterns of interactions among people, materials, equipment, product mixes, and delivery times. The use of computer modeling has been gaining popularity in recent years because of easy access to sophisticated modeling tools that can portray the interaction among a large number of variables with a high degree of accuracy and realism.[24]

Website for sample simulation software:
www.experiencepoint.com

> If the average waiting time in a service station before an employee approaches a customer is 5 minutes, simulations can be used to reduce the waiting time. The firm can build a simulated model that calculates additional human resources, process improvement, or system improvement necessary to bring this down to 2 or 3 minutes. It can also predict the expected waiting time for customers if the current staff strength is increased or if process improvements and system improvements bring in additional time savings.

Organizational Change Management When the focus is on changing an organization's culture and philosophy into one that supports continuous improvements, it is not enough to simply introduce technical changes. However, introducing system-wide changes (e.g., culture change) is by no means easy. The change agents must be well versed in the technical demands posed by changes and also must be able to facilitate organizational acceptance of new philosophies. These new philosophies of continuous improvement routinely use tools such as cause-effect analysis, root cause analysis, control charts, and models.[25f] Some of these techniques are discussed in Chapter 3 of this book. Training and communication system improvements, as well as persistence and patience are integral to the success of any such organizational change.

> The experience of Bull Information Systems, a British computer company underscores the challenges of achieving cultural change. Though the need for some fundamental

change was recognized as early as 1986, even in late 1990s the change process had not been completed. The progress was often slow and the budgets allocated were minimal. The change did not start with the top management, rather in one of the divisions of the firm that recognized the need for transforming the work culture to maintain effectiveness and ensure survival. Ultimately, it was the persistence and patience of the change team leader and other catalysts that resulted in progress toward the goal.[26]

Whatever the approach used, all benchmarking exercises go through several phases. These are discussed in the following section.

PHASES OF BENCHMARKING

All benchmarking exercises have four phases.

Phase 1: Planning All benchmarking exercises begin with the formation of a benchmarking initiation team that is entrusted with the task of starting and managing the process. In this phase, the team must:

- define responsibilities;
- identify the benchmarking focus. This may be products, services, equipment, processes, or a combination. Even employee skills can be benchmarked against competitors and industry leaders;[27]
- obtain support from management;
- provide detailed characteristics of the benchmarked item or process;
- describe how to measure these characteristics;
- plan data collection methods; and
- outline data analysis methods.

Once the plans on various aspects of the project are made, the team moves into the second phase of benchmarking.

Phase 2: Data Collection Necessary information for benchmarking is collected in two ways: internally and externally. Internal sources include:

- all readily available information such as reports, forms, charts, budgets and statements;
- information acquired through new, original research (e.g., profiles of customers);
- internal surveys and interviews with individuals who can provide insight into the activity under examination; and
- site visits, where internal departments or services are used as benchmarks.

External data are also of two types: information that is already available and information acquired through original research. Presently available information includes published annual statements, newspaper reports, reports of industry associations, Statistics Canada and Industry Canada reports, and a variety of other information sources (see Figure 2-3, page 3). Sometimes, even unconventional approaches may be used to collect new information. Consider how Apple Computers used reverse-engineering process to catch up with competition.

> In 1990, Apple Computers came out with its portable computer weighing only 18 pounds. The same year, Compaq came out a notebook computer weighing 6 pounds. After disassembling Compaq's notebook, Apple engineers realized that their current

Website for Statistics Canada:
www.statcan.ca

product couldn't be redesigned to match. Apple embarked on a major catch-up project and was able to introduce its own notebook, weighing only 5.1 pounds, in 1991. Other companies such as Motorola, Ford Motor Company, and Xerox routinely disassemble competitors' products to improve own designs. In Xerox's New York state plant, it is common to see 20 to 30 competitors' products carefully disassembled with each part characterized.[28]

Phase 3: Improving Performance

Once the relevant information is collected, it has to be used to improve products, services, or systems. Some of the questions to ask in this context are:

*   Why does a gap exist between a firm's current products or services and those of the benchmarked firm?

*   What are alternate ways to fill this gap and maximize future value for stakeholders? What constraints are faced in this context?

*   What actions are needed today? Tomorrow? By whom? In what order?

*   Can we model future-state solutions and use a flow chart to outline the action sequences?

*   What are the benefits of the change? What are the costs? Who will bear the costs?

A summary comparison of a company's own product (or other benchmarked item) with an industry standard or competitor's product often facilitates communication and the visual identification of present gaps. Figure 2-14 shows a sample comparison of a firm's product with two of its key competitors. As the chart shows, compared to competition, the firm's product scores lower on a number of dimensions, suggesting long-term and tactical solutions to the benchmarking team.

Once the best-value solution is identified and modified after review by internal experts, an implementation plan has to be developed. Typically, a team will be assigned the task of implementing the changes. An implementation budget will also need to be prepared and supported by top management. Planned dates for progress review and tactical plans for modifications will also be identified before implementation.

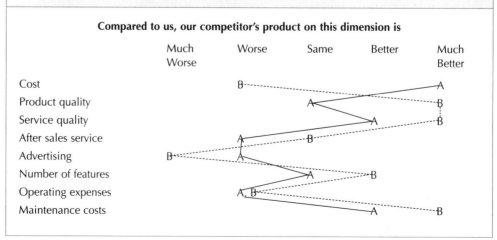

FIGURE 2-14   **Competitive Gap Analysis for Two of a Firm's Competitors**

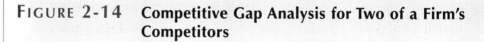

Phase 4: Continuous Improvement Benchmarking is not an isolated, one-time effort. To be beneficial it should be a continuous effort that is integrated into all relevant organizational activities and evolves as time passes. This should not be thought of as something relevant only for large, technologically sophisticated firms (although the changes in technology affect them most). Indeed, given today's technology, even very small businesses can easily create a culture of continuous innovation and improvement in products and service delivery. The process to identify future negative gaps requires an organization to:

- continually update the database on which decisions are made;
- periodically review the data for continued relevance (e.g., the environment may reflect new trends requiring new benchmark targets);
- consistently review the items (i.e., products, services, processes) that require benchmarking; and
- initially develop a mechanism to incorporate past learning into future benchmarking efforts.

Benchmarking procedures should themselves be periodically benchmarked against others to improve them.[29] Many firms formally entrust this responsibility to one or more persons or teams.

The new adage is "adapt or die." Adapting involves more than simply offering new products or services-often, it may involve fundamental rethinking of the business, its goals, and mode of operation as in the CNN example cited earlier. Proactive responses to environmental changes necessitate modifications to internal systems such as reward structure, training, employee development, and even changes in corporate philosophy. Several system wide improvements in compensation, counselling, and training are discussed later in this book. Before dealing with them, it is necessary to examine internal processes and individual employee performance in greater detail (see Chapter 3).

Implications for Practice

1. Specific and challenging goals provide direction and motivate employees. Clear, widely communicated goals should be the standard.

2. Most organizations have multiple goals which may, at times, conflict. To avoid confusion, you should prioritize the goals, attend to them sequentially, or even alter some.

3. The basic mission of the organization should be clearly linked to its goals and strategies.

4. Overall organizational goals should be cascaded down to divisional, departmental, team, and individual levels, making sure that these goals are mutually consistent and well linked.

5. Benchmarking can be used to improve, among other things, a firm's products, services, or manufacturing. Depending on the benchmarking objective, somewhat varying methods should be employed to identify the best future-state value.

6. Continuous environmental scanning and proactive actions are critical for success today. An organization's structure, strategy, and goals should be continuously aligned with the new environmental realities.

Key Terms for Review

Balanced scorecard, p. 34

Bargaining, p. 33

Benchmarking, p. 46

Domain, p. 30

Mission statement, p. 29

Prioritizing, p. 34

Satisficing, p. 33

Sequential attention, p. 34

Stakeholders, p. 32

Strategy, p. 39

Discussion Questions

1. What are some outcomes if a firm's strategies do not match its mission and goals?

2. If you were hired as a consultant to improve the overall effectiveness of an institution's strategic planning system, what steps would you take?

3. Why is benchmarking useful? What steps are used to identify benchmarks for a grocery chain?

Critical Thinking Questions

1. Consider two different organizations, both operating in an industry with which you are familiar (e.g., two fast food chains). What are their goals? What strategies and practices are apparent? In your opinion, are their strategies and operating practices consistent with their goals?

2. You are the manager of Supergraphics Inc., a software manufacturer owned by three partners. Recently, you and the owners were involved in setting future goals. During discussions, considerable differences of opinion emerged. A summary of these is given in Figure A. You realize that unless the owners come to some agreement, you will not be able to proceed. While you are prepared to compromise, you feel that, as the manager in charge, you should have some important input into the goal setting process. How would you go about reconciling the differences?

3. What are some effectiveness standards and outcome measures for this course? What concepts learned in this chapter are relevant to goal setting in this course?

Web Research

Visit the websites of at least two firms in a specific industry. Collect all information available on their goals, strategies, and constituents. Collect additional industry and environmental information from websites of Industry Canada, the Conference Board of Canada, Human Resource Development Canada, and any other relevant sites. What differences do you see between the firms in their goals, constituents, and strategies? What conclusions can you draw about performance management in these firms?

FIGURE A   Summary of Desired Goals by Owner

Desired goals	Owner A	Owner B	Owner C	Your view
1. Desired return on investment	15%	10%	7%	7-10%
2. Market share	Medium	High	Low	Low to medium
3. Liquidity	Low	Medium	High	Medium
4. Safety of investment	Medium	High	High	Medium to high
5. Importance of employee morale	Medium	Medium	High	High
6. Product reputation	High	Medium	Medium	Medium to high

CASE INCIDENT

Sandy Hines

Sandy Hines graduated from a reputable university with a Bachelor's of Commerce degree specializing in finance and marketing. Hines was an excellent student and was also active in a number of sports and extracurricular activities. Hines was very concerned with environmental issues and founded an association called Green Think that conducted seminars and published a newsletter to improve public awareness of the need for protecting world ecosystems.

Soon after graduation, Hines got a job as Assistant Marketing Manager with Maple Leaf Builders (MLB), a large building contractor and developer. MLB was headed by an aggressive young MBA named Terry Morand. Morand, who took over the leadership of the firm six years previous, had developed the business from an ailing, small, local organization to a profitable, medium-sized, regional organization. "I want MLB to be among the top two developers in this area within the next eight years. Given our track record in the last four years, I believe that this is entirely feasible," said a confident Morand at a recent staff meeting.

Hines made a big impression on Morand. Within one year of being appointed, Hines was given a promotion and made a member of the corporate planning group. However, the organization's indiscriminate cutting of trees to develop new buildings was increasingly concerning Hines. Hines raised this issue one day, but Morand, who wanted the firm to grow rapidly, was worried about such "mushy notions of a few far-left liberals."

Hines was also unhappy with several procedures employed by MLB, for example the recent abolition of interest-free loans to new buyers. MLB had also frozen its advertising budget in an effort to control costs, a step that Hines disagreed with. A new performance appraisal system and a point system of compensation introduced by Morand ("It is time we had some formal procedures for evaluating and compensating employees.") were disliked by most employees. In an effort to encourage creativity, the organization instituted a suggestion scheme; however, Hines questioned its effectiveness.

Questions

1. What problems, if any, exist in MLB's goal setting?

CASE

Pay and Save Groceries: Setting Goals

Pay and Save Groceries (PSG) is a regional grocery chain with 45 supermarkets spread over Eastern Canada. The firm, which began as a mom and pop store in Halifax 25 years ago, grew to its present size primarily because of the energy and vision of its founder, Charles Libbey. The firm currently employs 480 full time employees and a large number of part-time cashiers and other workers. While the exact number of part-time employees fluctuates seasonally, it usually ranges from 2300 to 2500. More details of the firm are given in the Case at the end of Chapter 1 (see pages 25-27).

Jane Werther, the human resource manager of the firm, made a list of the current key challenges facing the firm and her department. They include the following:

- Save More, a no-frill supermarket chain with extensive operations in Western and Central Canada, entered the Atlantic market and its competition decreased PSG's sales by 15% to 25% in some areas. Compared to PSG, Save More possesses vastly superior resources and cost advantages because of its "self-serve" and "bulk-purchase" strategies.

- A few larger national grocery chains had recently entered Atlantic Canada and had resources to buy prime locations and offer full services. These competi-

tors had fine-tuned their market analysis to offer a product mix catering to the specific needs of each neighbourhood and demographic group.

- High turnover and less-than-desirable performance of the firm's cashiers was affecting PSG. About 60% of the cashiers hired each year met the management's performance expectations on customer service, product knowledge, and the ability to perform assigned duties (e.g., inventory keeping, stock display) well.

- Cashiers were exhibiting high absenteeism and turnover. The turnover rate for full-time cashiers, most of whom were middle-aged women with between a Grade 8 and a Grade 12 education, was 20% and exceeded 35% for part-timers. Because the firm was dependent on part-time staff, the turnover figure was not only expensive, but also a major inconvenience when planning the daily and weekly schedules.

The management team recently met to define the firm's new strategy and identify the necessary changes. At university, Werther had studied goal setting and felt that some of the approaches she studied could be useful in this context. To start with, she decided to examine and enhance the per-

(continued)

formance of cashiers. Though not formally trained in business management, Charles Libbey was a very shrewd businessman who could get into the bottom of an issue and thoroughly evaluate her ideas for their usefulness and success potential. Werther knew that if her recommendations appeared sensible, he would support her efforts by allocating necessary budget and other resources.

Questions

1. *What concepts discussed in this chapter are relevant to Werther's objective of improving cashier performance?*

2. *What steps would you recommend Werther follow to implement the above concepts and achieve success in her goals? Detail your considerations at each stage of implementing change.*

CHAPTER

3 PROCESS AND EMPLOYEE PERFORMANCE

Organizational interface with internal and external stakeholders occurs at the performer level-where employees actually do the work required to produce products and services. The organizational and business process levels may be architectural masterpieces, but if performers cannot execute efficiently and effectively, performance quality and outputs will be negatively affected.[1]

Jerry Gilley, Nathaniel Boughton, and Ann Maycunich

CHAPTER OBJECTIVES

After studying this chapter, you should be able to:

- Discuss the four steps of organizational process improvement

- Define productivity and ways to improve it

- List the various steps to improve quality

- Discuss steps in conducting a job analysis

- Outline alternate approaches to setting employee performance standards

Coopers & Lybrand (C&L), one of the largest professional service firms with global operations, is dedicated to client service. C&L's management recognizes that a key competitive advantage of the firm is its ability to anticipate and meet client needs more effectively than its competitors. At the same time, the company management knows that they cannot take their intellectual capital (i.e., the sum total of their employees' capabilities, competencies, and commitment) for granted. To offer the best service to the clients, employee skills and commitment are focused and channelled towards organizational goals in support of its strategies. Under the direction of Judith Rosenblaum, then

Vice-Chairman of Learning, C&L developed a strategy called "Nexus" to integrate employee commitment and client service initiatives. Service benchmarks were established collaboratively-with input from the C&L work team dedicated to a specific client and the client's team. These teams met periodically to identify the best approaches to serve customers and to respond to their demands in the fastest manner possible. Over a period, C&L staff were better focused and served clients faster, utilizing C&L resources more fully.[2]

Management involves planning, controlling, coordinating and directing activities within the organization.

While effective **management** of human resources is important for all organizations, for service organizations like C&L, competent employees responding to customers in a timely and effective manner means the very survival of the company. The best formulated corporate missions and strategies may never get implemented in the absence of competent employees. Even the most competent employees may not be able to perform adequately in the absence of sound internal processes and systems. Figure 3-1 shows that all organizations must create conditions by which their employees can effectively and efficiently produce goods and deliver services. Existence of clear goals and processes is a must if employees are to work together to achieve organizational mission and success. This chapter introduces the important task of aligning larger organizational goals with internal systems and employee performance goals. More specifically, this chapter looks at the following two issues:

- How can internal processes be improved to achieve the larger organizational goals?

Performance standards are defined criteria against which expected levels of performance are measured.

- How can high and challenging performance standards for employees be identified? **Performance standards** focus on both the level and the quality of performance.

The chapter begins by looking at ways to improve organizational processes and systems. This is followed by a discussion on the steps used to identify employee performance standards and ways to achieve higher levels of performance. Some of the popular approaches for measuring and improving quality of performance and fostering employee competencies are examined. First, we must define what a process is

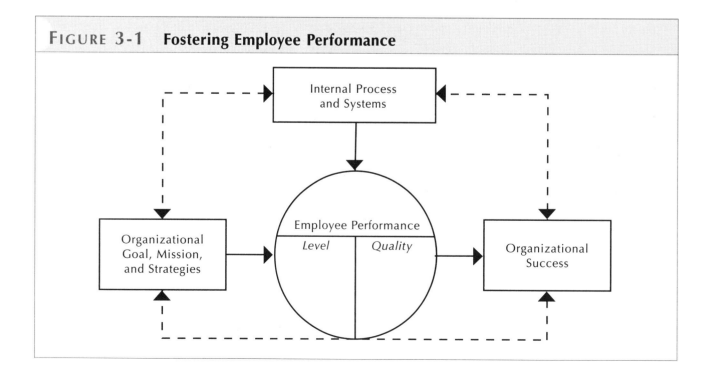

FIGURE 3-1   Fostering Employee Performance

and how different processes pose differing demands on the organization and its members.

ORGANIZATIONAL PROCESS IMPROVEMENT

Organizational process improvement involves four interrelated activities (Figure 3-2):

1. Defining the process and its components accurately;
2. Understanding and providing for interdependencies amongst them;
3. Improving process efficiency; and
4. Improving process quality.

Each step is discussed in some detail below.

DEFINING THE PROCESS AND COMPONENTS

An organization's **process**—also referred to as technology in its broadest sense-consists of all knowledge, tools, techniques, and behaviour used to transform organizational inputs into outputs. The outputs may be used by another organization or by a division, department, or group within the same organization.[3] Process or technology includes even the beliefs of employees.[4] Technology, in this sense, is pervasive, and impacts everything we do and how we do it. The technology employed varies considerably across organizations.[5]

Process is technology in its broadest sense and consists of all knowledge, tools, techniques, and behaviour used to transform organizational inputs into outputs.

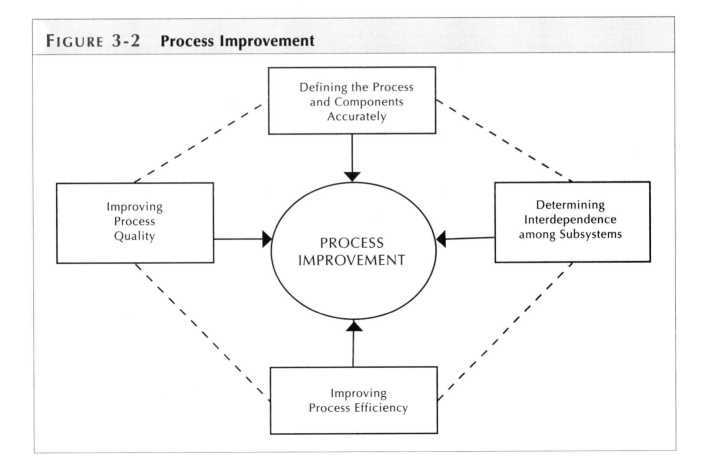

FIGURE 3-2   Process Improvement

In a cotton mill, the technology employed consists of, among other things, equipment, processes, and knowledge used in the breaker, carding, spinning, and weaving sections (i.e., the four activities that transform raw cotton into finished cloth). In between, the outputs of one section (e.g., carding) become the input of the next section (e.g., spinning).

In a university or college, the technology consisting of a variety of techniques such as classroom lectures, experiential exercises, case discussions, project assignments and diverse equipment (e.g., books, videos, computers) are used to "convert" new students into learned graduates.

Even within similar organizations, the technology employed can show remarkable differences depending on strategy, culture, employees, and history. This means that different organizations may start with identical inputs, yet produce qualitatively different outputs. Similarly, identical outputs may be produced from varying inputs. This is also true within a single organization changing over time. It is therefore important to focus on organizational processes carefully and critically for their appropriateness in the organizational mission and goals. Consider the following example of two MBA programs in Canada.

Two Canadian universities are almost identical in their requirements for admission into their Master of Business Administration (MBA) program. Both universities, located in the same region, admit only students with a B+ average in their undergraduate programs, a score of 590 or above in a standardized Graduate Management Admission Test, and satisfactory work and academic references. An analysis of the profiles of applicants to the two programs indicated that there were very few differences between them. However, the graduates of the two universities differ so much that it is difficult to recognize that both universities offer similar programs with similar courses. Graduates of University A are scholarly, competitive, and individualistic while University B's graduates are oriented toward team work and are practical in their orientation. Although both universities started with similar inputs, their outputs (the MBA graduates) are very different.

All modern work organizations are "open" to their environments. An organization routinely acquires inputs from its environment and exports outputs to its environment. The inputs include human resources, capital, material, knowledge, information, and technology, which are transformed by the organization to create outputs. The outputs of an organization are the various goods, services, and knowledge it produces. Figure 3-3 illustrates a fast-food hamburger chain as an open system. The conversion from inputs to outputs is done through a series of processes that are sometimes referred to as throughputs. Unless the internal processes are efficient and effective, the organization cannot survive in the long run.

Eaton's is an example of a firm that became extinct because of changes in the market place. The entry of aggressive volume discounters like Wal-Mart and Home Depot resulted in a steep decline in demand for Eaton's products. Eaton's was not able to convince its customers to pay a price premium (often exceeding 15%) for comparable products and brands.

In a large, complex organization, the various elements of the process can be hard to pinpoint. Some of the components of internal process are shown in Figure 3-4. It should be noted that even similar organizations might assign different levels of importance to these components that in turn affect their efficiency and overall effectiveness. For example, an organization can significantly enhance its operational efficiency through improved **information technology**. Wal-Mart is a good example.

Information technology is the process of receiving, generating, and analyzing information and converting raw data into meaningful facts.

Wal-Mart's managers maintain on-line linkage with the stores through phone, fax, and the Internet. In urgent cases, an executive can broadcast vital information on TV to all stores via a six-channel satellite system, which also gathers store data for its master com-

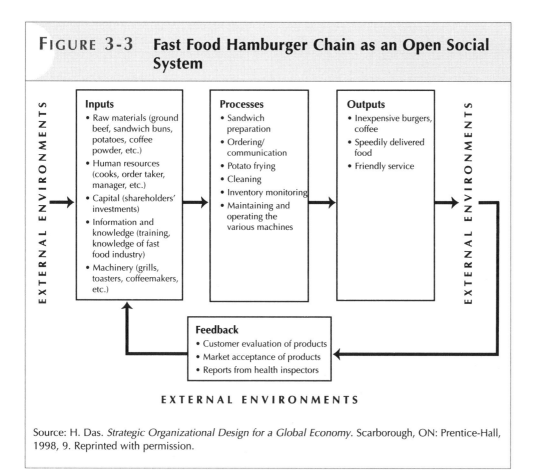

FIGURE 3-3   Fast Food Hamburger Chain as an Open Social System

Source: H. Das. *Strategic Organizational Design for a Global Economy*. Scarborough, ON: Prentice-Hall, 1998, 9. Reprinted with permission.

FIGURE 3-4   Components of Internal Process

Almost all modern organizations have the following components as part of their throughput process. In smaller organizations, they may be less visible to a casual observer; however, the functions are still performed by one or more individuals.[6]

Operations technology or the machines, equipment, and instruments used to transform physical inputs into outputs are the more visible part of internal process.

Information technology or the process of receiving, generating, and analyzing information and converting raw data into meaningful facts is another important component of internal process.

Maintenance or the process of ensuring the ready availability of equipment and people on a timely basis at the right place through planning and preventive actions (such as replacement of parts before they totally wear out).

Adaptation or the process of sensing changes that are occurring within or outside the organization and taking corrective actions to survive and prosper. In large organizations, this may be done through market research, organizational change attempts, elaborate training, and development of employees. In smaller businesses, it may simply take the form of querying the customers and employees and making changes in response to them.

Management or the process of planning, controlling, coordinating, and directing activities within the organization.

Supportive systems focus on the process of acquiring inputs and disposing of outputs from the system. While, technically, these are not part of the manufacturing part of the process, activities such as purchasing, marketing, and public relations are integral to the continued and predictable operation of internal process.

puter, handles credit card approval in five seconds, and tracks Wal-Mart's complex distribution system. Point of sale scanners track sales and monitor the supplies left on the shelves. Such integrated systems enable Wal-Mart to carry less inventory and reduce other operating costs that, in turn, enable it to offer "every day low prices" and effectively compete in the market place.[7]

UNDERSTAND AND PROVIDE FOR PROCESS INTERDEPENDENCE

The degree of dependence of employees, work groups, or departments on each other for materials, resources, and other inputs required to accomplish their respective tasks varies substantially across organizations.[8] In low interdependence situations employees or different departments can perform their tasks independently, without consulting, interacting, or exchanging resources with others. In a situation characterized by high task interdependence, workers can perform their tasks only by continuously monitoring, communicating, and adjusting their behaviours and tasks to those of others.

Depending on the technology employed, the manner of dependence also varies even within comparable organizations. In some situations, one employee may not be able to perform until another person has completed his or her task, but the other employee may not be dependent on the former. In other situations, both may not be able to perform without each other's help. Such differing types of interdependence have to be clearly understood if a manager is to plan activities effectively and efficiently.

Interdependence is not related to employees alone, however. The nature of dependencies among various constituents of an organization has to be recognized by the management if it is to take timely and appropriate actions.

> A firm that wants to improve its response time to customers should take into account the impact of such a decision on its suppliers or inventory policy. In several instances, a shortening of the response time may have to be followed by higher inventory costs unless the suppliers are willing to shorten their delivery times as well.

Based on the type and extent of interdependence, James D. Thompson,[9] an eminent sociologist whose writings on technology have been considered seminal, classified technology into three groups: mediating, long-linked, and intensive.

Mediating Technology
Some organizations employ mediating technology reflecting relatively low interdependence among their subunits or constituents, such as clients and customers.

> Commercial banks, insurance claim offices, real estate companies, and computer dating services are examples of organizations that employ mediating technologies, because they link clients and customers who are otherwise independent. An individual depositor in a bank, for all practical purposes, is not dependent on the borrower from the bank, nor is a typical real estate buyer dependent on a seller visiting the office. The agencies provide a useful service to the community by linking these otherwise independent units or constituents.

Similarly, the subunits of such organizations work, on a day-to-day basis, relatively independently of each other's activities.

> Consider the departments of a bank, such as its consumer loans, retirement investments, and estate management departments. Because of their impact on the bank's overall profitability and reputation, these departments are, indirectly, ultimately dependent on each

other. For example, if total loans were to rise sharply and suddenly push the interest rate up, it would have an impact on the volume of savings or type of retirement investments chosen by clients. However, on a daily basis, these departments operate independently.

Organizations employing mediating technology typically cope with external uncertainty by increasing the number of units (or customers) served.

An insurance firm tries to maximize the number of clients it serves to avoid the possibility of any one loss reducing the firm's overall effectiveness and ability to provide coverage to other clients. The same strategy is visible in the case of banks, real estate agencies, telephone companies, and auction houses.

Internally, to achieve coordination, firms rely on standardization of procedures and rules.

Almost all Canadian banks have rigid procedures and rules for approving and disbursing loans. Rules governing the type of information to be collected from borrowers, the type of risks allowed, and the nature of properties to be used as securities for a loan all facilitate standardization and coordination of activities.

Long-Linked Technology

The technology employed in an assembly line is quite different from the technology discussed above. In an assembly line (whether it produces an automobile or a safety razor), the raw materials and partly assembled products pass through a series of sequential operations, steps, motions, or modifications.

The conveyor belt symbolizes a situation where the first worker does a portion of the total task, then passes the product on to the second worker, who works on it and passes it on to the third worker, and so on. Here, the first worker's task must be performed before the product can be passed on to the second worker. The third worker is thus dependent for task performance on the second worker who, in turn, is dependent on the first worker to complete the task and hand it over to him or her.

Long-linked technology generates a sequential interdependence characterized by relatively little flexibility in day-to-day operations. In other words, work must be performed in a predetermined order.

Fast food cafeterias, sports relay teams, assembly lines, and food processing companies are examples of organizations using long-linked technology. In all cases, work has to be performed in a certain sequence, and the workers at the end of the sequence are dependent on the work of others preceding them in the line.

Internal coordination of employees, who are sequentially interdependent, is typically achieved through careful planning and scheduling. Since member interaction is high, the demands on management to coordinate and control the various activities are also high. Consequently, long-linked technology emphasizes predictability and encourages the production of a standardized product, repetitively and at a constant rate. Environmental uncertainty is primarily met through vertical integration or broadening operations to include a large number of manufacturing and selling steps.

Some orange juice producers have bought or developed orange farms. Some large aluminum companies have become involved in selling finished products, or have bought mining operations that produce bauxite. In each case, the intention is to bring more predictability into the firm's day-to-day operations.

Intensive Technology

The highest form of task interdependence arises when an organization uses intensive technology that generates reciprocal interdependence.

Consider a surgical team operating on a patient. The surgeons are dependent on the nurses for surgical tools and assistance and on the technicians who inform them about the patient's condition. The nurses, in turn, are dependent on the doctors and the technicians for their actions. The technicians have to observe the surgical process and take the necessary actions as it continues. Each professional is dependent on the actions of all the others and the success of the surgery depends on how effectively they work as a team.

Such intensive technology is visible in many organizations and work groups, including military combat units, basketball and ice hockey teams, and psychiatric centres. The demands for coordination are highest in the case of reciprocal interdependence. Yet there is no simple way to achieve coordination. Free-flowing communication and ongoing mutual adjustment by the task incumbents would seem to be the only way to coordinate their activities. Constant interaction among the people (or units) involved allows coordination of the activities and minimizes the cost of implementing them. Typically, organizations using intensive technology manage external uncertainty by improving their competence levels. They offer specialized services or products to ward off competition or to maintain and enhance their market position.

> Many Canadian hospitals continuously invest resources into research and sophisticated diagnostic tools. New knowledge and technology helps them to improve their expertise, reputation, and viability.

The relationship between interdependence and other organizational characteristics is summarized in Figure 3-5.

FIGURE 3-5   Technological Interdependence and Organizational Actions

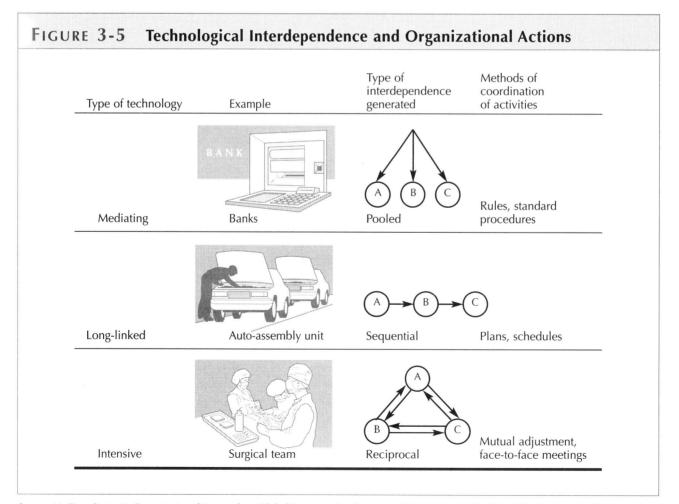

Source: H. Das. *Strategic Organizational Design for a Global Economy.* Scarborough, ON: Prentice-Hall, 1998, 135. Reprinted with permission.

A clear understanding of the task interdependencies is critical in project management. While large projects employing hundreds of people and extending over long periods of time (e.g., laying of a pipeline in the Yukon) simply cannot be carried out without a clear understanding of the interdependencies, even in a small project, activity and time planning are critical for success.

> A student project in a course such as this one requires careful planning to achieve satisfactory results. The various activities involved (e.g., library research, interviews with people, observation of events, data collection, data analysis) have to be clearly identified and the interdependencies identified before you can proceed clearly.

A useful tool in this context is a Program Evaluation and Review Technique (PERT) chart. Originally developed in the 1950s for coordinating the work of more than 3000 contractors and agencies working on the Polaris submarine weapon system, PERT was able to reduce the overall completion time of the project by as much as two years! A PERT chart is a diagram that depicts the sequence of activities needed to complete a project and the time and costs associated with each activity. With a PERT chart, the decision maker is able to determine which events depend on which others, what must be done first, and how long each activity will take (and cost). It enables the decision maker to foresee potential problem areas and bottlenecks before they occur. Figure 3-6 is a PERT chart without cost or time guidelines for the student team project example discussed above. The chart shows that some activities like library research and identifying interview sample can be done concurrently-one is not dependent on the other. However, the project cannot start until the individual student roles and responsibilities have been identified. Similarly, data collection cannot begin until interview sample has been identified and so on. A clear understanding of the interdependencies among the various activities is critical in managing mega projects such as pipeline laying or nuclear plant construction involving thousands of individual activities.

IMPROVING PROCESS EFFICIENCY

Efficiency refers to the ratio between an organization's resource inputs and its outputs. In other words, efficiency focuses on the amount of resources used by an

Efficiency is the ratio between an organization's resource inputs and its outputs.

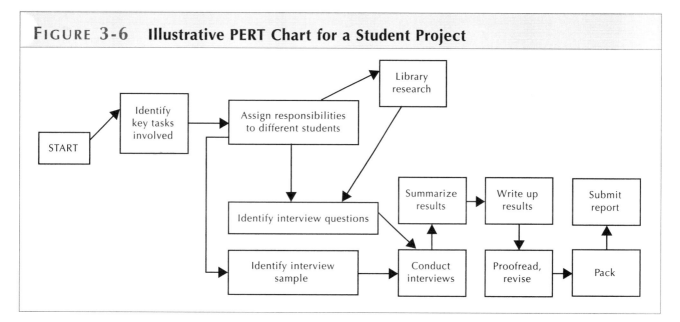

FIGURE 3-6   Illustrative PERT Chart for a Student Project

organization to produce a unit output.[10] An organization that uses fewer resources to produce a unit output is more efficient than a firm that uses more resources to achieve the same output.

When dealing with processes and manufacturing systems, it is common to think of productivity. **Productivity** is an efficiency concept generally identified as a ratio of output relative to input in some productive processes. While there is no single universally accepted definition of productivity and the meaning of the term may differ from discipline to discipline[11] (Figure 3-7 provides alternative conceptualizations of the term), most researchers and practitioners emphasize the need to look at both the outcomes and the inputs related to the activity under measurement. Employee productivity can be measured using output per worker or output per work hour while productivity of equipment may be measured by production per dollar of investment and so on. While productivity, like efficiency, links all inputs to outputs, it is more useful for managers to think in terms of labour productivity, productivity of machinery, etc. Sample measures of productivity are shown in Figure 3-8. Efficiency and productivity measures, like all performance measures, serve to provide direction and motivation, especially when targets or objectives are clearly specified.

Productivity, in productive processes, is an efficiency concept defined as a ratio of output relative to input.

> Productivity in the Canadian service industries grew by average annual rate of 1.2% between 1988 and 2000 thanks to the introduction of information technology. This does not include invisible savings in transactions, search, and processing costs, especially in business-to-business commerce.[12] The bad news is that productivity growth in our economy is nowhere close to what is seen in the U.S., our biggest trading partner. Productivity, as measured by the economic output per hour worked, is 19% higher in the U.S. Other countries also surpass Canada on this front. In 1990, Canada was third globally in gross domestic product (the total value of all goods and services produced) per capita; by 1999, it was fifth. By 2001, Canada had fallen to seventh. Had we maintained third rank, each Canadian family would be $10 000 richer today.[13]

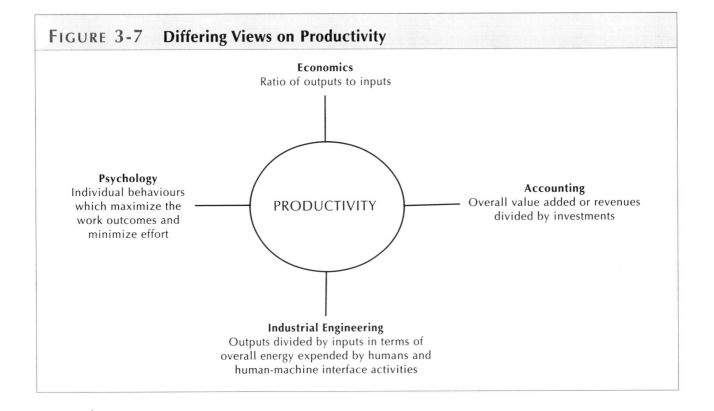

FIGURE 3-7   **Differing Views on Productivity**

Economics
Ratio of outputs to inputs

Psychology
Individual behaviours which maximize the work outcomes and minimize effort

PRODUCTIVITY

Accounting
Overall value added or revenues divided by investments

Industrial Engineering
Outputs divided by inputs in terms of overall energy expended by humans and human-machine interface activities

---

FIGURE 3-8 Sample Measures of Productivity

Machine, Equipment, or Process Productivity Indices

- Sales to inventory ratio
- Production to dollar investment in equipment
- Yield per unit of input or investment
- Sales revenue per square meter of office area
- Average sales revenue/donation per call
- Percent of total capacity utilized in a period (day, week, month, quarter, year)
- Capacity utilization per unit investment over different time periods
- Cost of different services compared to benchmarks, standards, or past accomplishments
- Ratio of actual production cost to standard cost

Employee Productivity Indices

- Output per employee
- Output per labour hour
- Ratio of actual labour hours to standard or planned hours
- Number of defects per 100 units produced
- Response time in minutes, hours, or days
- Customer satisfaction measures per employee
- Current labour cost per unit versus industry standards, budgets, or past accomplishments
- Lost time compared to standards, past figures, and/or industry benchmarks
- Costs of labour withdrawal from work (e.g., absenteeism, turnover)
- Average revenue per transaction, activity, or unit of service

---

In the recent past, several other countries-most notably the U.S.-have been able to reach great heights by using the new technology. Canada's growth, in contrast, has been mainly attributable to longer hours of work by our employees. As The Globe and Mail noted, "The U.S. worked smarter, Canada worked harder."[14] This means that both at the national and individual business levels, we have to make a concerted effort to improve our productivity and innovation record. Sample strategies for improving employee productivity are summarized in Figure 3-9.

FIGURE 3-9 Sample Actions to Improve Productivity

- Continuously upgrade technology where cost effective and feasible
- Identify competencies for all jobs and use these in hiring, training, and placement decisions
- Continuous training of employees to upgrade knowledge and skills
- Tie rewards to performance
- Communicate mission and goals widely and continually to all levels in the organization
- Redesign jobs to match job activities with organizational goals and workforce characteristics
- Assess and improve goal consensus at all levels
- Monitor environment continuously and respond to changes
- Invest in research and development
- Provide a sense of ownership to employees increasing their involvement

Effectiveness is the degree to which a process or an organiza- tion realizes its goals.

Closely related to the notions of productivity and efficiency is the construct of effectiveness. **Effectiveness** is the degree to which a process or an organization real- izes its goals. Performance effectiveness relates to the level of performance (production, service, sales) relative to the desired performance goals.[15] Thus, when a desired end is attained, we call the action effective.[16]

Efficiency and effectiveness are related but distinct concepts. High efficiency is typically achieved by using resources to the maximum and is characterized by an absence of organizational slack. In reality, though, an organization can be flexible and effective only when it has some slack (i.e., some elbow room) or surplus resources. Therefore it may be useful to think of the two terms as distinct concepts. "Effectiveness may be thought of as doing the right thing, whereas efficiency involves doing things right."[17]

Can an organization be effective without being efficient, or vice versa? Some firms have inefficient systems and procedures, but are still able to achieve many of their goals (in the same way that it is possible to kill a fly with a sledgehammer). Equally, it is possible for an organization to produce the wrong outputs efficiently.

> Thus, undue focus on cutting costs (an approach that improves efficiency) may result in public agencies not achieving their original goals of speedy response to clients and high cus- tomer satisfaction. Instead of this, the new goal of balancing the budget takes priority.

In the short term, then, efficiency and effectiveness need not be related to each other. In the long run, however, there is a close relationship between the two concepts. An organization that exhausts more resources on a per-capita basis than its competi- tors will find itself non-competitive and, thus, progressively ineffective. Similarly, an organization, however efficient, cannot continue to produce outputs not valued by its constituents. Thus, an ineffective organization will lose its legitimacy and find it dif-

Focus on Ethics:

How Does Our Technology and Consumption Impact Our Planet?

Alarming long-term environmental effects can emerge from products, the technology used to produce them, or the level of their consumption. Since these are often interrelated, it is hard to separate their effects. A product that may look harm- less may often require a process that emits poisonous gases or other wastes into the environment, which in turn endan- ger living organisms and the overall shape and structure of the planet. On the other hand, there may be harmful prod- ucts produced by a "safe" technology that poses relatively less danger to the inhabitants of this planet.

Cigarettes and paper towels are good examples in this context. Most people consider cigarettes to be harmful—cit- ing their negative effects even on non-smokers. Interestingly,

however, the technology employed to produce them is not tremendously harmful. Paper towels, a harmless product, create an abundance of pollution, thereby harming the envi- ronment. Some of the other conveniences we take for granted—including automobiles and airplanes—produce negative impacts on the environment both during produc- tion and when in use.

The ethics of processes, should, however, go beyond the simple matter of production. After all, products will not emerge and remain in the markets unless people consume them. This means that consumers have roles to play in decid- ing what products should be produced, in what quantities, and by what processes. Consider the following facts:

(continued)

1. A typical Canadian child, in the first five years of life, will use more of world's resources than an adult born in many poor countries.

2. An average Canadian throws out more garbage in a month than do residents of developing nations in their entire lifetime.

3. Advanced economies like Canada not only use up resources of their own territory, but also, in one way or the other, use up a disproportionate share of resources found in other countries.[18]

The difference in consumption between rich and poor countries has been steadily increasing as richer countries use advanced technologies to produce more and more products. Is it time we pause and ask ourselves questions about "eco-friendly" processes and consumption? Here is a sampler of questions that we may want to ask:

• More Canadians own automobiles-our icon of freedom and independence-and drive them today than ever before. But, are we really freer today because of them?

• Are we living better today because we replace our linens and utensils approximately every five or six years instead of owning them for a life time as in the past?[19]

• Are we healthier today because we buy bottled mineral water instead of drinking chlorinated water from our once pristine lakes and rivers?

• Are we more informed today because we have highly paid TV anchors convey news to us 24 hours a day?

• Has our quality of life significantly improved now that we have electric toothbrushes, moustache trimmers, and meat cutters?

• How much packing material is needed to safely transport a $1 value videocassette from the factory to our homes?

Ultimately, it is the common person in the street, the informed consumer, and the introspective worker, who can make a difference. After all, ethics, by its very nature, is based on human decisions.

What are some actions you can take to improve the present state of affairs? List three specific actions you can take to make this planet a better place to live. Compare your answers with those of your friends and acquaintances. Is there something you can do beginning today?

ficult to attract the resources needed to keep operating. In the long term, it is unlikely that a firm can continue to score very high on one of these dimensions without having at least minimal levels of performance on the other. Needless to say, successful organizations focus on improving both efficiency and effectiveness.

IMPROVING PROCESS QUALITY

There is hardly any process or system that does not have variation in its performance.

> The assembly line which produces widgets, the customer service staff who respond to queries, the instructor who teaches a course, the driver who makes routine deliveries, the actor playing the same role on different occasions-all exhibit variance in performance over time.

Variation can occur in quantity and quality of performance. Variation in quantity may be caused by, among other things, differing employee skills and motivation, differences in the quality of raw materials, differences in working conditions, variation in the state of equipment, or simply by random, unexplained factors. Similarly, variation in quality may be caused by a variety of factors attributable to employees, equipment, raw materials, working conditions, and so on. Figure 3-10 lists key factors that contribute to variation in quality. Whatever the reasons, unless careful attention is paid, unwanted variations in volume and quality of outputs—whether they are physical products or services—are bound to occur.

FIGURE 3-10   Factors Contributing to Variation in Quality of Products or Service

Employees.
Employees have differing abilities, skills, motivation levels, and understanding—all causing variation in performance. Even the same person usually shows some variation on several of these variables across time.

Equipment.
Even identical machines do not perform exactly alike and the same machine may produce differing volumes or quality of products across time.

Technology.
The production methods and shop floor procedures may show slight variation from one time period to the next. This is more common in non-automated and labour intensive operations.

Input materials.
Since a typical organization receives inputs from multiple suppliers, there are bound to be quality differences. Even the same supplier's products may show variation across time or over different batches.

Physical surroundings.
Workplace environment and factors such as heat and humidity have a decisive influence on process outcomes while changes in organizational policies, leadership styles, systems, and practices, etc. can cause variation both in volume and quality of production.

Measurement differences.
Unless the measures used are precise and reliable, some of the variation may be due to errors in scaling or computation.

Random fluctuations.
Even when all key variables are kept under control, there might be random fluctuations not clearly attributable to any observable factors. There can also be interaction among two or more of the above factors that may not be apparent but still cause variation.

Steps in Monitoring and Improving Quality Figure 3-11 summarizes the key steps in process monitoring and improvement. These are discussed in greater detail below.

Step 1: Describe the Process The first step is to describe the process in detail showing the various tasks and interdependencies among them. Usually, a flowchart that shows the interdependencies among various actions, the direction of flow of actions, and key decision points is used for describing the process. **Flowcharts** help to visualize present and future processes, possible obstacles for improving speed or quality of the process, and bottlenecks.[20] Opportunity flowcharts[21] can be particularly useful in improving quality or speed since they identify process steps that do not add value to the product or service.

Flowcharts are visual illustrations of the interdependencies among various actions, the direction of actions, and key decision points.

FIGURE 3-11   Steps to Improve Process Quality

Step 1:   Describe the process

Step 2:   Collect data

Step 3:   Assess process stability

Step 4:   Identify causes and cause-effect relationships

Step 5:   Implement changes

Step 6:   Monitor progress

Step 2: Collect Data Accurate data should then be collected to see how the process is currently performing. Several indices associated with the process performance are collected at this stage. Often, available company records will need to be supplemented with survey or interview data.

> To assess the performance of a customer telephone order section, indices such as number of calls received, number of orders received, response time, delivery time, value of orders over different time periods, number of missed delivery dates, number of customer complaints, and number of days taken to settle complaints are necessary.

Step 3: Assess Process Stability Control charts or plots of process performance related data over time as a graph enable the decision makers to assess process stability. Figure 3-12 is an example of a control chart of a manufacturer's on-time delivery of products. If the manufacturer has a goal of meeting on-time delivery on 95% of occasions, the chart indicates the weeks when the firm missed this target (in this instance in weeks 4 and 8).

Control charts are plots of process performance related data over time used to help decision makers assess process stability.

Step 4: Identify Causes and Cause-Effect Relationships Further in-depth examination of the control chart and associated data enables the decision makers to identify factors that caused variation. Even the most efficient processes will have some variation due to random and common causes such as variability in quality of raw materials, equipments, etc., as listed above. However, there are a number of occasions when specific causes such as changes in raw material procurement policies, organizational practices, and manufacturing processes may be the underlying cause for variation.

> A look at the company records may indicate that the week when the firm had its lowest delivery rate was the period when the vehicle repair shop was partially closed for equip-

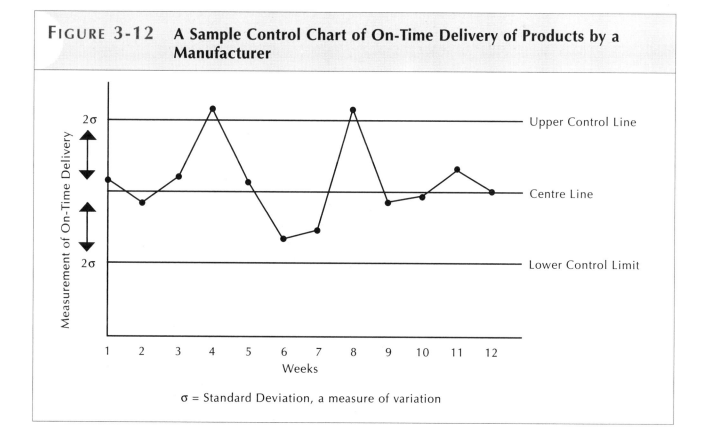

FIGURE 3-12 A Sample Control Chart of On-Time Delivery of Products by a Manufacturer

σ = Standard Deviation, a measure of variation

ment re-tooling. Similarly, an examination of company records may indicate that the employee turnover was highest in a week when the company announced a possible closure of one shift that was associated with missed delivery dates.

Step 5: Implement Changes Once the cause-effect relationship is identified, it becomes easier to determine what changes are necessary to improve the process. Specific counter measures such as better inspection of raw material, and more preventive **maintenance** of equipment can reduce routine and some of the random variation while radical changes may be needed to bring about improvements in other instances.

Maintenance is the process of ensuring the ready availability of equipments and people through planning and preventive actions.

> The firm may find that a newly introduced organizational procedure is holding up delivery. In this instance, abolishing or modifying the procedure may be necessary to achieve targets. When implementing changes, their impact on other processes or employee behaviour should be considered.

Step 6: Monitor Progress No single action ever produces lasting improvements. This means that continuous monitoring of the process and the outcomes is necessary for maintaining high predictability and consistency in operations. Any process improvement system should have a mechanism for periodically reviewing achievements and deficiencies. Radical changes in the process will require revision of the original flowchart.

ISO 9000 Standards Today, many organizations have realized that high quality is synonymous with survival and success in a highly competitive, global marketplace. Several have embraced management philosophies that stress stringent quality standards. ISO 9000 is the International Organization for Standardization's standard of quality management and quality assurance. The Organization also has a standard for environmental management (ISO 14000). ISO 9000 is rapidly becoming the most popular quality standard in the world with thousands of organizations already practicing it. Organizations of all sizes[22] and types (manufacturing, service, non-profit) can benefit from use of the standard. ISO distinguishes between four types of products: hardware, software, processed materials, and services. Hence, all work, including service activities, can be subject to stringent quality standards. The underlying philosophy of ISO certification can be summarized as below:

- All work is a process involving transformation of some input into outputs.

- The above means that an organization, whether large or small, is nothing but a network of processes. The success of an organization depends on how effectively it identifies and manages these processes in an integrated fashion.

- The overall process quality depends on how well the network of processes operate.

- To ensure high quality, the processes must be continually monitored for deviations. Continuous improvement of the process must be a high priority for organizational success.

- The quality management system is also a set of interrelated processes. The steps, interface, interdependencies, and sequence of the processes must be defined clearly if prompt and adequate quality control is to occur.

- The quality management system must have clearly defined procedures with documentation for defining processes, approving procedures, and implementing changes.

In Canada, the National Quality Institute is the body responsible for certifying auditors for ISO certification.[23] Certification usually requires a five-step process:

SELF-TEST:

How Quality Conscious Are You?

This exercise enables you to assess your overall concern for quality. Please answer all questions frankly. Answer *strongly agree* (SA), *agree* (A), *neither agree nor disagree* (NAD), *disagree* (D), or *strongly disagree* (SD). Note your answers on a separate sheet so that no one else may access it.

1. Before submitting my papers to the instructor, I check them for grammar and spelling.

2. I formulate a sketch or plan of my paper (even if it is in my mind) before I begin to work on it.

3. My best work partners are the ones who never question the quality of my work.

4. Prior to starting a major project, I check my ideas with others to see potential problems.

5. I always put my case analyses or term papers in a binder before submitting to the instructor.

6. When doing a group project, I do not encourage one member to criticize the quality of another's work.

7. When I receive my exams back, I go over the instructor's comments carefully to see where I can improve.

8. Before beginning to work on a project, I find out the exact expectations of my instructor.

9. People who are fussy about grammar and spelling often miss the creative aspect of a project.

10. If I received a grade or mark less than what I hoped for, I would meet with my instructor to find out the exact reasons and correct the deficiency next time.

11. Occasionally, I examine past papers or reports of others deemed to be of superior quality.

12. I do not pay much attention to term paper or project preparation guidelines provided by others.

13. Before I start work on a project or assignment, I divide the task into various components (e.g., library research, data analysis) and assign dates or times by which I should complete each part.

14. Most often, I am pressed for time when preparing my class submissions.

15. I do not clip the sheets together before submitting a report to the instructor.

Scoring

For all items except 3, 6, 9, 12, 14 and 15, assign a score of 5, 4, 3, 2, and 1 for SA, A, NAD, D, and SD. For items 3, 6, 9, 12, 14 and 15, assign a score of 1, 2, 3, 4, and 5 for SA, A, ND, D, and SD. Add up your score; it should range from 15 to 75.

Interpretation

Scores above 60: You are extremely concerned about the quality of your work and take considerable efforts to ensure that all your work meets a certain standard of quality.
Scores between 25 and 59. You are moderately concerned about the quality of your work. By focusing more rigorously on the quality, you might be surprised to find its positive impact on your performance at school.
Scores below 25. By focusing on the items where you scored 1 or 2, you can significantly improve the quality of your future project reports and other course submissions. You are bound to be surprised at how small behavioural changes can impact the quality of performance. Remember, quality does win results!

- Step 1: ISO assessment that involves a review of the organization's quality system and procedures.

- Step 2: Preparation of quality assurance manual that compiles the specific quality assurance techniques, procedures, and policies that will be followed in future.

Six sigma is a set of formally established organizational processes, tools, and techniques that aims to achieve less than 3.4 defects or mistakes per million outputs or service transactions.

- Step 3: Training of employees in the new ISO-based quality management system.

- Step 4: Documentation of work instructions which details all work procedures.

- Step 5: Registration audit where an ISO auditor reviews the organization's systems and approves if it meets required standards.

Research studies examining links between concern for quality and overall organizational success and performance have shown a positive relationship between them. This seems to be true even when controlling for the size of the organization.

> One study, which looked at 62 small businesses in Australia, indicated that concern for quality had the highest impact on overall competitiveness of the business.[24] The same study showed a positive impact on total sales and market share of the business. Another researcher who compared the performance of ISO certified Danish companies to those without ISO standards found that ISO registered companies had nearly 15% higher returns a year after registration.[25]

Encouraging reports such as the above have prompted several organizations to embark on quality improvement initiatives. Total Quality Management (TQM) and **Six sigma** have become popular today. Figure 3-13 outlines the Six Sigma concept. Chapter 5 will look at TQM in some detail.

IDENTIFYING EMPLOYEE PERFORMANCE STANDARDS

Even the most efficient and sophisticated organizational processes cannot make an organization effective if individual employees do not carry out their tasks effectively

---

FIGURE 3-13   Six Sigma and Quality

Six sigma stresses a management philosophy that recognizes that defects are expensive both in terms of costs of operation and customer loyalty. Six sigma is a set of formally established organizational processes, tools, and techniques that aims to achieve less than 3.4 defects or mistakes per million outputs or services. It is an effort to achieve near perfection in operations and can be applied in any process—from manufacturing to transactional and from product to service.
Like all quality improvement efforts, six sigma processes also have five major components:

Define: Goals, standards, and targets have to be explicitly defined and well communicated to all concerned.

Measure: There is an established, formal procedure to measure all relevant aspects of performance validly and on a timely basis. This means that measurement must be free from errors, happen frequently, and the results communicated to all relevant persons in time.

Analyze: The causes for variation are analyzed systematically and in depth. Where necessary, controlled experimentation is done to identify factors that cause mistakes or errors and others which simply co-vary with them.

Design: Based on findings, action plans to improve quality are established. These are also understood by all concerned and implemented systematically.

Control and Verify: The processes are continually monitored to see whether improvements occur as a result of the changes. Continuous monitoring of quality and focus on alternate ways of improvements to the system exist.

The six sigma systems, thus, have built-in procedures for continuous monitoring and improvement of quality. While many six sigma projects do not achieve their ambitious goal of 0.0000034 defects, it remains as the ideal goal and drives process operations. Like any other system, six sigma will succeed only if all are committed to well-defined goals and have necessary power and resources to take timely actions.

Focus on Small Business:

Root Cause Analysis to Improve Process Performance

In large organizations, process planning is a complex task requiring the use of sophisticated mathematical models and powerful computers. In small businesses, however, the scale of operations does not justify the use of such complex equipment or decision models. Indeed, planning may have to be done on the spot to meet unforeseen emergencies or challenges. Often, the only tool available to the small business manager may be a calculator.

The need for continuous process improvement and timely corrective actions for operational problems is all the more important in small businesses because of their inherent vulnerable nature (see Chapter 1 for more on this). Root cause analysis is a collection of techniques that help the small business manager to identify the real cause(s) of a problem (rather than mere symptoms). While a number of techniques are popular,[26] one simple technique of analysis may be to ask "why?" in sequence. Consider the following problem faced by a small hair styling salon.

> **Step 1: Statement of the problem by the Maple Leaf Hair Styling Salon:** In the last two weeks, a number of our female customers have complained about service.

> **Step 2: Ask why:** "Why have they complained?" Assume that the answer is: "They were not happy with the hair colouring."

> **Step 3: Ask the why again:** "Why were they not happy with the colouring?" Assume the answer is: "The colour they got was not quite what they had expected based on sample colour plates."

Step 4: Ask the third why: "Why was the colour in the bottle different from the sample colour plates on the shelf?" Answering this question may require a thorough look at all procedures of shelving, training of the hair stylists, work motivation, etc. Let us assume that the hair stylists were quite competent and motivated (or, at least, there was no obvious reason why their motivation levels should have been reduced lately). Further, let us assume that because of a holiday weekend, two stylists had been away and a temporary cleaning person had been hired to re-shelf the bottles after cleaning the premises. That person had put the wrong bottles on the shelf.

Step 5: Ask the fourth why: "Why did the cleaning person put the wrong bottles on the wrong shelf?" The answer can range from: the cleaning person was not well trained to the cleaning person was colour blind! Whatever the reason, the salon is able to identify the true cause of the problem and take remedial action (e.g., not to hire the same cleaning person, explain the circumstances to the clients and make amends).

Experts suggest that asking "why?" five successive times should unearth the root cause of problems in most situations. While, this simple technique may prove valuable in many situations, there are other instances where a more detailed analysis may be required. There are several other techniques[27] for root cause analysis.

and in a timely fashion. The best systems are no substitute for a highly motivated and competent workforce that has a clear understanding of the organizational priorities and objectives. Organizations that do not recognize this important truth sometimes get into problems. Consider the following scenario.

> Some organizations that take advantage of cheap labour in developing countries by locating their plants abroad often fall into a trap: they confuse wage rates with wage costs. While the wage rates in several of these countries may be lower, the overall productivity per hour may also be lower, thus resulting in higher labour costs. The costs of higher levels of defects, reduced customer responsiveness caused by distance, and opportunity costs caused by reduced innovation are also often not considered when computing total costs.

What factors characterize a highly productive workforce? While, there is no single set of attributes or conditions that seem to represent all productive work settings, past studies have identified some characteristics that determine individual performance (Figure 3-14).

This chapter primarily looks at abilities and goal awareness. Later chapters on reward systems, training, and counselling will look at the other important attributes associated with high performance.

FIGURE 3-14   Employee Characteristics Associated with High Performance Levels

Past research studies indicate that a number of characteristics are consistently associated with high performance including:

- **Abilities.** Relatively stable individual characteristics such as verbal ability, mathematical aptitude, and eye-hand coordination are important determinants of performance on many jobs since they enable individuals to carry out certain cognitive, psychomotor, or physical behaviours.

- **Knowledge and Skills.** Acquired, job relevant skills can determine performance in many instances. Persons with identical abilities may perform differently depending on their knowledge.

- **Effort levels.** Individuals differ in the efforts they are prepared to expend on their jobs; there are also differences in persistence levels.

- **Goal Awareness.** A person's performance is dependent on his or her awareness of the task demands.

- **Motivation.** Effort levels are dependent on goal acceptance and motivation levels of the task incumbents.

The task of identifying employee performance standards consists of a number of interrelated steps:

1. Defining performance;

2. Assessing performance requirements through job and task analysis;

3. Setting performance standards; and

4. Identifying and developing performance competencies.

The remainder of this chapter looks at these four steps.

DEFINE PERFORMANCE

For a number of jobs, there are clear and visible performance outcomes associated with the position. Thus, sales persons are expected to sell, painters are expected to paint surfaces or objects, and tax accountants are expected to complete tax returns. However, for several other jobs, such clear performance outcomes may not be available. There are also jobs where the jobholder only provides part of the total input-holding the person responsible for the entire outcome may not be appropriate or even fair.

> Consider a call centre sales person who is very competent and conscientious and makes the highest number of calls in the team, yet has substantial variation in daily sales (the outcome). This person may not even be the top salesperson in any particular period. A college instructor may be extremely knowledgeable and enthusiastic, but her students' learning (the outcome) is affected by a number of factors beyond her control.

Over concentration on outputs in such instances may detract the job incumbent from important non-quantitative aspects of the job.

> Simply emphasizing sales volume may encourage salespeople to focus only on that activity resulting in little attention paid to other important activities such as merchandise display, responding to customer complaints, and training new staff.

In such instances, the behaviours of the employee may be preferred as indicators of performance. All actions and behaviours that are relevant to the organization's goals and can be validly measured are included for defining performance. In this instance, performance is not looked at as the consequence or result of an employee's actions-the action itself is the performance. This means that all actions measured should be within the control of the employee concerned. Problems arise when an employee is expected to engage in specific behaviours but may not have the resources, time, or training to do so.

In most organizations, the term performance is used to denote both outputs and behaviours. Thus, salespeople are not only expected to sell a certain volume (an outcome) but also to be punctual, cleanly dressed, and courteous to customers (behaviours). The precise definition of performance for each job should be identified on the basis of corporate and departmental objectives (discussed in Chapter 2).

ASSESS PERFORMANCE REQUIREMENTS THROUGH JOB AND TASK ANALYSIS

A **job** consists of a group of related activities and duties. A single employee or several people may hold a job. For the purpose of performance planning and improvement, it should be distinguished from other related terms like **position** or **task** (Figure 3-15).

Job analysis involves the systematic collection, analysis, and interpretation of job information. The information collected is used for describing jobs, hiring suitable candidates for various jobs, and setting performance standards. **Task analysis** examines the various tasks that constitute a job, looking for interdependencies and overlaps. The immediate outcome of job and task analyses is a **task inventory** that lists all the tasks that form a job and the competencies required to perform them. Without accurate information about jobs and tasks, it is virtually impossible to provide fair compensation to employees, assess their performance, and counsel them when they face difficulties. Efforts to improve employee productivity levels and eliminate unnecessary job requirements that can cause discrimination necessitate careful study. In the absence of valid job information, an organization would also find it dif-

A **job** is a group of related activities and duties that may be held by a single employee or several people.

A **position** is the collection of activities, duties, and responsibilities performed by an individual employee.

A **task** is an identifiable, related activity that is part of a job.

Job analysis involves the systematic collection, analysis, and interpretation of job information.

Task analysis is the examination of the various tasks that constitute a job to look for interdependencies and overlaps.

Task inventory lists all the tasks that form part of a job and the competencies required to perform them.

FIGURE 3-15   Performance Related Terms

Job: A group of related activities and duties. A job may be held by a single employee or several persons.

Position: The collection of activities, duties and responsibilities performed by an individual employee.

Task: Each job has a number of tasks or identifiable and normally related activities. In a service department with one supervisor, three clerks, twelve service personnel, there are sixteen positions but only three jobs. Each job requires the job incumbent to do a number of tasks.

Performance Assessment Criteria: The various outcomes or behaviours associated with a job or position which are used to measure the effectiveness of performance of a job or position. A variety of criteria such as "quantity of production", "wastage", "response time in minutes", "punctuality", and "attendance" are used to assess performance.

Performance Standard: The level of performance expected or achieved on each performance assessment criterion. These are, usually, measurable, specific and time bound. "Achieve 93% customer satisfaction rate" or "reduce wastage by 2%" within specific time frames are illustrative of performance standards.

ficult to evaluate how environmental challenges or specific job requirements affect workers' quality of work life.

With hundreds, even thousands, of jobs, it is nearly impossible for a large firm to know the details of every job. It is, however, unnecessary to collect information on identical jobs separately. Consider this example.

> One large grocery chain has 390 cashiers. Each job is the same. Therefore, job analysis requires only a random sample of these positions. Data collection on a few of these jobs generates an accurate information base for all 390 positions.

Job analysis is a complex activity with six interrelated steps.[28] These are briefly examined in the following sections.

Website for meaning and uses of job analysis:
www.hrzone.com/topics/joba.html

Identify Objectives of Job Analysis

The specific details collected during a job analysis are influenced by the objectives of the study; hence, it is critical to crystallize the objectives early on. While the most common uses of job analysis are to establish performance standards, identify criteria for selection of employees, determine training needs, and design performance appraisal and compensation systems,[29] job analysis may also be done to eliminate discrimination against specific employee groups, for job re-design, or even to identify career paths for specific employee groups. The objectives determine which jobs are to be analyzed and in what sequence. While almost all job positions could benefit from an in-depth analysis, resource and time constraints often preclude organizations from this. Likely targets of job analysis are jobs that are critical to the success of an organization, jobs that are difficult to learn or perform (since this determines the extent of training), jobs where the firm continuously hires new employees (since identification of clear job requirements assumes great importance), or jobs that preclude minority members, women, and the physically challenged. Jobs should also be analyzed if new technology or altered work environments affect the way the job is performed.

> One job analysis study[30] found that the skills, knowledge, and abilities essential for performance in secretarial and clerical positions are very similar to those needed in entry-level management positions. If female or minority employees are concentrated in secretarial or clerical positions, information such as this can be used to move them into managerial positions. Employees can also utilize this information to make the best use of their work experience and training and plot future career paths.

Website on job analysis:
www.hr-guide.com

Website on relating employee practices to strategy:
www.chrs.net

Familiarization with the Firm and Jobs

Before studying jobs, it is important to have an awareness of an organization's objectives, strategies, structure, and culture. Job analysts should also study industry and government reports about the jobs to be analyzed.

Determination of the Sources of Job Data

Although the most direct source of information about a job is the job incumbent, a variety of other sources, both human and non-human, may be used for this purpose. If job analysis has been done before, previous records may be very helpful, although provision for changes in technology and work environment should be made. Existing job descriptions, process specifications, machinery design blue prints, maintenance manuals, and other reports may also help in establishing the nature of the various jobs. On many occasions, professional magazines and publications such as National Occupational Classification (NOC) in Canada and U.S. Department of Labor's Handbook for Analyzing Jobs also provide information on various jobs. Some other sources include the following:

- Job incumbents
- Supervisors, subordinates, colleagues, union officials

- Customers, other outside experts

- Company records including existing job descriptions, organizational charts, and mission statements

- Equipment design blueprints, maintenance and safety manuals, and training videos for machines

- Professional publications

- The Internet

Data Collection Instrument Design To study jobs, analysts most often develop checklists or questionnaires to collect job information uniformly. They uncover the duties, responsibilities, human abilities, and performance standards of the jobs investigated. Such questionnaires are particularly important when collecting information from human sources. Even in the case of non-human sources, however, the quality and comparability of information collected can be enhanced by the use of common checklists. It is important to use the same questionnaire on similar jobs. Analysts want differences in job information to reflect differences in the jobs, not differences in the questions asked. Uniformity is especially hard to maintain in large organizations. When analysts study similar jobs in different departments, only a uniform questionnaire is likely to result in usable data. Some of the more important items seen a typical job analysis questionnaire are summarized in Figure 3-16.

Website with a sample job analysis tool:
http://mime1.gtri.gatech.edu/ MM_Tools/analysis.html

There are a number of standardized forms currently available for job analysis. Two of the more popular ones are Functional Job Analysis and Position Analysis Questionnaire. Functional Job Analysis[31] rates the job on responsibilities pertaining to data, people, and things. In addition, it rates the job on a number of other dimensions such as reasoning, judgement, mathematical ability, and verbal skills needed. It

---

FIGURE 3-16   Sample Items in a Job Analysis Questionnaire

- Date of job analysis

- Person conducting the job analysis

- Job identification number, job title, and the department where it is located

- Nature of primary duties (Managerial, Technical, Professional, Clerical, Blue Collar, Other)

- List of duties and proportion of time spent in each task and activity

- Performance criteria for evaluating success

- Extent of training needed to perform the various tasks

- Responsibilities associated with the job (for tools, equipments, safety, material usage, other)

- Physical attributes necessary to perform the job (e.g., vision, hearing, strength, height, hearing)

- Mental attributes necessary to perform the job (e.g., mathematical skills, verbal skills)

- Education required

- Training needed to perform the job well

- Unusual psychological or physical demands on job holder (e.g., hot working area, abusive clients)

- Level of prior work experience needed to perform the job

- Safety or other health hazard associated with the job

- Performance standards for the various activities

Website for information on
job analysis approaches:
http://harvey.psyc.vt.edu/

is a more quantitative approach to job analysis that also sums up the training requirements and performance standards associated with each job.[32]

Position Analysis Questionnaire (PAQ)[33], designed to be applicable to all types of jobs offers a highly quantitative and finely tuned description of jobs. Using a five-point scale, the PAQ aims to determine the degree to which 194 different task elements are involved in performing a particular job (the five-point scale measures a continuum of "nominal or very infrequent" at the lowest level to "very substantial" at the highest). The PAQ allows grouping of job elements in a logical and quantitative manner and the number of job elements covered under various categories is large (e.g., there are 36 different elements that measure "relationships with other people"). This is claimed to make job comparison easy. Past research, however, has indicated PAQ to be more useful for lower level jobs.[34]

Choice of Data Collection Method
There is no "best way" to collect job analysis information. Analysts must evaluate the tradeoffs between time, cost, and accuracy associated with each method.[35] Once they decide which tradeoffs are most important, they use interviews, questionnaires, employee logbooks, observations, or some combination of these techniques.

Interviews Face-to-face interviews are an effective way to collect job information. The analyst has the questionnaire as a guide, but can add other questions where needed. Although the process is slow and expensive, it allows the interviewer to explain unclear questions and probe into uncertain answers.

Mailed Questionnaires A faster and less costly option is to survey employees using a mailed questionnaire. This can be done using interoffice mail, Canada Post, or the Internet. This approach allows many jobs to be studied at once and at little cost. However, there is less accuracy because of misunderstood questions, incomplete responses, and unreturned questionnaires.

Employee Log An employee log or diary is a third option. Workers periodically summarize their tasks and activities in the log. If entries are made over the entire job cycle, the diary can prove quite accurate. Logs, however, are unpopular since they are time-consuming. Managers and workers often see them as a nuisance and resist their introduction. Moreover, after the novelty wears off, accuracy tends to decline as entries become less frequent.

Observation Directly observing the job incumbent is slow, costly, and potentially less accurate than other methods. Accuracy may be low because the analysts may miss irregularly occurring activities. However, observation may be preferred when analysts question the validity of data collected using other methods or when language barriers exist as in the case of temporary foreign workers or new immigrants.

Combinations Since each method has its faults, analysts often use two or more techniques concurrently. Combinations can ensure high accuracy. It is also particularly attractive when all employees are at the same location.

Using Job Analysis Information to Make Decisions
The information collected about various jobs is put into such usable forms as job descriptions, job specifications, and job performance standards. A **job description** is a written statement that explains the duties, working conditions, and other aspects of a specified job. A **job specification** describes what the job demands of employees who do it and the human factors that are required. It is a profile of the human characteristics needed by the job. These requirements include experience, training, education, physical demands, and mental demands. The difference between a job description and a job specification is

Job description is a written statement that explains the duties, working conditions, and other aspects of a specified job.

Job specification describes what the job demands of employees who do it and the human factors that are required.

one of perspective. A job description defines what the job does; it is a profile of the job. Since the job description and specifications both focus on the job, they are often combined into one document. The combination is simply called a job description. Figure 3-17 illustrates a job description that also includes job specifications.

The key parts of a job description are: job identity, job summary, job duties, working conditions, and skills and competencies. All job descriptions also usually identify the author, the work supervisor, and the date on which it was prepared.

Job Identity The section on job identity typically includes job title, job location, job code, job grade, and status (whether exempted from overtime laws or not). Job codes use numbers, letters, or both to provide a quick summary. These codes are useful for comparing jobs.

Job Summary and Duties A job summary is a written narrative that concisely summarizes the job in a few sentences. It tells what the job is, how it is done, and why. Most authorities recommend that job summaries specify the primary actions involved. Then, in a simple, action-oriented style, the job description lists the job duties.

Working Conditions A job description also explains working conditions. It may go beyond descriptions of the physical environment. Hours of work, safety and health hazards, travel requirements, and other features of the job expand the meaning of this section.

Skills, Efforts, and Competencies A job specification should include specific tools, actions, experiences, education, competencies, and training (i.e., the individual requirements of the job). For example, it should describe "physical effort" in terms of the special actions demanded by the job. "Lifts 50 kg boxes" is better than "Lifts heavy weights." Clear behaviour statements give a better picture than vague generalities.[36] When preparing specifications, it is critical not to include needless job requirements since they not only exclude potentially qualified individuals from consideration, but also expose the firm to possible litigation from unsuccessful job applicants who feel they were unfairly discriminated against.

Approvals Since job descriptions affect most work related decisions, selected jobholders and their supervisors should review their accuracy. Then supervisors are asked to approve the description. This approval serves as a further test of the job description and a further check on the collection of job analysis information.

A job description is a broad-brush picture of the job on an analyst's canvas; a task inventory can be thought of as strokes with a finer brush.[37] The task analysis enables the analyst to list each task that is an integral part of the larger job and list the specific competencies, skills, and personal resources needed to do it effectively. Simple job descriptions cannot, often, highlight the differences in job responsibilities and duties between two firms or even two divisions in the same firm.

> The job description of a human resource manager in two different firms may look somewhat similar. In one firm, however, the person may be in charge of a large department with a $3 million budget and may supervise a team of professionals while in another firm, the person may be overseeing all human resource functions under severe budgetary constraints and a skeleton team. In both firms, all essential human resource functions must be carried out, although under qualitatively different conditions.

Figure 3-18 shows parts of a task inventory for a shipper in the Office Products Company. A task inventory is not a substitute for a job description; rather, it elaborates and explains several of the items that cannot be dealt with in detail in a summary document such as a job description.

Website with sample job descriptions of a government unit: *www.spb.ca.gov/*

FIGURE 3-17   A Sample Job Description that Includes Specifications

Office Products Limited
Job Description for Customer Service Representative

JOB IDENTIFICATION DETAILS

Job Title: Customer Service Representative	**Job Code:** CS 078
Date: May 13, 2002	**Author:** Greg MacKinnon
Job Location: Downtown Toronto Store	**Job Grade:** 6
Report to: Tim Cleary, Manager	**Status:** Not exempt from overtime

JOB SUMMARY

Interacts with customers on a daily basis, promptly responds to all inquiries in person or over the phone in a courteous and efficient manner. Encourages the sale of company products at every opportunity and applies exemplary customer relation skills. Provides information to customers about product features and substitutes when asked. Helps customers when they are faced with problems or need information.

DUTIES AND RESPONSIBILITIES

1. Responds to customer inquiries on product features, prices, services, and delivery terms.
2. Takes customer orders for products and communicates these accurately to supply and servicing personnel in the company.
3. Accepts returns of merchandise by customers and gives them credit for the same.
4. Displays and stocks merchandise on shelves.
5. Accurately prices items based on instructions received from the supervisor.
6. Prepares necessary documents and transmits/files copies to relevant offices within the company.
7. Responds to other miscellaneous inquiries especially those related to warranties, delivery terms, servicing frequencies (in the case of equipment).
8. Undertakes other tasks assigned by the supervisor.

WORKING CONDITIONS

Works in a well-ventilated office.
Must be able to work shifts.

SKILL, EFFORT, COMPETENCIES, AND OTHER SPECIFICATIONS

Education:	Ten years of general education or equivalent. Familiarity with popular computer programs and software highly desirable.
Experience:	Prior sales experience in an office-products industry is desirable. Familiarity with computers, scanners, and printers highly desirable.
Communication:	Strong interpersonal skills a must. Should have strong oral communication skills. Knowledge of French highly desirable.
Physical Demands:	Long periods of standing may be required in some instances. Should be able to lift products weighing 10 kilograms or less. Finger dexterity to operate a computer keyboard and cash register is essential. Should not be allergic to solvents used in printer ribbons, cartridges, or chemicals normally used in an office setting.
Mental Demands:	Ability to respond to customer inquiries regarding prices, service terms, etc. a must. This requires good short term memory. Ability to learn and remember product codes of popular items.
Other Competencies:	Ability to empathize with the customer a must. Ingenuity and ability to solve problems in a creative manner is associated with superior performance on the job.

The above information is correct as approved by:

(Signed) _____   (Signed)_____

Customer Service Representative   Manager

FIGURE 3-18 Parts of a Task Inventory for a Shipper

Office Products Limited
Task Inventory for Shipper

JOB IDENTIFICATION DETAILS

Job Title: Shipper
Date: May 13, 2002
Job Location: Downtown Toronto Store
Report to: Joan Hardy, Supervisor

Job Code: CS 083
Author: Greg MacKinnon
Job Grade: 3
Status: Not exempt from Over time

JOB SUMMARY

Receives delivery orders from customer service department, arranges them in sequence based on established criteria, packs products, addresses and attaches invoice in standard containers as per procedures detailed in operating manual and leaves them at the delivery counter for pick up by trucks. The shipper is responsible for the safety of the products at the delivery point and during transit to the extent that all packages and procedures meet the safety standards specified in the Operating Manual. The shipper is also responsible for following proper lifting procedures and safety of lift-truck and cart operation procedures.

PERFORMANCE STANDARD

100% accuracy in address labeling and 95% accuracy in shipping correct products is expected. At least 90% of the deliveries should be completed within 2 days after receipt of the delivery instructions from the customer service department.

	STANDARDS		
	Time (Minutes)	Accuracy (%)	Skills (Primary only)
TASKS			
1. Review delivery order tickets			
(A) Note quantity	1/2	98	C
(B) Note brand/style/grade	1/2	98	C
(C) Note delivery speed desired	1/2	97	C
(D) Note prepaid or to be billed	1/2	95	C
(E) Note address to be sent to	1/2	99	C
2. Obtain supplies and equipments needed to process order			
(A) Obtain shipping containers	2	95	C, P
(B) Obtain flatbed cart to transport containers	3	90	P
(C) Use forklift where necessary	4	90	P
(D) Retain order ticket and mark items collected in the boxes provided	-	90	C

....
....
....

Skills: C = Cognitive; P = Psycho-motor; A = Affective
The above information should be interpreted in conjunction with *Operating Manual* and *Safety Instructions*. In the event of any discrepancy between the above information and instructions contained in the *Operating Manual* or *Safety Instructions*, the latter will prevail. The Management reserves the right to assign other duties so long as they are not beyond the capabilities of the employee concerned and not in contravention to the current *Collective Agreement*.

The above information is correct as approved by:

(Signed) _____

(Signed) _____

Shipper

Supervisor

Many task inventories also provide some benchmarks or standards for performance, although this is, by no means, universal. The steps in establishing performance standards are discussed in the next section.

SET PERFORMANCE STANDARDS

Job analysis, when properly done, helps establish job performance standards that become objectives or targets for employee efforts. Once standards are met, workers may feel accomplishment and achievement. This outcome contributes to employee satisfaction. Without standards, employee performance may suffer.

Job standards are obtained either from job analysis information or from alternative sources. For example, industry standards may be used as benchmarks for performance in certain jobs (especially service functions like accounting).[38] Job analysis information is usually sufficient for jobs where:

- performance is quantified;

- performance is easily measurable;

- performance standards are understood by workers and supervisors; and

- performance requires little interpretation.

Jobs with short work cycles often exhibit these features. An example is an assembly-line job. For these jobs, questions on the job analysis checklist may generate specific, quantitative answers. When confirmed by supervisors, this information becomes the job performance standard. In the case of some service jobs, quantifiable "outputs" may not be readily available; but even here, performance can be appraised by looking at the behaviours of the jobholders.

ALTERNATIVE APPROACHES TO SETTING PERFORMANCE STANDARDS

Although job analysis information does not always provide a source of job standards, it is necessary even if analysts use other means to develop reasonable standards. The most common alternative sources of job standards are work measurement and participative goal setting (Figure 3-19).

Work Measurement Work measurement techniques estimate the normal performance of average workers; the results dictate the job performance standard. Such techniques are applied to non-managerial jobs and are created from company records, time study, and work sampling.

Work measurement techniques are methods used to estimate the normal performance of average workers, the results of which are used to form the job performance standards.

FIGURE 3-19   Setting Performance Standards

1. WORK MEASUREMENT
   a. company records
   b. time study
   c. work sampling

2. EMPLOYEE-INVOLVED GOAL SETTING

Company Records Historical data can be obtained from past records if job analysis does not supply performance standards. For example, the number of tables and chairs produced by a furniture assembly unit in a month indicates how many legs, drawers, tabletops, etc. should be made or assembled by each worker. One weakness of this approach is that it assumes past performance is average performance. Another weakness is that historical data are useless on new jobs. However, if production records are reviewed for longstanding jobs, historically based standards may be more accurate than standards drawn from a job analysis checklist. For jobs where production technology continually changes, this approach is unlikely to lead to satisfactory results.

Time Study Time studies produce standards when jobs can be observed and timed. Time studies identify each element within a job and then time the elements while being conducted by an average worker using the standard method of doing the job. The average times for each element of the job are summed up to yield the rated job time. Allowances for rest breaks, fatigue, or equipment delays are added to produce a standard time. The standard time allows the firm to compute performance standards.

> Assume a painter can paint 10 square meters of wall in an average of four minutes, based on several direct observations. To this rated job time of four minutes, allowances for moving ladders, changing drop sheets, and taking rest breaks are added. The total is a standard time of five minutes. This means that the painter's standard of performance should be an average of 10 square meters for five minutes, or 120 square meters an hour.

Work Sampling By taking random samples of work done by different job holders over a representative time period, the analyst can determine the number of minutes to add for allowances. Allowances are usually set through work sampling.

> By making 200 observations of different painters at different times during the day over a two-week period, analysts discover that the painters were actually painting 80% of the time. If four minutes of uninterrupted painting is required to paint 10 square meters, the standard time can be computed by dividing the rated time (four minutes) by the time spent working (80%). The result is a standard time of five minutes. Mathematically, the computation is rated time divided by observed proportion of work time used equals standard time.

Standards for some jobs cannot be determined by either job analysis information or work measurement. In service or managerial jobs, output may reflect changing tradeoffs.

> The time needed by a physician with each patient cannot be accurately determined as this depends on the seriousness of each illness.

But standards are still useful, even though they are difficult to set. In some cases, mutual agreement between the job incumbent and others-typically the boss-is more likely to be effective. This is discussed below.

Employee-Involved Goal Setting When a job lacks obvious standards, managers may develop them with the participation of subordinates. These conversations discuss the purpose of the job, its role in relation to other jobs, the organization's requirements, and the employee's needs. The employee gains insight into what is expected. Implicit or explicit promises of future rewards may also result. From these discussions, the manager and the employee reach some jointly shared objectives and standards. The process may even lead to greater employee commitment, morale, satisfaction, and motivation. More on employee involvement practices is discussed in Chapter 5. Since objectives are for individual positions (instead of jobs), they are seldom included in job descriptions.

Performance standards sometimes are set with the participation of union leaders. Labour leaders understand the important role of job analysis information, and they may insist on negotiating performance standards for jobs. These negotiated agreements are written into legally enforceable contracts.

> In one paper products company, management decided to increase production rates by 5% to meet customer demand. The union threatened legal action because the new standards conflicted with those in the labour contract. Management was forced to retain the old standard.

IDENTIFY AND DEVELOP PERFORMANCE COMPETENCIES

Competency is the knowledge, skill, ability, or characteristic used to perform a job successfully.

More recently, competency-based job descriptions and specifications have gaining in popularity. A **competency**, such as problem solving, analytical thinking, or leadership, is a knowledge, skill, ability, or characteristic associated with high performance on a job.[39] Others have defined the concept "an attribute bundle," consisting of task competencies, results competencies, and knowledge, skills, behaviours, and attitude competencies including work related values and beliefs.[40] Whatever the precise definition, the objective in most cases is to identify characteristics that are associated with superior job performance. Figure 3-20 lists illustrative competencies for a superviso-

---

FIGURE 3-20   Illustrative Competencies for a Supervisor in a Textile Firm

The operational measures attached to competencies listed below are specific to the firm and may have to be changed to meet the needs of other firms The weight shown against each competency is based on the relative frequency with which the competency distinguished superior supervisors from average supervisors in this firm.

Competency	Meaning	Weight
1. Professional expertise	Knowledge of all relevant professional practices including a sound awareness of situational factors which are to be considered in making decisions.	8
2. Interpersonal skills	Ability to communicate, negotiate, lead, and resolve conflicts with others in desired time frame and effectively.	14
3. Initiative	Tendency to initiate actions before being asked to do.	9
4. Planning	Consistency with which realistic production plans are made. Ability to anticipate production related challenges and take proactive actions.	12
5. Customer service focus	Focus on providing the highest quality service to internal and external customers on a consistent basis.	9
6. Flexibility	Ability to alter plans, practices, and behaviours in the light of emerging challenges and to respond to emergencies.	7
7. Analytical thinking	Ability to analyze situations thoroughly and validly seeing interdependencies among events and variables. Capacity to form valid conclusions and action plans.	4
8. Directiveness	The structure and action plan, focus on achievement and the tendency to lead (rather than follow) seen in behaviours.	6

ry position. In the case of the position described, interpersonal and planning skills are found to be most important for the position.

Competencies are identified after a careful analysis of the work of high performers. This may be done through observation, listings of critical behaviours or incidents at work, interviews, or employee logs. The job analysis information, combined with the information on an organization's goals and strategies, forms the basis of identifying competencies and their relative importance to the position under consideration.

A **competency model** describes the output from analyses that differentiate high performers from average and low performers. Competency models are represented in different formats, depending on the methods used to collect the data, customers' requirements, and focus of the persons developing the model. Some competency models identify specific competencies, provide a behavioural description for each one, rank order the competencies by importance, and establish a proficiency level for each of them. Competencies might include items such as integrity and tenacity. Competency models are useful not only for employee placement and performance planning, but also to facilitate hiring, training, and career planning for employees.

> A survey of 219 Canadian organizations by The Conference Board of Canada found that 45% of the responding firms used a competency framework for training and development activities. A large number of the respondents had also used it for hiring, compensation, and performance management. According to 85% of the respondents, the adoption of a competency framework had enabled their training programs to become more strategic while facilitating decision-making. This was because a competency framework allowed employees to quickly identify the success factors in their organizational and personal work.[41]

Competencies have to be carefully established and continually evaluated for their relevance to organizational strategy and processes. Employees must also be encouraged to acquire new competencies by relating competency building to internal reward systems. To be effective, employees should also have opportunities to use their newly acquired skills. The next chapter looks at some reward systems that encourage competency building. Chapter 5 looks at designing jobs that encourage employee involvement and competency building.

A **competency model** describes the output from analyses used to differentiate high performers from average and low performers.

Implications for Practice

1. An organization's mission and performance benchmarks need to be translated to process goals and day-to-day performance standards for individual employees and work teams.

2. An open system view of organizations is useful because it underscores the importance of process effectiveness and efficiency and the need for responding to environmental changes.

3. To improve labour productivity, a firm must pay close attention to a variety of factors such as knowledge and skills, goal clarity, abilities, motivation, and effort levels of workers.

4. Organizational processes reflect varying levels of interdependence among employees and departments to accomplish their respective tasks. In situations characterized by low interdependence, an organiza-

tion may be able to maintain effectiveness through rules and standards; when the tasks are sequentially interdependent, clear plans and goals have to be formulated. In situations characterized by intensive, reciprocal interdependence, only continuous adjustment on the part of everyone involved can produce timely and effective actions.

5. To ensure high quality, an organization should establish procedures that describe the process, collect data, assess process stability, identify causes and cause effect relationships, implement changes, and continually monitor progress.

6. Job and task analysis are critical in most organizations to clarify job duties, establish performance standards, identify valid selection criteria, avoid discrimination, and improve productivity and quality of work life. Using valid and cost-effective methods, job information should be collected, summarized,

and communicated to all concerned on a regular basis.

7. Competencies are to identified after a careful analysis of the work of high performers. This may be done through observation, listings of critical behaviours or incidents at work, interviews, or employee logs. The job analysis information combined with the information on an organization's goals and strategies should form the basis of identifying competencies and their relative importance to the position under consideration.

Key Terms for Review

Competency, p. 84

Competency model, p. 85

Control charts, p. 69

Effectiveness, p. 66

Efficiency, p. 63

Flowchart, p. 68

Information technology, p. 58

Job, p. 75

Job analysis, p. 75

Job description, p. 78

Job specification, p. 78

Maintenance, p. 70

Management, p. 56

Performance standards, p. 56

Position, p. 75

Process, p. 57

Productivity, p. 64

Six sigma, p. 72

Task, p. 75

Task analysis, p. 75

Task inventory, p. 75

Work measurement techniques, p. 82

Discussion Questions

1. What major actions improve organizational process?

2. How can the productivity of an assembly-line worker be measured? A college professor?

3. How does an organization's technology affect its member performance? Consider the examples of a bank, a bottling plant, and a firefighting team. Explain.

4. What is job analysis? What steps are needed to perform a job analysis of 300 assembly-line workers in a garment factory? Is the approach different if most workers are new immigrants?

5. Describe the various approaches to set performance standards. Identify the "best approach" and defend your position.

6. What specific steps can be taken by a fast food hamburger chain to improve quality?

Critical Thinking Questions

1. If you were part of a team asked to look into the quality of training offered in your college or university, what criteria would you employ to evaluate it? What specific actions would you recommend to improve internal systems and processes?

2. Consider the following two organizations:

	Organization A	Organization B
Number of employees	4200	22
Region of operation	All of Canada	Whitby, Ontario
Type of business engaged in	Banking	Psychiatric care
Size (by industry standards)	Medium	Small

What differences in processes and employee management practices are likely to exist?

3. Assume that you are asked to conduct the job and task analysis of the instructor in this course. How will you go about it? How should the process quality in each task should be assessed?

4. If you were identifying the performance standards for a group of assembly line workers and a group of lawyers in a small firm how would your approach differ? Why?

Web Research

Conduct a web search to find out about the specific actions taken to implement ISO 9000 or Six sigma in a small business. Write a report summarizing your findings. (Hint: You may begin your search with the websites listed in this chapter.)

CASE INCIDENT

Ontario Electronics Company Limited: R&D Division

Ontario Electronics Company Limited (OECL), a manufacturer of electronic, communication, aerospace, and audio equipment, currently employs over 500 workers, many of whom are professionals. The company's head office and major plant are located in Scarborough, Ontario, and its plants and sales offices are in four other Canadian provinces and in major U.S. cities. In the recent past the company has faired well financially, but top management is somewhat unhappy with the productivity levels seen in some plants. The management is particularly concerned about its Research and Development (R&D) division. Brenda Cole, recently hired in the capacity of Performance Analyst, looked into the performance of the R&D unit. She has just begun her review of the division-so far, having time to review some of the company records and talking to a few of the staff, including the division's leader of 2 years, Jim Nunn. When asked by Chuck Bridges, Vice President (Production), how her review was coming along, she had this to say:

"You know, Chuck, the R&D Division, historically, has not been a high performing unit. With 22 technically qualified persons, its workforce is quite comparable to similar Canadian hi-tech firms. So one asks, why is the unit not excelling in research?

I can't detect a specific reason or pattern so far. The salary and benefits we offer are at par with or exceed what is offered elsewhere. Our working conditions are excellent. True, the hours are long-but in today's work world, is there any job that does not involve long hours? From what I hear, the R&D group had always been fairly close-knit. There seems to be some horsing around, but not what I would call a major waste of time or resources.

Jim Nunn is a highly qualified, methodical, and very conscientious person. He literally lives, breathes, and sleeps his work. He's an ex-army officer who has won three gold medals for his work. The year he joined our firm, the R&D division came out only with two workable ideas. Jim introduced some new procedures and routine meetings in the division but so far, nothing seems to have improved the overall performance. Of course, now we have the additional challenge of having to find a replacement for Peter Kahn, the Research Supervisor, who has left us for Alpha Systems."

Later that day, Bridges met Jim Nunn in the boardroom where they were scheduled to have a strategy session. Both Bridges and Nunn were a few minutes early. When asked about Cole's review of R&D Division, Nunn said:

"Ms. Cole is collecting a lot of useful information. I am waiting to hear her findings, although, I suspect that she is as intrigued by the current situation as I am.

Mr. Bridges, as you know, the R&D division is actually composed of three distinct groups who all have different work patterns-the researchers, the preproduction designers, and the technicians. When I joined Ontario Electronics, these folks were haphazardly meeting each other and wasting a lot of time. I insisted that they have some formal meeting times so they now meet Tuesday mornings and Thursday afternoons. I also asked them to plan things ahead and write down every step they followed in their research. Initially, there was some resistance to my changes, but now, they are used to the formal meetings. What beats me is the overall performance of the unit. This year the division has come out with one just workable idea-and we were aiming for four!

You know, among the technicians, the absenteeism is now down by 15%; we have also reduced waste and scrappage by over 20%. The response to customer inquiries is 10% faster. Last week that I had an email from one of our major clients stating how happy they are with the improved service. But, when it comes to innovation, we just don't seem to be getting anywhere. I seem to have the most effect on the technicians and designers; but I cannot figure out the researchers. Finally, last week, I asked Mr. Kahn for an explanation and he wasn't at all happy with my question. I was totally taken aback when he tendered his resignation yesterday. I know that Alpha Systems is a good firm. There is some really good work going on there, but we are not behind them in anything, including our compensation package."

At this time, other board members entered the room and the discussion stopped abruptly.

Questions

1. Based on the material discussed in the chapter, what are some likely explanations for the poor performance of the R&D Division?

2. What actions plans would you suggest to Cole? To Nunn? Why?

Meadow Brook is an idyllic, quiet, Canadian farming town with less than 5500 residents. In the normal course of events, it would not have made into the national news or TV. However, recently, the entire media has been inundated with images of sick and dying town children, town people lining up with large bottles, and grief stricken faces of people in cemeteries. The TV viewer has become familiar with the image of a dazed parent striding from a chopper to hospital doors alongside a stretcher carrying a sick child.

The reason for all this media attention? In one word: water.

E. coli contaminated town water has left seven people dead and caused about 2300 others to fall ill. Everyone in this town knows someone who has died or was seriously ill. They have all attended the funerals; washed their hands with soap and water and then bleach to make sure the dangerous bacteria is gone. Some of the victims who survived face a lifetime of illness. For example, those diagnosed with Hemolytic Uremic Syndrome—a serious complication of E. coli infection—can permanently cause a decrease in the amount of urine produced, swelling in the face, hands, and feet, and fatigue. Many will continue to have abnormal kidney function and a few will require long-term dialysis. It will be months, perhaps years, before anyone turns on a tap in Meadow Brook without wondering if the water is safe.

E. coli 0157:H7 is a deadly microbe; once a person is infected, there is no proven medical treatment. All doctors can do is to prevent dehydration and wait for the infection to run its course. Many residents who had taken one gulp of town water or brushed their teeth with the polluted water experienced bloody diarrhea, abdominal cramps, and in some instances, kidney failure. Children and the elderly were most susceptible to the danger. Most of the adults who died were in their late sixties or older.

BACKGROUND

While everyone agrees that the town's water delivery system has miserably failed in this instance, there remains great confusion about what went wrong, who knew what things, and when, and how the information could have been utilized to prevent such a tragedy. Some claim that the bacteria invaded the system through faulty piping and weak barriers between surface water and the town's wells. As far back as 1978, tests revealed fecal coliform contamination in Meadow Brook's wells. A preliminary hydro-geologic investigation established that all the three water wells had possible pathways that would allow contamination to enter. In the months preceding the outbreak, the Environment Ministry's office received faxes from the lab that test results were positive for the presence of coliform bacteria in the town's water system. The lab manager said his company notified the Ministry about the problem five times in four months. But every time an alarm was raised, all officials

involved insisted that everything would be fine-as long as water was properly chlorinated and the provincial safety guidelines were followed. It did not happen.

At the centre of the storm is the Meadow Brook Public Utilities Commission (PUC), a two employee municipal water and power company, and its general manager Steve Kramer. The utility is overseen by a part-time board whose chairman, John Placek, is the owner of a home-building supplies firm in the town.

It was reported during a later judicial inquiry that the province's Environment Ministry received faxes in January and April indicating the presence of coliform bacteria (not E. coli) in the town's water system. The Ministry responded in April by a telephone call to PUC and was assured that measures were being taken to correct the problem. The Ministry did not receive any more positive test results and pursued the matter no further.

Meadow Brook Town switched to a different testing laboratory in early May. The laboratory found coliform in the town's water supply on May 5 and E. coli on May 17 and informed PUC of the results but not the Environment Ministry, claiming that it is not the responsibility of the testing laboratory to do so. Tim Allen, the Mayor of the town was not aware of the problems the PUC was having with its chlorination system, or of the warning the commission received about the safety of the water, until it was too late to prevent the epidemic. An approximate sequence of events taken from various testimonies and news reports is shown in Figure A.

In Canada, the provinces have jurisdiction over water quality control-federal government's involvement is limited to being part of the federal-provincial subcommittee on drinking water, which regularly updates water safety guidelines. However, these guidelines are not legally enforceable by Ottawa, leaving control with provinces. The drive to cut deficits has resulted in various provincial governments downloading the enforcement to municipalities. For example, in Ontario, the Ministry of the Environment cut more than 50% of its staff and 44% of its overall budget. Ministry laboratories no longer undertake drinking water analyses for municipalities. This often means that there is no reporting link from Ministry laboratories. The responsibility for notifying health authorities rests with the waterworks concerned.

Today, there are stark differences among provinces on how much control and enforcement they exercise. Only Alberta and Quebec have legislation mandating specific standards to be followed. There is no set procedure for sharing results of water quality tests between different levels of government and the general public. Quebec issues an average of 600 boil-water advisories each year-by far, the highest in the country; Alberta, in some past years, has issued only two such orders.[43] Most provinces receive the results of water quality tests from the labs directly; howev-

(continued)

FIGURE A   An Approximate Sequence of Events

May 5 (Fri)	The testing laboratory finds coliform bacteria in Meadow Brook Town's water supply system. Informs the Municipality by telephone and fax.
May 15 (Mon)	PUC takes routine sample of water supply.
May 17 (Wed)	PUC receives a fax from the testing laboratory confirming E. coli contamination in the water sample.
May 19 (Fri)	Region's Medical Health Office (MHO) first notified about several patients with bloody diarrhea. Later it is told that local doctors have been treating several patients with symptoms including bloody diarrhea, vomiting, and fever since May 16.
May 20 (Sat)	At least 50 people report to hospital with bloody diarrhea. PUC officials reassure the public that water supply is safe.
May 20 (Sat)	Mike Myer, an environment ministry employee who was hired a month previous at the spills action centre, receives four anonymous phone calls about adverse water samples in Meadow Brook Town. Myer frantically calls the police stations in communities near to Meadow Brook. The action centre does not have an emergency number for PUC.
May 21 (Sun)	At least 400 town residents have, by now, reported their illnesses. MHO officially warns residents not to drink the water. MHO takes independent water supplies despite being told by PUC that there is no contamination. Myer is able to reach Steve Kramer who tells him that "they have issued a boil water..." Kramer admits receiving adverse water samples two weeks earlier.
May 23 (Tue)	MHO's lab confirms that there is E. coli in the water supply. PUC tells MHO about the May 17 fax. Health officials are told that the equipment used for chlorination of the water has not worked for a while.
May 24 (Wed)	Fred Kramer makes changes to the water records—the day the E. coli claimed its first victim. Records for one well were neatly copied onto new sheets and chlorine residual readings were entered onto the sheets from May 3. The chlorinator in the well was disconnected from May 3 to 19, Fred told the judicial inquiry later.

er, governments in some provinces (e.g., Ontario, Quebec) rely on municipalities to inform the public when water is found to be contaminated. Sometimes, the public is altogether left out of the loop-as in Newfoundland when the government refused in November 1999, "CBC Radio's request for information on trihalomethanes in drinking water, claiming that it was a cabinet secret".[44] The funding for tests in Alberta, New Brunswick, Prince Edward Island, and Nova Scotia are at the municipal level; in Saskatchewan and Newfoundland it is at the provincial level; in British Columbia, it is provincial except for Vancouver and Victoria; in Manitoba, it is shared between the two levels of government. In all the territories, the responsibility for water safety rests with the territorial governments, except in Whitehorse.

THE GROWTH OF FACTORY FARMS AND WATER POLLUTION

Despite their image as centres of pollution, large cities may, in fact, have safer tap water than smaller, rural areas in many instances. Big cities can afford sophisticated water treatment plants. The quality of ground water in many rural areas is also adversely affected by the growth of large, factory farms-a new industry which the governments call "intensive livestock operations."[45] Even thirty years ago, tak-

ing care of 100 cattle was considered a big responsibility. Today, in Feedlot Alley, an area north of Lethbridge, Alberta, just one feedlot has as many as 25 000 cattle in a maze of outdoor corrals on a piece of land the size of a city block. Similarly, Ontario farmers, today, on average, manage 418 pigs each in crowded high-tech barns-more than four times the number they did 20 years ago. Just two hog factories account for nearly a quarter of the 5.6 million hogs produced in the province. Excessive grazing and stream use by too many cattle on too little land results in ground water pollution.[46] Intensive operations, while an economic boon to many towns, have also created industrial scale waste problems. A single 500 sow farm producing 20 piglets per sow each year can create as much effluent as a town with 25 000 people without any waste treatment.[47] Alberta's Feedlot Alley produces untreated waste from 1.3 million animals-sewage equivalent to that of eight million people.[48] Unless carefully monitored and controlled, these effluents can seep into the ground water thus posing a major health hazard. About 100 strains of dangerous E. coli now live in healthy cattle, which shed the organisms in their manure.[49] Even a few of them can start an infection. For example, a 25 000 head feedlot produces in excess of 50 000 tons of dung which contain a host of heavy metals because of mineral-rich diets and other bacteria. In several instances, very little of this dung is properly treated or removed from places which can cause potential water quality problems. Heavy rains-as experienced by Meadow Brook the week of the outbreak-and storms knocking out or flooding feces-treat-

(continued)

ment lagoons is a potential risk.[50] In some counties where intensive livestock farms exist, E. coli infection rate is 2.9 times the Canadian national rate. Some areas also report high incidence of gastrointestinal illnesses. A U.S. study showed that 25% of workers employed by hog barns suffer from bronchitis due to the corrosive nature of hog waste while even residents of counties with hog farms have been found to experience more headaches, sore throats, excessive coughing and diarrhea than residents of communities without hog farms.[51]

THE JUDICIAL INQUIRY AND AFTER

There have been varied reports about Stan Kramer's whereabouts for the first two days after the tragedy broke out. Some said that he was at his rural cottage while others said that he was helping provincial officials clean up the water supply. Later, a friend of Kramer informed the press that he was in the hospital either in a state of depression or with an E. coli infection. Kramer is considered by most members of the local public a "decent man, known for his integrity; a regular churchgoer who is dedicated to his family and friends." Kramer, who was assessed to be suicidal because of the tragedy, was given compassionate leave immediately. Outside Kramer's empty office door hung a poster: "Water is Life: dedicated to safe drinking water."

Dr. Dan McArthur, the medical officer of health who first went to the media with his concerns about water quality, was less enthusiastic in his endorsement of Kramer. He believed that the Meadow Brook Utility Commission and the town council officials withheld the information for five days, insisting the town's water supply was safe even though they had a lab report showing evidence of E. coli bacteria and had told Kramer that the chlorination system was malfunctioning. John Placek denied that the Utilities Commission had any knowledge of water impurity; he personally did not know anything about the contaminated water until Sunday, May 21, four days after the town's utility workers received a fax from the lab about the problem with the water. He said that the workers who received the fax were unaware of E. coli's deadly potential and didn't report the fax to their supervisors. He himself was "so busy trying to purify the water that he hasn't yet had time to read the report."

During a judicial inquiry, Fred Kramer, brother of Steve Kramer and PUC foreman admitted that water samples labelled as having been collected all over the town were frequently taken from a single source: the PUC's pumphouse. He admitted to wrongly labelling them as having come from various sources. Asked how often the samples were falsified, he replied, "I would say it was a regular event." Fred Kramer, who at the age of 17 joined his father when he was managing PUC, had no formal training nor had ever read the province's drinking water objectives. He was granted his water system operator's licence because of his work experience. He also did not know that E. coli could be deadly. "I always believed that we had good quality water in the town and if the chlorinator broke down, it

was not a major issue," he admitted. He grew up drinking unchlorinated water and never felt that there was any need to add foreign substances to water. He and other utility workers regularly drank untreated water at the town's wells. "It always tasted better," he admitted.

Fred Kramer also admitted to drinking alcohol on the job regularly. On one occasion, his brother sent him home from work because he had been drinking. Two years previous, when Fred was hospitalized for his second heart attack, Stan removed the refrigerator which contained beer from the PUC office and told him that "there would be no more alcohol in the shop."

Later, in a judicial inquiry, Steve Kramer revealed his lack of training for the job and admitted to faking reports. He also admitted that he knew the water was contaminated, but thought he could correct the problem and didn't tell either the public or town officials. According to Kramer, the samples "didn't look good" but he was never told in detail that coliform or E. coli bacteria were on the sample plate in the lab. He admitted knowing that the chlorinator was malfunctioning. Beginning May 19, he had an uneasy feeling about the water prompting him to raise the chlorination level. He firmly denied those actions as part of a cover-up. It "was a preventative measure" and he still believed that water was safe.

The following December, about seven months after the tragedy, Steve Kramer was relieved of his position. He was originally granted a severance pay of $98 000 which was later reduced to $84 000. The provincial government announced that it will spend $25 million on safe drinking water and clean air in the next budget. A Meadow Brook Compensation Plan was established by the provincial government to "do the right thing for the victims of the tragedy."

"There is a dramatic need for a new federal level water policy," commented Paul Muldoon, the executive director of the Canadian Environmental Defence Fund and one of the top water experts in Canada a year after the tragedy[52]— a sentiment that was echoed by the Federation of Canadian Municipalities, asking for mandatory national standards.[53] There is a growing consensus among all concerned that Canada, which possesses nearly 10% of the world's renewable fresh water supply, is squandering this valuable resource. The disagreement seems to be on who should be held responsible for what and how. Meanwhile, the world water use is to soar to crisis levels putting additional pressures on water-rich countries like Canada.[54]

Questions

1. *What concepts discussed in this chapter can provide additional insights into the tragedy? What factors seem to have contributed to this tragedy?*

2. *If you were hired as a consultant to improve water quality and delivery systems in rural Canada, what actions will you recommend? What criteria would you employ to evaluate the effectiveness of your recommendations?*

PART 3

PERFORMANCE FACILITATION

Even the most competent employees underperform if reward systems and work climate are not motivating. Establishing performance-reward linkage is critical to maintaining and enhancing performance. The rewards must be seen as fair and equitable and must be valued by the recipient. Reward system properties are discussed in Chapter 4. Chapter 5 examines how jobs can be designed to maximize intrinsic rewards like work autonomy and involvement, and in turn, enhance performance.

4 REWARDS AND PERFORMANCE

Reward systems can give people a reason to take desired actions by providing something positive for achieving a desired result... If reward systems are to reinforce desired changes in behaviours, they need to be redesigned from the ground up.[1]

Thomas B. Wilson

CHAPTER OBJECTIVES

After studying this chapter, you should be able to:

- List the types of rewards seen in organizations

- Outline the key factors used to design a compensation strategy

- Discuss the implementation of a pay system that fosters high employee performance

- Examine the methods of linking executive pay to performance

Fifteen years of overseeing carrot cutting and chicken skinning has brought a lottery-scale win for many managers of Sky Chefs Inc., an airline catering company that employed 33 000 and sold $2.6 billion worth of meals in 2001. The 299 middle level managers received an average of $1.34 million the year Lufthansa AG bought Sky Chefs from its parent company, Onex Corporation. Veteran kitchen supervisors, who for years focused on fresh buns and crisp salads, received $3 million each while the company's top 25 executives averaged $10.9 million. At privately owned Sky Chefs, management had an opportunity to buy stock at book value-public companies normally change hands at a premium of their book value. For every $3 of equity they bought, managers had to invest $1 themselves. Onex arranged a bank loan to cover the remaining $2. Annual bonus payments were structured, in part, to cover interest payments on the loan. The result of the stock ownership was a fundamental change in the managers' attitudes, putting a renewed emphasis on creating shareholder value. "We were able to start talking about what our day-to-day decisions meant to the price of their shares, and the team got very sophisticated," said Pat Tolbert, the Chief Financial Officer. Having managers who actually owned stock rather than stock options not only helped attract top talent to the firm but also created an organizational culture that worshiped shareholder value.[2]

Sky Chefs' strategy of stock ownership is, by no means, the norm for Canadian firms. Indeed, only a small percentage of companies in other sectors, like banking and hi-tech, that employ stock ownership programs. However, even in established or old-economy firms, well-designed stock ownership plans can be effective. As one compensation expert pointed out, "if old-line manufacturing companies come up with plans that are well designed and communicated, they tend to enjoy enormous support. There's usually a strong desire among employees to align themselves with the company through stock ownership."[3]

Pay systems are almost as varied as the organizations using them. This is because a large number of factors, including the specific objectives of the business and its management, affect the type of pay system implemented:

- The overall compensation philosophy (e.g., below market versus above market pay)

- The managerial objectives (e.g., whether to maximize employee performance or maximize loyalty and tenure)

- The business strategy (e.g., to remain a low cost producer versus innovative entrepreneur)

- The number of employees in the organization (e.g., 40 versus 40 000)

- The geographical operation of the business (e.g., a local business versus a large firm operating in eight countries)

Figure 4-1 summarizes key objectives of most reward systems. It is unlikely that any single pay system will achieve all the objectives. Depending on its goals, strategy, size, and culture, an organization has to identify specific compensation objectives.

This chapter is about rewards. Here, we will be looking at a number of approaches to rewarding employees-all aiming to achieve desired performance whether in outcome or behavioural terms (Figure 4-2). Desired outcomes usually include producing the appropriate quantity and quality of output while almost all organizations like their employees to exhibit certain behaviours such arriving on time for work, being courteous to customers and fellow employees, and generating useful

---

FIGURE 4-1   Reward System Objectives

- To attract and retain qualified employees
- To reward effective performance
- To foster innovation and entrepreneurial spirit
- To maximize productivity and employee contributions
- To build employee competencies and support career development
- To foster long-term commitment and tenure
- To attain equity in salary levels
- To maintain high employee satisfaction levels

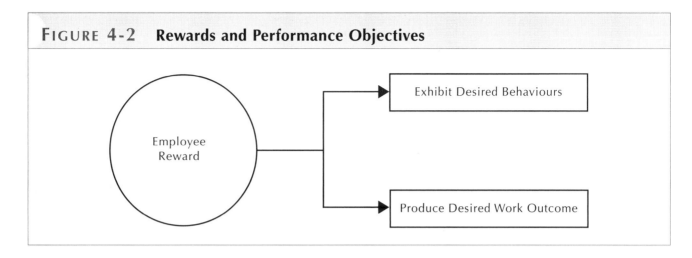

FIGURE 4-2 **Rewards and Performance Objectives**

ideas. For this purpose, the employer offers a variety of rewards and incentives. These are discussed in the next section.

TYPES OF REWARDS

Most organizations offer a variety of rewards to generate desired employee performance, although the mix and value of these rewards show considerable variation from one firm to another. Figure 4-3 shows current popular organizational rewards. Most likely, no single firm offers all types of rewards, just as no firm restricts itself to any single reward.

By and large, most rewards can be categorized into four groups: monetary and tangible rewards, social rewards, status enhancement rewards, and intrinsic job rewards.

MONETARY AND TANGIBLE REWARDS

Pay, raises, fringe benefits, work breaks, and holidays are commonplace in Canadian organizations. While a large number of monetary and tangible rewards exist, the impact of specific rewards on performance varies.

> Organizations that rely on pay raises and promotion to influence individual employee motivation may discover these rewards to be problematic because of the frequency with which they can be administered. On the other hand, financial incentives and bonus plans reinforce superior performance on a regular basis, but are not aimed at any single employee.

Similarly, while production and cost-reduction bonuses encourage greater productivity in a specific job, stock ownership and profit sharing encourage employees to take a broader, organizational level perspective. Employer-provided benefits such as insurance may enable employees to receive some services at a fraction of their actual cost and still enjoy substantial tax benefits-something a simple pay raise cannot provide. Vacations and time off not only reduce fatigue and enhance productivity, but also enable employees to achieve better balance between work and home life. Indeed, the more enlightened employers offer a variety of rewards to their employees to tap into their full potential. Consider the following organization.

> Exfo Electro-Optical Engineering Inc., based in the Quebec City suburb of Vanier, is among Canada's fast growing hi-tech firms. It is also rated as one of the top 100

FIGURE 4-3   Popular Organizational Rewards

Monetary and Tangible Rewards
Pay
Pay raise
Pensions
Profit sharing
Supplementary health and disability insurance
Other insurance programs (e.g., automobile, theft)
Use of company car
Product discount plans
Time off/ work breaks
Vacation
Training and education assistance programs
Bonuses
Promotion to a higher paying job
Free or priority parking
Sabbatical and other types of leave
Vacation trips
Home purchase assistance
Club membership
Subsidized food plans
Moving expense reimbursement
Free legal, financial, and other counselling
Tickets to popular shows/theatre
Flexible hours
Alternate work arrangements (including flextime, work-family balance arrangements, etc.)

Social Rewards
Praise
Informal recognitions
Positive feedback
Invitations to company parties/get-togethers
Company games
Other social gatherings
Compliments/greetings
Nonverbal signals

Status Enhancement
Office size
Office location (e.g., office with a view, on a specific floor)
Promotion to a higher rank
Carpeting
Other furnishings including paintings, drapery
Furniture
Wall plaque
Listing in "hall of fame"
Reports in company newsletters, annual reports, and other publications
Watches
Rings

Intrinsic Job Rewards
Job autonomy
Job variety
Job challenge
Job feedback
Participation in new organizational ventures
Authority to choose geographical location, work time, etc.

Canadian employers. Founded in 1985 by president Germain Lamonde and a partner-each with 50 ($1) shares of investment-the firm now has a market capitalization exceeding $350 million. The secret of its success? According to Lamonde, it's the employees. The firm, which now employs about 1200 people, still attempts to respond to each employee's needs as much as possible. All can participate in share purchase and profit sharing plans and earn quarterly performance bonuses. Exfo also gives its employees tickets for movies, live shows, and restaurants on the basis of performance. Most programmers can choose flexible work hours-some working only at night-and all are encouraged to be active in the social club which organizes soccer and hockey games and ice-canoeing on the St. Lawrence River.[4]

SOCIAL REWARDS

Humans, as social beings, are significantly influenced by the opinions of relevant others. Even opinions of strangers may, at times, influence a person's judgement.[5] Several research studies in varied work settings have indicated how others' expectations influence a person's performance.

> Simply communicating that someone will do a good or a poor job seems to make a person more likely to, in fact, do so. Thus, an instructor who conveys early on that a student is superior may influence the student's behaviour positively.

Recognizing this fact, many employers use a variety of social rewards-all fostering an employee's sense of self-esteem, self-worth, and social position and role. This has assumed greater importance today, especially in firms that attempt to retain valuable employees and employ teams for making day-to-day decisions. Great West Life Assurance Company of Winnipeg is a good example in this context.

> With 3800 employees and enough assets to pay $18 billion worth of death benefits and annuities, Great West Life Assurance Company should be a large, intimidating, and impersonal work setting. Not so, say a large number of employees whose positive evaluation of the company's employee practices helped the firm be on the best Canadian employer list in 2002. The Great West social club, which sponsors events such as an annual bonspiel (attracting over 500 curlers), is just one way employees get to know each other. The firm's hockey league-with inside statisticians meticulously calculating the goals and assists of over 400 employees who have skated in the league since 1980-is another place where employees make new friends and meet old ones regularly. The result? Even employees who originate from small towns and rural areas feel totally at home in the company. The company also moves employees from one division to another periodically, allowing them to develop large circles of friends and acquaintances.[6]

STATUS ENHANCEMENT

Almost all humans make social comparisons. Most individuals are motivated by a desire for self-definition-to know how one stacks up against some relevant individual or group. In an organizational context, symbols that enable employees to raise their own status through others have been popular since formal organizations emerged (the proverbial notion of receiving "key to the executive washroom" being a symbol of "having made it").

> In most organizations, it is common to see top managers and powerful employees having access to scarce resources such as valuable paintings and large, well-furnished offices with a good view.

Focus on Small Business

Reward Is More Than Money!

Both management and employees of small businesses are likely to view compensation from a rewards perspective.[7] That is, both tangible and intangible rewards are likely to be important from both the management's and employee's point of view. The management of a typical small firm can offer an informal, family-like work environment where every employee knows everyone else and may find the rules less impersonal and systems less bureaucratic. In return, employees may be willing to accept slightly lower pay or less job security. Many reward programs are also unique to specific organizations and may even be a source of competitive advantage[8] as it will be hard to replicate. Rewards offered in small firms include the following:

- Existence of a friendly organization culture
- Opportunity to engage in fun projects (especially in small hi-tech firms)
- More flexible work hours
- More personal supervision
- Support of further employee education and development
- High quality of life and better balance between work and personal life
- Personal treatment generating a family-like environment
- Provision of information on a continuing basis (i.e., what the firm is doing and where it is going), increasing employee involvement

Because of its very nature, employee trust is critical in small businesses.[9] If the employees do not trust the management, irrespective of the type of rewards given, they may still leave the firm or be poorly motivated.

AudeSi Technolgies Inc., of Calgary, rated as one of Canada's top 100 employers, is a good example in this context.[10] AudeSi develops embedded technology hardware and software that connect consumer products such as refrigerators to the Internet. Established four years ago, AudeSi's growth has been impressive, much of the credit going to its ever-growing workforce (last year, it created 15 new positions). AudeSi employees can work flexible hours and from home on many days. Employees enjoy free soft drinks and snacks and if they work through the noon hour, the employer buys them lunch. The company's offices are open concept both in design and philosophy and almost all employees have direct contact with customers-something rarely experienced in larger hi-tech firms. AudeSi actively organizes numerous staff and family activities including mountain biking, hiking, and camping trips. Employees are encouraged to participate in Calgary stampede breakfasts, golf days, and other celebrations. The company offers a number of benefits including eye and dental care, prescription drug coverage, and tuition subsidies. All employees are offered stock options on the first day of employment. For travelling employees, the company has a weekend travel policy by which the airfare savings for staying over a weekend are shared with the employee.

In March 2000, Windriver Systems Inc., a leading U.S. provider of software and services for smart devices on the Internet acquired AudeSi. The financial analysts expect the market for information appliances to grow rapidly in the near future from 11 million units in 1999 (valued at U.S. $2.4 billion) to 89 million units (U.S. $17.8 billion) in 2004. With that kind of growth trajectory, AudeSi employees should have even greater challenges and rewards.[11]

For more information visit the company website at www.windriver.com/press/html/acq_audesi.html

The culture of an organization defines the symbols of success. Thus two organizations operating in the same industry may have different symbols of status and success. Needless to say, status symbols in schools, business organizations, the military, churches, universities, and hospitals show considerable variation as well.

Intrinsic Job Rewards

Job autonomy, task variety, feedback of performance, and a sense of task accomplishment are important rewards intrinsic to many jobs. Given their positive impact on employee motivation, many employers have redesigned jobs to incorporate these features. Job redesign is discussed in detail in Chapter 5.

SELF-TEST:

What Motivates You?

This exercise assesses the relative importance of factors that motivate you to perform. Please answer all questions frankly. Note your answers on a separate sheet so that no one else may have access to it.

Indicate the importance of each item to you by answering *extremely important* (EI), *important* (I), *neither important nor unimportant* (NIU), *unimportant* (UI), or *extremely unimportant* (EU).

1. Pay

2. Other monetary benefits like rent allowance and pension plans

3. Employee discount plans

4. Supplementary insurance (e.g., disability, supplemental health, dental)

5. Production or service related bonuses

6. Number of paid holidays

7. Number of breaks

8. Paid leave

9. Ability to take time off work without pay

10. Flexible working hours

11. Job variety

12. Job autonomy

13. Getting performance feedback on a timely basis

14. Meaningful contribution in your work

15. Challenges in your job

Scoring

For all items, assign 5, 4, 3, 2, and 1 for EI, I, NIU, UI, and EU respectively. Total your scores for items 1 through 5, 6 through 10, and 11 through 15 separately.

Interpretation

Your total score on items 1 through 5 shows the importance you attach to money and other monetary rewards. Your total score on items 6 through 10 shows the importance you assign to free time (and in a sense work: family balance). Your total score on items 11 through 15 shows the importance you assign to rewards associated with the job.

DESIGNING A COMPENSATION STRATEGY

In formulating the compensation strategy, several considerations are paramount. Figure 4-4 shows the more important ones and they are discussed in some detail below.

Websites on compensation systems:
www.hr-guide.com
www.chrs.net

MONETARY VERSUS NON-MONETARY REWARDS

Almost all organizations employ both monetary and non-monetary rewards (e.g., interesting work, autonomy, and prestige) to generate superior performance. While many individuals are openly reluctant to assign high importance to pay, "money has been and continues to be the primary means of rewarding and modifying human

---

FIGURE 4-4   **Key Considerations in Compensation Strategy Design**

1.   Should the organization primarily use monetary or non-monetary rewards?
2.   How to maximize owner and employee needs?
3.   How to maximize effort-reward linkage?
4.   How to ensure equity in reward system?
5.   Should the organization primarily reward performance or membership?
6.   What and how many competencies and skills should be rewarded and how?
7.   Should the organization have an open or secret pay system?
8.   Should the organization have a centralized or decentralized compensation system?

---

behaviour in industry."[12] Pay "may rank higher (in importance) than people care to admit to others-or to themselves" and pay's role in motivating employees may be higher than often recorded in research.[13]

Several explanations currently exist as to why money is important to individuals. Some of these are:

- Attachment to money is learned.[14] Over time, socialization and upbringing may make acquiring money an even a neurotic need.[15]

- Money reinforces certain behaviours[16], acting as a conditioned incentive. Once these behaviours become important to the people, they need for money also increases.

- Money helps people achieve several outcomes[17] and engage in activities that they enjoy.

- Money often satisfies material and safety needs.

- Money compensates for sacrifice of time and effort. Since many other rewards cannot be accumulated or saved, money's role assumes great importance.

- Money often indicates a person's social status. Money may even provide a source of self-esteem.

- Money often acts as a "tangible sign of achievement"[18] to both the individual and outsiders.

For an average employee, money is likely to play an important part in shaping work motivation although money alone may not be sufficient to generate very high levels of commitment. Indeed, the available research indicates that there are considerable differences in the meaning and importance of pay to individuals.[19]

> Materialistic employees may prefer high pay, individualists may want individual pay plans, and high risk-averse (i.e., security minded) employees may want fixed pay.[20] People who assign greater importance to money have often been found to be high in self-esteem, need for achievement, and Type A behaviours and less likely to work for the sake of work itself.[21]

Similarly, gender and age differences with respect to money exist:

- Women tend to budget less; men tend to assign greater importance to money and manage it more.

- Older individuals tend to budget more and see money in less negative light.
- Better-educated individuals are more careful about money but less obsessed by it.[22]

In conclusion, pay's importance varies across individuals. Monetary rewards are an important component of the total reward package. However, the relative importance attached to monetary versus non-monetary rewards may differ depending on the industry, nature of work, and employee characteristics.

> Real Estate firms and auto-dealerships are well known for their emphasis on sales commissions—almost all rewards are monetary and contingent on job outcomes. In contrast, professors often settle for lower pay (compared to what many of them could make in industry) in return for the academic atmosphere, autonomy, and prestige associated with their work.

In general, organizations that emphasize monetary rewards want to reinforce high performance while those that emphasize non-monetary rewards focus on fostering commitment to the organization, tenure, and, in some instances, innovation. Greater emphasis on monetary rewards is typical of organizations facing volatile markets and those that can offer lower job security.

This chapter primarily looks at the monetary rewards; the next chapter will deal with some of the non-monetary rewards intrinsic to various jobs.

MAXIMIZING OWNER AND EMPLOYEE NEEDS

Agency theory regards the firm as a series of contractual relationships between owners and workers. Owners, also called principals, invest in firms to increase their wealth.[23] They contract with managers and other employees, also called agents, to produce goods and services. The connection between time and effort exerted by the agents and the "fruits of their labour" is not entirely under their control. The employee can influence the amount of work accomplished, but cannot control the output directly as a variety of situational factors affect the outcomes. The owner probably wishes to pay employees on the basis of outcome, since an hourly payment may not provide any incentive to the employees to exert themselves. However, the employee may prefer to be paid according to the hours worked, since pay for production shifts most production risks to the employee.

> An employee hired to dig postholes bears the risk of rocky soil, bad weather, the axe breaking, etc. if the payment is strictly based on number of holes dug.

The challenge, then, is to find an optimal compensation scheme that gives the highest expected profit to the owner and a compensation package to the employees that is attractive enough to make them accept the job and continue to strive while at work. In practice, this is not always easy.

> In many organizations, the employer can increase overall profits (at least in the short term) by hiring temporary and part-time workers. These people are not, typically, eligible for several of the expensive benefits offered to full time employees. However, from the employee's point of view, this reduces their sense of security and the overall rewards package to which they were entitled.

In instances such as the above, finding a solution that is acceptable to all stakeholders requires considerable thought and careful examination of various strategies for their long-term viability.

Agency theory postulates that a firm is a series of contractual relationships between owners and workers. Owners invest in firms to increase their own wealth and contract with employees to produce goods and services.

MAXIMIZE EFFORT-REWARD RELATIONSHIP

Expectancy theory suggests that employee motivation is affected by the performance-outcome relationship, the attractiveness of the outcome to the person concerned, and the perceived effort-reward relationship.

Past research findings suggest that employee behaviour is a function of the outcomes that are received for the work and the value of those outcomes to the individual.[24] The **expectancy theory** of motivation[25] probably offers the most practical application of this notion in the context of administering rewards. The three variables that affect employee behaviour are:

- performance-outcome relationship-employees must believe that performance leads to outcomes in order to perform highly;

- the value or attractiveness of the outcome-even if the above relationship is strong, performance may still be poor if the outcomes are not valued by the employee; and

- effort-performance relationship-an employee who feels incapable of performing at a certain level despite best efforts is unlikely to perform highly.

> Consider your own performance in a course. You are unlikely to put forth maximum efforts unless you believe that your efforts (e.g., studying, library research, field project work) will enable you to meet the course requirements well. The outcome of the course (e.g., the grade you receive, the knowledge you gain) should be dependent on your performance and valued by you. If, for example, you believe that grades do not matter or that a particular course does not provide you with any relevant or useful knowledge, you are unlikely to perform well even if it is an "easy" course.

To maximize the effort-reward relationship, a compensation system should:

- Establish clear and strong links between performance and outcome;

- Design flexible reward systems providing a variety of outcomes, at least some of which are attractive to individual employee;

- Ensure that employees have the ability to perform the job successfully; and

- Continually monitor employee needs, performance, and competencies to ensure that the rewards offered are valued and within reach.

MAINTAIN EQUITY

Internal equity is the perceived fairness of the pay structure within a firm.

External equity is the perceived fairness of pay relative to what other employers are paying for similar services or efforts.

Equity theory proposes that employees examine the relationship between their outcomes from a job (such as pay) and their inputs (such as education), by computing a ratio of these and comparing it to the ratios of relevant others.

Only if performance is fairly and equitably rewarded will employees experience job satisfaction. However, the notion of "equity" is, by no means, simple to define, measure, or implement. **Internal equity** refers to the perceived fairness of the pay structure within a firm. **External equity** refers to the perceived fairness of the pay relative to what other employers are paying for similar services or efforts. To make matters difficult, these two need not always move in the same direction.

> **Equity theory**[26] proposes that employees examine the relationship between their outcomes from a job (e.g., pay, recognition, promotion) and their inputs (e.g.,education, skill, experience, effort). A ratio of outcomes and inputs is computed (most of the time, unconsciously) and compared to the ratios of others (i.e., other employees doing the same job, other employees in similar industries, other employees with similar levels of training or education). If the ratios are perceived as inequitable, dissatisfaction results.[27]

Equity theory suggests the existence of three conditions.[28] First, people develop beliefs about what constitutes a fair and equitable return for their contributions to their jobs. Second, employees compare what they perceive to be the exchange they have with their employers with the exchange relevant others have with their employers. Finally, when an employee believes that his or her own rewards are not equitable (compared to those relevant others receive), they are motivated to do something about it. Each employee, for comparison purposes, computes ratios such as rewards/inputs compared with others rewards/inputs. When confronted with inequity, an employee may attempt to reduce it by adjusting inputs, outputs, or even leaving company.

> If an employee feels underpaid (i.e., compensation compared to inputs is lower than what relevant others with the same inputs receive), several options exist including asking for a raise (i.e., increasing rewards), decreasing inputs (i.e., produce less, work fewer hours if possible, reduce quality- and hence attention, a form of input), or leaving the organization altogether.

To ensure equity in pay, organizations employ job evaluation procedures. **Job evaluation** is a systematic process of assessing job content and worth according to a consistent set of job characteristics and effort requirements. Information collected through job analysis (discussed in Chapter 3) about job duties, responsibilities, specifications, and working conditions are further analyzed and supplemented by additional job data to arrive at total "points" for each job, reflecting its relative value to the organization. Figure 4-5 outlines steps in a point system job evaluation.

Maintaining equity in a pay system is no easy task. Depending on how the firm defines equity (equity with external market rates only, equity among various jobs inside the firm, or both), different salary structures may be necessary. Figure 4-6 provides an illustration of this dilemma.

A **Compa-ratio**[29], an index of how the salary of an employee relates to the midpoint of the relevant pay grade, is sometimes used to assess the compensation status of individual employees or a group and the overall equity in the pay system. The formula for an individual compa-ratio is:

$$\text{Compa-ratio for an employee} = \frac{\text{Salary of the employee}}{\text{Midpoint of the pay grade}}$$

A compa-ratio above or below 1 shows that the individual's salary is above or below the midpoint of the pay grade, which in turn is viewed as a benchmark for salary decision criteria such as performance, tenure, and experience.

A compa-ratio for groups can be calculated as:

$$\text{Compa-ratio for groups} = \frac{\text{Average of salaries paid}}{\text{Midpoint of the pay grade}}$$

In this instance, a ratio above 1 indicates that a large number of employees are bunched at the top of the pay grade. A ratio of below 1 may be caused by the presence of many new employees or may be an indication of high employee turnover. In any case, further investigation is warranted.

FOCUS ON PERFORMANCE VERSUS MEMBERSHIP

When designing reward systems, an organization may decide to focus solely on member performance-making pay contingent on job outcomes. In this instance, the pay received by individual employees can show substantial variation. Examples of **performance contingent compensation** which tie a substantial proportion of its employees' pay to job outcomes include piece rate plans, sales commissions, bonuses for perfect attendance, and merit pay based on performance evaluations.

Website on pay equity in Ontario: *www.gov.on.ca:80/mczcr/ owd/english/guide/equity.htm*

Job evaluation is a systematic process of assessing job content and worth according to a consistent set of job characteristics and effort requirements.

Website with salary statistics for over 450 benchmark jobs: *www.abbott-langer.com/*

Compa-ratio is an index of how the salary of an employee relates to the mid-point of the relevant pay grade.

Performance contingent compensation ties a substantial proportion of employees' pay to job outcomes.

FIGURE 4-5   Steps in Point System Job Evaluation

While there are several approaches to job evaluation, the point system of job evaluation is perhaps the most popular in industry. It has eight major steps.

1. **Determine compensable factors.** Based on a thorough job analysis, the critical factors (or aspects) of each job are identified. Usually, these consist of:

   1. Responsibility (e.g., responsibility for safety of others, responsibility for safety of equipment, responsibility for product or service quality)

   2. Skill required (e.g., work experience required, education and training required)

   3. Effort required (e.g., physical effort needed, mental effort needed)

   4. Working conditions (e.g., how unpleasant are the working conditions, what safety hazards are faced by the employee)

2. **Determine the levels or degrees of factors.** For each factor above, several levels of performance are created. Usually, four or five levels are used, although more or fewer levels may be needed for specific organization.

3. **Sub-divide the factors into sub-factors** (shown in brackets in Step 1 against each factor). The sub-factors should collectively exhaust all aspects of performance on various jobs.

4. **Allocate total points to sub-factors** to indicate their relative importance. For example, if a particular job has 1000 points, it may be distributed to the above four factors and sub-factors as follows:

A. Responsibility		**300**
1. Responsibility for safety	100	
2. Responsibility for equipment	50	
3. Responsibility for quality	150	
B. Skill required		**300**
1. Work experience required	200	
2. Education and training required	100	
C. Effort required		**250**
1. Physical effort required	75	
2. Mental effort required	175	
D. Working conditions		**150**
1. Unpleasant conditions	50	
2. Hazards	100	
TOTAL POINTS FOR JOB		**1000**

5. **Allocate points to various levels.** If the above 1000 points are the highest level of performance (say, level 4), then the points have to be identified to the other three levels to indicate their relative importance at lower levels of performance.

6. **Iterate points allocation for all factors, sub-factors and levels** until the points distributed accurately reflect the relative importance of factors, sub-factors, and levels of performance.

7. **Develop the point manual** which gives clear, written explanation of each job and each level of performance. For example, at Level 1 (lowest level) of responsibility for safety of equipment may only involve "report malfunctioning equipment to immediate supervisor on a timely basis"; however, the same sub-factor at the highest level (Level 4) may involve "the employee conducts major repairs to the machine without supervision".

8. **Implement the system.** Once the system has been de-bugged for errors or inconsistencies, it has to be implemented fairly and communicated to all concerned.

FIGURE 4-6 The Definition of Equity May Decide Your Pay Scales

Job	Job Evaluation Points	Salary in External Labour Market ($)	Option A External Equity only ($)	Option B Internal Equity only ($)	Option C External and Internal Equity ($)
A	1000	90 000	90 000	80 000	90 000
B	1000	80 000	80 000	80 000	90 000
C	900	71 000	71 000	72 000	81 000
D	800	65 000	65 000	64 000	72 000
E	600	47 000	47 000	48 000	54 000

To maintain equity, jobs with identical job evaluation points have to be paid similar salaries. However, this is not always easy to do in practice. If internal equity is to be achieved, all jobs within the organization with identical point value are to be paid equal pay. If we establish $80 as the point value, the salary levels for five jobs (A,B,C,D, and E) shown in the first column will be $80 000, $80 000, $72 000, $64 000, and $48 000 respectively (See Option B column). However, the salaries for Jobs A and D are lower than what are offered in the outside labour market; employee dissatisfaction and possibly high turnover in these jobs may be the result if point value is pegged at $80.

If the firm wants to maintain external equity only, it has to pay salary levels comparable to those in the external labour market (Option A). While this might prevent turnover of employees in Jobs A and D, this can create employee dissatisfaction since it can create internal inequity especially in Jobs C and E since compared to the value of their jobs, they are underpaid. For persons holding Job A, the payment is at the rate of $90 per point. For others, the figures are different: Job B= $80; Job C=$78.8; Job D=$81.25; and Job E=$78.33. There is likely to be considerable dissatisfaction emerging from perceptions of inequity.

If the firm raises the dollar value of each point from the current $80 to $90, it can achieve both internal and external equity. However, this can drive up the overall compensation costs, which can only be justified if the organizational needs can be better served by maintaining both internal and external equity. A firm whose business strategies call for a policy of leading the external market might choose this option—especially if the successful execution of requires highly competent and scarce human resources.

Alternatively, a firm might use a **membership-contingent compensation system** that offers the same wage to every employee in a given job, as long as the employee achieves at least satisfactory performance. In a membership-contingent compensation system, typically, salary progression occurs by moving up in the organization, not by doing the present job significantly better. In most white-collar jobs, this is the popular method of compensation where each employee has to work a certain number of hours each week and at a satisfactory level. What is deemed "satisfactory" varies across firms.

Membership-contingent compensation systems offer the same wage to every employee in a given job, as long as the employee achieves at least satisfactory performance.

Various factors including organizational strategy, culture, history, and employee characteristics influence which pay system emerges. Most firms that employ performance contingent pay tend to be small with few management levels, rapid growth, and clearly measurable performance indicators for most positions. Some times, the managerial values play a decisive role as well.

3M, a global firm producing a variety of products including Scotch Tape and Post-It notes holds the managerial value that "human beings are endowed with the urge to bring into being something that has never existed before . . . (hence) rewards have to be tied directly to successful innovation . . . the worst thing to do . . . is to base . . . rewards on how well they fit in with some preconceived management mould."[30]

JOB-BASED VERSUS KNOWLEDGE-BASED PAY

In most traditional organizations, especially for white collar jobs, salaries are determined by the value or contributions of individual jobs, not on the basis of actual performance or job related skills. Under this system, the job becomes the unit of analysis for determining the base of compensation, not the competencies of the individual performing it.

> Whether a grade 8 drop out or an M.B.A. graduate performs the job of a janitor, both will be paid the same amount as they are doing the same job.

Increasingly, several organizations-especially those operating in industries where quality of human resources determines success-use a knowledge- or skill-based pay where employees are paid on the basis of the competencies they possess, the jobs they can do, or the knowledge they possess.[31] The greater the number of different jobs a person can do, the greater their pay.

> The janitor holding an M.B.A. will be paid at a much higher hourly rate than the other as the latter will be able to do several tasks as the occasion demands (e.g., prepare a business plan, survey the employees or clients).

Knowledge- (or skills-) based pay systems reward employees on the basis of the competencies they possess, the jobs they can do, or the knowledge they possess.

Website on skill-based pay systems:
www.bizcenter.com/skillpay. htm

The focus of a **knowledge-based (or skills-based) pay system** is on fostering and taking advantage of employee competencies; this is particularly critical when jobs continually change and technology is unstable. Organizations experiencing high turnover because of labour market conditions also find it easier to meet the challenges of sudden shortage of employees by reassigning others within the firm who may possess the required job competencies.

However, a knowledge-based pay system has several associated costs. Typically, it is more expensive than a job-based system. It also violates norms of seniority popular in many organizations and can be confusing unless well designed. In general, job-based systems may work well when the technology is relatively stable and does not cause many changes in job duties, when employee turnover is low, or when long training is required to perform individual jobs.

OPEN-PAY VERSUS SECRET-PAY SYSTEM

Organizations vary markedly in the extent to which they communicate compensation practices or levels. In some firms, every employee's pay is a matter of public record while others expect each employee to sign an oath preventing them from divulging their pay to anyone-the penalty for breaking the oath may be as severe as termination. Most organizations fall somewhere in between these extremes.

Past research indicates that secret-pay systems cause greater employee dissatisfaction, as employees generally tend to overestimate the pay of coworkers and superiors. In other words, in the absence facts, they tend to feel more underpaid than they really are. Secret-pay systems may, in fact, be breeding grounds for favouritism and bias, as superiors do not have to defend their compensation decisions to their subordinates. Secrecy also reduces work motivation by failing to engender trust and by causing wrong perceptions of the performance-outcome linkage. Secret-pay systems also do not provide clear feedback on performance as an employee does not have any idea what performance leads to superior rewards and what value the organization assigns to performance. Equity comparisons become extremely difficult—even when they occur, they are based on inaccurate data or premises. The result, in general, is poor motivation.

Open-pay systems can cause problems as well. Even the best system may fail to satisfy all employees—this means that the superiors may have to spend a good portion of their time defending their pay decisions to disgruntled employees. To avoid time consuming and uncomfortable arguments with subordinates, many superiors choose to pay the same amounts to all without recognizing individual differences. This, in turn, can reduce motivation of superior performers and may even cause them to leave the firm. The cost of making a bad pay decision is also higher in an open setting. This may prevent managers from being innovative in their compensation decisions.

To conclude, open pay may not be appropriate for all organizations or all times. Research indicates that open-pay systems are more likely to succeed in organizations that have extensive employee involvement and an egalitarian culture that fosters trust and commitment. In fiercely competitive work climates, open pay may in fact cause conflicts and rivalries.

CENTRALIZED VERSUS DECENTRALIZED COMPENSATION SYSTEMS

In a centralized compensation system, all pay decisions are tightly controlled and monitored in a central location, normally, the human resource department in the corporate headquarters. In a totally decentralized system, pay decisions are delegated to the lowest supervisor.

In many instances, centralized pay is more cost-effective because of higher efficiency and ease of storage and retrieval of compensation data. Centralized systems also bring in significant economies of scale thus permitting the firm to hire compensation specialists who are experts in their field. In contrast, a typical supervisor may not be aware of the many technical and legal issues related to compensation policies. More professionalism in compensation practices and reduced possibility of legal violations may be the beneficial outcomes of using professionals. A centralized system is also likely to maximize internal equity since comparisons across individuals and departments are easier to do under such a system.

A centralized pay system, while it maximizes internal equity, may not achieve external equity. The reverse may be true of decentralized systems.

> This is especially true in the case of large, diversified global firms where corporate head office staff may be unaware of labour market conditions facing local managers. For example, firms like Bombardier, Royal Bank, and Air Canada, that operate in a number of countries, facilitate the decentralization of compensation decisions in order to respond to local market conditions. However, this can result in internal inequities where two persons doing identical tasks can get substantially different rewards.

Since an immediate supervisor is best qualified to evaluate an employee's performance, the link between performance and rewards is also likely to be stronger in a decentralized system. Because of this, it is not surprising that most organizations fall somewhere between the extremes of a totally centralized or decentralized compensation system. In an effort to maximize the relationship between performance and monetary rewards more firms are moving toward a decentralized system. Today, the emphasis is on teamwork, employee involvement, and creating a culture that is customer responsive. For this, a "bottom-up" approach to compensation planning may be necessary.

Website on pay and performance: *www.fraserinstitute.ca/ publications*

Focus on Ethics:

How to Maintain Equity in Rewarding Employees

There are several alternate principles that seem to guide and shape reward systems in organizations.[32]

1. Equity norm:[33] A person's reward should be commensurate to the person's contributions or inputs. Hence the ratio between outputs and inputs should remain the same across individuals.

2. Market norm: The price of any item-including human labour-should be strictly based on market supply and demand.

3. Need norm:[34] The share of total resources a person gets should be based on the individual's need, not inputs or abilities.

4. Equality norm: Every individual should receive an equal amount of resources without consideration of other factors including inputs.

5. Effort norm: The rewards should be based on an individual's efforts, not outputs. If someone tries hard but does not succeed, rewards should still be equal to someone who was successful.

6. Ability norm: The rewards given should be based on a person's abilities, knowledge, and competencies and not inputs or outputs which can be influenced by factors beyond the individual's control.

7. Equal opportunity norm: Every individual should have equal opportunity for completion of work free of any bias and discrimination.

As a management consultant, the author of this text came across a number of incidents relating to reward systems in organizations that had ethical implications. Five of these are listed below. Consider each of them against the above norms and see which, if any, is being violated. Suggest improvements where necessary and compare your answers with those of your friends.

1. The work supervisor allocates overtime to employees on the basis of personal preferences. Some employees who want to work over time are ignored while the others, liked by the supervisors, receive the overtime, which pays double wages. When confronted, the supervisors justify their actions on the basis of "their faith in employees who will get the job done on time."

2. A multinational firm that operates in a developing country pays large salaries and benefits (e.g., rent free house, car with driver, paid holiday travel) to their white, expatriate managers but considerably lower salaries and benefits to local employees. While the local employees receive a "decent" salary that compares favourably in local industry, the expatriate managers often receive 600 to 700 times the average salary of local employees. Note that the same ratio in the company's head office in a developed country is 20 to 30 times.

3. The employees in Division F of an organization believe that their jobs and competencies are very similar to those in Division K, although those working in Division K are paid approximately 30% more and have better working conditions. If anything, Division F employees believe they should be paid higher for the unclean and dusty working conditions.

4. A middle level manager of a geographically dispersed firm believes that the compensation levels in different regions, even after accounting for cost-of-living differences, show vast discrepancies. While the employees have not raised the issue, the manager feels that it is unethical to pay different levels for the same work, especially since some regions (which pay lower levels) employ more women and minorities. She worries that pointing out this matter to others may brand her a "troublemaker", thus reducing her chances of career advancement.

5. Plant supervisors in manufacturing facilities were accused of favouritism in assigning shift times, time allocated for completion of specific jobs, and reactions to lost work time. Favoured employees were given better shifts, granted informal extensions for work completion, and were not reprimanded when they were late from lunch or took time off to take care of personal business.

LINKING PAY TO PERFORMANCE

Depending on the nature of the industry and various organizational characteristics (e.g., size, business strategy, culture) various compensation approaches may be used. The same organization may have to use differing approaches to reflect changes in the environment and organizational and employee priorities. Despite this, all effective compensation systems share some common features, examined in detail in the following sections.

ATTRIBUTES OF EFFECTIVE COMPENSATION SYSTEMS

Figure 4-7 lists key attributes of compensation systems that maximize employee performance in many situations. These attributes are discussed below.

Control The employees should feel confident that their efforts result in higher performance and pay. Rewards received by employees should be related to their own efforts and competencies and not unduly influenced by environmental forces and events such as stock market fluctuations, and changes in governmental policies.

Objectives Both short-term and long-term objectives of the organization should be clearly linked to the pay plan. If the compensation system rewards achievement of some objectives but not others, it is virtually certain that the employees will not focus on "unrewarded" objectives.

> The household appliances section of a department store compensated its staff solely on the basis of sales volume. The result was that most salespeople only engaged in activities that helped them secure a sale. Other activities such as answering customer queries, after sales service, and display of merchandise were ignored by most employees. This was despite the fact that the store emphasized superior customer service in all its advertisements and public statements.

Meaningful If a firm wants to motivate its employees, it must offer them something of value-something that fills a need. The reward should be "worth the effort" either as reinforcement, recognition, or status. In the past, it was assumed that a 10 to 20% bonus or incentive to make the reward meaningful to an employee; however, more recent studies indicate that even a 3 to 5% bonus or raise can be powerful motivators if accompanied by other appropriate actions in performance measurement, feedback, and reinforcement. More on performance measurement and feedback will be discussed in Chapter 6.

Perceived contingency The system should consistently reinforce specific employee actions and behaviours. Not only should rewards be contingent on the achievement of desired results, but such contingency must be transparent and understood by all concerned.

FIGURE 4-7   Key Attributes of Performance Maximizing Compensation Systems

The acronym **COMPENSATE** summarizes the key ten attributes of performance maximizing compensation systems

Control

Objectives

Meaningful

Perceived contingency

Equity and fairness

Non-quantifyable performance dimensions

Simplicity

Achievable

Timely

Economical

Website on salary surveys: *www.salariesreview.com/ Surveys/methodology1.htm*

Equity and Fairness The employees should understand the rationale behind the system and must recognize the performance-reward contingencies as fair and equitable. Equivalent improvements in performance of two similar employees should result in both receiving identical extra rewards. Employees should also perceive equity between their own salary and what similar workers outside the firm receive. This means that employers have to continually survey the outside labour market for salary trends.

Non-quantifiable Performance Dimensions The reward system should focus not only on quantifiable performance indicators such as quantity of production, attendance patterns, and number of safety violations, but also on other, qualitative dimensions of performance that may not be easily amenable to numerical measurements (e.g., innovation, concern for customers, organizational citizenship behaviours). The qualitative measures should be aligned with the organization's strategy and culture.

Simplicity The system should be fairly simple to understand and the salary fairly easy to compute. Simplicity is important not only from the employees' point of view. Organizations also find it easier and cheaper to administer a simple compensation system.

Achievable The performance targets should be attainable. Work measurement practices (discussed in Chapter 3) should be employed to identify the normal performance levels of an average worker in a specific category. Bonuses for superior performance should be based on such data. Managers should not arbitrarily raise performance standards since employees and unions will construe this as "raising the bar."

Timely To reinforce performance, rewards should be provided soon after achievement of desired outcomes. Employees work harder to achieve goals when they can see a clear link between their job outcomes and rewards. This is more likely when the time gap between performance and rewards is minimal.

Economical The system should be cost effective for the organization. Two kinds of costs, namely, total compensation costs and costs of administering the system should be considered. If the compensation becomes a large and increasing proportion of the firm's cost of production, its overall competitiveness and profitability may suffer in the long run. Some compensation systems are expensive to administer. Cost-benefit analyses and systematic program reviews should be carried out to identify the level of service appropriate for the organization.

POPULAR PERFORMANCE BASED INCENTIVES

A variety of individual and team incentives have been offered in the past to bolster performance (Figure 4-8). The more popular incentives are discussed below.

A **piece-rate pay system** compensates employees for each unit of output.

Piece-Rate With a **piece-rate pay system**, the employee is compensated for each unit of output. Under the piece rate, each employee's earnings depend on a measure of productivity. This system dates back to the work of Frederick W. Taylor, who early in the 20th century, detailed his principles of "scientific management." Daily or weekly pay is determined by multiplying the output in units by the piece-rate per unit.

On several farms, workers are paid a specific amount per crate or bushel of fruit or vegetables picked. The wages earned at the end of the day depend on the productivity of the worker concerned, thus providing a powerful incentive to work hard.

FIGURE 4-8 Popular Performance Incentives

Individual Incentives	Team Incentives
Piece rate	Profit sharing plans
Commissions	Employee stock ownership plans
Production bonuses	Cost reduction plans
Merit pay	

Piece-rate, however, does not always lead to higher productivity. Past research indicates that work group norms may have a powerful impact on the quantity of production. In some instances, piece-rate may also result in poor quality of products. "Since workers are rewarded for the quantity of their output, the message the reward system sends is that nothing else matters, regardless of what a shop foreman might tell them."[35] Piece rate may also cause tension among employees. When an employee works at a pace that far exceeds the average production levels of other employees, it demonstrates to the management that production standards might be too low, resulting in upward revision of the standards. In general, piece-rate systems solely rely on extrinsic rewards and compensate only measurable outcomes. For the above reasons, piece-rate systems have fallen out of favour in many industries. Today, they are mostly seen in manufacturing, agriculture, and other production oriented jobs such as data entry. For some jobs (e.g., receptionist) the piece-rate system is simply not applicable.

Commissions
Still popular in many sales organizations, **commissions** are a percentage of the selling price or a flat reward paid for each unit sold. Some organizations pay a base salary in addition to commissions. When no base salary is paid, the entire income for the salesperson comes from commissions, making it very similar to a piece-rate system, except that the income depends on volume of sales rather than on production.

> Real estate firms, auto dealerships, and more recently, several dealers in office products and household appliances extensively use commissions to generate high performance.

As in the case of piece-rate system, commissions often result in extreme emphasis being placed on "getting a sale." It can also result in inter-member rivalry and sales-grabbing. An organization rewarding solely on the basis of commission may generate little loyalty-as soon as the employee can get a higher commission elsewhere, the person may leave the firm.

Commissions are a percentage of the selling price or a flat reward paid for each unit sold.

Production Bonuses
Production bonuses are incentives paid to employees for exceeding a specified level of output. Normally, under this system, all employees receive a base salary or remuneration using a predetermined wage rate. As long as only the "standard output" is achieved, the employee will only receive the base remuneration. For every unit produced over and above the standard, the employee becomes eligible for a production bonus. Another variation rewards the employee for saving time.

Production bonuses are incentives paid to employees for exceeding a specified level of output.

> If the standard time for painting equipment is twelve hours and an employee completes the task in ten hours, he or she is still paid for twelve hours. The John Deere Company, a large manufacturer of construction and farm equipment, has had great success with the

standard hour system. It is not uncommon to find some Deere employees producing consistently at 150 to 175% of the standard.

Production bonuses have several of the advantages and problems associated with piece-rates and commissions. Further, employees often distrust the standards established by industrial engineers. They may also be sceptical when these standards are changed although, in the eyes of the management, frequent upward revisions of performance standards may be legitimate and even essential.

Merit pay is a typically annual salary increase that reflects performance.

Merit Pay

Traditionally, many firms gave **merit pay** or typically annual salary increases to reflect performance with the idea that better performers receive higher pay increases. In concept, the raise given is independent of cost-of-living increase allowances and solely dependent on performance appraisal results. Until recently, merit pay was an integral part of compensation practices of many private sector firms though it was not very popular in the public sector and institutions such as universities, hospitals, and not-for-profit organizations. In a corporate environment, merit pay made intuitive sense-automatic step increases or across-the-board increases are alien to a value system that upheld meritocracy, a culture of excellence that most firms valued.

Despite its popularity, merit pay has not worked too well in the past. For many firms, merit pay budgets remain small-around 3 or 4% of the payroll-meaning that any individual increase above 5% cannot be done without denying pay increases to a large number of other employees.

> Many supervisors find it hard to deny raises even to poor or marginal performers since almost every employee has grown accustomed to an annual raise. This has significantly reduced the motivational properties of a raise.

Some management experts like Edward Deming, who spearheaded quality management efforts, were strong opponents of merit pay. Deming called individual performance appraisal one of the "deadly diseases" and argued strongly and persuasively that rewarding individual performance works against larger organizational goals.[36] His argument is that if employees are to focus on the larger mission of the organization, it is important to avoid reward systems that solely reinforce individual achievements.

Problems with the individual incentive plans have led some firms to drop them altogether and implement team or group based incentives. The three popular group incentives are discussed below.

Profit sharing plans pay employees their regular wages and a share of the company profits, usually on an annual basis.

Profit Sharing Plans

Profit sharing plans pay employees regular wages and a share of the company profits, usually on an annual basis. At least three major types of profit sharing plans are currently seen in Canada:

- Current distribution plans distribute a share of a company's profits to all employees in direct cash payments or company stock each period.

- Deferred payout plans give each employee a share of the profits, but the payout is done at a later date. The tax payments on accrued employee share of profits are also deferred until the actual date of profit payout.

- A combination plan combines some of the features of the two plans.

Profit sharing plans help employees focus on the larger goals of the organization, increasing its value in the marketplace and in the eyes of its stakeholders. Since all employees become eligible for a share of the profits, inter-member rivalry is replaced by a sense of teamwork for the common good. No wonder that, in Canada, the number of profit sharing plans increased from approximately 2000 registered plans in 1950s to 32 000 in 1982 and probably over 60 000 now.[37]

Dofasco of Hamilton, Ontario operates in the very competitive and technologically fast changing steel industry, has never been unionized, and has had only three unprofitable years since it introduced profit sharing in 1938. Employees contribute a maximum of $300 a year to the Employee Savings and Profit Sharing Fund. The company contributes 14% of its pre-tax profits for distribution to employees. Each employee's share is split in two, one half being deposited in the Fund along with employee contribution (to be saved for retirement). The company guarantees a payment of $900 each year. Employees can take the remaining half as cash or have it deposited into a deferred profit sharing plan. Over the nine-year period from 1988 to 1997, the average pay out has been $3446.[38]

Despite success stories, the effectiveness of profit sharing in motivating employees is far from clear. Although organizations with profit sharing plans tend to be more profitable, it is debatable whether their success can be attributed to profit sharing plans alone. In general, companies which have profit sharing plans tend to have open, two-way communication between management and the union, which may be one of the key reasons for the firm's success. Once again, whether improved communication is the cause or effect of the profit sharing plan is unclear.

Profitability is not always linked to employee performance-a number of factors including emergence of competition, changes in technology, and economic recession can reduce or eliminate profits despite a committed workforce. The immediate reinforcement value of the rewards is also low since, even in firms that use current distribution plans, employees have to wait until year's end to know the results of their efforts. In those firms that invest the employee's share of profits into their retirement plans, the motivational impact is, perhaps, even lower. In summary, in the best-case scenario, "profit sharing tends to contribute to higher motivation and productivity, but it does it in conjunction with other factors."[39]

Employee Stock Ownership Plans (ESOPs)

Employee Stock Ownership Plans (ESOPs), by which employees own actual company stock or representations of stock, have been steadily gaining in popularity in North America. One estimate is that over 54% of U.S. companies grant ESOPs. Because of a lack of tax incentives, only about 25% of Canadian companies offer an ESOP. Unlike profit sharing plans, ESOPs give employees genuine ownership and voting power.

> In 1994, General Printers, an Ontario firm, was unprofitable with a workforce that had poor morale and needed round-the-clock supervision. Then, the company changed its reward structure: it introduced an ESOP. The result? In less than seven years, the firm has grown by 80% and employees do a first-rate job with no supervision for 16 of the 24-hours in a workday. In 1997, the firm was named the Business of the Year by a local Chamber of Commerce.[40]

The simplest arrangement is one where employees hold actual company stock. There are also several instances where the employer awards stock with restrictions on transfer or invests the stock into an employee's retirement fund. In many instances, long-term (typically seven year) service (referred to as vesting period) is required before an employee can take the shares when leaving the organization. Some companies also award phantom or deferred interest in company stock as a reward. Apart from facing several of the limitations of the profit sharing plans, ESOPs can also hurt the company if the stock options of all employees have a common vesting date and a large number of employees choose to exercise or sell all their claims on that date.[41]

Employees whose regular income and retirement savings are dependent on a single employer may be exposing themselves to high financial uncertainty as the failure of U.S. giant Enron illustrates.

> The collapse of the giant U.S. energy company, Enron, left banks, pension plans, and other lenders with at least $5 billion at risk. More than 4000 Enron employees have lost

Employee stock ownership plans are plans in which employees own actual company stock or representations of such stock.

Website on ESOPs:
www.nceo.org/library/esops.html

their jobs and pension fund savings that had been invested in Enron stock. The shares of the company, which once represented material success reached penny stock status within a matter of a few weeks in early 2002.[42] Employees of several other American firms like General Electric, Procter and Gamble, and Microsoft have considerable stakes in their employer's welfare (in some instances, over 75% of employee pension funds is held in the form of employer's stocks).[43] Such practices significantly increase the financial risk for the employees as both their regular income and retirement savings are tied to the fortunes of a single firm.

Cost Reduction Plans Unlike profit sharing plans and ESOPs, which link employee performance to something that employees have little control over (namely, profits), **cost reduction plans** reward employees for something they can control: labour costs. Most cost reduction plans focus on the reduction of labour costs and the sharing of resultant savings among employees. There is an increasing interest on the part of most firms, especially those facing global competition, to cut labour costs. Cost reduction plans, also referred to as gainsharing by some writers and practitioners, recognize the fact that employees can influence day-to-day results and improve operating efficiency.

> Lincoln Electric, a manufacturing firm based in Cleveland, Ohio, was one of the early success stories of gainsharing. The payouts from gainsharing in several past years exceeded the typical worker's base salary.[44]

In a typical gainsharing plan, labour costs over a specified period are compared with the levels in a base period. If the costs are lower (i.e., worker efficiency or productivity has improved), the savings or gains are shared with the employees. Typically, employees receive 50% of the gain and the firm retains the balance. Several different gainsharing plans currently exist, of which Scanlon Plan and Rucker Plan are popular. While the exact calculations of gainsharing differ from one plan to the next, the underlying philosophy in all remains the same.

Traditional formats of gainsharing have several of the benefits and limitations of profit sharing plans. Normally, the payouts to employees do not occur until the year-end or other specified period, thus reducing the reinforcing value of the reward. Reducing labour costs is not the only performance goal for most organizations today; in this sense, cost reduction plans have a limited perspective. Some practitioners believe that goals are often set too low and the plan can become cost additive (that is, costs go up rather than down over time).

A close look at the popular incentives indicates that none meets all the criteria discussed in this chapter. Figure 4-9 provides a summary evaluation of incentives on the ten attributes identified earlier. One writer pointed out, ". . . pay systems can do more harm than good. That is, traditional pay systems have frequently been a disincentive rather than an incentive."[45] The following section provides some suggestions for modifying traditional pay systems for today's work settings.

MODIFYING TRADITIONAL PAY-FOR-PERFORMANCE MODEL FOR TODAY'S WORK SETTINGS

Traditional pay systems, which originated in the 1920s and 1930s, reflected a work paradigm and culture that assumed inherent conflict between labour and management. Beginning with Frederick Taylor, most writers and practitioners believed that management's role was to plan, direct, and control; the labour was merely adjunct to the machines "to do" jobs. Planning and evaluating the jobs were the prerogatives of the management. Beginning in the late 1970s, this assumption was questioned seri-

Cost reduction plans are plans that reduce labour costs and the sharing of resultant savings among employees.

Websites on gainsharing plans:

www.netnz.com/gainsharing/ Gainsharechapter.html

www.hr.com

FIGURE 4-9   A Summary Evaluation of Popular Incentives

Attributes of a Compensation System

	C	O	M	P	E	N	S	A	T	E
1. Piece rate	+	-	+	+	+	-	+	+	+	?
2. Commissions	+	-	+	+	+	-	+	?	+	+
3. Production bonuses	+	-	+	+	+	-	+	?	+	?
4. Merit Pay	?	?	?	?	-	?	?	?	-	-
5. Profit sharing	_	+	?	-	?	-	?	?	-	+
6. ESOPs	_	+	?	-	?	-	?	?	-	?
7. Cost reduction plans	?	+	+	?	?	-	+	?	-	+

Code: + indicates that this criterion is being met
- indicates that this criterion is not being met
? Indicates that this criterion is at best met only partially

ously. Deming was one of the earliest to highlight the important role of the lowest worker to ensure quality and customer satisfaction. The global competition and technological revolution of the 1990s made intellectual capital more important than ever before. Workers were no longer mere appendages to machines. To succeed in the new competitive world, employees had to play more active roles-they were, in many instances, equal partners to management in deciding the fate of the firm.

Figure 4-10 lists the major changes in the work paradigm that make it critical to design a new compensation system to recognize the role of the employee. Today's firm must design a compensation system that meets three distinct, though related, objectives: to develop a culture of high performance, to improve employee competencies that achieve immediate and longer-term organizational goals, and to be cost effective (see Figure 4-11). Below, an approach that modifies the traditional incentives to achieve these objectives is outlined.

FIGURE 4-10   Shifting Work Paradigm

Dimension	Old Assumptions	New Realities
Role of Management	Plan, evaluate, control employees	Inspire employees to mutually beneficial directions
Role of Employees	Only doing the assigned work	Plan, do, evaluate, and control in several instances
Knowledge Level of Typical Employee	Low	Much higher
Assumptions about Rewards Expected by Employees	Monetary rewards only	Monetary rewards, sense of self-fulfillment, ownership for work and products
Mobility of the Employee	Low	Very high
Valued Traits	Obedience, loyalty	Entrepreneurship, competence, innovation
Diversity of Workforce	Low	Very high
Environmental Uncertainty Faced by the Firm	Relatively low	Extremely high

FIGURE 4-11   **The Triple Goals of a Compensation System**

Improve Employee Competencies
to Achieve Organizational Goals

Develop a Culture of High
Performance   Be Cost-Effective

Step 1: Define Goals Clearly Any effort at designing a pay-for-performance model must begin with a clear definition of organizational goals, strategies, and the identification of exceptional business achievement that is attributable to sustained employee commitment and high performance. Among the questions to ask:

• What are the short- and long-term business objectives?

• What needs to be done to meet the objectives?

• What can employees and teams do to make it happen?

• What new behaviours and competencies do employees and teams need?

Step 2: Focus on Uniqueness Identify the unique characteristics of the industry and the organization (e.g., its history, culture) that have a bearing on the appropriateness of the planned pay system.

> Organizations operating in certain industries find it easier to quantify performance than those in other industries (e.g., apple picking versus teaching primary school). Even within the same organization, some jobs are more measurable than others (e.g., manufacturing versus counselling). Education levels and labour market conditions for certain employee categories may pose other challenges.

Step 3: Identify Competencies Identify the jobs, tasks, and competencies that are critical for strategic success using methods discussed in Chapter 3. Involvement of employees and teams in identifying job specifications and performance standards is vital, not only to ensure their accuracy, but also to gain employee commitment to goals. Where necessary, job-redesign, additional employee training, and provision of additional resources should be undertaken to ensure goal achievement.

Step 4: Consult and Compensate In consultation with employees, determine the mix of compensation that will maximize employee performance and organizational goal achievement. In general, compensation packages should have four components:

> Component 1: A base salary that is "fixed" and that meets legal requirements and recognizes market realities;

Component 2: Short-term incentives for achieving operational and financial goals in the short term with payout frequencies between one month and one year (typically, quarterly to minimize administrative expenses). In general, the rewards should be for results under the control of the employees (e.g., cost reduction, improving response time);

Component 3: Longer-term incentives based on two to five year performance objectives with payout when goals are achieved; and

Component 4: Business Growth Incentives such as stock options or stock ownerships which encourage employees to strive towards increasing the overall value of the organization.

Consulting the employees when identifying compensation packages helps achieve three objectives:

- First, the process becomes transparent, increasing the equity and fairness of the system.

- Second, a compensation package that recognizes the unique challenges of the firm can be identified.

- Third, two-way communication on performance standards and rewards fosters a sense of ownership of ideas, thus increasing the probability of its acceptance and commitment to the goals.

Needless to say, the financial state of an organization plays a decisive role in the final compensation package identified. The compensation plan should be affordable to the firm and have provisions for a possible downward turn in the market. This means that the fixed component of the package should be carefully identified only after a thorough review of alternate scenarios.

For an individual employee, the compensation package has two components:

- Fixed Part: A fixed part (base salary) and a variable part that recognize the person's performance and unique competencies. When the person performs at or below acceptable levels, only a base salary is received.

- Variable Part: For every improvement in competencies and performance, the person is rewarded. Figure 4-12 illustrates how two levels of variable incentives can be offered for differential performance and competency levels of employees. When performance or competencies are lower than desired, only the base salary

FIGURE 4-12 Variable Pay for Different Performance and Competency Levels

Performance Outcomes		Low	Average	High
	Exceeds	V1	V2	V3
	Acceptable	B	V0	V1
	Unacceptable	B	B	B

Competencies

Code:
B = Base salary only; corrective actions such as training, counselling, and in some instances other disciplinary actions may also be taken
V0 = No variable pay; only base salary is offered
V1 = Variable pay increase at Level 1 is offered
V2 = Variable pay increase at a higher Level 2 is offered

is provided and employee counselling and training are provided to bring the employee's performance to the levels desired. Above the minimum levels, the firm offers two levels of variable pay. Level 1 is for improvements in performance or competencies alone and a Level 2 is for improvement on both dimensions. The specific arrangement should be identified after a thorough review of the unique conditions facing the firm.

In rewarding competencies or skills, some firms have found it useful to differentiate between the number of competencies and degree of mastery of specific competencies. Figure 4-13 shows one possible way to differentially reward employees who score high on these two dimensions.

In this case, the highest rewards are given to workers who have broader skills and higher degree of mastery over them. Persons with a narrower range of skills and depth get the least reward and the others belong to somewhere in between. Smaller organizations may find such finer discrimination in competency assessment not cost effective and administratively complex. On the other hand, for organizations whose strategic success depends on human capital development, there may be no choice but to develop such systems.

When developing team or group incentive plans, care must be taken to differentiate between individual and group contributions. Balancing team and individual focus is not an easy task. The appropriate performance measures should be identified, bearing in mind those non-quantifiable performance criteria; attributes and competencies are as critical to organizational success as quantifiable ones. The more popular criteria for evaluating team efforts are shown in Figure 4-14.

Website with information on variable pay: *www.conferenceboard.ca*

LINKING EXECUTIVE PAY TO PERFORMANCE

Many managerial positions are highly attractive in terms of money and prestige. In Canada, top executives are among the highest paid members of society. To attract top talent, compensation levels running into millions of dollars are not uncommon.

In 2000, John Roth, then-President and CEO of Nortel Networks, had a total direct compensation of $70 754 000, of which $1 857 000 was base salary, $8 371 000 was

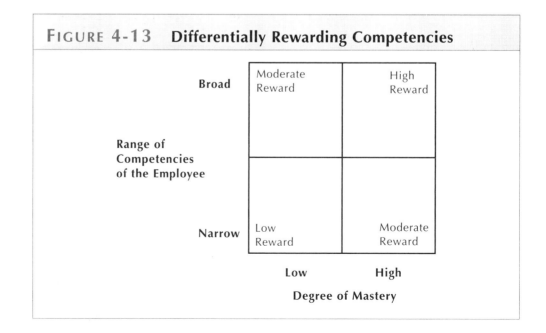

FIGURE 4-13   Differentially Rewarding Competencies

FIGURE 4-14   Some Indicators of Team Performance

OPERATIONAL

- Safety record
- On-time delivery record
- Errors, missed deliveries, wrong deliveries, etc.
- Cost reduction
- Process improvements

CUSTOMER RELATED

- Customer satisfaction measures
- Number of returns
- Number of services introduced
- New product/service introduction
- New account/market penetration

FINANCIAL

- Revenue growth
- Value added
- Earnings per share
- Value added per dollar investment

---

an annual bonus, and $60 527 000 was long-term incentive. The same year, Frank Stronach, Chairman of Magna International received a total pay of $48 529 000 and Jacques Bougie, President of Alcan, received $23 863 000.[46]

While such huge compensation packages are assumed to inspire top managers to steer their firms to prosperity and growth, researchers using different methodologies, measures, and statistical tools have "often found weak or even statistically insignificant relationships between pay and performance."[47] In a recent meta-analysis of the field, the pay-performance relationship was estimated to be 0.24, indicating that pay explains less than 7% of the performance variability.[48] Evidence from the field has also been unsupportive of a strong relationship between compensation and performance. Consider the following firms.

> During 2000-2001, when Roth received the highest compensation in the history of Canadian business, Nortel lost over 80% of its stock value resulting in a total loss of over $19 billion in market capitalization. The salaries of CEOs of a few other Canadian firms which lost their market values during the same year were (percentage loss in market capitalization shown in brackets): Ballard Power Systems: $18.04 million (-26.9%); Rogers Communications: $8.86 million (-47.6%); 360 Networks: $8.83 million (-82.8%).[49]

Such information attracts close scrutiny and criticism about the way senior executives in the industry are paid. Even in early 1990s, before the culture of astronomical salaries to senior executives emerged, the average salary for chief executives in the U.S. was 160 times the average assembly-line worker's wage.[50] In Japan, however, the ratio of managerial pay to pay level of workers is a modest 10 to 1. The large sums of money that corporate executives receive have been the target of press attacks-*Business Week*, for instance, has an annual spring issue on managerial pay. The general conclusion seems to be that the overall relationship between senior management pay and performance is low.[51] This raises an important question: How should managerial pay decisions be made?

While many of the incentives discussed above are also applicable to senior executives and managers, traditionally, managers have been provided with additional **stock options**—or the right to purchase the company's stock at a predetermined price. The price may be set at, below, or above the market value of the stock. The theory is that the manager, then, has an incentive to improve the company's performance in order to enhance the value of the stock options. Theoretically, stock options should only be given to managers who can have a significant effect on company profits.

In practice, stock options have not worked out as effectively as they were supposed to. When faced with lower stock prices, many firms identify new and lower price limits for exercising options or otherwise materially change the conditions under which managers can exercise them, reducing their future motivational property.

> In June 2001, Nortel Networks, faced with a downslide of its share prices, cancelled 111 million of its old stock options and reissued them under more favourable terms to those holding them.[52]

Stock options also encourage CEOs and other senior executives to acquire other firms, a practice that adds short-term value to the stock. Several acquisitions add value to the acquiring firm's stock even if the market is not able to fully value the acquired firm at the levels—increasingly, a large proportion of the purchase price accounts for "goodwill", or financially invisible value—of the firm purchased. The short-term gains in stock prices associated with options motivate executives "to chase potentially large gains from acquisitions even if such gains are not assured. Because option pay does not penalize executives for acquisition failures, it provides little disincentive to engage in acquisitions."[53]

Even junior officers, who have no significant role in corporate strategy planning, are often given stock options making options just another form of bonus or profit sharing. Stock options also encourage the managers to focus unduly on events that affect the value of the stock even if it is at the expense of the longer-term welfare of the company or its constituents. Stock options, which were, traditionally the rewards for exceptional performance have become an expected part of annual compensation today.

Several actions can be taken to improve their motivational properties of executive stock options. These are discussed in the following sections.

LINK EXERCISE OF OPTIONS TO GOAL ACHIEVEMENT

Such performance-based options are commonplace in Europe but North America, and particularly Canada, has been slow to modify its systems. As mentioned in Chapter 2, a balanced scorecard approach helps firms identify key expectations from managers and other employees. Rewards, including stock options, should be related to the accomplishment of these objectives, especially the bottom line performance figures. Specific financial and other measures should be identified reflecting business strategy. Figure 4-15 provides a sample balanced scorecard for an executive outlining expectations and payouts for a period. Clear, measurable targets such as these have to be established bearing in mind the unique organizational and environmental conditions.

Stock options represent the right to purchase the company's stock at a predetermined price.

FIGURE 4-15   Sample Balanced Scorecard for an Executive

Performance Dimension	Performance Measures	Weight	Target (%)	Actual (%)	Actual as a % of Target	Payout
Financial	1. Profit growth	30%	6	5	83%	75%
	2. Revenue growth		8	8.8	110%	130%
Market related	1. On-time delivery	25%	100	90	90%	95%
	2. Customer satisfaction		98	95	97%	98%
Employee related	1. Safety record	25%	95	80	84%	77%
	2. Employee competencies		85	63	74%	0%
Operational excellence	1. Cycle time	20%	80	100	125%	150%
	2. Percentage defect free		98	89	91%	96%

Note: For payout figure calculations in the last column, see Figure 4-16.

DETERMINE PAYOUTS CAREFULLY

Incentive zones, or the performance ranges over which bonuses will be paid, have to be carefully identified bearing in mind the firm's strategy, resources, and long-term goals. Payout curves, which define awards paid at each level of performance, also need to be carefully defined or the compensation package will become expensive and cost-ineffective. Figure 4-16 shows a payout curve for the managerial position shown in Figure 4-15. Depending on the firm's needs, the payout curve may be linear or curvilinear. In a linear curve, every incremental growth in performance brings the same increase in rewards; in a non-linear or curvilinear setting, a unit increase in outcome may generate differential incentive depending on when it occurs (typically, a unit increase at a higher level is considered more difficult and hence rewarded at a higher rate). Alternatively, there may be differential curves for different performance dimensions. A dimension which has lower "weight" may have a different curve slope compared to another dimension which is considered more important.

EXTEND VESTING PERIODS

The typical **vesting period**—the time between issue of options and their exercise for the first time—has been dropping over time to 2 or 3 years. In some hi-tech organizations, vesting periods are as brief as one month! While maintaining low vesting periods may be a necessity for some firms that operate in tight labour market conditions, it is in the interests of the firm to maintain a longer vesting period and the manager's commitment to the longer-term growth of the firm.[54]

> **Vesting period** is the time between issue of options and their exercise for the first time.

SELECTIVE GRANTS OF OPTIONS

Limiting option grants to employees who can influence the direction of the firm and its people may avoid some of the current problems associated with them.

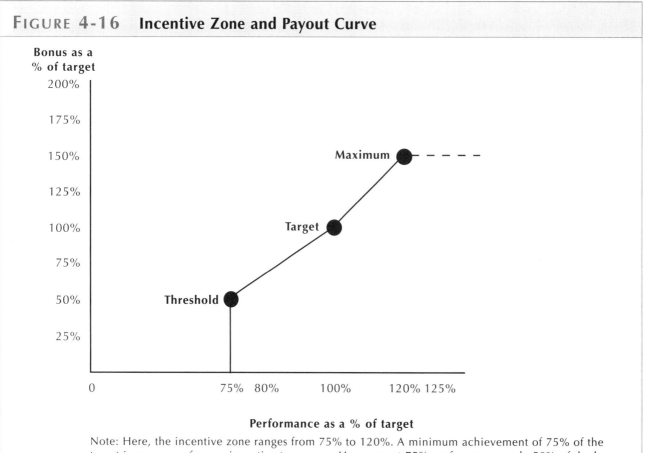

FIGURE 4-16 Incentive Zone and Payout Curve

Note: Here, the incentive zone ranges from 75% to 120%. A minimum achievement of 75% of the target is necessary for any incentive to emerge. However, at 75% performance, only 50% of the bonus will be given. At 129% of target (the maximum level of performance that is currently rewarded with a bonus or maximum performance that is deemed possible under current conditions), 150% of the bonus will be given. At 100% performance, 100% of bonus is given.

Note: The incentive zone ranges from 75% to 120%. A minimum achievement of 75% of the target is necessary for any incentive to emerge. However, at 75% performance, only 50% of the bonus will be given. At 120% of target (the maximum level of performance that is currently rewarded with a bonus or maximum performance that is deemed possible under current conditions), 150% of the bonus will be given. At 100% performance, 100% of bonus is given.

LIMIT VOLUME OF STOCK OPTIONS

The volume of stock options in any given year should be limited or the value of stock held by others will devalue.[55] Nortel, for example, issued 175 million options in 2000-or roughly 52% of all its outstanding options were handed out in a single year! The dilution in the value of shares for common shareholders can be imagined in such instances.

LINK OPTIONS TO SHARE OWNERSHIPS

Having options encourages executives to increase the value of shares so that they can sell them. Insisting that they own shares makes them want to increase shareholder value because they can keep them. By tying share options with ownerships, the managers can be encouraged to have a longer time for decision making.

STAY ON COURSE DURING MARKET VOLATILITY

If the market conditions become unfavourable, the firm should not change the conditions under which stock options are granted. After all, stock options were given with the intent of shaping the firm's fortunes in a changing market. If the managers come to believe that the terms of stock options will be changed when the firm faces adverse market conditions, there is simply no incentive for them to work harder when faced with obstacles.

CEOs who are relatively new on the job are much more likely to chase the potential "lottery" returns that option pay can provide.[56] However, even among long-tenured executives, option pay still positively affects acquisition and divestiture activity making them engage in risky deals which bring short-term gains in stock prices. This means that a firm's stock option plan has to be designed after a thorough review of its goals and situational contingencies to ensure longer-term value building.

> Canadian National (CN) Railway's stock option plan is a good example of how well formulated stock options can lead to achievement of organizational goals. When CN went public in the fall of 1995, it had the overriding objective of slashing its operating costs. One of CN's main tools was an innovative stock option plan for senior managers. CN's program held out the prospect of hefty personal profits, but two thirds of the options would be issued only if management pushed operating costs fast enough. The performance based options, still new to this country, were a success. The cost reduction goal was achieved two years early and managers drove down costs far below original targets. The result was a jump in the stock price from an initial $10 to over $60 in late 2000.[57]

As a recent study indicated, pay has different meanings to different managers.[58] To most managers, pay has at least four distinct meanings: an indicator of performance, a symbol of success, a reinforcement of specific behaviours, and an anxiety reducer. It may be possible for pay to meet certain managerial needs while ignoring others. To some, pay provides a feedback mechanism, to others, it is a measure of comparison of one's own efforts with those of relevant others, to others again, it is a sign of status and achievement. Motivating work behaviour through pay may be much more complex than is assumed by many practitioners and implied in some writings. Reward systems that assume managers are motivated by single needs may be misguided and ineffective.[59] To maintain effective compensation systems, organizations need to periodically conduct managerial salary surveys and assess internal and external realities.

Reward systems should also facilitate the successful implementation of a business strategy and encourage high performance. In some instances this may require a major re-design of traditional reward systems. Reward systems that simply focused only on the job duties may have to be replaced by those focusing on the individual's contributions and knowledge. Over time, many organizations have been getting flatter to be more responsive. In the foreseeable future, with the advancement of technology, this trend may continue necessitating a new system that encourages rewards based on the person rather than on the level at which he or she works. Figure 4-17 lists some emerging trends in reward systems.

As one researcher noted, not everyone in an organization needs to have an above average level of pay satisfaction. What is probably more desirable is to have one group of managers who are very much satisfied with their pay, a second and large group which is above average in its pay satisfaction, and a third group which is dissatisfied. If there is a good relationship between managerial performance and pay levels and no distortion in communication, the dissatisfaction and consequent turnover of the poor performers should not adversely affect the firm. What is critical

FIGURE 4-17 Traditional and Emerging Reward Systems

	Traditional	Emerging
Focus	Employee satisfaction	Strategic success by generating high employee involvement
Basis of rewarding	Job duties; Rank	Employee contributions, skill and knowledge
Hierarchical reward differences	Significant differences in reward across hierarchy	Minimal differences across hierarchy; Fewer layers
Attempts to encourage	Generation of loyalty	Build employee competence

is "to tie large differences in salaries directly to performance so that the good performer will be making substantially more than the poor performer."[60] As mentioned earlier, individuals make two types of pay comparisons: internal to the organization and external to it. For managers, the external comparisons may be more critical since if comparisons are poor, the concerned manager will leave the organization. Even if internal comparisons are adverse, the individual manager may not leave the organization if external comparisons are favourable.[61] However, feelings of internal inequity may prompt the manager to take actions that go against the overall interests of the organization. Hence, the importance of greater communication in organizations about the why, how, and what of the compensation system to avoid perceived inequity cannot be overemphasized.

Last, but not least, the old saying, "be careful what you reward, you will surely get more of it." Every day, we see examples of organizations that want their employees to exhibit certain behaviours but reward totally different ones. Thus, it is not uncommon to see organizations that continuously proclaim commitment to high quality but reward employees for shipping products on schedule, even with defects. Organizations want employees to be honest and creative, but often reward them for not disagreeing with their boss even when the latter is wrong. In mission statements and employee newsletters, several organizations underscore the importance of long-term growth and environmental responsibility, but then reward their managers on the basis of quarterly earnings. Several employers highlight the importance of teamwork and collaboration but reward only the best team members.[62]

Performance goals and measures have to be carefully chosen. They also should be clearly and frequently communicated to every one concerned. Plans, however well and carefully developed, will not succeed unless they are well understood and well implemented.

Implications for Practice

1. An organization's reward system affects practically all other human resource functions. Hence, it is critical to identify clear compensation objectives after an analysis of organizational goals, strategy, and size and organization character.

2. The mix of monetary and tangible rewards, social rewards, status enhancement, and intrinsic job rewards should be carefully planned after an exam-ination of the industry, the labour market, workforce needs, and organizational resources and priorities.

3. In formulating a compensation strategy, several considerations such as equity, effort-reward linkage, competency building, and openness are paramount. Specific system should be designed only after considering the unique market and internal conditions of a firm.

4. In all instances the compensation system should seek to have the ten attributes discussed in this chapter and summarized in the acronym COMPENSATE.

5. All traditional performance incentives are deficient on one or more of the ten attributes. When identifying incentives, attempts should be made to match the incentive with the firm's short-term and longer-term goals and strategies.

6. The traditional stock option for managers suffers from a number of drawbacks. A firm's stock option plan should be designed to overcome as many of these as possible. It may also be a good idea to combine stock options with mandatory stock ownership.

Key Terms for Review

Agency theory, p. 99

Commissions, p.109

Compa-ratio, p. 101

Cost reduction plans, p. 112

Employee stock ownership plans, p. 111

Equity theory, p. 100

Expectancy theory, p. 100

External equity, p.100

Internal equity, p. 100

Job evaluation, p. 101

Knowledge- or skills-based pay systems, p. 104

Membership-contingent compensation systems, p. 103

Merit pay, p. 110

Performance contingent compensation, p. 101

Piece-rate pay system, p. 108

Production bonuses, p. 109

Profit sharing plans, p. 110

Stock options, p. 118

Vesting period, p. 119

Discussion Questions

1. What are the popular monetary and non-monetary rewards seen in Canadian industry today? Do you think that money's role as a motivator is overestimated? Given our high standard of living, can money continue to motivate employees?

2. What factors must you consider when designing a compensation system?

3. What are the attributes of a good compensation system? Consider an organization where you have worked in the past. Which of these attributes were present in that firm's compensation plan? What suggestions would you make to the firm for improving its compensation plan?

4. Executives get paid in millions when other equally responsible job positions such as the Prime Minister of Canada, the Premiers of the provinces, and heads of major hospitals and universities get only a fraction of that. Why is this? Are there performance-linked rewards that can be introduced for these positions?

Critical Thinking Questions

1. What differences in the types of rewards and their administration would you expect between firms operating in the "old economy" (e.g., automobiles, mining) and "new economy" (e.g., hi-tech, biotech industries)? Why?

2. Consider an industry and job position that is dominated by female workers (e.g., grocery check-out clerks). Now consider another position and industry that has a concentration of male workers (e.g., mining). Would the considerations when designing compensation system be different in these two instances? How?

3. "Profit sharing plans require trust between management and the worker. Commissions require trust among workers," commented one manager. Do you agree? What kinds of industries are likely to benefit from profit sharing plans? Where would commissions be most beneficial?

4. "The things that get rewarded get done" goes the saying. If organizations fail, does that mean that the "right things" done by managers are not rewarded? Assume you are asked to design a compensation plan for senior executives in a highly volatile industry (like information technology). What challenges are you likely to face?

Web Research

Conduct an Internet search to find out the compensation patterns in three different industries (manufacturing, high-tech, and service). Are there differences in the compensation plans of organizations belonging to these industries? Why? Report the summary of your findings to the class with action guidelines for a future human resource professional employed in one of these industries. (Hint: Several private organizations and public agencies have websites that can be helpful. One useful site to start with is www.salariesreview.com/Surveys/methodology1.htm)

CASE INCIDENT
Ontario Electronics Company Limited: A New Compensation System for Plant D

Ontario Electronics Company Limited (OECL) is a manufacturer of electronic, communication, aerospace, and audio equipment. The company currently employs over 500 workers and operates in a highly environmentally turbulent hi-tech industry. The company's head office and major plant are located in Scarborough, Ontario, and its plants and sales offices are in four other Canadian provinces and in major U.S. cities. While in the recent past the company has faired well financially, the top management is somewhat unhappy with the productivity levels seen in some plants. The firm, which grew dramatically through acquisitions in the past two years, has embarked on an organization-wide effort to improve employee productivity and organizational growth. A variety of efforts including benchmarking, new performance appraisal procedures, changes in compensation systems, and new training and coaching programs are planned to achieve this twin objective.

The firm is now considering the introduction of a new compensation system in its new Plant D. Plant D makes radar equipment, signal systems, and digital communication modules and was recently acquired by the company from an ailing competitor and is geographically separated from the other plants. Therefore, OECL felt that it could conduct a pilot "experiment" of the new system in this plant. If it proved successful, it could implement the same (or a variation of the same) in the other plants. A major impetus for the present change was the difficulty in attracting highly skilled employees to the firm. A significant proportion of the firm's workforce are technically qualified professionals, currently in short supply in the local labour market.

The key components of the proposed compensation plan are:

1. The current flat salary system will be changed to encourage performance improvement. Under the new system, each employee will have a base pay and a variable pay dependent on the individual's or team's productivity for each quarter. The current performance figures will be used as standards to identify the variable component. For example, the signal module unit currently produces 1500 units a day or 30 000 units a month assuming 20 working days. A worker in the unit who currently gets $3000 per month will, in future, be paid a flat salary of $2000 plus $0.04 a unit, thus in future, making a total pay of $3200 a month.

2. The workers will also get an annual bonus related to net profits earned by the firm. The management believed that net profits, rather than gross profits or total revenue was a better measure of the workforce achievement since this provided an incentive for every one concerned to cut cost of production and administration. The bonus percentage is unspecified at this time.

3. For employees who were involved in sales or other revenue generating activities, a similar plan—but based on total sales—is planned.

4. Consistent with OECL's focus on improving the competencies of its employees and building a highly skilled and customer oriented workforce, each employee will also be rated by his or her supervisor on the following dimensions: Collaboration/Teamwork; Customer focus; Project management; Negotiation skills; Strategic vision; and Entrepreneurship. The ratings on the above dimensions on a five-point scale will be summed up. All who receive a score of 24 or above out of 30 will be eligible for merit pay. The amount of pay will vary from year to year depending on the total budget available.

Brenda Cole, who was recently hired in the capacity of Performance Analyst, was asked to comment on the above plan. OECL' s management wanted to install a simple system that was easy to understand and administer.

Questions

1. *If you were Cole, what comments would you make to the management?*

2. *What other actions or improvements, if any, would you recommend?*

CASE

Pay and Save Groceries: A New Compensation Plan

Pay and Save Groceries (PSG) is a regional grocery chain with 45 supermarkets spread over Eastern Canada. The firm, which began as a mom and pop store in Halifax 25 years ago, grew to its present size primarily because of the energy and vision of its founder, Jack Libbey. Today, PSG stores range from no-frills box stores to the trendy food villages and 24-hour superstores in several cities including Halifax, Saint John, Fredericton, Charlottetown, and Moncton. PSG has also made a limited entry into Quebec and Ontario through the acquisition of six local grocery stores. The firm currently employs about 480 full time employees and a large number of part-time cashiers and other workers. While the exact number of part-time employees fluctuates seasonally, it usually ranges from 2300 to 2500. More details about the firm are provided in the Case in Chapter 1 (pp. 25-27).

Despite the growth of the company, Jack Libbey maintained an informal atmosphere by avoiding installation of standard procedures which would "straight jacket" the firm. For example, there were no job descriptions for most positions nor any "organized" approach to employee planning, performance appraisal, and discipline. The store managers and work supervisors had a fair amount of discretion in routine decision making; all major decisions involving more than $3000 in new outlays had to be approved by top management.

The salary for new and part-time employees at PSG is 3 to 4% above the minimum wage. This is lower than what was offered by the competition. However, Pay and Save employees who stayed with the firm for three years or more often earned equal to or better than what they could have made elsewhere. While Pay and Save is not unionized at present, a national and a regional union have been making attempts to organize the employees. There are indications that these efforts are beginning to pay off.

Jane Werther, the new Human Resource Manager, recognized that good employee relations are critical to the success, even the very survival of the firm. Recently, Save More, a no-frills supermarket chain with extensive operations in Western and Central Canada, entered the Atlantic market. Compared to PSG, Save More possesses vastly superior resources and cost advantages because of its "self-serve" and "bulk-purchase" strategies. In the five stores it opened in Halifax, Saint John, and Moncton, it has been able to offer produce and goods at prices 15% to 20% cheaper than at PSG. Already, this has hurt PSG's sales (some PSG stores have lost as much as 15% to 25% of sales). Along with Save More came a few other larger, national grocery chains.

A pressing problem at PSG, in Werther's mind, was the high turnover and less-than-desirable performance of the firm's cashiers. Despite various employee training programs, only about 60% of the cashiers hired each year met the management's expectations with regard to customer service, product knowledge, and ability to do other assigned duties (such as inventory keeping, and stock display). High absenteeism and turnover were also a problem. The turnover rate for full time cashiers was about 20% while for the part-time cashiers the figure exceeded 35%. Since the firm depends on part-time staff to a great extent, the turnover figure was not only expensive but also a major inconvenience when planning the daily and weekly logistics.

In an effort to overcome the problems, the firm is currently considering the re-design of its compensation system for cashiers and other workers in the job family. A local management-consulting firm, Schlenker Associates Inc., was hired to design an alternate compensation system. Calvin Schlenker, a senior partner of the consulting firm, has been working on the project for the last three weeks and has now given some preliminary recommendations. Werther is expected to provide her evaluation of these recommendations in a board meeting scheduled for later this week.

In essence, the consultant's report recommended combining three positions: Cashiers, packers, and inventory clerks into a single job family called "Service Personnel". Employees in different groups will be cross-trained. Each employee will be expected to work in different capacities on the same day as the situation demands. This will, the consultant argued, result in better predictability for the organization and overall, higher wages for most employees. Relevant portions of the consultant's report are excerpted in Figure A. Earlier, the same consultant performed a job analysis of the cashier's position and made recommendations on the job specifications. The recommended job specification is shown in Figure B.

Werther knew that skill-based approach to compensation was popular in several organizations; however, she was unsure whether the concept worked in a setting such as Pay and Save's. She was also weary of some aspects of the consultant's proposal. She was wondering whether there are other, better ways of meeting the firm's multiple objectives of improved customer service, low costs, and reduced absenteeism and turnover among cashiers.

(continued)

FIGURE A Excerpts from the Consultant's Report

Job Categories:

Currently, Pay and Save has four job categories which require the same basic skills and aptitudes. These are: cashiers, grocery packers, labelers, and inventory display personnel.

About 60% of the total employees in the above three categories are cashiers; 15% grocery packers and the remaining 25% are labelers and inventory display personnel. By cross-training these personnel and requiring them to do multiple tasks, the firm will not only be able to meet its unexpected shortage of one type of personnel on any given day, but also reduce the overall costs. It is recommended that the entire job family be called "service personnel."

Pay Scales:

Different Pay and Save stores pay somewhat varying salaries to recognize the local realities. The pay rates also vary depending on the length of service. While the present system mostly works well, a uniform rate for these job categories will not only reduce the overall costs for the firm, but also act as a motivator for the various employee groups.

Example:

Take the case of Pay and Save on Bourbon Street which has 6 full-time and 10 part-time cashiers, 10 part-time packers and 4 full-time and 10 part-time lablers. While there are different pay rates for various persons in the same job category, let us take the average hourly rates for each job category. These are: cashiers: $7.80; grocery packers: $7.00; and labelers and inventory clerks: $8.00.

By cross training the workers in all the three tasks and assigning them to all three jobs, the firm can improve the productivity by about 50%.

For an 8 hour working day, the present payroll costs are:
Cashiers: $8 \times 16 \times 7.80$ or $998.40
Packers: $8 \times 10 \times 7.00$ or $560.00
Labelers: $8 \times 14 \times 8.00$ or $896.00
Total daily costs: $2454

Assume 300 working days a year. Total yearly costs: $736 200
After re-training, if we raise the salary levels to $10 for everyone, the daily costs will be:
$(8 \times 40 \times 10.00) \times 50\%$ (due to productivity gains)= $1600
Total yearly costs: $480 000
Yearly savings: $256 200
The above, of course, does not include other cost savings due to reduced absenteeism, turnover, and errors in pricing because of poor product familiarity.

FIGURE B Proposed Job Specification by the Consultant in a Past Assignment

SKILL FACTORS:

Education:	Grade 12 or better
Experience:	Prior cashier's experience in a small store is desirable
Communication:	Verbal fluency in English required; strong interpersonal skills a must

EFFORT FACTORS:

Physical:	Must be able to stand for six to seven hours
	Must be able to carry weights up to 25 kg
	Must have finger dexterity to operate a cash machine
Mental:	Need good short-term memory to respond to customer inquiries

Questions

1. *If you were Werther, what comments would you make on the consultant's proposal?*

2. *What further information needs to be collected?*

3. *What alternate compensation approaches might be viable in the present setting? What recommendations would you give?*

5 DESIGNING JOBS TO ENHANCE EMPLOYEE INVOLVEMENT

...top employers are emphasizing substance over style. Benefits like personal days off, flexible work hours and family leave are becoming tremendously important again. People want more time with their families-and employers are responding.[1]

D'Arcy Jenish and Berton Woodward

CHAPTER OBJECTIVES

After studying this chapter, you should be able to:

- Name the advantages of employee involvement in job and task design

- Discuss the factors to consider when designing jobs

- Outline the popular forms of employee involvement

- Examine steps to improve quality through employee involvement

At Harley-Davidson, employees more often wear a Harley T-shirt and a pair of Levis to work than formal business attire. Employees often attend rallies where they ride their bikes or bikes loaned to them by the company and join their customers in the Harley experience. The staffers in Hallmark's creative department are encouraged not only to develop innovative cards, but also to have fun in the process. They decorate their work-stations, have brainstorming sessions, meet with customers, and seek other ways to provide outlets for their creativity and personalities. Southwest Airlines requires its employees to take the safety regulations very seriously, but it also asks them to go out of their way to help passengers enjoy flying. Flight attendants have been known to sing, dance, and climb into overhead bins to entertain passengers while performing their required duties.[2]

Welcome to the work world of the new millennium! While organizations like Harley-Davidson, Hallmark, and Southwest Airlines are not typical, there is a growing realization on the part of business leaders that without a committed and competent workforce, survival in the new global market place is impossible. Different organizations adopt varying strategies to bring out the best in their employees-the above organizations believe that accomplishing high performance goals is facilitated by a work setting that energizes, excites, and even amuses employees. Other organizations have developed alternate organizational cultures. However, the objective for all remains the same: to succeed and survive in an extremely turbulent environment. High employee involvement is no longer a desirable goal; often, it spells the difference between success and failure and growth and extinction.

This chapter introduces you to some important ideas that will help you design jobs and organizational systems that encourage high employee involvement. First, we need to look at the rationale for employee involvement.

THE RATIONALE FOR EMPLOYEE INVOLVEMENT

Employee involvement consists of a variety of systematic methods that empower employees to participate in the decisions that affect them and their relationship with an organization.

Employee involvement (EI) consists of a variety of systematic methods that empower employees to participate in the decisions that affect them and their relationship with the organization. Through EI, employees feel a sense of responsibility, even "ownership" of decisions in which they participate. To be successful, EI must be more than just a systematic approach; it must become part of the organization's culture and management philosophy.

> Organizations such as Hewlett Packard, IBM, and Tektronix have had such a philosophy ingrained in their corporate structure for decades. Several other organizations are attempting to create a corporate culture that values employee involvement.

Employee involvement is based on two principles that effective managers have known about and practiced for many decades. First, individuals tend to support systems or decisions that they helped make. For example, if an employee was actively involved in developing a new equipment maintenance procedure, this individual is likely to ensure that the new procedure is carried out correctly. Second, employees who actually perform a task know more about it than anyone else, including their supervisors. Asking for information from employees who actually perform the job can provide insights not available from supervisors or outside experts.

> An employee survey in a major Canadian food-processing firm showed that the firm was not paying enough information to safety in one of its plants. Many employees complained that the floors were slippery. Loaders had to go up a deck using steps they considered "treacherous". The plant manager formed a safety committee with plant workers to look into the problem. The committee's suggestions, when implemented, increased speed of the entire assembly unit by over 14% as workers could now move faster and more freely without worrying about a possible fall. The total cost for the new procedures? A mere $428!

Why is employee involvement critical today? At least four major reasons (Figure 5-1) can be offered.

EMPLOYEE INVOLVEMENT IMPROVES PRODUCTIVITY

Employee productivity is significantly affected by two factors: ability and attitude. Ability is simply whether or not the employee is able to perform the job. Ability is

---

FIGURE 5-1   Beneficial Impact of Employee Involvement

1. Improves productivity
2. Reduces overall employment costs
3. Facilitates strategy implementation
4. Generates creative solutions resulting in product or process improvements

---

influenced by training, education, innate aptitude, tools, and work environments. Attitude, on the other hand, refers to an individual's willingness to perform the job. Attitude is influenced by a myriad of factors, such as level of motivation, job satisfaction, and commitment to work. Employee involvement practices help improve both the ability and attitude of the employee (Figure 5-2). When employees are involved, they tend to learn more about the various tasks and how they all fit into the larger picture. They are also likely to enhance their skills to do multiple tasks. The synergy of employees working together often results in improvement in quality of work environments and employee productivity.

EMPLOYEE INVOLVEMENT CAN REDUCE EMPLOYMENT COSTS

Employees who are highly involved in their jobs are absent less frequently from work. When they find their jobs meaningful, they are also likely to stay with the firm longer, reducing recruitment and training costs significantly. Over the years, the relationship between employers and employees has undergone a dramatic change. As one writer pointed out, "if the traditional lifetime employment relationship was like a marriage, then the new employment relationship is like a lifetime of divorces and remarriages, a series of close relationships governed by the expectation going in that they need to be made to work and yet will inevitably not last."[3] To keep highly skilled employees with the firm, the employer may have to offer considerable autonomy, freedom, and flexibility. Further, a high involvement workplace gives an organization a recruiting advantage, as most job applicants would like to work for an employer who offers them a meaningful job and where their ideas are valued. Consider the case of hospitals attracting nurses.

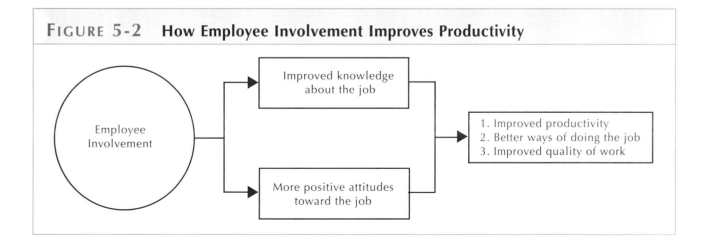

FIGURE 5-2   How Employee Involvement Improves Productivity

Nursing has a high burnout rate and continuous advances in medical science necessitate retraining for nurses who have been away from work even for a short period. Because the workforce is largely female, many nurses leave the workforce for a few years for childcare considerations. Faced with a 22% turnover rate, Midtown Hospital initiated a program wherein all employees, including nurses, were involved in identifying organizational mission and hospital policies including working hours, re-training, etc. The results were astonishing. The turnover rate dropped to less than 6% and the number of lost hours was reduced by 40% in a year.

INVOLVEMENT RESULTS IN EFFECTIVE IMPLEMENTATION OF ORGANIZATIONAL STRATEGIES

In Chapter 2, the importance of clear organizational goals and strategies was discussed. Goals and strategies, however well formulated, must be well executed. This means that employees should be committed to the achievement of the goals. Unless employees understand their roles and are rewarded for exhibiting desired behaviours, it is unlikely that the organization will be able to generate grassroots support for its plans. High employee involvement facilitates more effective communication of goals and strategies to all. When employees understand the importance of their contributions to organizational success, they are more likely to engage in activities that further goal accomplishment. This improved understanding comes with involvement.

INVOLVEMENT OFTEN GENERATES INNOVATIVE SOLUTIONS

Most employees, as they gain task experience, think of better ways of doing the task. If an employer is able to tap the creative solutions provided by workers, it often results in newer, better, and cheaper products or processes, safer working conditions, and reduced down-time for equipment. Such innovation has become a critical success factor today, especially in industries where continuous product improvement, value addition and cost control spell survival and success. It is also critical for small businesses that are very vulnerable to the environment and where only continuous improvement can ensure survival and success. By tapping into the creativity and entrepreneurial spirit of their employees, several organizations have identified new businesses, new ways of doing old business, and methods to add new value to old products.

> Operators at one of PanCanadian Petroleum's plants always knew that their gas field had additional reserves. They assumed that management knew this. Hence, they never communicated this information until a new employee involvement program sought their suggestions. Acting on the information provided by the employees, the firm was able to dramatically increase its gas production and profits.[4]

Before proceeding any further, it should be pointed out that employee involvement does not happen in the absence of trust, fairness, and mutual respect between employees and management. A company's corporate culture, leadership, and working climate have an effect on the motivation and job satisfaction of its employees. Effective communication systems, effective supervisory practices, providing meaningful jobs, and flexible work schedules that help balance work and private lives are other conditions that facilitate high employee involvement.

Focus on Small Business:

How Innovative Is Your Small Business?

Innovation and creativity are critical for success and the very survival of small businesses. However, establishing a culture that encourages creativity is no easy task. Based on past research studies that examined the level of creativity seen in different organizations[5], the following questions were formulated. While the questions on innovation listed below are designed for classroom use and not tested for their validity, they will sensitize you to the activities and systems that encourage creativity.

Consider a small business with which you are familiar and respond to each of the following questions "Yes, always", "Yes, sometimes", "No, sometimes", and "No, always". If you are unsure of a question, do not rate it.

1. Are employees formally rewarded for suggesting new ideas or processes in any form?

2. Is timely completion of work according to plans highly valued?

3. Are employees continually encouraged to improve product quality?

4. Does the management punish employees who try different approaches and, at times, fail?

5. Do employees trust their supervisors?

6. Do the supervisors punish employees who question present ways of doing things?

7. Does the firm reward workers in any manner for reducing waste or inefficiency?

8. Do the supervisors discourage employees from discovering new problems?

9. Do employees always have access to all necessary resources to do a job well-including adequate time?

10. Do the employees feel that they have too much work to do?

11. Are the job duties and job descriptions of employees continually changing or evolving?

12. Does this firm emphasize that employees follow policies and rules in day-to-day work?

For odd numbered questions, score 4, 3, 2, and 1 respectively for "Yes, always", "Yes, sometimes", "No, sometimes", and "No, always". For even numbered questions, reverse the scoring (i.e., a "Yes, always" get a score of 1 and "No, always", a score of 4). Add up the scores and divide the total score by the number of questions that you answered. This is the average innovation quotient for the firm you selected. It will lie anywhere from 1 to 4.

Interpret the scores using the following guidelines. A score of 3.5 and up indicates that the firm is highly innovative and encourages its employees to come up with creative solutions using a variety of structural, process, and managerial tools. A score of 2.75 to 3.4 indicates that the firm encourages innovative thinking on several occasions or to a moderate degree. A score of 2.74 or less suggests that the firm focuses more on stability and predictability of employee actions. Given their environments, competitive pressures and industry characteristics, perhaps, predictability is seen as more important by their managements for continued success.

Of course, only a detailed analysis of the organization can establish whether the management assumptions and strategy are appropriate for any particular setting.

This chapter looks at one of the above factors-namely the job-in greater detail. Here we look at the way jobs can be designed to achieve greater efficiency, improve employee productivity and satisfaction, and attain larger corporate goals. We begin our discussion by examining the various considerations in job design.

DESIGNING JOBS THAT ENCOURAGE INVOLVEMENT

Consider the following conversation between Jerry Sierargo, an employee of Sherwood Electronics Ltd., and Nancy Fox, his work supervisor.

Jerry: Oh, God! I hate this job. Day after day, all I do is to sort and add labels to the disks and CD ROMs. I realize that someone must do it, but surely the job could be more fun.

Nancy: I know how you feel; in fact, I sense that some of the other employees feel the same way. But the plant manager's big concern is maintaining productivity. Any changes we make must not mean fewer units per day. Any suggestions?

Website with articles on employee involvement: *www.pmihrm.com/articles. htm*

Jerry: I know high production is necessary to compete against foreign manufacturers. But why can't several of us on the line be responsible for entire subassemblies instead of being responsible just for these individual tasks?

Nancy: Well, what difference would that make?

Jerry: Probably not much. But when we get bored with one job we could swap with someone else. Besides, when someone got behind, we could all pitch in. And who knows? We might even produce more if we are not bored!

Nancy: Now, that seems like a great idea. Thanks Jerry. Why don't I raise this in our lunch meeting tomorrow? I am sure that we can find a solution that meets everyone's needs.

The above conversation reflects the multiple considerations in job design. Boring jobs result in employee dissatisfaction and apathy; however, jobs must also achieve larger organizational and societal objectives. Figure 5-3 lists the four key considerations-the needs of the organization, the employees, the technology, and the larger environments-of designing jobs. Each is discussed below.

ORGANIZATIONAL CONSIDERATIONS OF JOB DESIGN

Simply put, each job should maintain and enhance an organization's effectiveness and efficiency.

Effectiveness The overall organizational mission is accomplished through a series of inter-related tasks or activities. If the organization is to remain successful and grow, these tasks and activities should be performed competently and on a timely basis. Above all, they should meet the organizational objectives and the needs of the customers, employees, suppliers, and other constituents.

We are currently living amidst a revolution-the information revolution. While this is its very beginning, it is already starting to overwhelm us. It is reshuffling our economy, redefining our workplaces, antiquating our practices and laws, and redefining our very concept of reality.

Why is this revolution different from any other revolution (e.g., the industrial revolution of the 18th and early 19th centuries)? The answer is simple: The revolution that we are experiencing is far bigger, more serious, and more profound than any previous change in the history of humans. As Ed Roberts, who created the very first personal computer, the Altair, about 25 years ago noted, "the computer gives the

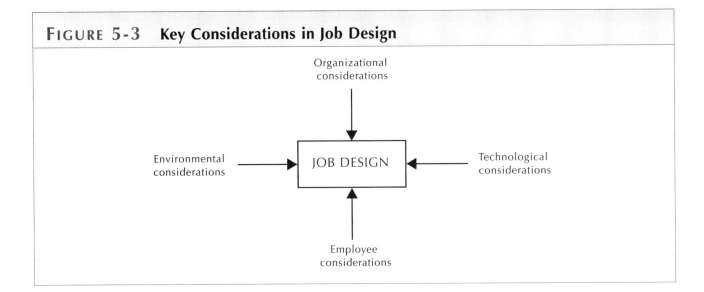

FIGURE 5-3   Key Considerations in Job Design

average person, a high school freshman, the power to do things in a week that all the mathematicians who ever lived until 30 years ago couldn't do."[6] As the new millennium unfolds, we are already on the threshold of a new way of living where traditional notions of work, leisure, hierarchy, and decision-making will become increasingly irrelevant. Figure 5-4 shows how the emerging technology impacts on various aspects of managing organizations. The new organization has already undergone "delayering" (removing layers of management and staff) and increased decision-making power and access to a wider range of information may further reduce the need for many middle management positions. The office of tomorrow may not have any front line staff who mediate between the customer and the product or service provider. This is already the methodology in most Internet-based virtual organizations. The networked interactive computing system will enable customers to make informed, comparative choices without assistance. The concept of a job as defined by place and reporting structure is also fast giving way to flexible notions of work at anytime and anywhere. Tomorrow's workers may have many contracts, may work from home or at the office, alone or with others, and may have more than one employer.

In the context of job design, to remain effective, organizations may have to redefine jobs, eliminate others, and combine tasks considered independent now. Even small businesses may be able to compete and win against giant, well-entrenched organizations by skilful use of new technology, so continuous monitoring of environments and redefinition of jobs is a must to succeed and survive in the new economy.

Efficiency Concern for high task efficiency or maximum output with minimum expenditure of time, effort, or other resources was first underscored by **scientific management**. This is the systematic approach to job design propounded by Frederick Taylor that attempted to determine the best way to perform each activity and minimize (wasted) human effort. **Industrial engineering**, which evolved from this movement focuses on analyzing work methods and establishing optimal time standards by finding the best ways to do jobs.[7] As discussed in Chapter 3, time standards are established by recording the time needed (typically using a stop-watch or video monitor) to complete each element in a work cycle. Industrial engineers study work

Scientific management is the systematic approach to job design, proposed by Frederick Taylor, that determines the best way of performing each activity and minimizes human effort.

Industrial engineering focuses on analyzing work methods and establishing optimal time standards by finding the best ways to do jobs.

FIGURE 5-4   **How Technology Necessitates Redefinition of Organization**

	In the Past	Now
Products	Standardized, uniform	Customized
Price	Fixed; pay-per-product	Variable; Often, pay-per-use
Typical Manufacturing Process	Assembly line	Uses a variety of approaches including outsourcing lean-manufacturing systems, and virtual operations
Focus of Distribution	Place ("where")	Customer ("who")
Structure of Manufacturing Operations	Hierarchical with many levels	Fewer levels; team decision making popular in several instances
Employee Characteristics	Technically skilled, Narrow skills	Knowledge worker with broader skills

cycles to determine which, if any, job elements can be combined, modified, or eliminated to reduce the overall time needed to perform. Task specialization was suggested as a key strategy to improve efficiency. When workers are limited to a few repetitive tasks, output is usually higher. This is because specialized jobs lead to short job cycles. The automotive industry is a good example of such industrial engineering practices.[8]

> In the early years of this century, Henry Ford became rich and famous by building automobiles on an assembly line. Every Ford worker did a specific, repetitive task. For example, an assembly line worker might install a right headlight, another the right front wheel, and a third, the right front door. As the auto chassis moved on the conveyor belt, other workers would add left headlight, left front wheel and so on. The worker in charge of installing the right headlight would pick it up, plug it in, twist the adjustment screws, and pick up the next headlight within thirty seconds. This worker's job cycle is therefore 30 seconds. The job cycle begins again when the next headlight is picked up.

Headlight installation is a specialized job. It is so specialized that training takes only a few minutes. And the short job cycle means that the assembler gains much experience in a short time. Said another way, short job cycles require small investments in training and allow workers to learn the job quickly. Training costs remain low because the worker needs to master only one job.

The above approach stresses efficiency in effort, time, labour costs, training, and employee learning time. Today, this technique is still widely used in assembly operations. Typically, the output measures used to calculate efficiency ratios include production volume and value. However, more progressive employers are beginning to recognize that a number of other variables such as technological improvement, innovation, and meeting employee expectations are as important for the long-term health of the organization. Despite this, traditional notions of efficiency are given high importance especially when dealing with poorly educated workers or workers who have little industrial experience.

TECHNOLOGICAL CONSIDERATIONS

Three key technological considerations-task interdependence, technical constraints, and ergonomic requirements-have to be considered here. Each is briefly discussed below.

Task Interdependence
The flow of work in an organization is strongly influenced by the nature of the product or service. The product or service usually suggests the interdependence among various tasks and the sequence in which they should be performed. As pointed out in Chapter 3, the degree of task interdependence may be high or low with implications for work design.

> Consider the consumer loans, estate management, and retirement investments divisions of a bank. Because of their impact on the overall profitability and image of the bank, these divisions are, indirectly, ultimately dependent on each other. For example, if total loans were to rise sharply and suddenly push the interest rate up, it would have an impact on the volume of savings or the type of retirement investments chosen by the clients. However, on a daily basis, these divisions can operate independently.

Now contrast the bank example to the auto assembly example we used earlier. The frame of a car must be built before the fenders and doors can be added. Once the sequence of jobs is determined, the balance between jobs is established.

> Suppose it takes one worker twenty seconds to install each headlight so that in one minute, three headlights can be installed. If, however, it takes two minutes to install the three headlight receptacles, the job designer must balance these two interrelated jobs by

assigning two people to install the receptacles. Otherwise, a production bottleneck results. Since the work flow demands two receptacle installers for each headlight installer, one worker specializes on the right side receptacles, and another specializes on the left.

Technical Constraints Almost all managers at some time face situations characterized by resource scarcity combined with multiple objectives. A simplest case is when the same machine, plant, or process can produce any one of two alternate products and the total capacity cannot be significantly increased in the short term. This means that the increase in the production of one item is always associated with a reduced production of the second item.

> Consider a machine that can produce either Product A or Product B. The machine takes one hour to produce Product A and only thirty minutes to produce Product B. If the total number of machine hours is limited to 60 hours per week, it can produce a maximum of 60 units of Product A or 120 units of Product B or any other combination of A and B all of which would require a maximum of 60 hours.

The above situation is graphically represented in Figure 5-5. The graph shows the region of feasible solutions. So long as the combination of Product A and Product B volumes are within this region, production plans are feasible. In practice, managerial decisions are far more complex. Often several constraints including those relating to resource availability, market demand, managerial and human resource availability, and corporate priorities, have to be worked into the decision-making model. In such instances, complex mathematical modelling techniques including linear programming, waiting line and queuing theory, and stochastic modelling techniques have to be employed to identify the tasks that need to be carried out and the order of their execution.

Ergonomic Considerations Derived from the Greek words "ergo" meaning work and "nomos" meaning laws, **ergonomics** means the "laws of work" and focuses on how human beings physically interface with their work.[9] Optimal productivity requires that the physical relationship between the worker and the work be considered in designing jobs. The study of ergonomics is multi-disciplinary, using principles

Ergonomics focuses on how human beings physically interface with their work.

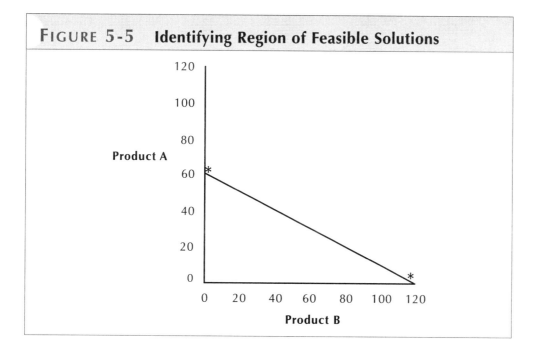

FIGURE 5-5   Identifying Region of Feasible Solutions

drawn from biology (especially anatomy and physiology), the behavioural sciences (psychology and sociology), as well as physics and engineering. Although the nature of job tasks may not vary when ergonomic factors are considered, the locations of tools, switches, and the work product are evaluated and placed in a position for ease of use. In other words, ergonomics focuses on fitting the task to the worker in many instances rather than simply forcing the employees to adapt to the task.[10]

> On an automobile assembly line, for example, a car frame may actually be elevated at a workstation so the worker does not become fatigued from stooping. Similarly, the location of dashboard instruments in a car is ergonomically engineered to make driving easier.

Attention to details of work settings can lead to improvements in efficiency and productivity as in the case of Saturn Corporation, a General Motors subsidiary that produces Saturn cars.

> In Saturn's plant, cars pass through the assembly line on hydraulic lifts that allow employees to raise or lower the cars to suit their own height. Employees are allowed to ride the platform and take up to six minutes to finish the tasks correctly (traditional assembly lines allot less than one minute). Industrial engineers videotape employee actions and simplify operations to minimize motion. In one instance, employees saved one-third of the steps walking to and from cars.[11]

EMPLOYEE CONSIDERATIONS

While ergonomic principles do consider employee safety and welfare, the primary focus is still on minimizing efforts and energy and maximizing efficiency. However, jobs cannot be designed by using only those elements that aid efficiency. To do so overlooks the human needs of the people who are to perform the work. While expectations from jobs vary across people, a large portion of employees look for jobs that offer them a challenge, a chance to learn and develop skills, and contribute meaningfully (Figure 5-6).

In general, as jobs are made more specialized, productivity climbs until factors like employee boredom and lack of control offset the advantages of further specialization (Figure 5-7). Indeed, many firms had to offer higher wages (some call it discontentment pay)[12] to compensate for the job dissatisfaction caused by narrowly defined jobs and jobs with short job-cycles. Employees in highly specialized jobs see

---

FIGURE 5-6   Common Employee Expectations About Their Jobs and Employers

While no single list of expectations characterizes the entire workforce, most employees seem to desire certain job and employer attributes. Here is a partial list of questions that go through the minds of most employees:

- Is this job meaningful and challenging?
- Does my supervisor tell me clearly his or her expectations?
- Do I get feedback about how well I am doing on a regular and timely basis?
- Have I been told why this job is important from the company's point of view? In other words, does my work really matter?
- Am I treated fairly and equitably?
- Do I get the necessary training to do a good job?
- Is the equipment I use safe and adequate?
- Does this employer provide me with an opportunity to grow and develop as a person?

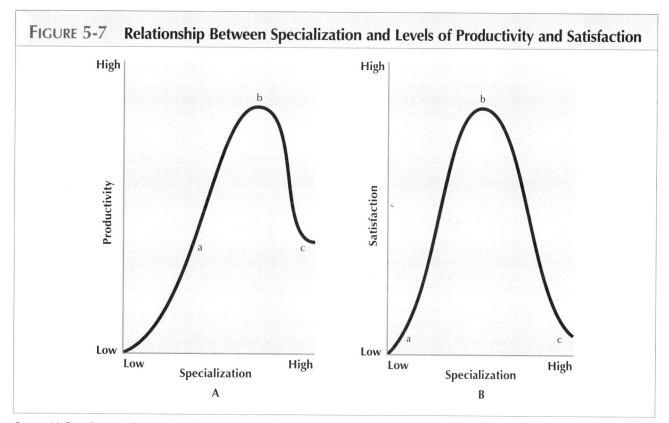

FIGURE 5-7   **Relationship Between Specialization and Levels of Productivity and Satisfaction**

Source: H. Das. *Strategic Organizational Design for a Global Economy*. Scarborough, ON: Prentice-Hall, 1998, 138. Reprinted with permission.

only a small part of the production process, making it difficult for them to identify with customer needs. This has resulted in quality control challenges. Higher employee turnover, absenteeism, and even sabotage, along with reduced productivity in the long term have been other costs of specialization. Past experience in several large assembly lines indicates that highly specialized jobs are tedious and socially isolating[13]—alienating workers from their employer and their jobs and reducing their overall mental health and motivation levels.

To overcome the negative effects of specialization, five core job dimensions are often improved: variety, autonomy, task identity, task significance, and feedback (Figure 5-8).[14] These are briefly discussed below.

Variety
Variety refers to the use of different skills and talents to complete work tasks and activities. For example, a body shop worker who, in the past, had the only duty of spraying paint may now be asked to do other auto body work, rebuild engines, and interact with customers. By injecting variety into jobs, not only is employee interest and motivation heightened in many instances, other benefits like reduced fatigue may exist.

Variety is the use of different skills and talents to complete an array of work tasks and activities.

> In a garment factory, several employees stitched buttons to apparel for eight to ten hours a day, depending on the market demand. Many employees, especially the younger ones, found this activity so boring that accidents and injuries were common. In a job redesign, the management formulated teams of employees who were given an opportunity to rotate their jobs. Thus, those who in the past only sewed buttons were trained to stitch other parts, label, or even cut clothes. The result? Fatigue related errors were reduced by over 65% in six months.

Job rotation or moving employees from job to job is frequently used to increase variety. Jobs are not changed; the workers are rotated. Rotation breaks the monoto-

Job rotation involves moving employees from job to job.

FIGURE 5-8   Job Characteristics that Encourage High Involvement

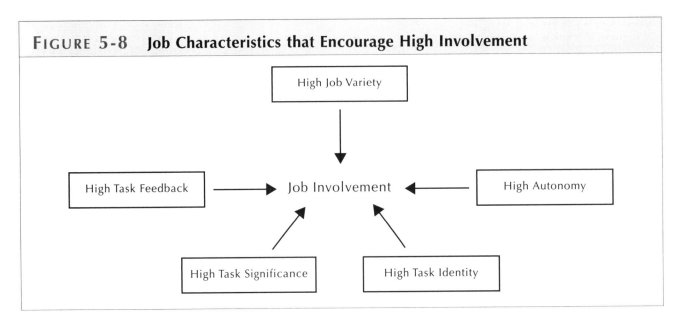

ny of highly specialized work by calling on different skills and abilities. The organization benefits because workers gain competency in several jobs. Knowing a variety of jobs helps the worker's self-image, provides personal growth, and makes the worker more valuable to the organization.

Autonomy refers to the freedom, independence, and discretion to plan and schedule the work and determine the procedures used to carry it out.

Autonomy
Autonomy is having the freedom, independence, and discretion to plan and schedule the work and determine the procedures to carry it out. It is the freedom to control one's response to the environment. In autonomous jobs, employees make their own decisions rather than rely on detailed supervisory instructions. While employee personality influences the relationship between autonomy and specific task performance,[15] in most instances, jobs that give workers the authority to make decisions tend to increase the employee's sense of recognition, self-esteem, job satisfaction, and performance. The absence of autonomy, on the other hand, can cause employee apathy or poor performance.[16]

> On the bottling line of a small brewery, teams of workers were allowed to speed up or slow down the rate of the bottling line as long as they met daily production goals. Although total output per shift did not change, there were fewer cases of capping machines jamming or breaking down for other reasons. When asked about this unexpected development, the supervisor concluded, "Employees pride themselves on meeting the shift quota. So they are more careful to check for defective bottle caps before they load the machine."

Task identity is the degree to which a job requires completion of a whole or identifiable piece of work.

Task Identity
Task identity is the degree to which a job requires completion of a whole or identifiable piece of work. In many instances, this means doing something from beginning to end rather than just a part of it. One problem with highly specialized jobs is that they lack task identity. Workers cannot point to a complete piece of work. They have little sense of responsibility and accomplishment and may lack pride in the results. When tasks are grouped so that employees feel they are making an identifiable contribution, job satisfaction may be increased significantly. Workers may be given "whole jobs" where they can identify their unique contributions and take pride in their accomplishments.

> A cabinet maker who designs a piece of furniture, selects the necessary materials and tools, and completes the project has high task identity as do most surgeons, newspaper columnists, and artists.

Job enlargement, or the expansion of the number of related tasks in a job, may aid in improving task identity. By adding similar duties to a job, it may also provide the employee with greater variety. Enlargement reduces monotony by expanding the job cycle and drawing on a wider range of employee skills.

> Maytag Company, through job enlargement, was able to improve production quality and reduce overall labour costs. Employee satisfaction and overall efficiency also increased.[17]

Job enlargement (horizontal loading) is the expansion of the number of related tasks in a job.

Task Significance

Task significance is the degree to which a job has a substantial impact on the organization and/or the larger society. Task significance, knowing that the work is important to others in the organization or outside it, makes the job even more meaningful for incumbents. Their sense of importance is enhanced because they know others are depending on what they do. Pride, commitment, motivation, satisfaction, and better performance are likely to result.

> Firefighters, Canadian Coast Guard members, teachers, and nurses enjoy high task significance because the quality of their work affects the safety and welfare of others.

Task significance is the degree to which a job has substantial impact on an organization and/or society.

Feedback

Feedback refers to the degree to which employees can tell how well they are doing based on direct sensory information from the job. When jobs do not give the workers any feedback on how well they are doing, there is little guidance or motivation to perform better. Some jobs offer regular feedback to employees.

> A website designer gets almost instant feedback about the accuracy of installed applications and links. Some data entry jobs also get almost instant feedback about accuracy of information entered. In contrast, some of the traditional, large auto assemblies and breweries provide little feedback to job incumbents on a daily basis.

Feedback is direct sensory information, received from the job, that enables employees to determine how well they are doing.

In summary, jobs are the central link between employees and the organization. Poorly designed jobs not only lead to low productivity, but can cause employee turnover, absenteeism, complaints, sabotage, unionization, resignations, and other problems. Hence employee needs must be recognized when designing jobs.

In the past, several employers have attempted to enrich jobs to meet the above needs of employees. **Job enrichment** refers to the vertical expansion of jobs increasing the degree to which employees plan, execute, and evaluate their jobs. Unlike job enlargement, which horizontally loads similar jobs to a position without adding to overall autonomy, job enrichment attempts to provide a more complete job to the incumbent by increasing autonomy and control responsibilities. These additions coupled with rethinking the job itself often lead to increased motivation and other improvements.

Job enrichment (vertical loading) is the vertical expansion of jobs that increases employees' job planning, execution, and evaluation.

> A large oil refinery changed the job duties of its data entry clerks in the human resource department. Unlike in the past when they simply entered the data, these clerks were now required to enter all data relating to specific worker categories, process the information, identify key trends, and pass on their findings to work supervisors who used the information to make human resource decisions. The new jobs not only provided greater challenge and autonomy, but also increased the task identity, significance, and feedback associated with the job. The productivity and employee satisfaction was up by over 40% in less than a year.

Job enrichment, however, is not a cure-all. Job enrichment techniques are merely tools and they are not applicable universally. As discussed below, environmental conditions have to be examined carefully before enriching jobs. Union resistance, resistance from supervisors who may fear the loss of power, high costs of change and training, and adverse cultural values make it impractical in some instances.

SELF-TEST:

How Involved Were You in That Course?

This exercise helps you assess the motivational properties of a course you took in the recent past and how far your involvement went. Consider a course that you have recently completed. Do not select a course that you are currently taking nor one done in the distant past. Please respond to the following statements *strongly agree* (SA), *agree* (A), *neither agree nor disagree* (NAD), *disagree* (D), or *strongly disagree* (SD). Since your first reaction to a statement is critical, do NOT change your response once you have indicated it.

1. The course encouraged me to use a number of my skills (e.g., writing, critical thinking, memorization) rather than a very narrow range of them.

2. The instructor encouraged the students to do independent study and research, interfering only when the students asked for assistance.

3. The instructor helped us understand how the course fit into the overall program.

4. The material taught in the course was important.

5. I received feedback on a continual basis about the quality of my performance.

6. I could readily see the practical relevance of much of the material taught in the course.

7. The material taught in the course made "sense" in the light of the overall program objectives.

8. In that course, a considerable portion of my final grade depended on activities over which I had total control.

9. The feedback received from the instructor helped me to improve my performance in the course.

10. The course used a variety of pedagogical techniques such as lectures, films, discussions, student projects, and student presentations.

Scoring

For all statements assign scores of 5, 4, 3, 2, and 1 for SA, A, NAD, D, and SD respectively. Total your scores for items 1 through 10.

Interpretation

Your total score will range from 10 to 50. A score of 40 or above indicates that the course provided you with all key motivators like variety, feedback, task identity, task significance, and autonomy. A score of 20 or below indicates serious deficiency on one or more of these dimensions. In the latter instance, you were probably not highly involved in the course.

ENVIRONMENTAL CONSIDERATIONS

When designing jobs, the environments within which the firm and job exist also need to be examined. Three items are of particular significance here: social expectations, workforce availability, and work practices (Figure 5-9).

Social Expectations In designing jobs, the surrounding societal expectations must be considered to avoid possible worker dissatisfaction and resistance. For example, working conditions that would be deemed acceptable in some societies may not be acceptable in others. Even in the same society, the passage of time brings about dramatic changes in social expectations. For example, jobs that would have been acceptable to some early Canadian immigrants are no longer suitable to for the present generation.

> At the time when rail lines were being laid across Canada, many people had to work long hours of hard labour. Often, they had fled countries where jobs were unavailable. This made any job acceptable. Today, employees in the same industry are much better educated and have higher expectations about the quality of work life.

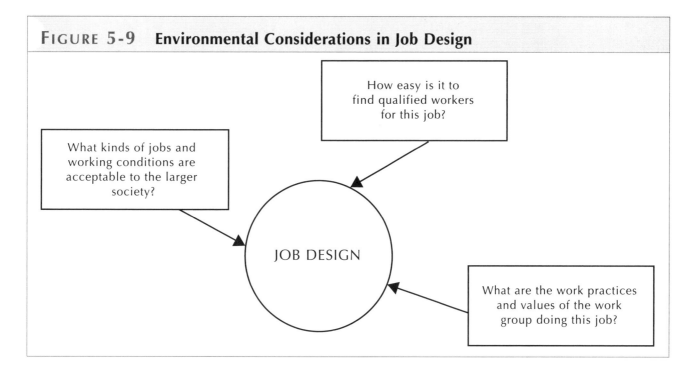

FIGURE 5-9   **Environmental Considerations in Job Design**

How easy is it to find qualified workers for this job?

What kinds of jobs and working conditions are acceptable to the larger society?

JOB DESIGN

What are the work practices and values of the work group doing this job?

Today's employees expect their employers to recognize the importance of a balance between work and non-work life. It is estimated that employee productivity increases by about 20% after companies implement work/life balance programs. Employee turnover falls by up to 50% when employees are offered benefits such as childcare and eldercare programs and flexible work hours.[18]

Workforce Availability Job requirements should be balanced against the abilities and availability of the people who are to do the work. An extreme example underlines this point.

> A developing country imported sophisticated oil refining equipment from the West to replace its existing aging equipment. Little did the political leaders of the country realize that their workforce did not have the skills to operate and maintain the equipment. As a result, government leaders had to hire Europeans to operate and maintain the refinery, boosting the overall costs of production.

In less developed nations, the major risk is jobs that are too complex. Jobs that are too simple can produce equally disturbing problems in industrialized nations with highly educated workers.

> Even when unemployment rates are high, many simple and overly-specialized jobs are hard to fill, as longstanding newspaper want ads for janitors demonstrate.

Work Practices Work practices are set methods of performing work. These methods may arise from tradition or the collective wishes of employees.

> A metal sheet and appliance fabricator aimed to increase productivity by redesigning the workflow. This not only changed the job demands but also broke up existing friendship cliques and social interaction patterns. Employee complaints and absenteeism significantly increased along with a drop in productivity.

The next section looks at some current practices that aim to improve employee involvement at work. Many of these are normally team based and seen in medium size or large organizations although the core principles of employee involvement are applicable in individual and small organizational settings.

Focus on Ethics:

How Far Does the Responsibility for Work Safety Extend?

Consider the following situations that focus on safety. How far do you think a firm should go to protect employees? Once you have made your decision in each case, compare your answers with those of your friends. Which of the ethical approaches discussed in Chapter 1 underlies the various positions?

1. Your firm, an office products manufacturer and retailer is a fast growing company that has been aggressively expanding into foreign markets. In the last four years, it has entered seven different countries in Asia and South America and has been successful in capturing a significant market share in each country within a very short period. Your company's products were originally designed for North American markets where the average office temperature is much cooler than in Asia or South America. Also, unlike in North America, office staff is not well trained in many of these foreign countries. When the copiers and printers are used in higher temperatures, especially by inadequately trained people, there is a very slight probability of a solvent in the equipment expanding and leaking. If humans touch the solvent, it can lead to burns and allergies, some of which are long lasting and may even leave permanent scars. The likelihood of this happening is estimated to be less than 1/5000. Substituting another harmless solvent will eliminate all possibility of this event, but will increase the cost of the units by over 20%. Further, such a change will disrupt your company's production schedules, resulting in an additional cost of 10% per year.

2. Tim Rock, one of your firm's Regional Managers located in an Asian country, was rumoured to routinely have sexual relations with his office staff-often coercing or coaxing them. On an earlier occasion, an employee in his office complained to the Human Resource Manager who later had a "chat" with Rock. However, nothing much seems to have changed. Since the Human Resource Manager recently left the firm, there is no one to look into the matter. You joined the firm only recently and although Tim reports to you at the head office, given the culture of the firm and the fact that he is the company's President's first cousin and close friend, you realize that you have to handle the situation carefully. Recently, you received an anonymous letter from an employee supervised by Rock requesting you to look into the matter. The country in question does not have any laws governing "acceptable practices" in offices. Past company records indicate that Tim is an effective manager.

3. Of the three processing plants your firm has abroad, one is located on a remote island in a developing country. This particular plant produces products for eight months a year and remains closed during the four winter months to save costs. The road to your plant runs through government land; however, the government has little resources to maintain 6 km of unpaved road and two bridges forming part of it. Your firm has routinely done all the essential repairs for the eight months it is used. Since your plant's opening, several new residents have moved into this part of the island and a number of shops have sprung up as well. The local population is poor and their literacy levels are less than 30% for males and much less for females. During the last two winters, there were half a dozen accidents on the road with vehicles, persons, and livestock slipping off the icy road and falling off the bridges. Last month, one child fell off the bridge into the cold water and died instantly. You are unsure what to do now.

EMPLOYEE INVOLVEMENT PRACTICES

Ottawa's AIT Corp., a developer of technology for reading airline tickets and other travel documents that employs 85, encourages employee participation in various aspects of work from the simple idea of putting a chocolate with a motivational saying on desks every Friday morning to being part of a staff committee that examines key employment issues. It was an employee committee that introduced a well-equipped exercise room and a quiet room with couches for software developers who need a nap during a long day. An open meeting held every Friday morning keeps every employee current on new developments in the company and how it is doing in the marketplace. The result? The company had an annual revenue of $16.5 million in 2001 and boasts an employee turnover below 10% annually in an industry where a 20% change in staff is the norm. The firm was also rated among the top 100 employers in the country in 2001.[19]

Employee involvement practices show variation across organizations. The level of employee involvement in deciding work practices and working conditions may show substantial differences even among similar organizations depending on their organization character (see Chapter 1). Below, we discuss four popular approaches to employee involvement, all of them sharing some common features (Figure 5-10).

AUTONOMOUS WORK GROUPS

Autonomous work groups are teams of workers without a formal, company-appointed supervisor who decide among themselves most matters traditionally handled by a supervisor. These groups typically decide daily work assignments, the use of job rotation, orientation for new employees, training, and production schedules. Some groups even handle recruitment, selection, and discipline. Gaines Pet Foods of the U.S. was an early example of an autonomous work group.

> At the Gaines Pet Food plant, jobs were radically changed. No longer were workers assigned specific tasks in traditional jobs. Instead, teams of workers were held responsible for a group of tasks that previously constituted several separate jobs. For example, a work group was held responsible for packaging and storing the completed products, instead of each worker performing only a few tasks in the packaging and storing operations. Employees were assigned to a work group, not a job. They were free to participate in group decision-making processes. Members developed work schedules, interviewed new employees, performed quality control checks, maintained machinery, and carried out other diverse activities. The workgroup enrichment led to reduced overhead, higher productivity, better product quality, and lower turnover and absenteeism.[20]

In Canada, autonomous work groups have been slower to emerge. In a past survey of 650 Canadian organizations, it was found that one in three responding firms had autonomous work teams.[21] Where implemented, beneficial outcomes generally emerge. When teams are empowered, they have decision-making authority over some

Autonomous work groups are teams of workers without a formal, company-appointed supervisor who together determine how to handle matters traditionally handled by a supervisor.

FIGURE 5-10   Common Features of Employee Involvement Practices

Most employee involvement practices share three common features.

1. Formation of natural work units. Tasks and jobs are usually combined in a logical fashion to provide task identity, greater autonomy, and an improved sense of ownership to the individuals or teams.

2. Vertical loading. The employee or team is now given the responsibility for the whole job—they plan, execute, monitor, and take control actions where necessary. The degree of discretion given to employees shows some variation across firms depending on their unique culture and circumstances; however, the focus is on improving the autonomy and power of the job incumbents. Choice of work methods, scheduling activities, quality control, and even managing budgets are sometimes delegated to the job holders. In turn, they are held accountable for the entire outcome.

3. Knowledge of results. Performance feedback is provided to employees and teams on a regular basis. In some organizations, the job holder is responsible for dealing with clients in which case the feedback is received directly from the user. In other instances, clear performance standards and performance measures are identified to provide feedback to the job holder. Gauges, charts, mechanical instruments, and other devices may also be provided to the job holders to check their own performance without waiting for supervisory feedback.

aspect of their jobs. The authority may extend not only over job context factors (e.g., working conditions) but also job content (e.g., what steps to follow; how to assess quality). Figure 5-11 shows some attributes of successfully empowered teams.

> Pratt & Whitney is one of the many Canadian firms employing autonomous work groups and benefiting from it. In its Halifax plant, which assembles over 100 varieties of expensive castings for aircraft engines, there are no middle managers, virtually, no supervisors or foremen, no fancy work titles, and no executive washrooms. Instead, a team of eight mangers sets overall strategies and plans and several self-managing work teams decide how best to meet them. This has resulted in expensive re-tooling being completed in a matter of hours rather than days, flexible manufacturing plans that can change product mix almost immediately, and a highly satisfied workforce. Employee morale is high and absenteeism is extremely low.[22]

> Steinberg Limited, a grocery store chain with branches in Quebec, Ontario, and New Brunswick, created autonomous and semi-autonomous production groups in its frozen foods distribution centre in Dorval. The frozen foods section outperformed other divisions on various dimensions: its productivity was 35% higher and absenteeism 7% lower than other divisions.[25]

FIGURE 5-11   Successful Team Empowerment

The word "empowerment" has a somewhat different meaning to different writers and practitioners depending on how much delegation of authority and employee involvement occurs.[23] On the one extreme, an empowered team may not only identify team goals (so long as they are in tune with the larger organizational goals and within budgetary constraints) but also implement them and evaluate their success. In such a setting, employees and teams may be encouraged to take risks and act as entrepreneurs within the organization. When defined very narrowly, the empowered team may only have power to execute already developed goals. Whatever the extent of involvement, all successful team empowerment appears to have some common characterisitcs:

1. Clarity of roles: The team is clear about its authority on various matters and responsibility for outcomes.

2. Clarity of goals: All members of the team clearly understand the tasks that needs to be accomplished and the benchmarks for performance outcomes. These benchmarks must be clearly linked to the evaluation of the team performance.

3. Discretionary power: Whatever the level of empowerment, the team has power to act in some area. It is not micromanaged by supervisors.

4. Competence: To be successful, the team members must have competence or relevant skills in the area. If necessary, before empowering a team, members may have to be provided with additional training.

5. Sense of impact: The team members must believe that they and the larger team can, in fact, influence work outcomes. If others in the organization do not listen to the team, over time, the team members may get discouraged.[24]

6. Size: While teams of varying size have proved successful in the past, by and large, teams much larger than seven or eight members may begin to face coordination and communication difficulties. If the teams grow much larger, it may be worthwhile to split them into two or more groups ensuring coordination of their activities.

7. Resources: To successfully achieve the goals, the team must be entrusted with adequate resources including time.

In organizations such as Air Canada, where the self-management team notion was implemented on a more limited basis, the results have still been encouraging.[26]

Website for an example of autonomous work group: *www.ganesha.org/sdwt/*

SOCIO-TECHNICAL SYSTEMS

Socio-technical systems aim to integrate the social and technical elements of a job by restructuring the work, work groups, and relationship between workers and the technologies they use to do their jobs. The systems are based on two premises. First, all organizations consist of the relation between a human and technical system. Rather than suggesting individuals conform to technical requirements, the socio-technical system emphasizes the needs of both the employees and the technology. The second premise is that the emerging socio-technical system in an organization must relate and respond to the surrounding environment. Semi-autonomous work groups capable of self-regulation are considered to be the essential building blocks of an organization that can effectively respond to turbulent environments.

> Among organizations that have implemented some form of socio-technical system are Alcan, AT&T, Digital Equipment, Exxon, General Foods, Shell Canada, and Hewlett Packard.[27]

In all instances implementing a socio-technical system involves more radical changes than just enlarging or enriching a job. Often, it leads to a fundamental change in the way the work is done as the following example shows.

> At a Siemens plant in Karlsruhe, Germany, workers assembling electronics products used to perform simple tasks repeatedly, spending less than one minute on each unit as it moved along a conveyor belt. A job redesign resulted in groups of three to seven employees at well-designed "work islands" where they can avoid boredom by rotating jobs, socializing, and working in cycles of up to twenty minutes rather than a few seconds.[28]

Figure 5-12 provides a comparison of traditional and socio-technical system work designs. Such rearrangement of the social and technical relationships offers workers an opportunity for greater quality of work life. In the past, Germany led the world in such "humanization" of the workplace, where the government even funded 50% of selected work restructuring and retraining efforts of private industry.

The organizational settings where a socio-technical system was implemented in the past vary significantly, from textile mills to petrochemical processing units to pet food plants. In most studies, the implementation of socio-technical systems has been followed by improved performance and quality and reduction of accidents, absenteeism, and turnover.[29]

Socio-technical systems integrate the social and technical elements of a job by restructuring the work, work groups, and relationship between workers and the technologies they use.

CODETERMINATION

An early attempt at worker participation was made in the former West Germany under the name "codetermination." **Codetermination** ushered in a new era of industrial democracy, allowing workers' representatives to discuss and vote on key management decisions that affect them in formal meetings and sessions with company management. This form of industrial democracy has since spread through most of Western Europe. As a result, decisions to close plants or lay off large numbers of

Codetermination allows workers' representatives to discuss and vote on key management decisions that affect them in formal meetings and sessions with company management.

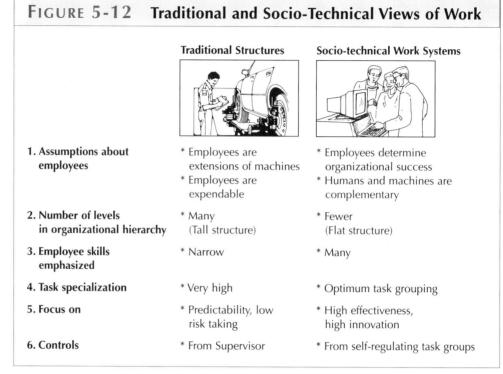

FIGURE 5-12   Traditional and Socio-Technical Views of Work

	Traditional Structures	Socio-technical Work Systems
1. Assumptions about employees	* Employees are extensions of machines * Employees are expendable	* Employees determine organizational success * Humans and machines are complementary
2. Number of levels in organizational hierarchy	* Many (Tall structure)	* Fewer (Flat structure)
3. Employee skills emphasized	* Narrow	* Many
4. Task specialization	* Very high	* Optimum task grouping
5. Focus on	* Predictability, low risk taking	* High effectiveness, high innovation
6. Controls	* From Supervisor	* From self-regulating task groups

Source: H. Das. *Strategic Organizational Design for a Global Economy*. Scarborough, ON: Prentice-Hall, 1998, 140. Reprinted with permission.

workers meet with far more formal resistance in Europe than in North America. On the plus side, European firms are forced to plan more carefully their human resource needs and to seek export markets to offset national economic cycles.

> In Germany, an employer with more than five employees must allow those employees to elect a representative Works Council, which has formal power in matters related to hiring and firing, work scheduling, and changes in work practices. The Works Council also plays a key role in the event of plant closures and work relocation. Past experience indicates that the Council cannot prevent a plant closure, but it can delay one. In larger organizations, workers are entitled by law to elect representatives to the firm's Supervisory Board that has the power to select managers and identify organizational strategy.[30]

Canadian organizations have been very slow in giving such powers to worker representatives. The prevailing argument is that since employee and management interests in matters such as plant relocation and downsizing are naturally opposed, worker participation in management can create inefficiencies and even result in lower effectiveness. The assumption is that "no union will be in favour of losing work for its members. Hence, when such actions are important for increased efficiency and profits of the firm, worker authority in these matters must necessarily be obstructionist."[31]

Such a simple argument ignores the reality that employees have a number of interests (e.g., higher pay, job security, safety for self and others, need for job challenge) and trade-offs are possible. They may be prepared to ship some of the work to low-cost countries if the gains are shared with them or used for expanding facilities elsewhere. However, for such effective labour-management cooperation to emerge, three conditions are necessary. First, there must be trust between the management and the employees. Second, management must be genuinely interested in power sharing and be convinced of the benefits of such a strategy. Finally, the employees must be competent to analyze various decision alternatives and assess consequences. This, in turn, may require continuous upgrading of employee skills. It is only a handful of companies (e.g., the Saturn plant of General Motors) that have attempted this radical form of empowering employees.

INTRAPRENEURIAL UNITS AND TEAMS

More recently, other approaches have been introduced to increase employee involvement at workplace. Some organizations have attempted to develop and maintain intrapreneurs (i.e., internal entrepreneurs) by creating the "right" organizational climate. The **intrapreneurial units** themselves may be individuals, teams, or divisions depending on the firm's unique realities. However, in all instances, some common characteristics can be observed across these highly entrepreneurial work settings.

Intrapreneurial units are entrepreneurial employees, teams, or divisions within an organization that have resources and responsibility to participate in entrepreneurial risk-taking activities.

Tight Link Between Rewards and Performance In no ambiguous terms, the linkage between superior performance and rewards is conveyed to the employees. The rewards themselves may take several forms and include financial incentives or the potential to assume greater responsibility, ever expanding roles and the opportunity to make things happen. Opportunities to be creative and take ownership are also highly valued by many employees working in these organizations and are often provided by the management as rewards for excellence. In any case, the reward systems in these firms continuously and consistently reinforce entrepreneurial behaviours-the employees who take the initiatives and see projects through successfully receive superior rewards to those who wait to be led by others.

Offer of Widespread Opportunity The firm's management takes a genuinely entrepreneurial approach to managing and developing its employees. Big opportunities are provided very early in the employee's career and individuals are expected to "figure it out for themselves."

Risk-Taking Climate The management expects employees to take risks. It is assumed that mistakes will be made. So long as the risks and mistakes do not overly endanger the firm, they are treated as lessons in learning new competencies.

Selection of Human Resources While selecting employees, there is a strong bias in favour of self-driven individuals and initiators of ideas. In several organizations, this translates into a "self-selection process." The end of the hiring process is a session focused on the issue of mutual fit: do you share these overall beliefs of the firm? Do you see a match between where you want to go and where we might be?

Clearly, entrepreneurial form is not easily viable in many businesses. The mission, the prevailing culture, and technological and other constraints might make it unsuitable for a number of organizations unless they are prepared to reinvent themselves. This structure has been most visible in some of the new hi-tech start-ups where entrepreneurial spirit is the key for success and each employee or section is involved in developing a specific process or product. Consider, the case of BMC, a software company.

> BMC, located in Silicon Valley, made its mark in the industry a short time after inception by producing 3270 Super Optimizer, a utility that dramatically improved terminal input and output operations of IBM's popular mainframe computer 3270. BMC's products offered much greater value to customers than any competitive offering. The company's workforce was broadly grouped under two heads: designers and marketing staff. The designers created high-value software to fit specific customer needs, that could

be described and sold over the phone or Internet, but that was difficult to develop and imitate. The marketing staff had to secure, retain, and nourish customers mainly over the phone. The sales staff were energized by the high earnings opportunity of serving key customer accounts correctly; in the case of the designers, the money was good, but creativity and ownership were important rewards too. Above all, each had the individual freedom to do what he or she wanted. The results? The firm claimed one of the highest productivity records in the software industry. Its average gross profit per employee, U.S.$275 000, compared very favourably with peer-company averages of U.S.$110 000 and with Microsoft's U.S.$265 000.[32]

While an entrepreneurial structure may be easier to implement in a software firm such as the above where highly skilled professionals work independently, with appropriate modifications it may be viable in several other settings. For example, one pet foods manufacturer went to great lengths to avoid hierarchical barriers to entrepreneurial efforts:

> Hills Pet Nutrition, Inc., the world's leading supplier of premium pet food, has been widely recognized for its accomplishments. Its management also goes to great lengths to foster a highly results oriented work climate. During a four year period, it doubled the number of products sold, increased sales volume by 70%, cut costs by U.S.$28 million, increased manufacturing productivity by 52%, and reduced down time by 20%. The company goes to considerable lengths to eliminate all barriers that might affect individual performance. For example, the company does not use any hierarchical symbols. The production facility has only one entrance. Everyone dresses the same; there is no employee of the month and no plant manager parking. "If you want a good spot, get there first."[33]

In Canada, work itself is increasingly being organized around teams and processes rather than activities or functions. Over 40% of the respondents in a national survey by the Conference Board of Canada reported use of teams in their workplaces.[34] Self-managed and autonomous work teams are also slowly, but steadily, becoming a normal part of several organizations. Several firms have also been employing teams for improving product and service quality. This will be discussed in the next section.

QUALITY ENHANCEMENT THROUGH EMPLOYEE INVOLVEMENT

Today, many firms have discovered that employee involvement potentially results in higher quality decisions as they have the most accurate and valuable information about the worksite. Other benefits of employee involvement in decision making include improved commitment to the decision, increased speed in implementing the decision, lower communication errors, higher employee satisfaction, and improved employee competencies. These in turn, lead to higher productivity, higher quality, lower absenteeism, and lower employee turnover.

> A cross section of Canadian organizations including CIBC, Xerox Canada, and Vancouver City Savings have found that employee teams result in better quality, lower turnover and absenteeism, and a sense of accomplishment for their workforce.[35]

This section discusses two important approaches to employee involvement that aim to improve overall quality: quality circles and total quality management.

QUALITY CIRCLES

A **quality circle** is a small group of employees drawn from the same work centre, with a common leader, that meets regularly to identify and solve work-related problems, especially, product and process quality issues.[36] Quality circles (QCs), popular in Japan since the 1950s and typically composed of six to ten volunteers, are useful for developing solutions for work- and quality-related problems. Quality circles have become popular in North America since the 1980s. Over 1500 Canadian companies, including B.C. Telephone, General Motors of Canada, Ford Motor Company of Canada, Northern Telecom, McCain's Food, and the Toronto Dominion Bank have instituted QCs in the past.[37]

> Ford Motor Company of Canada in Windsor, Ontario, successfully implemented quality circles, resulting in significant cost savings, quality improvements, reduction in rejects, and improvements in efficiency. "[The employees] love solving problems. Not the big ones, just the little ones; the kind that everybody used to walk by and say "somebody should do something about that."[38]

In-house training usually precedes the creation of quality circles. Supervisors typically get two or three days of training. Most of the time is devoted to discussions of small-group dynamics, leadership skills, and indoctrination in the QC philosophy. About a day of the training is spent on different approaches to problem solving and quality control techniques. Once the supervisor is trained, his or her employees are usually given one day of intensive training, primarily in problem-solving techniques. Part of this training also explains the supervisor's role as the group's discussion leader and the concept of the quality circle. Once the supervisor is trained, he or she, with the help of a facilitator, trains the other "volunteers." The groups also use experts from within and outside the firm when specialized expertise is needed to solve a problem.

Japanese QCs spend upwards of 50% of their meeting time discussing productivity, cost-reduction and safety problems.[39] In Canada, too, these groups often go beyond narrowly defined boundaries of product and service quality. In analyzing problems, QCs use a number of tools, including:

- Graphs and control charts: These include charts and diagrams that show variation in quality or process over a period of time.

- Cause-effect diagrams: These "fishbone" diagrams help analyze problems into causal categories such as machines, human resources, materials, and processes/methods.

- Check sheets: These are used for classifying events into various categories or groups.

- Pareto analysis: An analytical technique used to separate causes of key, recurrent problems from more trivial problems. Figure 5-13 shows an example of a Pareto diagram of repair complaints of a computer manufacturer. Charts like these help prioritize the action needed to improve service quality.

Participation in a quality circle is voluntary except for leaders of the circles, for whom it may or may not be voluntary. Typically, the circle selects problems that are to be analyzed and meets for one hour each week during regular working hours to solve the problems. When the number of quality circles becomes large, the appointment of a coordinator may become necessary. The coordinator's role is to liaise between the facilitators, the quality circles, and other managers.

Usually no monetary or other rewards are given to members of the quality circles; yet past research indicates a positive relationship between implementation of quality circles and improvements in productivity, job satisfaction, and worker morale.

Quality circle is a small group of employees, drawn from the same work centre and with a common leader, that meets regularly to identify and solve work-related problems, especially product and process quality issues.

Websites for articles on quality circles:

www.geocities.com/Heartland/ Acres/3257/quality.html

FIGURE 5-13   An Example of a Pareto Diagram for a Computer Repair Unit

Assume that a computer manufacturer has received a number of complaints about its repair service. A detailed look at the 500 complaints it received in a time period showed that the complaints could be categorized under five major heads:

	# of Complaints
Complaint 1: Even after multiple repairs, the problem was not resolved satisfactorily.	25
Complaint 2: The customer had to take the computer more than once to get the problem resolved.	100
Complaint 3: The repair time was unduly long.	250
Complaint 4: The staff at the repair unit was unfriendly and discourteous.	50
Complaint 5: Reaching the repair unit over the phone was difficult.	75
	500

In a pareto diagram, the above complaint categories are depicted as bar charts whose percentages total to 100 pecent. The causes of the problem can be sorted in increasing importance wth bar height descending from left to right. The pictorial representation shows that Complaint 3 had the highest frequency followed by Complaint 2. Indeed, these two categories accounted for 73% of all complaints, thus indicating where immediate action is needed.

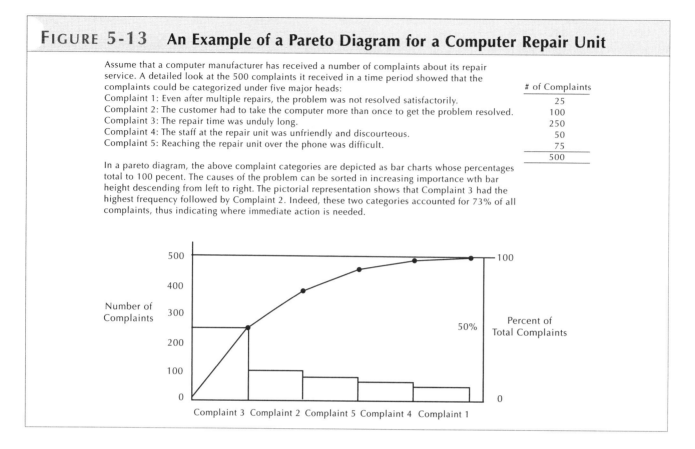

The QC group is permitted to select the problems it wants to tackle. Management may suggest problems of concern to it, but the group decides which ones to select. Ideally, the selection process is made not by democratic vote, but by consensus, in which everyone agrees on the problem to be solved first. (If management has pressing problems to be solved, they can be handled in the same way that problems were resolved before the introduction of quality circles.) This process allows employees to take on problems of concern and inconvenience to them.

> In an agricultural appliances company, employees were frustrated by the lack of power hand tools. They studied the lost production time caused by waiting for tools and showed management how to save more than $30 000 dollars a year by making a $2200 investment in additional hand tools.

The employees at this company did not select this problem to save management money; they did it because of the inconvenience that insufficient tools caused them. The fact that it saved more than a dozen times what it cost to fix is a typical by-product of successful quality circle efforts.

> Lockheed Corporation reported a saving of six dollars for each dollar it spent on implementing a quality circle. Morale went up after the implementation of quality circles, and defects in manufacturing were reported to have declined by two-thirds. Results from organizations such as IBM, Xerox, Digital Equipment, and Westinghouse also indicate beneficial effects of quality circles.[40]

Quality circles, when properly implemented, augment organizational efficiency by promoting adaptation and increasing worker productivity, employee satisfaction, and organizational efficiency.[41] To reap the full benefits of QCs, unconditional management support for the QC process is necessary.[42] When management representatives routinely attended steering committee meetings, QCs were found to solve problems faster.[43]Research indicates that QCs lead to better group cooperation and cohesion, improved group problem solving processes, and reduced grievance and absenteeism rates.[44] However, the exact outcomes may depend on the organizational contexts and culture.[45]

Quality circles may not, however, be applicable to all organizations or to all types of problems in an organization. To be successful, the managers must be willing to allow genuine worker participation.[46] To many Westerners, QCs symbolize Japanese management's commitment to ringi seido; bottom-up management philosophy. Training managers and work supervisors to be ready for genuine worker participation may take time and effort. It should also be noted that QCs can make significant but not fundamental contributions to a company's quality problems. In this sense, they are no substitute for good management and technological upgrading of production processes. QCs are perhaps best thought of as one element of a much wider process known as total quality management, discussed below.

Website of the National Quality Institute: *www.nqi.ca/english/index.html*

TOTAL QUALITY MANAGEMENT

Total quality management (TQM) is a set of organized, well-integrated, and continuous activities involving everyone (that is, both managers and workers) with the objective of improving performance and quality at every level so as to improve customer satisfaction. Different writers have interpreted the term differently but almost everyone agrees that total quality management comprises multi-faceted initiatives directed toward achieving a common goal: excellence in the quality of organizational outputs. It delivers "bottom line"-related improvements in productivity, profitability, and overall competitiveness.[47] The key elements of TQM are summarized in Figure 5-14 and discussed below.

Total quality management (TQM) is a set of organized, well-integrated, and continuous activities involving both managers and workers to improve performance and quality, and therefore, customer satisfaction.

A Corporate Culture of Quality When an organization commits to TQM, there is also a transformation in its corporate quality culture.[48] Quality control is no longer considered the responsibility of the quality control department or quality engineers alone. Rather, it is replaced by the maxim, "quality is everyone's concern." TQM uses a very broad definition of quality-it relates not simply to the products, but also the handling of deliveries, complaints, and maintenance requests, and even how politely, effectively, and timely phone inquiries or other messages are responded to.

Focus on the Customer Most TQM efforts focus on customer satisfaction as their ultimate goal. Thus, TQM firms seek to gain a competitive advantage based on their product and service quality. The "customer" includes not only outsiders who buy the firm's products and services but also internal constituents such as accounts payable staff or managers of other divisions who use the material. Since the quality of the final product is also dependent on the raw materials, TQM also emphasizes the importance of vendor management. Recognizing the value of reliable suppliers, many

---

FIGURE 5-14   Key Elements of Total Quality Management

1. A culture of quality
2. Focus on the customer
3. Focus on continuous improvement
4. Top management support and philosophy
5. Accurate measurement
6. Cross functional teams
7. Open communication
8. Empowerment of employees
9. Training

TQM firms send cross-functional teams to vendor sites to determine whether the supplies will satisfy the needs of different departments such as purchasing, design engineering, and quality control.[49]

Focus on Continuous Improvement

Continuous efforts are made to design and test product prototypes, so the firm can be sure of the quality and robustness of its products. In a sense, TQM is a commitment to never being satisfied! The assumption is that products, processes, and systems can always be improved. In this sense, reaching excellence is not enough. Quality can always be improved. The Japanese notion of Kaizen encourages a circular (rather than linear) notion of quality improvement-the better the results, the more the possibilities for improvement.

> Toronto-based NRI Industries Inc., which turns used tires and waste rubber into parts for the automotive industry is a good example. Although the firm achieved an average of zero defective parts per million (ppm) for four of its five largest customers, its ppm for its fifth largest customer, Daimler-Chrysler, was 28. Though Daimler-Chrysler requires only a ppm of 150, NRI did not stop its quest for improving its quality record.[50]

Top Management Philosophy and Support

The senior managers must be totally committed to improving the organization's quality management practices. As W. Edwards Deming (whose name has become synonymous with strategies to infuse "quality" into manufacturing) noted, top management "support is not enough: action is required."[51] Only management has the power to change "systems," which are responsible for 85% of all defects and poor quality.[52] Some organizations show their management's commitment to TQM by creating the position of a corporate quality officer.[53]

Accurate Measurement

TQM uses a variety of statistical tools to measure every performance dimension. Performance on these dimensions is compared to standards or benchmarks. TQM's measurement bias is best illustrated in benchmarking.[54] Organizational processes are dissected into homogeneous components. A search is then undertaken for industry leaders who excel in each of these processes. One's own performance is evaluated against the industry leader's performance in that area and efforts are taken to improve performance level. Sometimes, firms operating in other industries may be considered for benchmarking purposes.[55] (Benchmarking is discussed in detail in Chapter 3 of this text).

Cross-Functional Teams

Yet another critical element of TQM is cross-functional management. Whether to establish a customer-driven master plan or a daily management plan, the horizontal integration of many people and departments is achieved through cross-functional teams. In some organizations, a Quality Function Deployment team is formed to plan the best products and services. This team has been found to be instrumental in reducing new product introduction time, identifying potential product ideas, and promoting dialogues between suppliers, design and manufacturing engineers, and marketing staff.

Open Communication

Open, direct communication is necessary for successful TQM. Management must have close informational links with various employee teams who must communicate effectively with one another and with the members of other teams.

> Motorola communicates with employees through a variety of media: e-mail, talk sessions, town hall meetings, site publications, and video news magazines. To ensure that these messages are being received, Motorola uses focus groups and surveys employees.[56] Federal Express uses in-house television networks where employees can call in questions to managers.[57]

Empowerment of Employees If the employees' responsibility for quality is to be meaningful, they should have decision-making power on matters that affect quality. This means that almost all TQM efforts imply considerable degree of employee empowerment. Teams are widely used in TQM programs as empowerment tools for solving problems.

> In Japan, when an autoworker spots a quality problem in the production process, the worker has the authority to immediately shut down the entire assembly line. In Canada, such extreme empowerment of workers has been slow to emerge.

Training Most TQM experts stress the importance of training employees in problem-solving tools. It is usually recommended that the training go beyond simple statistical tools for measuring and analyzing quality (such as control charts and pareto analysis) and include advanced problem-analysis tools such as matrix diagrams and affinity diagrams. Managerial personnel should also be trained to use these tools in the strategic analysis of the firm.[58]

Anecdotal accounts of TQM results are encouraging, but mixed. There have been a number of cases of successful implementation of TQM yet there are also several instances where it has not resulted in noticeable improvement in quality or overall organizational effectiveness. The successful cases are found not only in the private sector but also include some public sector organizations or divisions.

> University of Alberta Hospitals, North York, Ontario's school board, and divisions of the province of New Brunswick have, in the past, successfully introduced TQM.[59]

Research studies carried out in Europe and North America have provided some support for the beneficial results of TQM in private, public, and healthcare[60] sectors, but they have also underscored some of the problems in implementing the change.[61] In a survey of 300 electronics companies, 73% of the respondents reported having a total quality program under way. But of these, 63% had failed to improve quality defects by 10%.[62] Unsuccessful TQM efforts are characterized by several common features including a focus on activities (rather than results), simultaneous inclusion of too many programs under TQM effort (rather than small, focused programs), and the use of too many staff consultants (rather than allowing operating managers and employees to take control). However, systematic and controlled research studies on TQM have only just begun to emerge. Part of the reason lies in the magnitude of changes attempted in TQM. TQM time horizons are exceedingly long and controlling the effects of extraneous variables such as international economic trends and technological breakthrough are hard to accomplish.[63]

Finally, the applicability of any employee involvement practice is to be examined in the light of specific organizational conditions. For instance, the complexity of the task involved, the prevalence of shift system, the skill levels of employees involved, and the historical relations between management and the workers may determine the applicability of such systems in a particular situation.[64] Introduction of team management, if not accompanied by changes in other systems (e.g., performance appraisal, compensation) may cause frustration, while lack of trust between management and union may result in the employees viewing all involvement attempts as simple ploys to increase production. One major study examining the TQM and other employment involvement in 14 organizations in eight European Union Member States found that part-time workers, administrative staff and shift staff often receive much less training and communication on company performance matters than full time, permanent, professional, or senior staff.[65] Such limited employee involvement practices may, in fact, increase the gap in information and involvement between employees. To be successful, the management should be truly committed to the notion of employee empowerment (i.e., granting employees power to initiate change and take charge of what they do) and focus on all employees. This is often difficult to implement in practice.

Implications for Practice

1. Employee involvement (EI) help generate a sense of responsibility and ownership of decisions in the minds of employees. To be successful, EI must be more than just a systematic approach; it must become part of the organization's culture and management philosophy.

2. Boring jobs result in employee dissatisfaction and apathy. However, jobs must also achieve larger organizational and societal objectives. When designing jobs, the needs of the organization, the employees, the technology, and the larger environment must be considered.

3. The various jobs and tasks should be planned to maintain and enhance an organization's effectiveness and efficiency.

4. While specialization increases productivity to a level, it also makes the jobs repetitive and boring. To overcome the negative effects of specialization, where feasible, five core job dimensions (variety, autonomy, task identity, task significance, and feedback) should be improved.

5. While employee involvement practices show variation across firms, most of have three underlying principles: forming of natural work units, vertical loading of tasks, and knowledge of performance. Depending on the culture and constraints of the organization, the specific attributes of employee involvement practice should be identified.

6. Two major employee involvement approaches that focus on quality improvement are quality circles and total quality management. Each of these requires specific conditions for its success. A careful examination of the organization and its contexts should precede any effort at implementing EI programs.

Key Terms for Review

Discussion Questions

1. What factors make employee involvement critical today?

2. What key job attributes seem to be linked to a high involvement workforce?

3. What are the characteristics of autonomous work teams? How are they different from the teams seen in typical organizations?

4. Do you think TQM is applicable to all organizations? Why?

Critical Thinking Questions

1. John Brennan, a manager in a construction company had this to say about employee involvement:

   > Employee involvement? That's a lot of gibberish coined by business professors and consultants. Do you think that employees ever consider the interests of their employers over their own? Show me one employee who thinks of the firm first and then about himself. Then, there is also the issue of their ability to participate meaningfully. Even if employee participation is possible in hi-tech and professional occupations, in an industry like ours where most workers are not highly skilled and only looking at the clock waiting for the quit time, it is simply impractical.

   What is your assessment of Brennan's statement? What counter arguments, if any, can you provide?

2. If you were asked to redesign the jobs of workers in a small furniture-making unit in Atlantic Canada employing 20, what factors would you consider? Would your approach be different if you were thinking about redesigning jobs in a downtown Toronto law firm with over 50 lawyers?

3. Consider a work team that you were part of in the past (either within this institution or outside). Were the team members highly involved? Why? What could either you or the leader have done to improve involvement of the team members?

4. Assume that the educational institution where you are currently enrolled as a student has decided to adopt TQM in its course delivery. What aspects of its operations will have to undergo changes?

Web Research

Select two countries or two industries within a country. Conduct an Internet search to find out the type and frequency of employee involvement programs in the countries of your choice. Report a summary of your findings to the class. Hint: You may begin your search by visiting the websites of newspapers, professional bodies (like human resource associations), management journals and magazines, or research agencies (such as the Conference Board of Canada or Fraser Institute).

CASE INCIDENT

Atlantic Computers[1]

When Mike Osborn started Atlantic Computers in 1988, it was a small firm catering to the special needs of a few large clients. Osborn found a market niche that had not been filled by large mainframe computer manufacturers or small personal computer (PC) firms: medium-sized firms who wanted an "organization-wide system" that was easily accessible to all employees through their PCs, but without the exorbitant cost of brand name mainframe manufacturers. His initial clientele included small schools, town agencies, and organizations employing 50 people or less. Soon, his firm's reputation for low prices and moderately high quality (especially in relation to price) resulted in more organizations joining his client list. His fast on-site service also appealed to organizations located in remote towns of Nova Scotia and New Brunswick that had found servicing to be a problem with large brand name companies. Osborn's products, sold under the brand name TriStar, became associated with inexpensiveness and fast service.

In 1991, he began manufacturing PCs to take advantage of his growing reputation in the market. In the early 1990s, the reduction in prices of fast processors such as the 486 and Pentium chips made it possible to design powerful PCs that could do the work of the earlier mainframe computers. What began as a modest PC operation in the early 1990s grew rapidly. In the beginning of the new millennium, Osborn had employed over 15 workers.

Then came the market crash in the hi-tech industry in mid-2000. While, the brunt of the losses was faced by firms specializing in wireless and Internet related products, the PC market was also down significantly. Established firms like Dell, and Compaq were cutting prices for their products almost on a weekly basis. The market for PCs also seemed to be approaching maturity. Osborn had to cut his labour force by almost half and continuously monitor production and material costs. Osborn recognized that his success, and even survival, was dependent on cost control. A small assembler like Osborn could hope to survive only by offering higher value than brand name manufacturers at lower prices.

Currently, Osborn's PC assembly section consists of eight workers in two shifts of four people. In the past,

Osborn left procedure and methods to each workgroup, as long as production orders were filled on time. The workers in the PC assembly section had arranged their work area in a diamond shape (see Figure A). This permitted them to converse with each other and to keep informed of each other's productivity and problems. The workers in each team not only achieved high production standards but also got along well outside of work, going bowling and out for Saturday evening beer sessions. Each worker had all the tools and equipment at his or her workstation to produce a complete PC. Two workers worked on the main drives and monitor assembly, while the other two worked on CD-ROMs, back-up tape drives, and sound and videographics systems. Almost every day, they traded their jobs to decrease monotony. On average, each shift was able to assemble three computers a day, considered impressive given the complexity of the product involved. The two shifts also competed with each other (especially when faced with tight deadlines in December and March) and occasionally produced four computers a day: often working extra hours without receiving overtime pay.

When a consultant told Mike Osborn that a new working system could improve his unit's productivity and help him cut costs, Mike was somewhat sceptical. Through the use of elaborate time and motion studies, the consultant was able to show that by a simple rearrangement of the plant, Mike would be able to increase production to four computers a day, and possibly to five. The layout suggested by the consultant is shown in Figure B. The consultant pointed out that the physical layout of the workplace did not facilitate the efficient flow of components. Further, the packaging department was located at a corner of the plant (see Figure A), quite far from where the final product emerged. The consultant suggested that the packaging department be brought in line with the assembly and that work should proceed in a linear fashion.

One long weekend, the plant was shut down and the machines reassembled according to the consultant's specifications. After three weeks, Osborn noted that productivity in the PC assembly section had declined rather than

(continued)

FIGURE A   Initial Layout of Atlantic Computers' PC Assembly

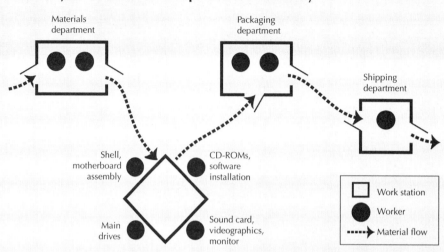

increased. Instead of producing four computers, the day's production was typically only three with some days as low as two. When Osborn asked the workers why, they could not articulate the reason for poorer performance. They could only tell him "something has changed which makes it harder to work now."

Osborn waited another two weeks to see whether any improvements occurred. Finding none, he raised the problem with the consultant, who responded, "I see no obvious reason for this decline. I haven't changed any technical procedures; I only altered the flow of the material, which does not constitute any problem. In fact, the workers themselves admit that the flow of material is not the problem. The group is composed of the same people doing the same work. How can a better layout lead to poorer results? I believe the

workers have slacked off on purpose to get your attention. This is maybe their way of trying to get a raise. Give them a pay raise and you will see a major change in performance!"

Questions

1. *What, in your assessment, led to the present outcomes?*

2. *What can Osborn do now to remedy the situation? Is a pay raise the answer?*

---

[1] Adapted from H. Das. *Strategic Organizational Design for a Global Economy*. Scarborough, ON: Prentice-Hall, 1998, 151–154. Reprinted with permission.

FIGURE B   Rearranged Layout of Atlantic Computers' PC Assembly

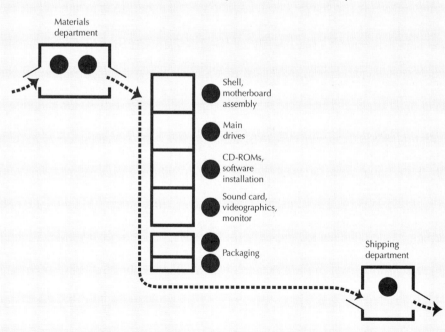

CASE

Founded in 1963, Kanata Food Outlets Limited (KFO) is a Canadian public company focused on retail food service business. It is one of the largest integrated food service companies in North America that prepares and distributes food to the consumers through various brand name restaurants, catering operations, and other food outlets. It also holds majority stock in two firms: The Sizzling Cup, a coffee chain, and Bean and Wine, a chain of restaurants that primarily focuses on the emerging vegetarian customer market. A summary of the firm's financial picture for the current year and last year are shown in Figure 1.

The firm has four major chains of restaurants and operational units: Northern Delights, Texan Delights, Traveller Delights, and Service Delights. Almost 75% of the chain restaurants are operated by franchisees.

Northern Delights is a full-service restaurant chain in Canada and the northeastern U.S. specializing in rotisserie chicken, ribs, and steak. It also serves seafood to a limited extent. This year, the chain served over 25 million customers in its 115 restaurants bringing in a total of $340 million sales.

Texan Delights focuses on highly seasoned, spicy steaks, Mexican dishes, and pasta. It generated over $43 million sales through its 30 restaurants.

Traveller Delights is aimed at the traveller and fast food customer. A leading quick service restaurant chain, most of the units are located close to highways, train stations, airports, and large hotels. Hamburgers, chicken burgers, chicken fingers, and fish sandwiches are offered at competitive prices and to suit individual customer tastes. For example, unlike McDonald's or Burger King, the firm offers three kinds of fish sandwiches-not to mention the half a dozen types of hamburgers and chicken burgers. Among the four divisions, perhaps, Traveller Delights faces the greatest competitive challenges. The fast food sector is dominated by multinationals like McDonald's, Wendy's and Burger King. Within Canada, there are other chains like the Harvey's and Dairy Queen. Increasingly, other firms like Tim Horton's and Subway, have been taking away a portion of the market that traditionally went to fast food chains. Through its 200 restaurants, Traveller Delights served over 25 million customers last year bringing in about $196 million in sales.

Service Delights, a new division started about five years ago has already made a name for the quality of its airline catering. It serves food on 23 domestic and international airlines in the world and trains in two European countries. The services are offered through the dozen flight and railway kitchens employing over 900 and serving over 10 million meals a year. The division brought in more than $177 million in revenue this year.

The present decision problem deals with Northern Delights division of the firm.

FIGURE 1   Financial Performance of KFO

	This year	Last year
	(in thousands of dollars except for share data)	
Gross revenue	732 849	707 728
EBITDA	75 299	68 399
EBIT	48 914	43 131
Earnings before unusual items such as sale of business	25 440	20 670
Net earnings	6 741	17 206
Dividends	0.16	0.13
Number of shares outstanding	53 000	53 000
Shareholders' equity	159 000	106 000

NORTHERN DELIGHTS

Northern Delights' efforts at brand imaging and branding paid off in the past by its above average industry growth rates. The company continuously monitored each restaurant's performance and renovated or closed underperforming units depending on market potential in the area. For example, this year, the company opened four new restaurants while closing six under-performing ones. (See Figure 2 for details of the number of restaurants). The company takes pride in its value-focused, guest-experience driven initiatives, and has consistently increased its market share in core markets. Some of the other relevant operating details include:

- Abode, the upbeat bar introduced in about 20% of the restaurants, has been extremely successful. The bar is particularly popular with younger customers.

- More recently, the firm has introduced several new menus with lighter fare and less fat content to attract younger and more health conscious customers.

- Delivery sales offer a significant growth opportunity and have contributed to 12% of the total system sales. Two years ago, delivery was only 2% of the total sales. It is expected that in the next three years, delivery will account for almost one-fifth of total restaurant sales, especially in larger centres.

- The firm continuously employs mystery shoppers and customer surveys to monitor and benchmark quality, service, and cleanliness.

From its inception, the management of Northern Delights recognized that the firm's survival and success depended on its employees. It was only a committed work-

(continued)

force that could execute the corporate mission and plans. The firm spent considerable effort and money hiring the right employees (called "associates"), training them, and rewarding them. The firm is proud of the fact that its wages are among the highest in the industry.

So, when a recent customer survey indicated that the overall service quality was barely "very good " (a rating of 3.9 on a 5-point scale of poor (=1), fair, good, very good, and excellent), the management was worried. Clearly, this was a major decline from the 4.2 rating the chain received in last year's survey. Indeed, the firm had hoped to get a rating of 4.5 this year. There were no major changes introduced in the past year and the wages and benefits offered by the firm had been at par or better than the best in the industry.

Intrigued, the management hired a consulting firm to conduct an employee survey. The firm selected a statistically valid sample of 640 employees and conducted a survey of employee attitudes. A 10-item questionnaire, which the consultant had used in the past with acceptable reliability and validity, was used to collect employee attitudes on a variety of matters. All items were scored on a five-point scale (1=very low or poor and 5=very high or excellent). The higher the score on an item, the more positive the response.

The consultant found differences in scores across job categories (Figure 3). Subsequent data analysis by the firm showed differences across different groups of employees formed on the basis of their gender, age, and work experience. The results of the analysis are shown in Figure 4.

FIGURE 2   Number of Northern Delights Restaurants

	This year	Last year
Company owned and operated	27	19
Company owned and franchise operated	52	55
Franchisee owned and operated	36	39
Total	115	113

FIGURE 3   Summary of Survey Results Classified by Job Categories

	Job Category (n=630)		
Questionnaire Item	Cooks (n=208)	Service Staff (n=220)	Maintenance Staff (n=202)
1. My supervisor helps resolve work problems.	4.3	4.29	3.6
2. I get regular feedback from my supervisor.	3.7	4.15	4.4
3. I enjoy the variety of duties this job provides.	4.1	4.13	3.3
4. I find the job challenging.	3.9	4.04	3.1
5. I am treated with respect by my supervisor and co-workers.	4.0	4.27	3.3
6. I believe that I have a future in this firm.	3.8	4.17	3.4
7. My suggestions are taken seriously by the management.	3.9	4.16	3.6
8. I am proud to say that I work for Northern Delights.	3.8	4.01	3.7
9. The compensation and benefits I receive are adequate.	4.1	4.36	4.2
10. Overall, I like my job.	3.8	4.14	3.5

(continued)

FIGURE 4   Survey Results Classified by Employee Categories

Code for employee categories:
Gender: M=Male (n=260); F=Female (n=370)
Age: Y=30 years or younger (n=435); O=31 years or older (n=195)
Length of service: S=Less than 5 years (n=405); L= 5 years or more (n=225)

| Questionnaire Item | Employee Category (n=630) | | | | | |
| | Gender | | Age | | Length of Service | |
	M	F	Y	O	S	L
1. My supervisor helps resolve work problems.	4.6	3.7	4.3	3.6	4.2	3.8
2. I get regular feedback from my supervisor.	4.2	4.0	4.2	3.8	4.1	4.1
3. I enjoy the variety of duties this job provides.	3.5	4.1	3.7	4.2	3.7	4.1
4. I find the job challenging.	3.4	3.9	3.8	3.5	4.0	3.1
5. I am treated with respect by my supervisor and co-workers.	4.4	3.5	3.9	3.8	3.9	3.9
6. I believe that I have a future in this firm.	3.8	3.8	3.8	3.8	3.8	3.8
7. My suggestions are taken seriously by the management.	4.6	3.4	3.7	4.3	3.7	4.3
8. I am proud to say that I work for Northern Delights.	3.9	3.8	3.6	4.4	3.7	4.1
9. The compensation and benefits I receive are adequate.	4.4	4.1	4.4	3.8	4.2	4.3
10.Overall, I like my job.	4.0	3.7	3.7	4.1	3.6	4.2

Questions

1. What conclusions can you form on the basis of the survey results, assuming that the survey was properly conducted?

2. What recommendations can be made to the management?

---

[1] Case prepared by Professor H. Das, Department of Management, Saint Mary's University. All rights reserved by the author.

PART 4

PERFORMANCE ASSESSMENT

Performance assessments not only provide feedback to employees but also are critical for identifying training needs and compensating employees. However, to be useful, all critical dimensions of job performance should be measured validly and on a timely basis. This part introduces the important task of assessing performance and the popular tools used for this purpose.

6 ASSESSING INDIVIDUAL AND TEAM PERFORMANCE

It seems quite probable, as we continue to question our current practices, that most systems of performance appraisals...will be unmasked as detriment to human spirit.[1]

Dick Richards

CHAPTER OBJECTIVES

After studying this chapter, you should be able to:

- Define the attributes of an effective performance appraisal system

- Discuss the strengths and limitations of popular individual appraisal systems

- Examine popular approaches to assess performance of employees working in groups

- Outline an approach to assessing performance that attempts to minimize errors and biases

With over $234 billion in assets, $1.4 billion in annual revenues and over 42 000 employees working in over 50 countries, Scotiabank group is one of North America's premier financial institutions and has been rated as one of the best employers in Canada. In part, the bank's success is attributable to its performance management system. Scotiabank's performance management program is extensive. The process begins on the first day of employment with a multimedia orientation program that highlights the bank's history, culture, operations, and customers. During annual performance reviews, employees conduct self-assessments, identify goals for the upcoming year, and receive feedback and support for these goals. There are other methods of recognition for their contributions and achievements. Throughout the year, regular meetings encourage open communication between employees and their supervisors. In addition, there are several opportunities for two-way communication between an employee and the organization on performance-related matters. A regular employee survey ("Viewpoint") solicits feedback on management, bank policies, working conditions, and programs. The bank has a toll-free telephone service ("Team voice") that allows employees to provide anonymous feedback in both official languages. Feedback from the employees is included as a regular agenda item in executive meetings. Employees also provide feedback on managerial performance through a 360-degree survey that collects anonymous ratings from supervisors, peers, and internal customers.[2]

By no means is Scotiabank's elaborate performance management system typical. In many Canadian firms, performance appraisal is a yearly or semi-annual exercise that is not well integrated into the firm's overall organizational philosophy, strategy, or workforce culture. However, more and more Canadian organizations are recognizing the vital role of effective performance management systems in their success and even survival. When performance is below standard, actions have to be taken to bring it up; employees who perform at standard levels or above have to be encouraged to strive continually for growth and improvement (Figure 6-1).

This chapter introduces popular approaches in assessing the performance of individual employees and teams. After discussing some of the limitations of existing systems, this chapter provides an alternate approach to designing effective performance management systems. To do this, we first need to identify the attributes of an effective performance management system.

ATTRIBUTES OF EFFECTIVE APPRAISAL SYSTEMS

The word "apprise" originates from the Latin word pretiare, meaning to value. Performance appraisal, thus, is the process by which we evaluate, judge, or estimate the value of someone's performance. For the purpose of the present discussion, performance appraisal may be simply defined as the process of evaluating an individual's or a group's performance after a specified period of time or after completion of a specific task cycle or set of duties. There are two interrelated aspects of performance appraisal:

- An appraisal method consisting of the approach taken to evaluate an employee's or team's performance, usually through special scales or a processes. This is the most obvious aspect of the system and is instantly recognized by all employees.

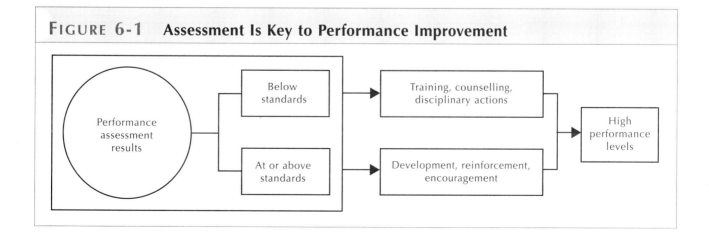

FIGURE 6-1 Assessment Is Key to Performance Improvement

- An appraisal system consisting of interlocking processes that are linked to the larger human resource management practices of the firm. The system should provide for timely conduct of the appraisal, recording the results accurately and making it available for making human resource decisions like training, compensation, transfer, and development of employees. The system also focuses on improving appraisal procedures (including training of supervisors and employees) in the process.

A well-designed appraisal system makes the results synergistic-that is, the outcomes of the system are larger than the sum of its parts. For this to occur, the various elements of the appraisal system should be well integrated and work smoothly together.

ELEMENTS OF AN APPRAISAL SYSTEM

Figure 6-2 shows the four key elements of a typical appraisal system: performance criteria, performance standards, performance assessment, and use of the appraisal information for employee feedback and human resource decisions.

Performance criteria are indicators of successful job performance.

Performance Criteria **Performance criteria** are indicators of successful job performance.

> Among the various criteria used to evaluate a call centre operator's performance are use of company procedures (e.g., correctly communicating prices and service policies, following company rules and regulations), pleasant phone manners (speaking clearly and courteously, staying calm), and call-placement accuracy.

If performance criteria are not job-related, the evaluation can lead to inaccurate or biased results. Not only is performance feedback distorted, but also, errors in employee records can lead to incorrect human resource decisions and even legal problems.

> All employees of a large organization were rated twice a year and the ratings were used for promotion, employee development, and compensation decisions. However, most of the questions in the ratings form referred to personality attributes such as ambition, and co-operation which had little direct relationship with day-to-day job performance of

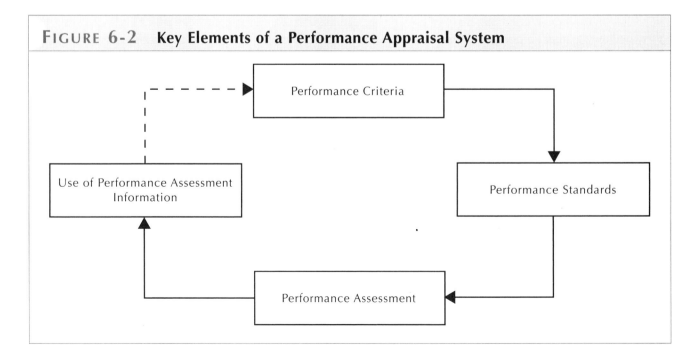

FIGURE 6-2   Key Elements of a Performance Appraisal System

most individuals. Several employees who were denied promotions and raises filed charges against the firm citing racial and sexual discrimination. The firm was unable to prove that the performance measures were job relevant and valid and subsequently lost the case.

In the above instance, problems arose because the performance criteria employed were personality traits that had only a weak relationship with actual job performance or success. Since a performance appraisal form is a legal document, only job relevant performance criteria should be employed to avoid potential court challenges by employees who lost a job or an opportunity for advancement as a result of inadequate job performance. It is the employer's responsibility to show that the performance criteria were valid and used consistently. Problems emerging from irrelevant criteria can be avoided if performance standards are established by a thorough job analysis and recorded in a job description. Figure 6-3 lists some performance criteria used by one secondary school to assess teachers.

Website on performance measures: *www.zigonperf.com/resources/pmnews.html*

Performance Standards Performance evaluation requires **performance standards** or benchmarks against which performance is measured. Even if valid performance criteria are being used, the evaluation may be invalid if the standards are inappropriate. Standards cannot be set arbitrarily. Typically, standards are established after a careful examination of jobs, tasks, and work procedures as discussed in Chapter 3. However, even validly established performance standards may have to be changed over time to reflect technological or environmental changes.

Performance standards are benchmarks against which an individual employee's or team's performance is measured.

> Consider the work of a checkout clerk or a typist. The arrival of electronic scanners, sophisticated computer programs, and data analysis procedures has made it necessary for employees to possess new skills and meet new performance standards compared to those employed even a decade ago.

Performance standards should reflect organizational and employee goals, current technological constraints, and working conditions. In the case of some jobs, standards may be unclear or lacking, in which case standards may have to be developed from observation of the job or after discussion with the job incumbent and immediate supervisor.

Performance Assessment The extent to which an employee or team meets the performance standards is typically evaluated using some sort of form, checklist, or other instrument. A variety of ratings scales, checklists, and other assessment tools and techniques are currently available. The more popular of these will be discussed in the next section. These assessment techniques can be divided into two general categories: direct or indirect.

FIGURE 6-3   Criteria Used by One Secondary School to Assess Teacher Performance

1. Plan and delivery of course content
2. Management of the classroom
3. Student performance assessment
4. Implementation of administrative policies and procedures
5. Relationship with students outside class
6. Liaison with parents
7. Self and professional development

Direct assessment occurs when the rater actually sees the performance.

Indirect assessment occurs when the rater can evaluate only substitutes for actual performance.

Direct assessment occurs when the rater actually sees the performance. **Indirect assessment** occurs when the rater can only evaluate substitutes for actual performance.

> A supervisor's monitoring of an operator's calls is direct observation. A written test evaluating knowldege of the company's procedures for handling emergency calls is indirect observation.

Indirect observations are usually less accurate because they evaluate substitutes or "constructs" for actual performance. Since constructs are not exactly the same as actual performance, they may lead to errors.

> In the above instance, the call operator may exhibit knowledge of correctly handling emergency calls, yet may not actually demonstrate these required behaviours when occasion demands. It is also possible that fast readers would score better in a written test even if their on-the-job behaviour is no different from slower readers.

Verifiable performance measures are indicators of job performance that can be observed and checked by others.

Performance assessment may also be verifiable or non-verifiable. **Verifiable performance measures** are indicators of job performance that can be observed and checked by others.

> If two supervisors monitor an operator's calls, they can count the number of misdialed ones. The results are more objective since each supervisor gets the same call-placement accuracy percentage.

Non-verifiable performance measures are those ratings that cannot be seen or checked by others.

Usually, verifiable measures are quantitative. They typically include units produced, scrap rates, number of computational errors, number of customer complaints, and so on. **Non-verifiable performance measures** are those ratings that cannot be seen or checked by others. Usually, such measures are the rater's personal opinions and are more susceptible to biases and inaccurate measurements.

Performance appraisal is the process of evaluating an individual's or a group's performance after a specified period of time or completion of a specific task cycle or set of duties.

Use of Appraisal Information
In most work organizations, **performance appraisal** procedures affect the employees' sense of who they are and what they can be. Employee competence, key job attitudes, and work-related self-concept are often shaped by the existing performance appraisal system, making it an important aspect of the organizational culture and management style. This means that performance appraisal information must be carefully monitored, stored, and retrieved for making important human resource decisions such as employee training and development, compensation, promotion, placing, and job redesign. When this linkage is effective, performance improvement, more equitable compensation systems, timely identification of training and development needs, avoidance of discriminatory job practices, and career development of employees occur (Figure 6-4). In contrast, devoid of an effective appraisal system, promotions, transfers, and other staffing decisions are subject to trial and error. In addition, human resource development suffers in the absence of systematic performance feedback.

The use of performance appraisal results must also meet all legal requirements. It is a legal requirement that a reasonable timeframe be set for performance improvement. The specific timeframe depends on the job.

> While it may be reasonable to expect an office clerk to improve performance within a few weeks or months, it may take a manager a year or more to show improvement.

Despite their importance, performance appraisal systems in many organizations have not been very effective or popular with employees. A survey by the Society of Human Resource Management found that more than 90% of appraisal systems were not successful.[3] Another survey found that most employers expressed "overwhelming" dissatisfaction with their performance management systems.[4] In a survey by Industry Week magazine, only 18% of respondents considered their performance

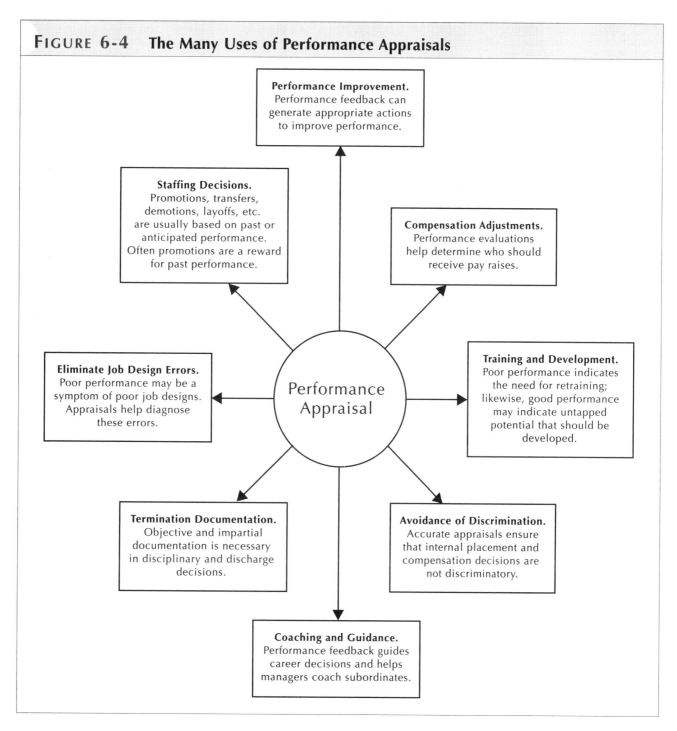

FIGURE 6-4   The Many Uses of Performance Appraisals

Performance Improvement. Performance feedback can generate appropriate actions to improve performance.

Staffing Decisions. Promotions, transfers, demotions, layoffs, etc. are usually based on past or anticipated performance. Often promotions are a reward for past performance.

Compensation Adjustments. Performance evaluations help determine who should receive pay raises.

Eliminate Job Design Errors. Poor performance may be a symptom of poor job designs. Appraisals help diagnose these errors.

Performance Appraisal

Training and Development. Poor performance indicates the need for retraining; likewise, good performance may indicate untapped potential that should be developed.

Termination Documentation. Objective and impartial documentation is necessary in disciplinary and discharge decisions.

Avoidance of Discrimination. Accurate appraisals ensure that internal placement and compensation decisions are not discriminatory.

Coaching and Guidance. Performance feedback guides career decisions and helps managers coach subordinates.

reviews to be accurate—nearly 50% called them "second guessing sessions."[5] Given such a discouraging state of affairs, the total abolition of performance appraisal systems has been suggested since, "taken as a whole, the research decidedly demonstrates that appraisals are ineffective and cause a spate of undesirable, unintended effects."[6]

Why are so many appraisal systems ineffective or unpopular with employees? There is no simple answer. Effective appraisal systems tend to have a number of characteristics. If one or more of these characteristics are missing, the employee and supervisor may find apathy, frustration, and alienation from the system. Below, the characteristics of effective appraisal systems are discussed.

Focus on Small Business:

Treating Your Employees Right

Small firms do not have the resources, time, or systems necessary to implement complex appraisal procedures. Yet, employees with high levels of job commitment are critical for their success. How can a small firm achieve high employee commitment and performance without installing elaborate measurement systems and bureaucratic paperwork?

The answer is contained in two principles-at least according to the late Ewing Marion Kauffman, who founded Marion Labs with U.S.$5000 capital in 1950 in the basement of his home (the company later grew into Marion, Merrell Dow Inc. and has over U.S.$2.5 billion in sales)[7]. First, treat others as you would like to be treated, and second, share the wealth that is created with all those who contributed to its creation. Simple as they may sound, these principles guided (and continue to guide) the firm's operating philosophy.

What are some things you can do to inspire and energize your employees and teams?

1. Treat them with respect, as equals and not simply as paid service personnel who are there to "sell" their services for a number of hours for a price. Take their ideas and suggestions seriously. After all, they know more about the problems of the tasks they are responsible for than anyone else.

2. Set clear performance expectations. These should be easy to understand and measure and should be directly related to employee efforts—not overly affected by environmental or other situational factors.

3. Measure employee performance and reward everyone who meets or exceed expectations.

4. Do not create too many rank differences in benefit programs. After all, each individual has a meaningful contribution to make to the firm (other wise, you would not hire the person in the first place!). People should be judged on the basis of their performance, not on their position in the hierarchy. This is a powerful incentive for performance improvement.

5. Do not punish employees for legitimate innovation or risk-taking behaviour. Do not evaluate ideas before they are elaborated and communicated.

6. Do not tolerate mediocrity. Repeatedly convey your goals, expectations, and future challenges. Offer training or counselling if the performance gap is attributable to skill or communication deficiencies.

7. Continuously re-assess your performance management system and leadership style. As times change, employee needs change, requiring new approaches and new styles of leadership. A senior worker is likely to need less of your monitoring than a person just hired.

CHARATERISTICS OF EFFECTIVE APPRAISAL SYSTEMS

To be effective, an appraisal system must possess the eight characteristics (Figure 6-5) discussed in more detail in the following sections.

Validity Validity refers to the legitimacy or correctness of the inferences that are drawn from a set of measurements or other specific procedures. Figure 6-6 describes several types of validity. To be valid, the assessment must relate to job performance or other relevant criterion (e.g., potential for promotion). As discussed in an earlier section, invalid (job-irrelevant) criteria lead to erroneous conclusions. Different approaches can be used to assess a measures validity.

> Results are the most valid criteria since they tend to be objective. It would be difficult, for example, to question the relevance of a 15% increase in profits when conducting a performance assessment of a manager in charge of a department.

Reliability is closely related to validity. **Reliability** refers to the consistency in measurements. If the same rater gives two totally different ratings for the same employee even over a short period (say, a week), then the assessment process lacks reliability. Reliability, thus, is the degree to which the measurements are free from

Validity refers to the legitimacy or correctness of the inferences that are drawn from a set of measurements or other specific procedures.

Reliability is the degree to which the measurements are free from random measurement errors.

FIGURE 6-5 Characteristics of Effective Appraisal Systems

The acronym "VITALISE" summarizes the attributes of effective appraisal systems. The question to evaluate the presence of each dimension is listed next to it.

Validity: Are the performance measures and instruments used valid?

Involvement: Did all persons concerned and affected by the system have input at the system design stage?

Training: Did all persons concerned (raters as well as ratees) receive training in the system before it was implemented?

Acceptable standards and targets: Are the performance standards and targets well communicated to job incumbents and accepted by them?

Linked to other systems: Do the appraisals have consequences especially on matters such as job placement, rewards, and career growth of job incumbents?

Input into appraisals: Do the job incumbents get an opportunity to participate in the evaluation process and offer their input?

Sources of information: Are different assessors and sources of information employed to improve overall accuracy and checked for consistency?

Employee feedback: Do the job incumbents receive valid and timely feedback on their performance with guidance to improve the same in the future?

---

random measurement errors. It is a basic minimum for a valid measure but does not, by itself, ensure validity. In other words, a measure may be reliable yet not valid; however, an unreliable measure cannot validly reflect performance.

> Consider a clock that is consistently five minutes fast. It is reliable since it always systematically adds five minutes to the actual time. However, it is not valid, since it is not showing the correct time.

Reliability, although highly desirable, is difficult to achieve in an organizational setting because of different raters, different instruments, and changing work environments. By using more verifiable and direct measurements, reliability can be enhanced (Figure 6-7). Even here, high reliability does not guarantee validity.

Involvement Employee participation in the development of performance criteria, appraisal instruments, and the appraisal system increases significantly the probability of acceptance of the system by both supervisors and employees. It gives employees the feeling of ownership. While employees hired after a system has been installed will not have had input into it, the knowledge that it was developed with their colleagues makes it more acceptable.

Training Raters need to be trained in observation techniques and **categorization** skills (e.g., the use of diaries or critical incidents). Raters also have to be familiar with the many potential rating errors (Figure 6-8) and the ways to minimize them. Rater training has been shown to be very effective in reducing such errors. To ensure that a performance appraisal system is well understood by employees and accepted, ratee training should also be implemented. The ratee training could be part of the process of developing the performance appraisal system, thereby serving two purposes.

Acceptable Standards and Targets If the supervisors unilaterally set performance standards, then they become "management standards" and receive little employee commitment. This does not mean that employees should set their own performance standards, but rather that the standards should be set in consultation with the employees to gain their commitment. A thorough job and task analysis coupled

Categorization is the process of classifying and storing data.

Websites on Performance Management:
www.p-management.com
www.work911.com
www.hr-guide.com

FIGURE 6-6   The Many Faces of Validity

Content Validity. If the measures include reasonable samples of skills, competencies, and outcomes related to the job, the assessment is judged as content valid. For example, if a supervisor assesses the performance of a salesperson by simply focusing on sales volume and tardiness, the assessment may not be content valid since it omits important aspects of job performance such as quality of customer service and merchandise display.

Criterion-related Validity. Are the competencies and skills assessed strongly related to criteria such as job performance and potential? If the answer is yes, then they have criterion-related validity. Of course, the criterion used must be legitimate and a fair representation of job success. Simply because the assessments are related to a criterion or a set of criteria does not make them valid unless the criteria used are relevant in the first place. For example, if a vehicle operator's performance assessment is simply related to the speed of operating the vehicle and not the safety (an important criterion), the assessment may still be considered invalid.

Predictive Validity. If the performance assessments can predict future performance and potential, they score high on predictive validity. Such valid assessments are critical for training and development of employees—especially, in the case of poor performers, valid assessments enable the organization to initiate remedial training programs which improve their future performance. In this context, the still widely used personality traits, such as intelligence, may be of questionable value for performance assessment. They are characteristics the employee brings to the job, not a job outcome. Even though traits may relate to performance—an intelligent employee will probably do better than a less intelligent one—this does not justify their use as sole performance measures in several instances.[8]

Concurrent Validity. To be concurrently valid, the measures used should be able to separate current high and low performing employees. For example, an attribute (e.g., clean work table) does not separate good performers from poor performers (that is to say, there are several high and low performers who don't keep their work tables clean); yet many supervisors erroneously consider a neat table as an indicator of superior performance.

Construct Validity. Construct validity is the degree to which a set of measures or an assessment procedure captures the essence of an abstract concept. Several constructs such as creativity, job commitment, and organizational citizenship are popular in the appraisal context today, yet, very few organizations can offer supporting data validating the construct being measured. Establishing construct validity is a complex process often necessitating data collection over an extended period of time and knowledge of sophisticated data analysis tools.

Face Validity. Face validity is high when the assessments appear to be valid even on a superficial examination by all concerned. While this is essentially a non-scientific approach to establishing validity, it is still important in practice, since measures not understood or considered credible by managers and employees may not be accepted by them. A practical system is one that, first of all, is understood by evaluators and employees; a complicated, impractical approach may cause resentment and nonuse. The confusion can lead to inaccuracies that reduce the effectiveness of the appraisal.

FIGURE 6-7   Types and Reliability of Performance Measures

Whether performance measures are variable	Whether performance measures are seen by the assessor	
	Direct	*Indirect*
Verifiable	High reliability	Moderate reliability
Non-verifiable	Moderate reliability	Poor reliability

with a review of available resources and work environments should precede setting of performance standards.

When establishing performance standards, it is critical to look at the interdependence among jobs and tasks (see Chapter 3). When job incumbents have to rely on the contributions or co-operation of their colleagues, they should not be held responsible for job outcomes that are out of their control. It is the responsibility of the manager, as a coach and counsellor, to set goals that are seen as achievable by the employee; otherwise, the employee will be discouraged, often resulting in a self-fulfilling prophecy: "That's too high for me, I can't do it." In some instances, it may be

Website detailing ten managerial errors in conducting performance appraisals: *www.work911.com/ performance/particles/ stupman.htm*

FIGURE 6-8   Appraisal Errors and Biases

Leniency error denotes the tendency to give very generous ratings to everyone. Most likely to occur when performance standards are very vague and organization has a highly political climate (the supervisor wants his or her people to advance).

Severity or Strictness error is the opposite of leniency error and occurs when the raters are too harsh on the ratees. This is again common when performance standards are vague. The tendency to rate others harshly is often linked to the type of ratings the rater receives from others—thus, supervisors who have received poor ratings are more likely to rate others more harshly.

Halo error denotes the tendency to carry over the rater's overall favourable or unfavourable opinion about the job incumbent on one dimension of performance to other dimensions. For example, a high-producing employee may be rated as more analytical or a tardy employee rated as uncooperative when they are not justified. Most likely to emerge when using indirect and non-verifiable measures and when the rater is asked to evaluate friends or others with whom (s)he has positive social relations.

Central tendency or range restriction error reflects a predisposition to cluster most job incumbents in the middle point of a rating scale. For example, when a five-point-rating scale is used (with, say, a 1 indicating poor, 3 average and 5 outstanding), the rater may give a rating between 3 and 4 on most dimensions to all job incumbents. Most likely to occur when the rater has to justify extreme ratings (such as a 1 or 5) either to the human resource department, union, or the employee concerned.

Recency error occurs when the ratings are unduly biased by the most recent actions—good or bad—of the ratee concerned. This is most likely to occur when appraisal occurs annually or after a long lapse. Encouraging raters to keep a log of all critical behaviours and achievements of the employee as well as more frequent assessments help reduce this bias.

Stereotypes are rater's prejudices against specific groups who share one or more common attributes. Many individuals have stereotypes (e.g., "accountants are not out-going people" or "women cannot be good in technical jobs") which unduly bias their ratings of members of such groups.

Attribution errors occur because of the human tendency to attribute favourable outcomes to ourselves and unfavourable outcomes to external forces or working conditions. For example, individuals may attribute successful job performance to their own traits (e.g., I am intelligent) or work habits (e.g., "I am a hard worker") and assign poor performance to external conditions ("The equipment is obsolete"). When the achievements of others are being evaluated, many assign reverse attribution—that is another person's success is usually attributed to luck, working conditions, etc. and failure to the person's incompetence.

Personal prejudices are the rater's personal like or dislike for the job incumbent which influence his or her assessment of that person's performance. On many occasions, the rater may not even be aware of his or her subconscious like or dislike for the other persons which complicate the picture. The rater's generalized assumptions about a job also bias the ratings in some instances—for example, when evaluating a holding a traditionally male job.

Self-serving errors are biases which encourage raters to inflate ratings to make themselves look good. For example, supervisors who are responsible for training or mentoring others may inflate the ratings to improve their own status as a trainer or mentor.

necessary for a manager to start out with a lower standard for a new or poorly performing employee until he or she has developed some experience and more self-confidence. Here the skill of a manager as a coach becomes crucial, as does open communication, trust, and support by colleagues. More on coaching is discussed in Chapter 8.

Linked to Other Systems

For the appraisals to be motivating, everyone concerned has to see that appraisal results are taken seriously and are followed up by management. All too often, evaluation results end up in the personnel file, unread and this can lead to cynical employees and frustrated supervisors. Superior performance should result in extra rewards (see Chapter 4 for some ideas). For maximum positive outcomes, employees must see the appraisal linked to other systems (shown in Figure 6-2).

Input into Appraisals

Allowing job incumbents a high level of participation in the appraisal process (and not merely in appraisal system design and goal setting) increases employee satisfaction and morale. It can also improve the overall social climate of an organization. A trusting relationship between managers and employees tends to foster two-way communication processes and leads to mutually agreeable performance goals. Because trust in the system is crucial, it is questionable whether a performance appraisal should be done at all in organizations with low trust levels.

> In Western Pulp and Paper Products Company, several supervisors believed that employee promotion and reward decisions were made haphazardly by the higher management. To ensure that their unit employees had a fair chance of getting promoted, several supervisors inflated the ratings of their employees. Often, everyone was given an outstanding rating that reduced the validity and usefulness of assessments.

Sources of Information

Relying on one source of information (typically, the immediate supervisor) increases the possibility of errors and biases. When the measures are subjective and non-verifiable, solely using one person's judgement can result in extreme rating errors. Using different sources either confirms an assessment if all or a majority point in the same direction, or raises a caution flag if assessments vary. Using multiple sources of information also acts as a check on the reliability of the measures used.

> Soon after she joined Western Paper and Pulp Products Company, Pat Sullivan, the new human resource manager realized that the performance appraisal system was deficient in a number of respects. In a reformulated system, more objective and verifiable performance criteria and standards were introduced. Sullivan also introduced the system of multiple raters. Information relating to an employee's performance was now gathered from direct supervisor, secondary supervisors (where relevant), the employee, and even customers where feasible. In the case of managers, feedback coming from subordinates was also summarized and passed on, helping them focus on areas that needed improvement.

Employee Feedback

Most organizations still conduct appraisals annually. It is debatable whether this achieves any useful purpose.[9] Ideally, performance feedback would be given by the supervisor immediately after effective or ineffective job behaviour was observed. However, this may be unrealistic in many organizational settings. A compromise may be feedback sessions on a monthly or quarterly basis. These sessions should be seen by employees as opportunities to receive advice and support from their supervisor, not to be appraised or judged.

POPULAR PERFORMANCE ASSESSMENT APPROACHES

Most organizations use a variety of devices, including budgets, variance reports, performance appraisal reports, and profit and expense indices to assess the performance of employees. The types of assessment used by an organization to monitor and control member performance show wide variation depending on size, culture, strategy, industry characteristics, and other factors. Consider how two different types of organizations monitor member performance.

> A major transit company monitors the performance of their drivers continually through observation and random inspection. The organization has a lot of rules, safety procedures, and clearly spelled out duties and schedules of performance to guide its operators in every aspect of their work. In contrast, several large, geographically diverse churches are able to control member performance through shared values. By rituals of recruitment, passage, and renewal, the churches are able to promote a common purpose and a set of core values among their clergy and other workers. Very few bureaucratic rules or procedures are found necessary to monitor or assess member performance.

As shown in Figure 6-9, the performance assessment tools used within the same organization show considerable variation across managerial levels. At the board and top management levels, the basis for measuring a job incumbent's performance is the achievement of corporate and societal objectives as well as ethical standards used by the firm. **Market control** or market-related indices such as market share, sales volume, and profit levels are normally used to assess the performance of senior executives and managers who are heads of profit centres or autonomous product divisions with total control over their operations. As one moves down the organizational hierarchy, a variety of **bureaucratic controls** including conformity to rules, standards, policies, and established procedures and performance assessment by others assume greater importance. At the middle management level, a superior's rating of accomplishments, at times in conjunction with peer and self-ratings, are common. As one proceeds down the hierarchy, internal reports along with management information system monitor performance. At the lowest level in the hierarchy, employees may be evaluated both in terms of their outputs or performance and behaviour (such as punctuality and sociability).

A large number of appraisal formats and practices currently exist. It is beyond the scope of this book to exhaustively discuss each one. Below is a discussion of major appraisal methods currently found in Canadian industry. For the purpose of the discussion, the approaches are grouped into three major categories: past oriented, present oriented, and future oriented.

PAST-ORIENTED APPROACHES

Past-oriented approaches focus on performance that has already occurred. This means that, to a degree, it can be measured. The obvious disadvantage is that past performance cannot be changed. However, employees can get feedback about their efforts in the past and this feedback may lead to renewed efforts at improved performance. The most widely used appraisal techniques that are primarily past oriented include the rating scales, checklists, critical incident method, and the behaviourally anchored rating scales.

Website outlining best appraisal practices: *www.zigonperf.com/resources/pmnews.html*

Website with a best practice checklist: *www.centerpointsystems.com/BSTframeset.htm*

Market control refers to the use of market-related indices such as market share, sales volume, and profit levels to assess the performance of managers who are heads of profit centres or autonomous product divisions.

Bureaucratic controls include conformity to rules, standards, policies, and established procedures and performance assessments by others.

FIGURE 6-9   Performance Assessment Tools at Different Levels of an Organization

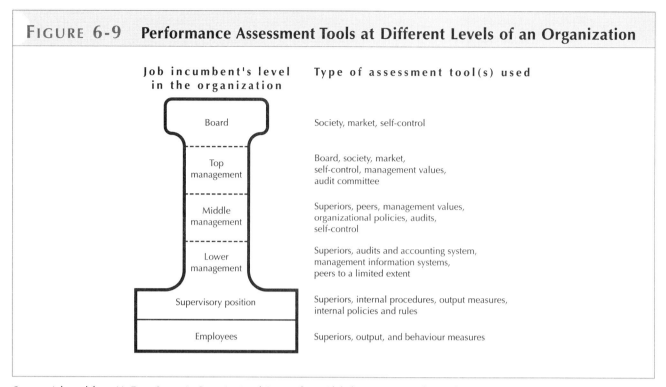

Job incumbent's level in the organization	Type of assessment tool(s) used
Board	Society, market, self-control
Top management	Board, society, market, self-control, management values, audit committee
Middle management	Superiors, peers, management values, organizational policies, audits, self-control
Lower management	Superiors, audits and accounting system, management information systems, peers to a limited extent
Supervisory position	Superiors, internal procedures, output measures, internal policies and rules
Employees	Superiors, output, and behaviour measures

Source: Adapted from H. Das. *Strategic Organizational Design for a Global Economy*. Scarborough, ON: Prentice Hall, 1998, 251. Reprinted with permission.

Rating scale requires the rater to provide a subjective evaluation of an employee on a number of job related dimensions along a scale from low to high.

Rating Scale Perhaps the most widely used form of performance appraisal is the **rating scale**, which requires the rater to provide a subjective evaluation of an employee on a number of job related dimensions along a scale. It can be easily constructed and understood, thus enhancing its face validity. It is also one of the oldest approaches to assessing employee performance. An example appears in Figure 6-10. As the figure indicates, the evaluation is based solely on the opinions of the rater. In many cases, the criteria are not directly related to job performance. Although subordinates or peers may use it, the immediate supervisor usually completes the form by checking the most appropriate response for each performance factor. Responses may be given numerical values so that scores can be computed and compared to other scores and to an average score. The rating scale is inexpensive to develop and administer and raters need little training or time to complete the form. For these reasons, it has high levels of user acceptability. Because of its simplicity, the rating scale can be applied to a large number of employees and individual total scores can be compared against other scores for making placement and compensation decisions.

Although there are advantages to using a rating scale, disadvantages are numerous. Some scales provide only very general and ambiguous anchors to the rater without specifying what "good" or "satisfactory" means (Figure 6-11). A consequence of this ambiguity is that the same rating across different raters may show substantial variation, reducing the usefulness of the total score to compare employees. A rater's biases are likely to be very high in a subjective instrument of this type. Further, raters and ratees may have different interpretations of the anchors thus reducing the developmental value of the feedback. Specific performance criteria may be omitted to make the form applicable to all or most jobs in an organization.

The performance criterion "safety in use of equipment" may be left off a rating scale because it applies to only a few workers. But for some employees, that item may be the most important part of their job. These omissions tend to limit specific feedback.

FIGURE 6-10   A Sample Rating Scale

Ontario Leather Products
Performance Rating Scale

Instructions: For the following performance factors, please indicate on the rating scale your evaluation of the named employee.

Employee's Name: **Department:**
Appraiser: **Date:**

	Excellent 5	Good 4	Acceptable 3	Fair 2	Poor 1
1. Quantity of production	❏	❏	❏	❏	❏
2. Quality of production	❏	❏	❏	❏	❏
3. Initiative	❏	❏	❏	❏	❏
4. Dependability	❏	❏	❏	❏	❏
5. Concern for safety	❏	❏	❏	❏	❏
6. Cooperation	❏	❏	❏	❏	❏
....					
....					
....					
12. Resourcefulness	❏	❏	❏	❏	❏

Total score received by the employee: _____

Additionally, descriptive evaluations are subject to widely variable individual interpretations. When specific performance criteria are hard to identify, the form may rely on irrelevant personality variables that dilute the meaning of the evaluation. The result is a standardized form and procedure that is not always job-related.

Checklists The checklist requires the rater to select statements and adjectives describing an employee's job-related behaviours and performance or other characteristics. Again, the rater is usually the immediate supervisor. If the rater believes the employee to have exhibited a particular behaviour or trait, the item is checked. The rater leaves items unchecked if the employee is not believed to possess those traits. The number of checks represents the employee's score. In weighted checklists, weights are assigned to different items on the checklist to reflect their relative importance (weights are unknown to the rater). The items with higher weights are either deemed to be more predictive of success or are more critical for the success of the organization's strategy. When weights are used, the total score is computed by the human

Checklist requires raters to select statements and adjectives describing an employee's job related behaviours and performance or other characteristics

---

FIGURE 6-11:   Ambiguous Rating Scale Anchors

Safety: High|_____|_____|_____|_____|Low

Safety: ◯Outstanding ◯Very good ◯Good ◯Satisfactory ◯Marginal ◯Unsatisfactory

Safety: Outstanding ❏   ❏   ❏   ❏   ❏   ❏   ❏ Poor

resource department after accounting for the weights of individual items. Figure 6-12 shows a portion of a checklist. The weights for each item are in parentheses here, but are usually omitted from the actual form. If the list contains enough items, it may provide an accurate picture of employee performance.

The advantages of a checklist are economy, ease of administration, limited training of raters, and standardization. Although this method is practical and standardized, the use of general statements reduces its job-relatedness. When the weights are unknown to the rater, some of the biases may be reduced or eliminated; however, when the items refer to personality traits or are subjective, many of the deficiencies of the rating scale may apply. Other disadvantages include susceptibility to rater biases (especially the halo effect), misinterpretation of checklist items, and use of improper weights by the human resource department. Moreover, it does not allow the rater to give relative ratings. For example, in the above form, employees who gladly work overtime get the same score as those who do so unwillingly. This has resulted in many systems moving towards more objective and behaviourally-based measures.

> The Western Paper and Pulp Products Company historically used a checklist for all types and levels of employees. Pat Sullivan, the new human resource manager realized that the performance criteria for different jobs were vastly different. In consultation with the relevant groups, she created three new formats: one for the managers and supervisors, another for clerical and sales staff, and a third for operating personnel in the factory and field. Personality based items (such as dependability and resourcefulness) were replaced by more behavioural and work outcome measures.

Critical incident method
requires the rater to record statements that describe extremely good or bad employee behaviour related to job performance.

Critical Incident Method

The **critical incident method** requires the rater to record statements that describe extremely good or bad employee perfmormance-relat-

---

FIGURE 6-12   Parts of a Weighted Checklist

Canada Office Products

Instructions: Check ALL items that apply to the employee.

Employee's Name: _____   Department: _____

Appraiser: _____   Date: _____

Weights		
(6.2)	❏	Greets customers in a friendly manner and smiles
(4.0)	❏	Keeps work station or desk well organized.
(3.9)	❏	Is cooperative.
(4.3)	❏	Plans actions before beginning job.
(6.0)	❏	Utilizes suggestive selling.
(4.0)	❏	Works overtime when asked.
(7.0)	❏	Serves customers promptly.
(5.5)	❏	Is conscientious.
....		
....		
(0.2)	❏	Employee listens to others' advice, but seldom follows it.

Total Score: _____
(Computed by the Human Resource Department)

Note: The weights are unknown to the rater and not shown on the form.

ed behaviour. The statements are called critical incidents. Critical behaviour differentiates between successful and unsuccessful performance in a particular work situation. Incidents are recorded for each employee very soon after they occur. Recorded incidents include a brief explanation of what happened. Several typical entries for a water works employee appear in Figure 6-13. As shown in the figure, both positive and negative incidents are recorded. Incidents are classified (either as they occur or later by the human resource department) into categories such as safety, quality control, and employee development.

The critical incident method is extremely useful for giving employees job-related feedback. It can also reduce the recency bias. It would almost seem a natural performance appraisal as supervisors can focus on actual job behaviour of the person concerned rather than on vague personality traits or general characteristics.[10] When a large number of critical incidents are collected and analyzed, they can provide valid indications of employee training needs and organizational improvement efforts.

> A year after she joined Western Paper and Pulp Products Company, Pat Sullivan embarked on a project to develop a behaviourally-anchored rating scale for the clerical and sales staff. Over 670 critical incidents were collected from the employees for this purpose, helping Sullivan to identify seven major dimensions of performance and associated behaviours. During the development of the scale, she also identified a number of areas that needed further improvement. Among these were: training the supervisors in communication and diversity management, training sales persons in handling difficult customers, and time planning skills for project heads.

Of course, the practical drawback is the difficulty of getting supervisors to record incidents as they occur. It is time consuming and burdensome to record behaviours and events on a daily or even weekly basis. Many supervisors start out recording incidents faithfully, but lose interest over time. Then, just before the evaluation period ends, they add new entries. When this happens, the recency bias is exaggerated and

---

FIGURE 6-13   Critical Incidents for a Performance Dimension of a Water Utility Employee

Town Waterworks

Instructions: In each category below, record specific incidents of extremely good or poor employee behaviour.

Employee's Name: _____

Appraiser: _____   Period: January 1 to December 31, 2002

Safety

Date	Behaviours/Incidents
Positive	
2/1	Put out small trash fire in the storeroom promptly
2/5	Reported broken rung on utility ladder promptly
....	
Negative	
12/3	Left leaky hose in front of storeroom causing wet and slippery floor
4/6	Smoked in the chemical supply room
3/8	Smelled of alcohol after lunch
4/9	Poured acid into plastic container ruining counter top
....	

employees may feel that supervisors are building a case to support their subjective opinions. Even when the form is filled out over the entire rating period, employees may feel that the supervisor is unwilling to forget negative incidents that occurred months before. The incidents, in their narrative form, do not lend themselves to quantification; this means that individual or group comparisons of performance are impossible. To overcome this, two suggestions have been proposed. One solution is to convert commonly occurring behaviours (or incidents) into a checklist or rating scale form. A second suggestion is to modify the incidents into a behaviourally-anchored rating scale (discussed below).

Behaviourally Anchored Rating Scales (BARS)

Instruments that assess employee behaviours may focus on the frequency of specific behaviours or their value to the organization. Behavioural observation scales require supervisors to record how frequently various behaviours listed in the instrument occurred. However, ratings which assess the value (rather than frequency) of specific behaviours are more common in organizational settings. Perhaps the best known behavioural scale is the behaviourally-anchored rating scale. **Behaviourally anchored rating scales** (BARS) attempt to reduce the subjectivity and biases of subjective performance measures by focusing on specific and critical work behaviours rather than traits or personality characteristics. From descriptions of good and bad critical incidents or behaviours provided by incumbents, peers, and supervisors, experts create performance-related categories such as employee knowledge and customer relations. Then specific examples of these behaviours are placed along a scale (usually from 1 to 7).

> The various behaviours of a department store sales supervisor for the performance dimension "employee supervision" are illustrated on the rating scale shown in Figure 6-14. Since the positions on the scale are described in job-related behaviour, an objective evaluation along the scale is more likely. The form also cites specific behaviours that can be used to provide performance feedback to employees. The BARS are job-related, prac-

Behaviourally anchored rating scales (BARS) attempt to reduce subjectivity and biases of performance measures by focusing on specific and critical work behaviours rather than on traits or personality characteristics.

FIGURE 6-14   BARS for a Sample Performance Dimension of a Department Store Supervisor

Maple Leaf Department Stores
Store Supervisor: Performance Dimension K: "Employee Supervision"

Outstanding performance	7- Can be expected to conduct a workshop for new sales persons providing them with adequate skills to be among top 10% of the salesforce in the department
Very good performance	6- Can be expected to publicly praise for job well done and constructively criticize in private those who did not perform to expectations offering the latter guidance for future
Good performance	5- Can be expected to provide great confidence to his or her salespeople by delegating important tasks to them
Satisfactory performance	4- Can be expected to keep timely, accurate human resource records and conduct salary reviews on time
Marginal performance	3- Can be expected to remind salespeople about their duties and ask them to come for duty even if they are ill
Poor performance	2- Can be expected not to honour promises on transfer or compensation
Extremely poor performance	1- Can be expected to blame the salespeople for own mistakes

tical, and standardized for similar jobs. But the rater's personal biases may still cause ratings to be high or low. Provision of specific behaviours that "anchor" the scale provide some criteria to guide the sincere rater, reducing personal biases to an extent.

If the rater collects specific incidents during the rating period, the evaluation is apt to be more accurate and a more effective counselling tool. Unlike rating scales that use vague anchors like "poor" and "excellent," BARS's anchors are more concrete, thus making them more legally defensible. When both raters and ratees are involved in the process of generating BARS, they are also better understood and accepted, improving overall reliability and validity.

One serious limitation of BARS is that they only look at a limited number of performance categories, such as customer relations or employee supervision. Each of these categories has only a limited number of specific behaviours. While the anchors (or points on the scales) are clear and behavioural in description, they are only examples of behaviours an employee may exhibit. The fact that some employees may never exhibit specific behaviours listed on the scale can potentially cause confusion to raters. Like the critical incident method, most supervisors are reluctant to maintain records of critical incidents during the rating period, reducing the effectiveness of this approach.

> Encouraged by her successful development of a behaviourally-anchored scale for the clerical and sales staff, Pat Sullivan of Western Paper and Pulp Products Company considered the same format for the manufacturing and field staff. She soon gave up the idea. For one thing, she knew that in many cases, the supervisors did not actually observe several of the behaviours exhibited by their subordinates on a regular basis. Further, there was often not a close correspondence between someone's behaviours and the performance outcomes. For many of the jobs, the employees preferred a more objective measure of their performance. She also knew that the top management was planning to introduce a performance-linked pay system which required more outcome-related measures.

Many supervisors find the behavioural focus unnatural-having been mostly exposed to trait-based rating scales. Supervisors required to make behaviourally-based evaluations may simply translate their trait impressions into behavioural ratings, thus reducing the overall accuracy of this approach.[11]

PRESENT-ORIENTED APPROACHES

Two major approaches are currently popular to evaluate an employee's present performance and competencies and skills: field review and performance tests. Each of these is briefly discussed below.

Field Review
In the **field review method**, a skilled representative of the performance management department (like a qualified performance analyst or psychologist) goes to the actual job site and either assists the immediate supervisor with ratings or, in some instances, rates the employees after consulting everyone concerned. To produce valid assessments, the analyst must be very competent, consult all involved (including the employee), and observe the job incumbent for sufficient time. After this, the analyst prepares a summary report that is sent to the supervisor for review, changes, approval, and discussion with the job incumbent. Since a highly qualified analyst far removed from the actual job is conducting the assessment, biases may be fewer and overall reliability high. However, the high cost associated with the use of a qualified analyst makes such field review too expensive for most firms.

Field review method is a process where a skilled representative of the performance management department goes to the actual job situation and either assists the immediate supervisor with ratings or does the ratings alone.

Performance Tests
For some jobs, **performance tests**, which assess the knowledge or skills possessed by the job incumbent, may be appropriate. A variety of paper

Performance tests assess the knowledge or skills possessed by the job incumbent.

and pencil, psycho-motor, and cognitive tests are currently used. While the paper and pencil tests may assess a person's knowledge of specific concepts, practices, or legal requirements, psycho-motor and cognitive tests assess a person's ability to do specific tasks including an assessment of the person's eye-hand coordination, ability to visualize, and so on. To be useful, the tests have to be both reliable and valid and must be administered in conditions identical (or at least very similar) to the conditions under which the actual job is performed. Developing valid tests takes time and considerable resources. In addition, tests may be applicable to only to a minority of jobs.

> Pilots of all major airlines are subject to evaluation by airline raters and Transport Canada. Evaluations of flying ability are usually made both in a flight simulator and during an actual flight. The evaluation is based on how well the pilot follows prescribed flight procedures and safety rules. Although this approach is expensive, public safety makes it practical, and the methods are job-related and standardized. For example, in August 2001, an Air Transat airplane lost all its fuel and had to do an emergency landing. This near disaster resulted in Transport Canada ordering the airline's pilots to take remedial training. A post-accident inquiry indicated that the pilots lacked adequate knowledge of safety procedures in the event of a fuel line leak.[12]

FUTURE-ORIENTED APPROACHES

Past- and present-oriented approaches to performance appraisal only tell where the employees have been or are, not what they are likely to achieve in future. Future-oriented appraisals focus on future performance by evaluating employee potential or setting future performance goals. Included here are three techniques: self-appraisal, management by objectives, and assessment centres.

Self-appraisal

Self-appraisal involves evaluating one's own past and present performance and knowledge, accompanied by an identification of future performance standards, skill repertoire, and areas for self-development.

Self-appraisal permits employees to evaluate past and present performance and knowledge and, in several instances, identify future performance standards, skill repertoire, and areas for self-development. It is particularly appropriate when the goal of evaluation is to further self-development. When employees evaluate themselves, defensive behaviour is less likely to occur. Thus, self-improvement is more likely. When self-appraisals are used to determine areas of needed improvement, they can help users set personal goals for future development. Obviously, self-appraisals can be used with any evaluation approach: past-, present-, or future-oriented approaches.

Past research indicates that self-appraisals suffer from leniency-employees who are given the opportunity to evaluate themselves tend to inflate their ratings.[13]

> One study reported that the average self-ratings were at least one standard deviation higher than their supervisory ratings.[14] The range of ratings given by the employees for their own performance may also be much narrower, making employee comparisons harder.

Some of these problems can be reduced by using specific anchors when ratings are used. For example, one study showed that relative anchors (e.g., "one of the best" or "above average") rather than absolute anchors (e.g., "good", "outstanding") result in less lenient ratings. The same study also showed that skewed anchors (e.g., 1=below average, 2=average, 3=above average, 4=well above average, 5=one of the best) had less leniency than symmetrical anchors (1=one of the worst, 2=below average, 3=average, 4=above average, 5=one of the best).[15] Figure 6-15 illustrates a self-assessment form for a salesperson in an electronics retailer.

Despite the above negatives, some organizations have recognized self-appraisals as an integral part of their employee development process. It is also indicative of their commitment to employee involvement in the appraisal process. Bechtel is a good example of this type of organization.

SELF-TEST

How Do You Evaluate Your Own Performance?

This exercise enables you to assess your performance in this course. Consider your behaviours, performance, and understanding of various concepts. Please rate each item truthfully using the anchors *outstanding* (O), *very good* (VG), *good* (G), *fair* (F), or *unsatisfactory* (U). Since your first reaction to a statement is critical, do NOT change your response once you have indicated it. If a particular statement is not relevant to the course, do not rate it.

1. My understanding of the course objectives.

2. My understanding of the performance requirements of this course.

3. My performance in this course as indicated by the grades and informal feedback I received from the instructor.

4. My class attendance.

5. My concern for quality in all the assignments and reports I submit to the instructor.

6. My efforts at finding better ways of studying and improving my overall performance.

7. The overall efforts I have put into group or team projects.

8. The number of hours I have spent preparing for quizzes or tests.

9. The library or Internet search I do to supplement text material and in-class learning.

10. The overall interest I have in learning about performance management.

Scoring

For all statements, assign scores of 5, 4, 3, 2, and 1 for O, VG, G, F, and U respectively. Total your scores for items 1 through 10.

Interpretation

Your total score will depend on the number of items you have rated and cannot exceed 50. If you got 80% or more (i.e., 40 or more assuming you have checked all statements), your self-rating of your performance is outstanding. In most instances, higher scores are likely to be related to higher grades indicating that specific behaviours help you achieve greater success in this course.

At the Bechtel Company, the largest privately held construction and engineering firm in the world, the performance planning system involves the employee in a process of self-appraisal. The process starts with the supervisor telling the employee what is expected. The employee gets a worksheet and writes down his or her understanding of the job. Ten to fifteen days before a performance evaluation is done, the employee completes the worksheet by filling in the portions that relate to job accomplishments, performance difficulties, and suggestions for improvement. Not only does it encourage the employees to generate new and innovative ideas for performance improvement, but the completed sheet also indicates to the supervisor what he or she needs to do to eliminate roadblocks to meeting and exceeding job standards.[16]

Management by Objectives Approach

Management-by-objectives (MBO) is a goal-directed approach in which employees and superiors jointly establish performance goals for the upcoming evaluation period and use these as the standards by which performance will be judged. Ideally, these goals are mutually agreed upon and objectively measurable. If both conditions are met, employees are apt to be more motivated to achieve the goal since they have participated in setting it. It also enables employees to adjust their behaviour to ensure attainment of an objective since they can, in most instances of MBO, measure their progress toward

Management-by-objectives (MBO) is a goal directed approach in which each employee and superior jointly establish performance goals for the upcoming evaluation period and use these as the standards by which employee's performance will be judged.

FIGURE 6-15   Sample Self-Assessment Form for a Salesperson in an Electronics Retailer

Future World Electronics

Name: _____   Department: _____

Employee Number:_____   Supervisor: _____

Please rate yourself on the following statements. Your comments will help us not only to recognize your full contribution to this organization but also identify areas where we can help you to improve by offering additional support (e.g., training, developmental opportunities).

PART 1. PERFORMANCE MEASURES

Please use the following rating scheme to indicate your self assessments: 1= below established standard; 2= at established standard; 3= above established standard; 4= well above established standard.

1.   Your sales since last assessment   ❏
2.   The number of days you were away from work   ❏
3.   The number of hours spent on merchandise display (on average)   ❏
4.   Number of customers handled each week (on average)   ❏
5.   Number of hours you spent training other salespeople each week (on average)   ❏

What are some of your accomplishments since last review?

_____
_____
_____

PART 2. YOUR ASSESSMENT OF PERFORMANCE-RELATED VARIABLES

Please rate the following statements using the following scheme: 1= Need to improve; 2= Fair; 3= Good; 4= Excellent. Your candid responses will help us improve the systems so as to serve you and the customers better in future.

1.   Your overall knowledge of the organizational goals and priorities   ❏
2.   Your knowledge of all job related procedures   ❏
3.   Your knowledge of product features in your section   ❏
4.   Your training to deal with different types of customers   ❏
5.   Your time management skills   ❏
6.   Your knowledge of ISO standards and required work procedures   ❏
7.   Your ability to train others   ❏
8.   Your ability to work in a team or group   ❏
9.   Your involvement in committees and task forces   ❏
10. Your overall accuracy rate in pricing (e.g., properly including discounts)   ❏

What are some actions, if any, that can be taken by yourself or by the organization to help you achieve higher performance levels? (Include here all activities such as training and counseling which can help you achieve higher levels.)

_____
_____
_____

Does your job description continue to reflect your daily activities? What changes would you recommend?

_____
_____
_____

What improvements would you recommend in the working conditions which could help you do your job better?

_____
_____
_____

Date:_____   Signature:_____

(Please return the completed form to Human Resources Department in the enclosed envelope)

the objective. In general, biases are reduced to the extent that goal attainment, rather than personality traits is being measured.

In practice, MBO programs have encountered difficulties. Objectives are sometimes too ambitious or too narrow. The result is frustrated employees or overlooked areas of performance. Further, a purely outcome-based approach may be seriously deficient when unforeseen emergencies or crises arise.

> Consider a situation where production machinery breaks down. In most organizations, it is the best worker-rather than the mediocre or typical employee-who is asked to fix the problem, even if the person is not using the particular machine. Fixing a problem may take an entire shift or even a workweek, resulting in the employee who is fixing the problem not meeting standards for the period. The superior's judgements and subjective evaluations continue to remain vital in such instances.

If care is not taken, objectives may unduly focus on narrow quantitative measures rather than on factors like quality, service, and innovation which are harder to measure objectively. However, these are equally (if not more) critical for several organizations. When employees and managers do focus on subjectively measured objectives, special care is needed to ensure that biases do not distort the manager's evaluation.

Assessment Centre

Assessment centres assess employee competencies and future potential using multiple types of evaluation such as interviews, in-basket exercises, games, and multiple raters. Typically, the assessment centre technique is applied to supervisory and middle-level managers to evaluate their potential to move up the ranks. During a brief stay at the assessment centre, which is usually located away from the job site, candidates are evaluated with the use of in-depth interviews, psychological tests, personal background histories, peer ratings by other attendees, leaderless group discussions, ratings by psychologists and managers, and simulated work exercises. The simulated work experiences usually include in-basket exercises, decision-making exercises, computer-based business games, and other job-like opportunities that test the employee in realistic ways. The psychologists and senior managers who rate the strengths, weaknesses, and potential of each attendee compare and merge their estimates to arrive at some conclusion about each member of the group.

Assessment centre findings are valuable if the tests and other assessment procedures used have predictive and construct validity. Otherwise, rating errors and rater biases are likely to reduce the usefulness of the approach. More recently, assessment centres have gained widespread use, and human resource researchers are finding ways to validate the process. Assessment centres can be expensive and time consuming, making them impractical for many organizations.

> **Assessment centres** assess employee competencies and future potential using multiple types of evaluation such as interviews, in-basket exercises, games, and multiple raters.

ASSESSING GROUP AND TEAM PERFORMANCE

Many organizations have realized that process-focused and multi-functional groups and teams can facilitate higher productivity, better customer service, and higher employee morale. In the case of groups and teams, two distinct types of evaluations are critical. First, the overall effectiveness of the team or group has to be evaluated. Second, the contributions of individual team members have to be assessed. Differential rewards and performance feedback have to be given to team members to recognize and improve performance.

Most organizations have not changed their appraisal systems to meet the needs of groups and teams. Popular indices used to gauge the overall effectiveness of teams

Website with articles on performance appraisal: *www.shrm.org/hrmagazine/archive/*

and groups include project cost, meeting project deadlines, market share, and customer retention figures. Many of the current approaches use global, outcome-oriented measures such as market success and profitability; only a few organizations focus on team-specific process criteria. Later in this chapter, we will offer sample process-criteria to assess team performance.

A variety of comparative evaluation methods are currently used to identify individual team member performance. The primary focus of most-if not all-existing systems is to enable comparison of one employee's performance with that of another's. We begin this section by examining the popular approaches to evaluating individuals who work in a group setting.

COMPARATIVE EVALUATION METHODS

Comparative evaluation methods are a collection of different methods that compare one person's performance with that of coworkers.

Comparative evaluation methods are a collection of different methods that compare one person's performance with that of coworkers. These can be conducted in one of two ways: by the supervisor alone or by using multiple raters including other managers and employees. Typically, comparative evaluations are conducted by the supervisor and the results are used for determining merit pay increases, promotions, and organizational rewards because they can rank employees from best to worst. Some larger organizations use a more elaborate group evaluation method. This method reduces biases because multiple raters are used. When the raters get an opportunity to compare their ratings with those of others, more valid future evaluations are likely. Usually, the comparative ratings are not shared with the employee fearing that it might result in loss of cooperation among employees.

The most common forms of comparative evaluations are the ranking method, forced distributions, and the point allocation method.

Ranking requires the rater to rank employees from best to worst.

Ranking
Ranking requires the evaluator to rank employees from best to worst. Ranking has the advantage of forcing the rater to differentiate among employees. When rankings are not mandatory, a supervisor may have the tendency to rate everyone the same, thus reducing the system's usefulness for reward and placement purposes. However, ranks do not provide any information about absolute performance or the difference between employees who hold different ranks. All that can be said is that certain employees are better than others, not by how much. Ranks can be particularly confusing when the performance of two work teams (Figure 6-16) is compared.

> In Figure 6-16, although both Ann and Tom hold the first ranks in their respective teams, Ann's performance is superior to Tom's. The difference in performance between two ranks is also very different in the two teams. Kevin and Mark, both of whom hold second rank not only have different performance levels but also differing distances from the first rank holder. Indeed, the third rank holder in work team 2 has higher absolute performance than the second rank holder in work team 1.

Ranking is also susceptible to halo and recency effects, although rankings by two or more raters can be averaged to help reduce biases. Its advantages include ease of administration and explanation to ratees.

Forced distributions require raters to sort employees into each of several classifications or categories based on performance.

Forced Distributions
Forced distributions require raters to sort employees into each of several classifications or categories based on their performance. For example, a certain proportion must be put in each category (such as "outstanding" and "poor"). Figure 6-17 illustrates how a rater might classify the overall performance of ten subordinates. Raters may also be asked to classify their subordinates on a variety of other criteria such as reliability, service quality, and safety. As with the

FIGURE 6-16 Ranks and Performance Levels in Two Work Groups

Performance Level (10= highest)	Work Team 1	Work Team 2
	(Ranks of employees in parentheses)	
10	Ann (1)	
9		Tom (1)
8		Kevin (2)
7		Rajesh (3)
6	Mark (2)	
5	Su-Yin (3)	Sonia (4)
4	Mohammed (4)	
3	Francois (5)	Matt (5)
2		
1		

ranking method, relative differences among employees are unknown, but this method does overcome the biases of central tendency, leniency, and strictness. Some workers and supervisors dislike this method because employees are often rated lower than they or their supervisors think correct. However, the use of a forced distribution requires some employees to be rated low.

Point Allocation Method Point allocation method requires the rater to allocate a predetermined number of points among the employees in the group to reflect their relative performance, competencies, or skills. Figure 6-18 illustrates how better employees in the Pilkington Foundry (shown in Figure 6-17) are awarded more points than poor performers, thus helping the firm recognize the extent of performance difference among employees. This method may also reduce central tendency, although the halo effect and the recency biases may continue to distort ratings.

Point allocation method requires the rater to allocate a predetermined number of points among the employees in the group to reflect their relative performance, competencies, or skills.

A SUGGESTED EMPLOYEE ASSESSMENT APPROACH

None of the approaches discussed above is devoid of weakness or capable of eliminating all rating biases. This has encouraged several employers to adopt a 360-degree appraisal system that combines supervisory, peer, subordinate, and self reviews

360-degree appraisal system combines supervisory, peer, subordinate, and self reviews.

FIGURE 6-17 The Forced Distribution of Performance of Ten Employees

Pilkington Foundry
Forced distribution rating of overall performance of employees

Outstanding (Top 10%):	Terry Jones
Very Good (Next 20%):	Rick Schwind, Mike Ryan
Good (Middle 40%):	Ted Miner, Jack Gale, Albert Summers, Russ Mills
Fair (Next 20%):	Dale Woods, Cathy Rider
Poor (Bottom 10%):	Pat Cormier

FIGURE 6-18 The Point Allocation Method of Appraisal

Pilkington Foundry
Point allocation among employees based on overall performance

Instructions: Allocate all 100 points to all employees according to their relative worth. The employee with the maximum points is the best employee.

Points	Employee
17	Terry Jones
14	Rick Schwind
12	Mike Ryan
11	Ted Miner
11	Jack Gale
10	Albert Summers
9	Russ Mills
6	Dale Woods
6	Cathy Rider
4	Pat Cormier

Websites with information on 360-degree appraisal systems:
www.360-degreefeedback.com
www.mapnp.org/library/emp_perf/perf_rvw/360_rvws.htm
www.zigonperf.com/resources/pmnews/360fb_amok.html

(Figure 6-19). While such an approach has shown promise in identifying performance dimensions and problems not visible to any particular assessor and reducing single rater biases, it may not be feasible in several organizational settings. Some emerging research evidence indicates that peer and subordinate appraisals may be beneficial only when used for developmental feedback rather than for administrative (e.g., compensation, placement) decisions. Peer and subordinate evaluations may also jeopardize coworker relations and may cause jealousy and retributive actions.[17] Further, the same behaviours or traits rated as desirable by one group may not be desirable to others. Thus, managers who were seen as challenging the status-quo and encouraging subordinate's independent action were rated lower by their superior managers, but rated higher by their subordinates.[18]

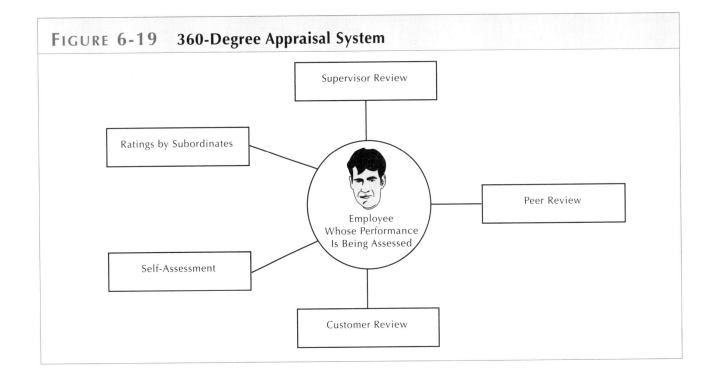

FIGURE 6-19 360-Degree Appraisal System

FIGURE 6-20 Questions that Help Employees Evaluate Performance.

- What are the three most important aspects of my present job? Is there any likely conflict among these? If yes, how should it be resolved? Which should get higher priority?

- What are the performance standards on these and other dimensions?

- What are my specific accountabilities?

- What are some examples of where I showed superior performance?

- What areas of my job could I have handled better? What specific actions can I take to improve my performance?

- How are my performance standards related to my department or team goals?

A performance assessment system that focuses on current performance and future potential is likely to meet the needs of most organizations. While no single system can equally apply to all organizational settings or is strong in all respects, certain actions can help reduce systemic deficiencies. These actions are discussed in the following sections.

CLARIFY OBJECTIVES AND PERFORMANCE CRITERIA

To have a valid base for evaluating performance, performance expectations from individual employees and teams should be identified and periodically updated. The performance criteria (or measures) and their relative importance have to be identified on the basis of inputs from all important constituents-top management, the supervisor, the employee, the coworkers, and other users and customers-and reflect the organizational priorities. Figure 6-20 lists some questions that the employee should ask to gauge and improve performance. Performance review is a two way process-both the rater and ratee should contribute to the process.

To identify multiple performance dimensions of a job, a balanced scorecard approach may often prove useful. In any event, an explicit and exhaustive listing of the jobholder's duties and outcomes and their linkage to other jobs is necessary. Figure 6-21 shows illustrative duties and linkages of an advertisement designer.

In the case of multi-functional teams, traditional measures like profits, market-share, and cost may not be useful for keeping track of performance. Nor do such measures tell team members what they must do to improve their performance.[19]

> The popular measures for assessing product development teams are schedule and cost. However, the fact that a project is eight months behind schedule or $1 million over budget may not tell the team what went wrong or how to fix the problem. In any case, it will not help the firm avoid potential cost overruns or delays before they actually occur.

Instead, tracking team process measures which are understood by and under the control of each team member might help the team to take timely corrective actions. Illustrative process measures for a service team are shown in Figure 6-22.

> Tracking staffing levels or service time per customer or activity can tell a team where it is heading and enable it to take action before things get too far out of control.

Website with balanced score-card approach to performance criteria:
www.zigonperf.com/resources/pmnews/making_bsc_payoff.html

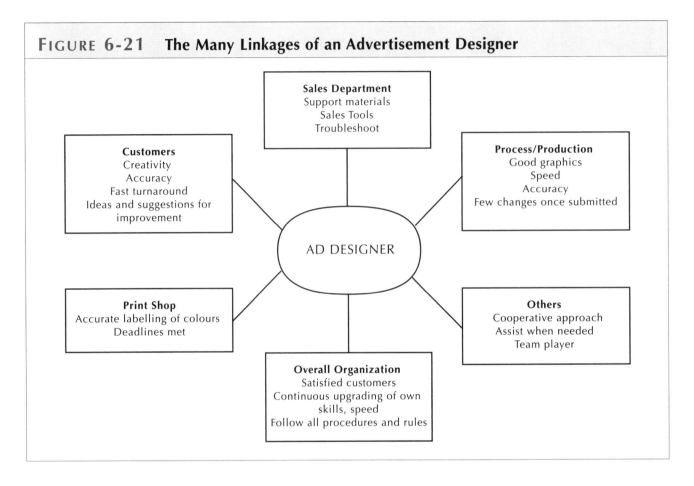

FIGURE 6-21   **The Many Linkages of an Advertisement Designer**

JOINTLY IDENTIFY PERFORMANCE STANDARDS

The standards for results and desired behaviours should be identified in consultation with the job incumbent. When behaviours rather than quantifiable outcomes are used as performance standards, the specific conditions and frequency with which they should occur must be specified. Almost every performance appraisal event includes a significant amount of time spent on performance defining activities-whether they are called so or not. Supervisors and employees often disagree about ratings, when they are in fact disagreeing about the way performance is being defined, and the standards used to judge it.[20] When individuals participate in setting standards, they develop a better understanding of what is expected and tend to be more committed to the standards.

> In a large, geographically dispersed firm, supervisors did not have a clear idea of the conditions under which their subordinates performs. For example, salespeople in tropical countries could not travel because of bad weather or roads during monsoon season. The non-availability of certain materials prevented production staff in a unit located in a developing country from meeting standards established by the head office. When dissatisfaction from field staff over ratings was made apparent to the human resource manager, the firm altered performance evaluation procedures. The field supervisor's ratings were given higher weight than the uniform, company-wide performance criteria. The firm also made it mandatory to get all employees' input when setting standards.

Of course, the culture of the organization and the prevailing management philosophy on employee participation impact the degree to which employees participate in setting standards. Meaningful participation requires a good superior-subordinate relationship and a history of mutual respect.[21]

FIGURE 6-22   Illustrative Process Measures for a Service Team

Time
- Service time for this time period compared to previous periods or business plans
- Delivery time for materials or service in this period compared to past or plans
- Time elapsed between identification of an error or omission and its resolution

Cost
- Cost of providing unit service compared to past trends and objectives
- Labour cost as a percentage of total margin
- Labour cost as a percentage of product or total service cost

Quality
- Number of errors or mistakes
- Customer satisfaction index compared to benchmarks and past trends

Performance
- Number of customers served (absolute number, comparisons with indexes)
- Number of customers who can be served concurrently
- Performance ratings by customers
- Innovation in procedures or service routines

Member tenure
- Average length of tenure of team member
- Member turnover rate

RECOGNIZE THE NEED FOR MULTIPLE APPRAISALS

Since appraisals serve several purposes, there are different appraisal approaches, which achieve different objectives. Five different types of appraisals have been identified:[22]

- appraisals done for the purpose of work planning,
- appraisals focusing on compensation review,
- appraisals focusing on employee developmental planning,
- appraisals focusing on employee career planning, and
- appraisals which facilitate human resource planning.

Each type of appraisal differs in application, focus, purpose, superior's role, job incumbent's role, and power distribution.

> Compensation reviews are intended to motivate employees by rewarding their past achievements and identifying future rewards and performance-reward linkage. In contrast, developmental planning review aims to improve employee's knowledge, skills, and attitudes. The focus here is on skill building and future action planning.

Combining different types of appraisals, focusing different activities and outcomes into a singly event, can cause major distraction to all concerned and reduce overall effectiveness.

DETERMINE PERFORMANCE APPRAISAL CYCLES

Because appraisals need to serve multiple organizational objectives, it is desirable to have different appraisal cycles for different kinds of appraisals. Most firms need to have at least two performance appraisal cycles:

- one that focuses on immediate performance improvements and feedback, and
- one that deals with longer-term career, development, and retention issues.

The two performance appraisal cycles need not be on the same time schedule, use the same measures, or even involve the same individuals. In fact, they may be best separated since they are being done for very different purposes. Success lies in how well the varied purposes are balanced.

There is no simple answer about how long a performance cycle should last. Given today's technology, for some assembly-line type jobs and service jobs (e.g., Internet/telephone customer service), **continuous performance monitoring** is possible. With the use of machines, the quantity and often the quality of task performance is automatically recorded and monitored by the job incumbents and supervisors for immediate corrective action.

> According to the American Management Association, three-quarters of U.S. businesses now electronically monitor employees in some fashion. Web and e-mail monitoring software not only track when an employee views sexually explicit material, but potentially any intimate subject. Voice-mail retrieval software does the same. Keystroke and screen-capture software can check what an employee is working on at any time. Field sales representatives have their movements tracked by location-based tracking systems in phones and some hospitals require nurses to wear badges on their uniforms so that they can be located at any time.[23]

In Canada, the state of affairs is nowhere close to that described above. However, with more regular performance monitoring of jobs such as telemarketing, call centre operations, and assembly line production, it becomes easier to assess performance deviations. In such instances, some emerging approaches to performance rating such as performance distribution rating may be possible. **Performance distribution assessment** (PDA) methodology conceptualizes performance as a distribution of outcomes achieved by each job incumbent and uses measures of central tendency (such as average, median, mode) and variability (e.g., standard deviation, range) to gauge the level and consistency of a person's performance. Figure 6-23 illustrates the usefulness of PDA methodology. In other cases, where daily measurement of performance is not possible for technical or other practical reasons, appropriate performance cycle length should be identified-always recognizing the importance of providing feedback soon after (and during) performance to improve it.

TRAIN RATERS AND RATEES

There are at least two critical players in a performance appraisal process: the appraiser and the appraisee. Each has a distinct role to play, and each must be prepared for that role. Performance appraisal does not come naturally to most individuals; indeed, some cultural norms may work against valid appraisal of others and oneself. In the absence of sound training, performance assessment may end up being a useless ritual incapable of generating valid information about the job incumbent, the work, or the future potential of the individuals involved. Figure 6-24 lists key items that warrant **attention** in any rater-training program. Companies such as the Royal Bank and Air Canada solve this knowledge gap through training.

How Ford Motor Company weeds out poor performers: *www.zigonperf.com/resources/pmnews/fordemplperf.html*

Continuous performance monitoring is a system where the quantity and quality of task performance is automatically recorded by machines and monitored by the job incumbents and supervisors for immediate corrective action.

Performance distribution assessment (PDA) methodology conceptualizes performance as a distribution of outcomes achieved by each job incumbent and uses measures of central tendency (such as average, median, mode) and the variability (e.g., standard deviation, range) to gauge the level and consistency of a person's performance.

Attention is the process by which the appraiser consciously or subconsciously records certain stimuli because they are relevant to a task performed.

FIGURE 6-23   An Illustration of the Usefulness of Performance Distribute Assessment (PDA) Methodology

Kane proposed the PDA to minimize the biases in performance assessment and improve its validity and comparability across employees. He suggested that performance be conceptualized[24] as a distribution of various job outcomes and measured using both central tendency and variation-based parameters. Central tendency measures reflect the average or typical level of performance, whereas the variation-based measures reflect the degree of consistency (or conversely, the variability) in performance. Two employees might have the same average performance; however, from the firm's point of view, the employee who has less variability in performance is preferable. Similarly, there are certain levels of performance—called Negative Range—which are totally unacceptable from the point of view of the firm. The employee who avoids these negative ranges is more preferable than an employee who might be an occasional high performer but frequently falls into the negative range. Since PDA requires some degree of familiarity with statistical tools and utility analysis, what is attempted below is to illustrate how PDA can offer greater insights than traditional performance appraisal measures which look at only raw performance data.

Assume that for a particular job position, a firm has established a minimum performance level of 10. The following data relate to the performance of three employees measured on 10 occasions:

Performance of three employees (units of output)

	Employee A	Employee B	Employee C
	12	15	19
	13	18	18
	12	12	17
	14	15	9
	13	10	6
	13	14	18
	14	13	18
	13	11	8
	13	10	7
	13	12	10
Average:	**13**	**13**	**13**
Standard deviation:	**0.67**	**2.54**	**5.40**

The average performance of all three employees are identical; however, Employee A has less variability (a statistical tool called standard deviation is computed to gauge variability). Between Employees B and C, Employee B is preferable since C drops into Negative range territory (i.e., production less than 10) on 40% of occasions. C's performance variability is also much higher although C reaches highest production figures on some occasions.

A knowledge of performance variability enables the firm to further investigate the reason for it. Performance variations attributable to the employee (e.g., ability, motivation, disposition, availability) can be separated from changes in the job (e.g., changes in work layout, new technology) and job contexts (e.g., new supervision) and appropriate and timely corrective actions can be taken.[25]

Training workshops are usually intended to explain to raters the purpose of the procedure, its mechanics, likely pitfalls or biases, and answers to specific questions. The training may even include trial runs of evaluating other classmates just to gain some supervised experience. The Royal Bank and Air Canada use videotapes and role-playing evaluation sessions to give raters both experience and insight into the evaluation process.

FIGURE 6-24   Key Items in Rater Training Programs

Whatever the nature of the system and measures used, raters need to be trained in the following areas:

- **Purpose of evaluation.** Just knowing whether the appraisal is to be used for compensation or placement recommendations may change the rater's evaluation of those being rated.

- **Consistency in rating.** A major problem is rater understanding and consistency of evaluations. Some human resource departments provide raters with a rater's handbook that describes the employer's approach. Guidelines for conducting the evaluation or for providing ratees with feedback are often included in the handbook. The raters have to be warned of the various types of rating errors likely to emerge and ways to overcome them.

- **Definition of key terms and criteria.** Key terms—such as "is cooperative" or "provides leadership"—need to be defined and at times included in the handbook.

- **Evaluation climate.** Not every manager has the required skills to build a supportive, nonthreatening atmosphere where the employees can own up mistakes and deficiencies without being afraid of punishment. Not many managers have the skills to provide constructive feedback either. This means that they have to be trained in this area. Often videotaping their behaviours during mock appraisal interviews helps managers to recognize their own behaviours and improve them.

Website on rater training:
www.zigonperf.com/resources/pmnews/train_mgrs_apprais.html

In the past, rater training has focused on rating errors such as the halo effect, leniency bias, and central tendency. The emphasis has shifted now to the cognitive aspects of the rating process. This refers to the ability of raters to make valid judgments based on relatively complex information. (Figure 6-25 provides one model of cognitive training.)

Training in performance assessment is a time consuming task that involves the presence of skilled trainers. It can be done by the internal training staff, outside consultants, or both. Perhaps the best approach may be a combination-namely, internal staff train everyone concerned under the guidance of an outside, expert consultant. Using internal staff can build a sense of commitment and ownership among employees while the outside consultant, because of their experience, may be able to educate everyone about current trends and emerging practices in the field. The outside consultant, because of their expertise and stature, may also be more credible to top management.

PLAN CORRECTIVE ACTIONS

Developmental evaluation interviews are performance review sessions that give employees feedback about their past performance and future potential.

Normally, the evaluation results are conveyed to the employee during an interview. **Developmental evaluation interviews** are performance review sessions that give employees feedback about their past performance and future potential. A poorly conducted interview can antagonize and demoralize a good employee and a well-executed one can result in significant, future improvement and exhilaration. Adequate prior preparation and data collection, good planning of interview steps, clear focus on objectives, and a positive tone that highlights achievements and potential rather than negative personality traits are necessary to make the interview a useful one. The interview will not result in positive changes unless all performance related information has been collected, synthesized, and fed back to the employee in a positive tone.

The evaluator may provide this feedback through several approaches. Three approaches are popular: tell and sell, tell and listen, and problem-solving.

FIGURE 6-25   A Model of Cognitive Training for Raters

One model divides the performance appraisal process into four steps: attention, categorization, recall, and information integration.

1. **Attention** refers to the process by which the appraiser consciously or subconsciously records certain stimuli because they are relevant to a task performed. The more deviant the observed behaviour is from the expected norm, the more strongly the attention-arousing stimuli work. If, for example, an employee is rude or insults a customer, the supervisor is much more likely to pay attention to the observed behaviour than if the person were to give friendly smiles to coworkers. Part of the training is to help appraisers improve their ability to observe even weak stimuli that may be critical for organizational success.

For example, a casual suggestion from an employee may have triggered off a major new product/process idea or other improvement. Unless the appraiser is able to recognize the source of the new idea, not only will the employee not get credit for his or her innovation, but also may not be encouraged to come up with other innovative ideas.

2. **Categorization** refers to the process of classifying and storing data. Several studies have shown that human beings have a limited capability of perceiving and processing information simultaneously, the upper limit being approximately seven items. Categorization helps us to make quick judgments with limited information about something. Stereotyping is one type of categorization that, as we all know, may result in biased conclusions.

3. **Recall** is the use of information that is already processed and stored in memory. Depending on the strength of an impression, some items may be recalled more easily than others.

For example, more recent behaviours are usually recalled first (recency effect). In many instances, information that supports prejudices or biases may be recalled more easily. When the performance cycle is one year, the probability of appraisers recalling all the important information about an employee's work is very low. Only if a conscious effort to record such information is made, by writing down critical incidents, for example, will raters be able to do an accurate evaluation.

4. **Information integration** requires the appraiser to recall all relevant information about an employee and to generate an integrated picture of the employee. However, due to the attention-arousing process (only strong stimuli are recorded), the categorization process (limited information is stored), and the recall process (a limited number of events is remembered), the final picture that emerges will be understandably biased.

- The tell-and-sell approach, which works best on new employees, reviews the employee's performance and attempts to convince the employee to perform better in the future.

- The tell-and-listen approach aims to remove employee defensiveness by allowing the employee to explain reasons and excuses for poor performance and by counselling the employee on how to perform better in the future.

- The problem-solving approach identifies problems that are interfering with employee performance and attempts to remove these through training, coaching, or counselling. Goals for future performance are also set at this time.

Regardless of the approach, all developmental evaluation interviews should follow some guidelines (Figure 6-26). The focus of the interview should always be to create a positive, performance-improving dialogue. By stressing desirable aspects of employee performance, the evaluator can give the employee renewed confidence in his or her ability to perform satisfactorily. This positive approach also enables the employee to keep desirable and undesirable performance in perspective, because it prevents the individual from feeling that performance review sessions are entirely negative. The review session concludes by focusing on actions that the employee can take

FIGURE 6-26   Action Guidelines to Conduct Developmental Evaluation Interviews

An appraisal interview should always aim to create a positive, performance-enhancing dialogue. The supervisor should provide the employee with renewed self-confidence to achieve improved performance targets. This means that such interviews have to be carefully planned. There are four key steps in evey successful interview: Prepare, Conduct, Assess the evaluation process, and Record results.

Step 1: Prepare for Evaluation

- Select an appropriate time to conduct the evaluation—preferably right after the task cycle or completion of a project. Definitely *not* immediately before an important project deadline, month-end report or vacation.

- Choose a location where manager and employee can be together without being distracted by phone calls, visitors, or other colleagues. No one should be able to observe the interview through a window or glass door.

- Carefully go through all performance-related records and make a note of key accomplishments and potential growth areas. Ask the employee to do the same.

Step 2: Conduct the Evaluation

- Emphasize positive aspects of employee performance and convince the appraisee that the evaluation session is to improve performance, not to discipline.

- Focus criticisms on performance, not on personality characteristics. Make criticisms specific, not general and vague. Emphasize apparisee's strengths whenever areas for improvement are discussed.

- Listen actively, without interruption to appraisee's ideas and action plans.

- Demonstrate understanding of the appraisee's point of view and be willing to change your mind on occasions.

- Focus on future, not past performance.

- Stay calm and do not argue with the appraisee.

- Identify specific actions to be taken to improve performance.

- Emphasize the evaluator's willingness to assist the employee's efforts and to improve performance.

- Conclude the session by stressing the positive aspects of performance and reviewing plans to improve performance.

Step 3: Assess the Evaluation Process

- Ask yourself questions such as: 1. How could I have made the meeting more productive? 2. Am I happy with the outcomes of the meeting? 3. What changes in my behaviour and plans are needed to make future meetings more productive and positive in tone? 4. What did I learn new about my approach to questioning, listening and handling difficulties?

- Look at the performance of employees whom you had interviewed in the past. Can you see any notable improvement in their performance? What separates employees who had improved performance after the interview from those who did not? What actions on your part seem to separate the two groups? Where would you place this interview (based on past results)?

- What do you need to do to improve future interviews?

Step 4: Record Results

- Make a complete record of discussions and agreed upon plans for future and keep it in a safe place.

- Ensure that the employee is aware of future performance standards or required behaviours.

- Provide written performance feedback summary (agreed upon during the interview) along with supportive documentation identifying performance deficiencies if any.

to improve areas of poor performance. In that concluding discussion, the evaluator usually offers to provide whatever assistance the employee needs to overcome the deficiencies discussed.

LINKING APPRAISAL RESULTS TO OTHER SYSTEMS

Appraisal is not, itself, an end. Unless the appraisal results are used for developing, rewarding, planning, and improving future performance, appraisal becomes a meaningless ritual that generates apathy and defensiveness. Employee behaviours are affected by a variety of factors including the way their jobs are designed, the perceived linkage between specific behaviours and rewards, perceived career growth opportunities, existing training programs to improve employee skills and behaviours, and so on. A change in any one of these factors has major implications for all human resource decisions. Thus, the human resource practices designed to manage employees must be coordinated and managed as a system.

> Before Pat Sullivan's arrival at Western Paper and Pulp Mills, the company had not used the appraisal results for anything other than periodic pay raises. Even then, it was not systematically done and there was no direct correspondence between an employee's ratings and the raises received. Under Sullivan's new system, employees received differential raises depending on their ratings (which also considered variability in performance from one time period to another). The ratings were used to plan training programs for marginal workers. The better workers were offered opportunities for development and possible moves to supervisory jobs in future. The company also initiated steps to develop a human resource information system where all future ratings will be deposited and used for making employee promotion, transfer, and counselling decisions.

Figure 6-27 shows the complex relationships between appraisal and other key HR activities. The strength of the linkage between appraisal and other HR activities ultimately defines the credibility of the overall system and generates desired employ-

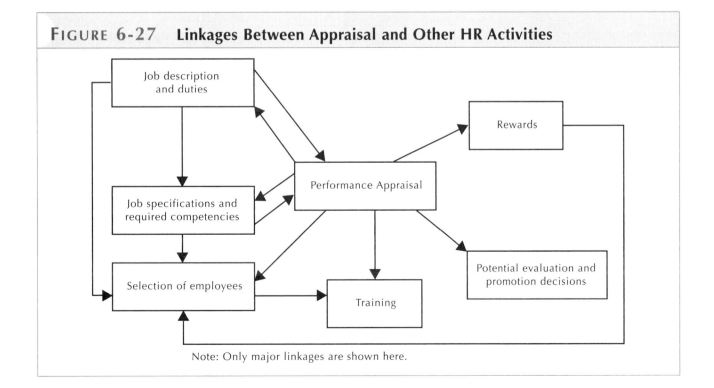

FIGURE 6-27   Linkages Between Appraisal and Other HR Activities

Note: Only major linkages are shown here.

Focus on Ethics:

How Watchful Should a Firm Be?

With advances in technology, monitoring employees has become increasingly easier. However, some of these are ethically questionable. Evaluate the ethical appropriateness of the following situations.

1. Before making formal job offers to managers, Firm M routinely hires private investigators who conduct background checks through court documents, perform media searches, root through the candidate's garbage (looking for remnants of drug or other compromising acts such as child pornography), and ask around about the habits and lifestyles of the candidates.

2. Firm M, which is planning to acquire Firm T, wants to ensure that T's employees are the "right fit." It hires people to create embarrassing situations at Firm T to test how its employees would respond under stress.

3. Firm W, a financial institution, routinely monitors its key employees via spy software to see whether any of them visit Casinos or gambling websites.

4. Firm Q installed video cameras in its cafeteria, washrooms, and staff lounges to ensure that none of the employees uses drugs, carries weapons, or wastes work time.

5. Firm N monitors how frequently its employees use profane or obscene language at work and incorporates this into its annual appraisal results.

6. Firm K will not hire a manager (or will get rid of the person on some pretext) if his or her spouse is not in a socially respectable position to protect the company's reputation in the larger society.

ee behaviours. For example, appraisal will only give useful feedback to the employees about performance no matter how well it is designed. In the absence of other supporting HR activities (e.g., rewards, career growth potential, design of challenging jobs), sustained high performance may not be forthcoming.

CREATING A LEARNING ORGANIZATION

Learning involves the innovative use of information available to an organization and the awareness of patterns and consequences of one's experiences. Members of a learning organization learn from their experiences rather than being bound by their past experiences and history, innovating and re-engineering systems and procedures continually to improve them. An organization and its employees can learn from several sources including the external world (competitors, customers, suppliers), the organization's past actions (its strategies, responses to problem situations), the existing processes and their consequences (e.g., the rules governing various activities), and the collective consciousness (the experience of all of the above). However, because of factors such as strong bureaucratic structures, high task specialization, and focus on short-term (financial) performance measures, only rarely do organizations take full advantage of learning opportunities.

Learning can occur at two levels: adaptive or transformational.

- An adaptive organization focuses on making incremental improvements to processes, strategies, systems, and products.

- A transformational organization makes quantum leaps in its processes, products, and technology and makes radical changes in its structure and strategies to accomplish them.

Whatever the scope of learning, a critical ingredient of the model is the human resources. If the employees are to make appropriate decisions, they must have valid information. In **learning organizations**, information sharing reaches extraordinary levels. Various techniques such as reports, meetings, financial statements, newsletters, e-mail, voice-mail, intranets, and broadcasts are used to facilitate information transmission.

> One firm routinely feeds the results of customer surveys to all employees, along with company performance on 100 key operational dimensions.

Establishment of a learning culture is vital as well. To achieve this, a firm must encourage "unlearning." This needs to start with the top management and includes every single employee. According to some researchers, "first, top level executives and senior managers must unlearn their own 'arrogance of accomplishment'... [that is] the attitude so often seen at the top of the organization that assumes, by virtue of my position and my record of achievement, I am excused from the need for further learning...until management unlearns...it cannot model the learning it expects of workers."[26]

Successful learning organizations also assume that everyone is capable of learning new things and will create a rewarding, supportive environment where employees are encouraged to experiment. Further, task assignments and promotions are also planned with the learning agenda in mind. When employees are hired, their ability to learn rather than their ability to do the present job is crucial.

> A past president of Pepsi-Cola focused on infusing the organization with learners. According to him, the best way to start is to hire a group of proven managers without having any particular jobs in mind for them. As job openings emerge, they can be fed into them; meanwhile, the company has access to the skills of proficient managers who are not overly influenced by the internal culture and past ways of doing things.[27]

Chapter 8 provides more details on the actions needed to create a learning organization.

> **Learning organizations** learn from their experiences (instead of being bound by past experiences and history) innovating and re-engineering systems and procedures continually.

Implications for Practice

1. Performance appraisal is a critical activity aiming to provide an accurate picture of past performance and future potential of employees. It affects practically every other organizational activity and, hence, has to be carefully planned and executed.

2. Clear, outcome oriented, realistic performance standards should be established where possible to ensure that actual performance is measured directly and objectively.

3. A combination of appraisal procedures that matches the organization's strategy, culture, and needs should be selected. The appraisal procedure should not only review past performance but also focus on developing future potential and improving future performance. The appraisal process should be designed with consultation and involvement from other parts of the organization.

4. To reduce appraisal biases and errors, it is important to train raters and appraisees in the appraisal procedure.

5. The development interview should attempt to balance positive areas of performance and those areas where performance is deficient, so that the employee receives a realistic view of performance.

6. If an employee's performance is inadequate, the cause has to be investigated. If it is a lack of skill or experience, the necessary improvements have to be made part of the goals discussed with the employee. Ideally, a step-by-step plan will be the outcome of the interview process.

7. Managers and human resource specialists need to be keenly aware that poor performance, especially when widespread, may reflect problems with management styles and human resource systems. A thorough review of the current managerial practices and systems is necessary in this instance.

8. To be effective in today's quickly changing world, it is important to design learning organizations that are able to adapt continually and respond to changes. Creating a learning culture begins with top management who should be prepared to "unlearn" past successful strategy and experiment

with new strategies and systems to respond to the new realities.

Key Terms for Review

360-degree appraisal system, p. 183

Assessment centres, p. 181

Attention, p. 188

Attribution errors, p. 169

Behaviourally anchored rating scales (BARS), p. 176

Bureaucratic controls, p. 171

Categorization, p. 167

Central tendency (range restriction) error, p. 169

Checklist, p. 173

Comparative evaluation methods, p. 182

Concurrent validity, p. 168

Construct validity, p. 168

Content validity, p. 168

Continuous performance monitoring, p. 188

Criterion-related validity, p. 168

Critical incident method, p. 174

Developmental evaluation interviews, p. 190

Direct assessment, p. 164

Face validity, p. 168

Field review method, p. 177

Forced distributions, p. 182

Halo error, p. 169

Indirect assessment , p. 166

Learning organizations, p. 195

Leniency error, p. 169

Management-by-objectives (MBO), p. 179

Market control, p. 171

Non-verifiable performance measures, p. 164

Performance appraisal, p. 164

Performance criteria, p. 162

Performance distribution assessment (PDA), p. 188

Performance standards, p. 163

Performance tests, p. 177

Personal prejudices, p. 169

Point allocation method, p. 183

Predictive validity, p. 168

Ranking, p. 182

Rating scale, p. 172

Recency error, p. 169

Reliability, p. 166

Self-appraisal, p. 178

Self-serving errors, p. 169

Severity or strictness error, p. 169

Stereotypes, p. 169

Validity, p. 166

Verifiable performance measures, p. 164

Discussion Questions

1. If you were asked to evaluate the performance appraisal system of an organization, what attributes or dimensions would you consider? Explain and illustrate where relevant.

2. Choose one evaluation approach each from the various past-, present-, and future-oriented approaches discussed in the chapter for an organization of your choice and explain why you consider this approach to be appropriate in this instance.

3. If you were asked to assess the performance of a work team, what approach would you take? Why?

4. For an organization that widely uses temporary project teams but rewards employees on an individual basis for their contributions, what appraisal procedure would you suggest? What precautions would you take?

Critical Thinking Questions

1. The institution where you are currently enrolled as a student has hired you to look into the appraisal procedures for its support staff. What criteria would you employ? What questions would you ask?

2. Consider a fast food outlet employing 15 cashiers/cooks and an electronic firm employing 50 software programmers. What appraisal system and evaluation criteria are likely to be relevant in each case? Why?

3. How would you go about designing an appraisal system for a team of seven construction workers who move from one construction project to another continually?

4. "Appraisal must result in learning just as learning must precede appraisal," commented one writer. Evaluate the statement based on the material discussed in this chapter.

Web Research

Visit popular recruitment websites (such as Monster.com or Workopolis.com) and collect four different recruitment ads for a senior managerial position (e.g., Human Resource Manager, Financial Adviser, Marketing Manager). What performance criteria do the ads reflect? Do you see overlaps in the performance criteria suggested by different firms? How do they compare to the concepts discussed in this chapter?

CASE INCIDENT

Office Products Limited

Office Products Limited is a medium sized distributor of a number of office machines and equipment. It has a policy of on-site service for all the equipment it sells. Aggressive marketing and introduction of a performance-based compensation system has resulted in the fast sales growth of the firm. In just two years, the company's sales have increased by 220%.

Customers were beginning to note delays in service and maintenance of equipment. About one-third of the customers noted that they had to make a second call to Office Products before the service personnel arrived at the site. At the end of each service trip, the customer was expected to complete a form evaluating the service of the technician who attended the call. The relevant portions of the form are

FIGURE A

Office Products Limited
Client Survey

Date Service Requested: _____   Today's Date: _____   Time: _____

Name of the Attending Technician: _____

We strive to deliver a high quality service to you. Please take a minute to fill the following details. The information you provide will help us to provide even better service in the future. If you rate "need to improve" for any item, please write detailed comments below.

	Excellent (5)	Good (4)	Satisfactory (3)	Fair (2)	Need to improve (1)
Did the technician:					
1. explain everything properly?	❑	❑	❑	❑	❑
2. appear professional?	❑	❑	❑	❑	❑
3. appear knowledgeable?	❑	❑	❑	❑	❑
4. service the call with speed?	❑	❑	❑	❑	❑
5. appear polite?	❑	❑	❑	❑	❑
Your overall evaluation of this service call:	❑	❑	❑	❑	❑

Comments:

....

....

This part of the form to be filled by the service technician:

Details of the problem/service job: _____

Time arrived: _____   Time departed: _____

Materials used: _____

_____

1. What is your assessment of the situation?

2. What improvements would you recommend to the various procedures, especially in the context of evaluating service technicians?

(continued)

shown in Figure A. The technicians were given a straight monthly salary plus a bonus based on their overall performance including number of clients visited in each period.

By and large, the quality of work of most technicians was rated as satisfactory; the average rating for the team of 11 service personnel was 3.4 on a 5-point scale. However, the technicians were not doing any preventive maintenance when they visited the site. Preventive maintenance routines include dusting, adjusting, oiling, and replacing parts that are worn out or nearly worn out. Many clients felt that more preventive maintenance by the technicians would have resulted in fewer service calls and delays.

Questions

1. *What is your assessment of the situation?*

2. *What improvements would you recommend to the various procedures, especially in the context of evaluating service technicians?*

CASE

Metro Water Utility: Ensuring Safety

One of the outcomes of the tragedy that struck Meadow Brook Town (see the case at the end of Chapter 3 for details) was the provincial government's decision to tighten and upgrade safety regulations in all waterworks. Some of the smaller municipality waterworks were also amalgamated to reap economies of scale and install uniform testing procedures. The present decision situation involves Metro Water Utility, a new, amalgamated water utility that has 50 operating personnel including 15 safety and quality inspectors and 20 mechanics/plumbers.

Two of the waterworks that now form part of Metro had no formal appraisal procedures for their staff in the past. One had an informal system where the supervisors kept track of critical incidents and communicated the events annually or, in rare instances, semi-annually. One waterwork had used a short rating form for all its employees. The form expected each supervisor to rate all subordinates on a four-point scale of poor, average, good, and very good on five dimensions (performance, attitude, cooperation, initiative, and absenteeism). The total score for each employee was summed up and those with 15 or above each year were given raises. In general, 70% of the staff received raises.

The amalgamated utility is now planning to introduce a new performance appraisal system. Everyone agrees that a prime focus of the new evaluation procedure should be on water safety. One suggestion was to slightly modify the existing rating form to include "concern for safety" as a sixth dimension. There was no support for this idea, however. In the end, the utility decided to hire a consultant to look into the current situation and suggest a course of action.

Questions

1. *If you were the consultant, how would you go about designing a new appraisal system for the utility? What steps will you take?*

2. *Is it adequate to modify the current rating form? Why?*

3. *Elaborate the various dimensions and components of an appraisal system that you would design for the utility.*

PART 5

PERFORMANCE IMPROVEMENT

This part discusses two important activities for improving individual and group performance. Chapter 7 looks at various training approaches that enhance performance while Chapter 8 discusses employee counselling and disciplinary systems.

7 TRAINING AND PERFORMANCE ENHANCEMENT

Skill needs of employees continue to escalate and are in continuous change. Learning is now a life-long requirement with organizations needing to provide the infrastructure to support continuous learning.[1]

Dana Robinson and James Robinson

CHAPTER OBJECTIVES

After studying this chapter, you should be able to:

- Outline the steps in performance gap assessment

- Determine when training is appropriate to solve organizational problems

- Discuss the steps in training needs assessment

- Detail the various learning principles involved in determining which training programs to use

- Discuss popular training approaches to enhance employee performance

- Describe the major approaches to evaluate training effectiveness

- Outline an approach to facilitate continuous learning and create a learning organization

The regional division of Canadian Insurance Company employed 320 employees. Recent competition from large global firms, department stores, and banks (entering the lucrative field of insurance or with associates in the field) was beginning to cut into the firm's market share and profits. Customer surveys indicated that the firm's service was at par with or slightly below that of key competitors. Employee surveys also indicated that role requirements were not always clear and employees often faced conflicting demands from supervisors. A significant percentage of employees also noted the inability of supervisors to deal with the demands of a diverse workforce. After a detailed analysis of the relevant facts, the regional human resource manager requested a major increase in the training budget for the next period. After considerable deliberation, the budget was granted and the firm embarked on a large training program. The firm focused on three major types of training and with the help of a local university and two industry experts, it focused on providing the latest technical and service related facts to sales staff. Each sales person had to undergo training for eleven weekends on a variety of topics including developments in the insurance industry, response to customers, sales techniques, and claims processing routines. They were also trained to recognize the task interdependencies among various job incumbents and divisions and the need for information sharing. All supervisors underwent leadership and diversity management skills training. All clerical and administrative staff were introduced to new workplace technology with particular focus on information processing and retrieval, customer tracking, and profiling. The cost of the entire program was $800 000! However, the firm's management felt that it had more than recouped the costs when the customer base showed a 6% increase in the next 18 months (compared to a decline of 0.5% in the previous year). Customer satisfaction surveys indicated that the training program had improved customer service. Internal employee surveys carried out six months after the training gave higher ratings to supervisors for their leadership and people management skills.

Not all training programs are as successful as the above. While most firms engage in some type of training, carefully planned and executed training programs are still not frequent. Indeed, Canada's past record on training is not impressive.

> A study by the Conference Board of Canada report that, compared to many other countries, Canadian employers invest far less into training their workforce. The average training investment for each employee in Canada was $859 in year 2000, roughly the same as in 1993. This compares with an average of $1278 in Europe, $1206 in Australia and New Zealand, $1091 in Asia, and $957 in the United States.[2]

With an aging workforce and scarce skills, innovative ways to leverage existing human resources to achieve organizational success are needed. New employees have to be trained quickly. The highly diverse workforce also requires new interpersonal and communication skills for both supervisors and employees.

Yet, training is not a panacea for all performance related problems. There are several instances where performance improvement is linked to other factors such as system improvement, staffing plan, and job design. Further, if training is not well planned and executed, the organization may not reap many of the benefits as discussed in the next section. Additionally, even well planned training programs may not always produce desired results. This means that training programs have to be continuously evaluated for their effectiveness.

This chapter introduces a variety of training approaches that enhance employee skills and competencies. As well, approaches to evaluating training programs are detailed. Finally, the challenge of creating a dynamic learning organization is discussed.

Figure 7-1 shows the sequence of steps involved in training to enhance performance. First, the level at which performance gap exists has to be identified. Training, rather than changes in organization structure, technology, or other variables, should be confirmed as the solution to removing performance deficiency at this time. After this, a second step identifies precise training needs after a thorough analysis of the organization, the job, and the individuals involved. This, in turn, defines the training objectives, program content, and training methodology. The criteria to be used for

Publications on training:
www.trainingsupersite.com/

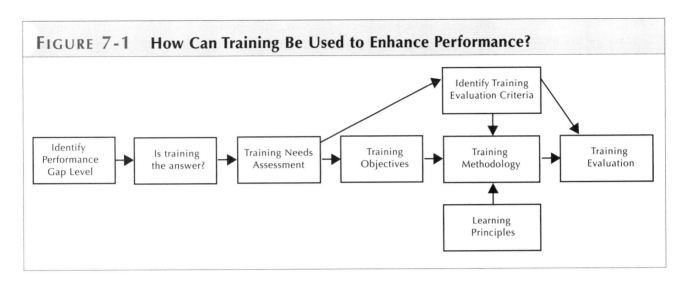

FIGURE 7-1   How Can Training Be Used to Enhance Performance?

training evaluation have to be identified and used to assess the overall value of the training. The learning emerging from the overall exercise has to be used for refining training program objectives and training methodology.

The next section looks at the first step: identifying the level and reason for performance deficiency.

PERFORMANCE GAP ANALYSIS

To be successful, an organization must be effective at four levels: organization, structural and system, process or task, and individual employee (Figure 7-2). **Performance gap analysis** involves a careful examination of the firm's functioning at organizational,

Performance gap analysis involves a careful examination of a firm's functioning at organizational, structural and system, process or task, and employee levels in order to identify performance deficiencies.

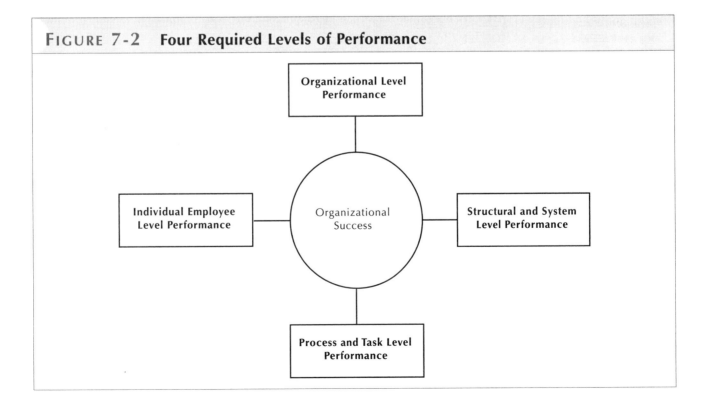

FIGURE 7-2   Four Required Levels of Performance

structural and system, process or task, and employee levels in order to identify performance deficiency.

LEVEL 1. ORGANIZATIONAL LEVEL

To be effective, an organization's mission, goals, managerial philosophy, and strategy must be compatible with needs of the larger environments and reflect changes in the priorities of its constituents. This means that a firm should, among other things:

- respond to the needs of its customers by offering the right products and services;
- have a clear idea of where it is going and where it wants to go;
- be competitive;
- focus on a strategy that recognizes the firm's inherent competitive strengths;
- acquire resources from the environments on a timely and efficient basis;
- respond to the needs of its constituents including the larger society within which it operates; and
- change, even reinvent, on a timely basis to meet the emerging challenges.

LEVEL 2. STRUCTURAL AND SYSTEM LEVEL

A firm's internal structure and systems should facilitate the achievement of organizational goals and strategies and timely response to stakeholder demands. This, in turn, requires that a firm:

- be structured to facilitate effective and efficient delivery of products and services to the market;
- have internal systems and procedures that help accomplish the organizational mission;
- measure performance at various levels using procedures in alignment with basic strategy;
- have human resource systems that support organizational strategy accomplishment; and
- take timely corrective actions to remove performance gaps at different systems levels.

LEVEL 3. PROCESS OR TASK LEVEL

A process is a series of steps or actions that convert a specific input into an output.

> The various processes (including lectures, student projects, student presentations, and field projects) in a college or university convert incoming high school diploma holders (raw materials) into graduates and post-graduate degree holders (products).

A process is further divided into jobs and tasks (see Chapter 3). Despite the best goals and structure, an organization can succeed in the long term only if internal processes are logically and efficiently planned and executed to maximize efficiency, quality, and member commitment. This, in turn, means that an organization should:

- align its process goals with overall organizational goals;

- have adequate systems and processes to achieve organizational strategy;

- ensure consistency in systems and processes;

- have adequate and relevant criteria to measure process effectiveness and efficiency; and

- continuously monitor and improve processes.

LEVEL 4. INDIVIDUAL EMPLOYEE LEVEL

Finally, in the absence of skilled and motivated employees, goals are unlikely to be met regardless of how clearly defined they are. To ensure adequate employee performance, an organization should ensure that employees:

- are aware of their job requirements and standards of excellence expected;

- possess adequate levels of motivation;

- have all the required skills, knowledge, and competencies; and

- possess appropriate work related values.

While training can contribute to improved performance at all levels, its maximum impact is at the individual employee level. For this reason, our primary focus in this chapter is employee training. The approaches discussed in Chapters 2, 3, and 4 aim to improve performance at organization, system, and process levels.

Information on training needs analysis:
www.hr-guide.com

IS TRAINING THE ANSWER?

As already mentioned, employee training might not achieve the desired results if the problem is primarily at the system or task level. Consider the following example.

> If the production capabilities are constrained by machine availability or availability of raw materials, no amount of employee training is likely to produce results. If demand for products is affected by a general market slump (as during a recession), simply training the salesforce may not produce any tangible results in the short run.

To determine whether a particular performance deficiency is correctable through training, it is useful to look at two factors:

- First, if the performance deficiency is limited to just a few individuals, it is more likely to be caused by lack of training. On the other hand, if there is a general performance deficiency in the workforce, it more likely reflects a systemic deficiency like poor hiring practices, inappropriate performance standards, inadequate rewards, or poor communication. Simply training the employees without changing the other systems may not produce desired results.

- Second, it is useful to examine whether the deficiency is limited to simply one area of performance or all aspects of performance. If there is deficiency on several dimensions of performance, then, again, it is more likely attributable to some systemic deficiency not correctable thorough training alone.

> Thus, if a supervisor's performance deficiency is visible only in poor communication skills, a training problem is more likely than if the deficiency is seen in every aspect of planning, organizing, directing, controlling and rewarding subordinates. In the latter

FIGURE 7-3   Is Training Appropriate?

		How Many Employees Face the Same Deficiency?	
		Few	*Many*
On How Many Dimensions Is the Performance Deficient?	*Few*	Training is appropriate	Training is probably appropriate
	Many	Training is probably inappropriate	Training is inappropriate

instance, it is, once again, more likely to be a systemic issue like a poor hire. Simply training the supervisor may not solve the problem.

Given the above, there are four possible scenarios (Figure 7-3). Training is ideally suited when only a few employees are deficient on a few performance dimensions. For other settings, careful analysis should precede a decision to embark on a major training program. Figure 7-4 lists the alternate, appropriate responses for some sample situations. As shown in the figure, training is relevant only in some of these settings. Other actions such as job redesign or resource acquisition are necessary in other settings.

Identification of appropriate solutions requires more in-depth analysis of performance gap at each of the above four levels. The performance at each level has to be assessed on specific criteria or using performance variables as multiple variables or factors may influence overall outcome.[3] For this purpose, five performance related variables are considered: direction, capacity, consistency, motivation, and expertise. In total, 20 possibilities have to be considered for the possible performance gap (Figure 7-5).

DIRECTION

Performance is affected by the direction or focus of the firm, system, or person under study. There are several firms that have clear goals, mission statements, and systems

FIGURE 7-4   Performance Gaps Require Different Responses

If performance gap seems to be caused by the employees...	The solution may lie in...
Lacking required tools or materials	Provision of resources
Not supported by appropriate technical specialists	Increased technical support
Perceiving no clear and equitable linkage between efforts and rewards	Changes in reward system
Not being aware of policies, objectives	Provision of more information
Working with inferior technology or equipment	Process/Task redesign

FIGURE 7-5 Questions Used for Performance Gap Analysis at Four Levels on Five Performance Variables

Level/Variable	Organizational	Structure and System	Process or Task	Employee
Direction	Do the organizational mission, strategy and goals fit internal and external realities?	Are the organization's systems supportive of the organizational strategy? Is the structure appropriate given the strategy?	Are appropriate processes and technologies present? Do the present jobs and tasks further organizational success?	Are individual employee's goals consistent with organizational goals? Are employees fully aware of organizational mission?
Capacity	Are resources and leadership adequate to achieve organizational goals and mission?	Can the structure facilitate timely and correct decisions? Is the information processing capacity of various systems adequate?	Can the processes and tasks produce the right quantity and quality of products and services at the right time?	Do the employees have the physical, mental and other capacity to perform well?
Consistency	Are the strategies, goals, and mission mutually consistent and consistent with environmental needs and internal strengths? Does the strategy take advantage of competitive advantage and minimize risk?	Is the degree of specialization and integration of various functions appropriate given the strategy? Are the various functions and systems mutually consistent in their demands on the organization and its members?	Are the various tasks and processes mutually consistent? Are the decision rules employed to integrate various tasks logical and cognizant of the interdependence among tasks?	Do individual employees understand and support the various systems and decisions? Are the actions of various employees and functionaries mutually consistent?
Motivation	Do the organization's culture and managerial philosophy result in high motivation on the part of everyone concerned?	Do the structure and various systems encourage behaviour that is consistent with organizational mission and strategies?	Do the various tasks and processes have motivating property? Do the jobs provide a sense of meaning and task identity to the job incumbent?	Are individual employees motivated to excel in whatever they do?
Expertise	Are the top managers true leaders? What level of expertise do the Board and the Chief Executive possess? Can the CEO and key managers inspire high performance?	Do the structure and various systems facilitate the creation and maintenance of required expertise?	Are the processes and tasks continuously being modified to take advantage of emerging expertise and knowledge? Does the organization invest in upgrading its technology?	Do the employees have all required skills, knowledge, and competencies to perform well?

thus providing focus to member efforts. In the case of less successful firms, such clarity in focus is missing.

CAPACITY

All systems have limitations on their capacity or capabilities. Successful organizations are able to acquire adequate resources (including human resources) from outside environments on a regular basis. But even these organizations may not be able to change process capacity in the short run.

CONSISTENCY

It is not enough to have clear goals and procedures; these must also be mutually consistent. If a firm's performance evaluation system is not consistent with its reward system or training system, problems emerge. Within each activity and system, the various components should also be mutually consistent.

MOTIVATION

The drive, the desire to excel, and the overall persistence of efforts characterize successful organizations and individuals. There are some structures that energize individuals while others create apathy, indifference, and frustration.

EXPERTISE

Information on technology and training: *www.itworldcanada.com/*

Do the members have the necessary expertise to perform at a high level? Is the technology sophisticated enough to be a source of competitive strength? Are managers (from the top level to lowest level supervisor) qualified to lead? Answers to such questions indicate how far and how fast an organization can go.

Before venturing into training programs, the firm must ask the precise reason for performance deficiency and ensure that the deficiency is correctable through training. Sample questions to ask at each level are shown in Figure 7-5. Once training is identified as the solution, the precise training needs have to be identified. The steps involved are discussed in the next section.

TRAINING NEEDS ASSESSMENT

Training needs assessment is a careful diagnosis of environmental, organizational, operational, and human challenges that can be met through training and the future challenges to be met through long-term development of employees.

Training needs assessment involves a careful diagnosis of environmental, organizational, operational, and human challenges that can be met through training or the future challenges to be met through long-term development of employees. For example, changes in the external environment may present an organization with new challenges. To respond effectively, employees may need training to deal with the change. Consider the experience of several firms after the enactment of human rights legislation and the arrival of a multicultural and diverse workforce.

> After enactment of human rights legislation, several firms had to train their managers and supervisors to ensure that they did not ask questions during job interview that might violate federal or provincial laws. Later, with the emergence of a highly diverse work-

force, the same managers had to be trained in managing diversity. Communication and appraisal practices that were appropriate earlier were no longer acceptable given the profile of the new workforce. Supervisors were alos trained in creating a work environment that was friendly to women, visible minorities, and the physically challenged.

The environmental challenges are often reflected in changes to a firm's strategy, structure, systems, or processes. For the purpose of identifying training needs, three levels of analysis (Figure 7-6) are critical. These are discussed in some detail below.

ORGANIZATIONAL LEVEL ANALYSIS

Organizational level analysis involves a study of the firm at the macro-organizational level, including character and culture, resources, mission, goals, strategy, and environments to identify the general training requirements. It looks at broad, organizational level variables that create a need for training. For example, a new strategy or new product can necessitate new training for employees.

> In the past, Xerox encountered this challenge when it decided to produce computers. Sales personnel, programmers, and production workers had to be trained to produce, sell, and service this new product line.

The first step in an organizational analysis is identification of organizational mission, strategies and short-term objectives in precise terms. The gaps between current and future goals and strategies can provide vital clues to the training and developmental needs.

> For example, if an organization, which historically competed on a low cost strategy, may have plans in the future to compete on the basis of high quality or exemplary service.

Organizational level analysis is the study of a firm at the macro-organizational level including its character and culture, resources, mission, goals, strategy, and environments in order to identify the broad training requirements.

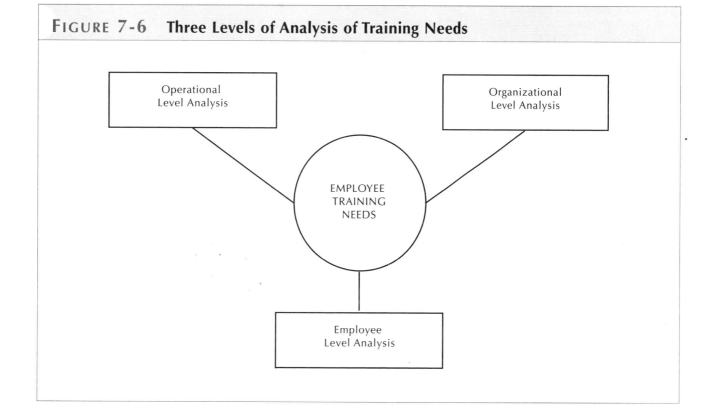

FIGURE 7-6   Three Levels of Analysis of Training Needs

FIGURE 7-7   Illustrative Questions for Organizational Level Analysis

- What changes are likely to occur in our mission or goals? What new competencies or attitudes are required as a result of these changes?

- What employee capabilities and attitudes are critical for our strategic success? What can be improved through training?

- What new skills, competencies, or attitudes are required for future strategic success? How prepared are we for the future on this dimension?

- What environmental changes and trends have implications for our workforce behaviour?

- Do our employees understand and respect corporate culture? Is further training needed?

- Are we attempting to change the corporate culture? What training is needed now?

- Do we consistently achieve our goals and benchmarks? What relevant human variables can be improved through training?

- What are our future challenges? What employee developmental needs are indicated by these?

This in turn necessitates major re-training of production and front-service personnel so that they are ready in time for the introduction of the new strategy.

Illustrative questions for organizational level analysis are shown in Figure 7-7.

OPERATIONAL LEVEL ANALYSIS

Operational level analysis is the study of a firm's systems, processes, and jobs in order to assess training and developmental needs through the systematic and detailed collection of data about each main process, activity, or job in order to identify skill or competency gaps that can be reduced or eliminated through training.

Operational level analysis involves the study of a firm's systems, processes, and jobs in order to assess training and developmental needs. It requires a systematic and detailed collection of data about each main process, activity, or job to identify skill or competency gaps that can be reduced or eliminated through training. Based on a thorough job and task analysis (see Chapter 3 for details), the analyst lists the specific competencies, skills, knowledge, and attitudes that should be acquired or enhanced at various job or activity levels. Illustrative approaches to operational level analysis are shown in Figure 7-8.

FIGURE 7-8   Illustrative Approaches to Operational Analysis

- Interviews with managers, supervisors, and employees to find out about production problems.

- Observation of jobs to identify inefficient or inconsistent practices.

- Surveys of managers and staff using questionnaires, telephone, fax, or internet.

- Examination of blueprints of newly acquired machines to assess skill requirements.

- Examination of company records (including rejection and wastage records, customer satisfaction reports, employee grievance records, safety, and accident reports).

- Examination of company records on staff movements, supervisory requests for various categories of employees, and a comparison of expected demand for and supply of employee categories.

- Focus groups of employees or managers to identify problems to be avoided through training

- Flowcharting of the various activities to identify redundancies or bottlenecks.

- Information from outside constituents like customers, suppliers, members of the public, etc.

Where feasible, industry standards and benchmarks must be employed to compare the firm's performance on various dimensions. This, in turn, provides information on current and future training needs. When time permits, customers, suppliers, and other outside constituents are contacted to gauge their satisfaction with the firm's performance. The views of these outsiders may often provide objective data about service quality and product performance that can give important clues on training needs within the firm. Internally, the views of managers and staff provide important insights into current and future training needs.

EMPLOYEE LEVEL ANALYSIS

Employee level analysis focuses on the training needs of individual employees or work teams comparing their current expertise and attitude levels to those ideally required to perform tasks at optimal levels. This level of analysis is done to find out whether:

- employee performance is substandard and whether training can help improve it;

- employees are capable of undergoing training. This is commonly referred to as "readiness for training" and refers to whether the potential trainee has the necessary ability, attitudes, beliefs, and motivation necessary to successfully undergo the training and apply it on the job; and

- the employee's work environment facilitates transfer of knowledge to workplace.

Training needs for each employee must be determined. Various approaches and documents can be used to gauge employee needs for training (Figure 7-9). Needs may be determined by the performance management (or human resources) department, supervisors, self-nomination, or a combination.

Supervisors see employee performance daily so are a valuable source of recommendations for training. Figure 7-10 lists sample survey questions given to supervisors in a food processing plant to help assess the training needs of operational personnel. The exact questions vary depending on the type of company and the operations involved. Supervisory recommendations, while useful on most occasions, can

Employee level analysis focuses on the training needs of individual employees or work teams comparing their current expertise and attitude levels to those ideally required to perform tasks at optimal levels.

FIGURE 7-9 Assessing Training Needs at the Employee Level

- Performance appraisal records of employees indicating consistent deficiencies.
- Results of performance or job knowledge tests.
- Company records indicating performance deficiencies of specific sections or teams. (Examples: late deliveries, downtime, repairs, equipment utilization, customer complaints)
- Critical incidents reported by employees and supervisors.
- Requests from supervisors for specific types of employees who are in short supply.
- Employee surveys indicating their desire for specific training programs.
- Supervisory feedback on training needs of their subordinates.
- Observation (especially in areas such as leadership, communication, counselling).
- Records of exit interviews with employees indicating absence of developmental training.
- Industry information on skill levels of employees in similar firms.
- Equipment/process blueprints indicating required operator/maintenance skills.

FIGURE 7-10   Sample Questions in a Supervisory Survey Form for Assessing Employee Training Needs

Prince Edward Island Potato Processors

This form collects some important information on the training needs of your employees. The information you provide will assist the human resource management in planning and conducting future training programs for your employees. We would very much appreciate it if you can spend a few minutes to reflect on the performance of your subordinates and indicate your evaluations below.

Your Name: _____   Your Section: _____
Job Title: _____   Number of employees you supervise: _____
Date: _____

This survey has three parts. Please complete all parts.

PART 1

For the purpose of responding to these statements, consider all your employees as a group. We are interested in their typical behaviours or practices. Please indicate your assessment of the current state of affairs below using the following scale:
5= Outstanding; 4= Very good; 3= Good; 2= Fair; 1= Needs improvement

  1. Concern shown by your employees for safety   ❑
  2. Concern shown by your employees for workplace cleanliness   ❑
  3. Overall work quality   ❑
  4. Meeting performance or output standards   ❑
  5. Absenteeism record   ❑
  6. Overall efficiency (consider lost time, wastage, etc.)   ❑
  7. Teamwork and cooperation exhibited by the employees (where relevant)   ❑
  8. General understanding of organizational goals by the employees   ❑
  9. Overall work commitment by the employees   ❑
10. Overall employee morale   ❑

PART 2

In this part, we would like you to respond to a few questions which may have implications for work practices or skills needed by your employees. Please answer each question using the scales: 3= yes, very much; 2= yes, to a limited extent; and 1= no

  1. Have there been any changes in the processes in the last year?   ❑
  2. Has your unit installed any new machinery in the last year?   ❑
  3. Has your unit introduced any new product in the last year?   ❑
  4. Have the demographics of your workforce changed very much in the last year?   ❑
  5. Have there been any new quality standards introduced in the last year?   ❑

PART 3

Below, please provide information on the skills that could improve the performance of your employees. In the case of employees who are already doing well, please feel to suggest training or development programs that might benefit the person in the long term.

	Employee name	**Suggested skill improvement**
1		
2		
3		
4		
...		
N		

Thank you for taking the time to fill out this survey. Please return it to the Human Resource Department in the attached envelope.

be biased. Suggestions may be made to banish troublemakers, "hide" surplus employees who are temporarily expendable, or reward good workers. Since these are not valid reasons for training, the human resource department often reviews supervisory recommendations to verify the need.

Often, employees are encouraged to nominate themselves for various training programs. Many organizations also use high accident rates, low morale and motivation, and other problems as indicators of training needs. Production records, quality control reports, grievances, safety reports, absenteeism and turnover statistics, and exit interviews can indicate problems that should be addressed through training or development efforts. Training needs may also become apparent from career planning and development discussions or performance appraisal reviews. Although training is not an organizational cure-all, undesirable trends may be evidence of a poorly prepared workforce.

Finally, if the overall organizational culture or management philosophy does not support newly acquired skills or values, the training may be wasted. Before embarking on a major training program, the firm should ensure that the newly acquired knowledge and skills are valued by everyone in the organization and the existing systems and culture will reinforce new learning. International Harvester's experience is noteworthy in this context.

Articles on succession planning: *www.chrs.net*

> At International Harvester, supervisors who received two weeks of training designed to increase consideration for their subordinates showed improvement in attitudes immediately following the training program. However, six months later, only those who believed their bosses wanted them to be considerate maintained their new attitudes. A deterioration in human relations practices also resulted when a supervisory training program taught practices in conflict with union norms.[4]

TRAINING OBJECTIVES

Training objectives, which are formulated after a thorough training needs analysis, specify the performance outcomes and changes in trainee behaviours and outcomes that are expected from the proposed training program. To be useful, these objectives should clearly specify:

1. Performance outcomes or behaviours of the trainee after training.
2. Quality or level of performance of the trainee.
3. Time period within which they are to be accomplished.
4. Conditions under which they should occur.

Training objectives, formulated after a thorough training needs analysis, specify the performance outcomes and changes in trainee behaviours and outcomes that are expected from the proposed training program.

The objectives offer a standard against which individual trainee performance (after training) and the effectiveness of the training program can be measured.

> The objectives for a call centre operator might be stated as follows: (1) Greet all customers in both official languages, offer service in one of the languages, and route the customer to the appropriate agent; (2) Provide product and price information to call-in customers within 45 seconds; (3) Offer contact phone numbers on additional warranty or service information and transfer the call to appropriate personnel within 30 seconds; (4) Take customer orders accurately within two minutes; and (5) Maintain an overall customer satisfaction rating of 4 or above (on a 5-point scale) 90% of the time.

Objectives such as these give the trainer and the trainee specific goals that can be used by both to evaluate their success. As the example illustrates, objectives should:

- be a statement about the trainee;

- refer to specific behaviour or performance of the trainee. Rather than simply stating "the training should result in improved call centre operator performance," it defines what "improved service" means in specific terms;

- focus on terminal learning, outcomes, or performance. It is a description of the end-state, not of the process;[5]

- specify the conditions under which the outcome will be measured. In the above case, the trainee's behaviour will be measured in a call-centre when responding to customers using a telephone. If the trainee is expected to use a specific instrument or appliance (in the above case, a telephone), this is also specified; and

- describe the level of performance deemed necessary. In the above case, the time within which service is to be provided as well as the service quality measure (e.g., customer satisfaction measure) are detailed.

To be useful, the training objective should be linked to the larger strategic direction of the firm. Different strategies emphasize different employee characteristics and performance focus. To get the maximum return on the training investment, training objectives should be closely aligned to the overall mission and strategic direction of the firm. Figure 7-11 illustrates how business strategy shapes training objectives.

One writer suggested that training programs have three levels of objectives, which are listed below in the ascending scale of excellence and difficulty:[6]

- Regular training objectives are recurring or routine and are seen in training programs such as new employee orientation, new product training for salespeople, and supervisory skills training for new supervisors. The objectives for such training programs are based on historic data (e.g., figures from same quarter last year) and a range of possible outcomes (e.g., highest and lowest levels of performance after the training) and establish the minimum standards of performance for the trainer.

- Problem solving objectives help the training department identify and solve human behaviour problems through applied training.

- Innovative goals comprise the highest level of excellence and challenge for the trainer since the focus is to impart new ways of thinking or new behaviour that improves the overall organizational or divisional performance through creative solutions.

> While the focus of both problem solving and innovative training programs is to find good solutions to problems, there is a qualitative difference between the two. A training program that introduces statistical quality control techniques, helping control a process that has gone out of control (in terms of quality), focuses on problem solving. A training program that trains employees in work simplification (cuttine costs or time), re-engineering (adding value to products or reducing costs), or teamwork (generating group synergy) is going beyond "fixing a problem" and is adding real value to the organization. The added earnings are a direct result of the creative thinking and behaviour of the trainees.[7]

Whatever the type of objective, clear, measurable goals communicate to the trainees what they are expected to do when they complete the training. The objectives also tell the trainer what to focus on, how to train, and how to evaluate training effectiveness. Despite the obvious advantages of clear objectives, formulating them to perfectly match with later job responsibilities or task behaviours is not easy. When the job is complex, the trainee cannot be expected to exhibit the same behaviours of a job incumbent who has been performing the task for several years. In such instances, one set of objectives and criteria may be used for initial training evaluation and other supplementary criteria used for evaluating performance at a later time.[8]

Some jobs or processes are not analyzable. An **analyzable process** is one that can be reduced to explicit steps, techniques, instructions, and programs.[9] Unanalyzable tasks are ones without clear knowledge about cause and effect, or about what steps should be taken to achieve the solution. With such tasks, the employee has to use intuition, trial and error, or knowledge gained from past experience. The employee "muddles through" these problems and faces considerable uncertainty while resolving them.

Analyzable process is a process that can be reduced to explicit steps, techniques, instructions, and programs.

> What makes a person a great film actor or a champion figure skater? Obviously, such factors as the dedication of the performer, past training, knowledge, and ability of his or her trainer have important bearings on the outcome. However, there are few standard procedures that make someone an exceptional performer. Other commercial activities such as fashion designing, advertising layout, and creative writing, while "trainable" to an extent, need years of practice and intuitive learning. Establishing clear training objectives in such instances becomes harder.

The training program's content is shaped by the needs assessment and the learning objectives. This content may seek to teach specific skills, provide needed knowledge, or try to influence attitudes. Whatever the content, the program must meet the needs of the organization and the participants. If company goals are not furthered, resources are wasted. Similarly, participants must view the content as relevant to their needs or motivation to learn may be low.

LEARNING PRINCIPLES AND PROGRAM DESIGN

Although it is widely studied, the learning process continues to remain a puzzle. Part of the problem is that learning itself cannot be defined, at least, not in a sense that is acceptable to everyone who is active in the field. Learning cannot be observed; only its results can be measured. Often, we must infer learning by looking at the behaviours or attitudes of learners. Yet, learning is not synonymous with behavioural change.

> Learning about the moon's terrain or the lifestyle of Romans in 200 B.C. may not immediately result in any behavioural change.

In some instances, learning has to be assessed by the way learners respond to information. Hence, for our present purpose, **learning** is defined as changes in attitudes, behaviours, other observable effects, and in the content or storage of information. Often, learning may only represent the mental processing of information. These may, in several instances, lead to new behaviours. However, not all learning is immediately accompanied by behavioural changes.

Learning reflects changes in attitudes, behaviours, other observable effects, and relatively enduring changes in the content or storage of information.

> An engineering designer may learn several concepts that will help a person build a better product. However, in the absence of the right materials and rewards, the innovative behaviour may not emerge. This, of course, does not mean that the person has not learned. It only means that the right circumstances that are needed for the behaviours to emerge have not yet occurred.

LEARNING PRINCIPLES

If learning itself is hard to define, it is easy to imagine the difficulties involved with listing learning principles. **Learning principles** are guidelines to the ways people learn

Learning principles are guidelines to the ways people learn most effectively.

FIGURE 7-11	Link between Corporate Strategy and Training Objectives	

Business Strategy	Typically, the firm's emphasis is on	Training objectives focus on developing
1. Cost leadership strategy[10] focusing on achieving the lowest cost of production and distribution so that it can price lower than its competitors and win a large market share (e.g., Wal-Mart, Texas Instruments)	Cost reduction in production and distribution Predictability in operations Repetitive, efficient operations	Efficiency, productivity Employee skills in a narrow range Fit among operations Improvement of predictability in operations
2. Differentiation strategy where the firm concentrates on creating a highly differentiated product line and marketing program so that it comes across as the class leader in the industry (e.g., IBM, Procter & Gamble)	Creativity and innovation Responsiveness to customers	Service quality Innovation Broad range of skills
3. Focus strategy where the firm focuses on serving a few market segments well rather than going after the entire market (e.g., Rolls-Royce, Calvin Klein)	Product refinement to meet needs of specific customer groups Maintenance of high quality standards Responsiveness to customers	Quality control Customer service Product improvement ideas
4. Product leadership[11] **strategy** where the firm provides superior value by offering a continuous stream of leading edge products or services that make their own and competing products obsolete (e.g., Cognos, Corel)	State of the art products Innovation Improvement in product features	Innovation Creativity Knowledge levels Breadth of skills Ability to work in groups

most effectively (Figure 7-12). Several of these were formulated after decades of research into learning and training. The more learning principles present in a training setting, the more effective training is likely to be. However, not all the principles listed below have equal weight or importance in all training settings.

Learning-Reward Link If the learner perceives a close connection between learning and desired rewards, the learner is more motivated to learn the new material. Learners begin to associate a favourable outcome to a specific change in behaviour or attitude. The more frequently a newly learned response is associated with a desired reward, the more likely it is to recur.

Participation Learning is usually quicker and longer lasting when the learner can participate actively. Participation improves motivation and engages more senses to reinforce the learning process. Once you learn to ride a bicycle or learn to swim, you are unlikely to forget.

Figure 7-12 Key Learning Principles and their Implications for Training Program Design

Learning Principle	Implications for training program design
1. Learning-Reward Link	• Identify positive outcomes of the training early on in program. • Divide the training goal into smaller goals and reinforce achievement of each smaller goal. • Ensure that organizational reward systems are in line with newly learned behaviours. • Recognize that different employees value different rewards (e.g., praise, involvement, money). Plan reward system carefully. • Hook trainees with their own needs early in the training. Find out why the trainees want the training and plan the program accordingly.
2. Participation	• Involve trainees when deciding the pace of training. • As much as possible, use training methods which involve the trainee in the training process. Discussions, role plays, and job rotation score high on involvement while simple lectures or videos involve passive participation.
3. Repetition	• Reinforce a concept using several different examples. • Repeat difficult concepts several times while reviewing learning.
4. Relevance	• Where possible, link the training matter to day-to-day life events. • Emphasize the practical job implications of the newly learned matter. • Do a thorough training needs analysis to ensure that only relevant trainees attend the training session. • Use examples relevant for trainee group when illustrating a concept. • Develop links between previous learning and current material.
5. Transference	• Obtain support from all relevant personnel (e.g., supervisor, senior management) to facilitate transference of learned material to workplace. • Ensure that organizational reward systems reinforce newly learned work behaviours or knowledge. • Develop clear, time-based goals for transference of training. • Identify potential obstacles to transference and deal with them during training.
6. Feedback	• Provide feedback on how well the trainee is doing; as much as possible, use positive reinforcement to strengthen learning. • Provide time to evaluate performance level accomplished.
7. Spaced Approach	• Provide time in between training sessions to think about and practice the newly learned concepts or practices. • When dealing with complex concepts, split them into manageable chunks of information and give a rest period after training in each segment. • Consider the education, maturity level, and life experiences of the trainees when planning rest periods. In general, trainees who score low on these dimensions may need more rest periods than those who were exposed to considerable training earlier.

Repetition Although it is seldom fun, repetition apparently etches a pattern into our memory. Studying for an examination, for example, involves memorization of key ideas to be recalled during the test. Likewise, most people learned the alphabet and the multiplication tables by repetition.

Relevance Learning is helped when the material to be learned is meaningful. For example, trainers usually explain the overall purpose of a job to trainees before explaining specific tasks. This explanation allows the worker to see the relevance of each task and the importance of following the given procedures.

Transference Transference is the application of training to actual job situations. The closer the demands of the training program match the demands of the job, the faster a person learns to master the job. For example, pilots are usually trained in flight simulators because simulators closely resemble the actual cockpit and flight characteristics of a plane. The close match between the simulator and the plane allows the trainee to quickly transfer the learning to actual flight conditions.

Feedback Feedback gives learners information on their progress. With feedback, motivated learners can adjust their behaviour to achieve the quickest possible learning curve. Without feedback, learners cannot gauge their progress and may become discouraged. For example, test grades are feedback on the study habits of test takers.

Spaced Approach A six-hour training program can be done in several ways: a one-day training program lasting six hours, a two-day program with three hours each day, a three-day program with two hours each day, etc. Past research indicates that a **spaced approach** with time gaps for rest and reflection during training is most effective. This helps trainees reflect on the new learning's relevance and to facilitate retention and further learning. Such a spaced approach is particularly important when the training involves learning complex subject matter. However, a longer training cycle may result in cost escalation since the facilities, trainees, and trainers have to be committed to the training program for more time. The performance management department needs to be creative in developing training programs to facilitate spaced practices.

> Instead of the traditional one-day workshop, it may be possible to hold eight one-hour workshops. Instead of a five-day training program, it might be possible to redesign the training program in such a way as to train employees once a week for five weeks.

Finally, it should be pointed out that most employees arrive at the training location with an already well-established cognitive structure. They already know about the firm, their work, and themselves (i.e., their capabilities, strengths, and limitations). Often, to improve a trainee's effectiveness, the existing belief system and cognitive structure of the employee has to be changed. However, any change creates anxiety and stress. Fear of the unknown ("how will the training affect the way I do things at work?"), losing rewards ("will my pay, autonomy or workplace friendships be affected by the new way of doing things?"), incompetence ("I don't know whether I will be able to do learn this new approach"), and of lost investments ("I spent a lot of time and effort to learn to do this; now, they are going to change everything again") are present in many training settings. The trainee's motivation to learn will depend on the answers to these questions.

TRAINING METHODS

Perhaps, there are as many training approaches and combinations as training objectives themselves-a fact that makes the choice of a particular training program very difficult. In selecting a particular training technique, there are several trade-offs. No technique is always best; the best method depends on:

- cost effectiveness of a specific training method;
- training objectives;

Transference is the application of training to actual job situations.

Spaced approach provides time gaps for rest and reflection during training.

SELF-TEST

What Is Your Preferred Learning Method?

This exercise assesses your preferred learning method. Please answer all questions frankly using the anchors *strongly agree* (SA), *agree* (A), *neither agree nor disagree* (NAD), *disagree* (D), or *strongly disagree* (SD). Since your first reaction to a statement is critical, do NOT change your response once you have indicated it.

1. I like courses with periodic quizzes or tests that force me to study on a regular basis.

2. A good instructor is one who makes you question and wonder about things rather than someone who teaches you specific concepts.

3. I like courses where the instructors lectures or plays an active part in teaching the material.

4. The best course is one where the student sets the course objectives and identifies ways of achieving them.

5. I like courses that have elaborate guidelines and datelines attached to all assignments.

6. As a rule, I study the various course materials on a regular basis; I do not need time lines to prompt me to study.

7. The best courses I have taken clearly spelled out course objectives.

8. I often use my own evaluation criteria, exceeding standards used by the instructor, to test my learning in a course.

9. A good course is one where the instructor identifies all quizzes and exams without being influenced by student preferences.

10. I prefer Internet-based courses as they let me learn at my pace and on my time.

Scoring

For statements 1, 3, 5, 7, and 9, assign scores of 5, 4, 3, 2, and 1 for SA, A, NAD, D, and SD respectively. For items 2, 4, 6, 8, and 10, assign scores of 1, 2, 3, 4, and 5 for SA, A, NAD, D, and SD respectively. Total your scores for items 1 through 10.

Interpretation

Your total score will range from 10 to 50. If you scored 40 or above, you prefer a directed, structured course where the instructor plays a key role and provides you encouragement, reinforcement, and evaluates your knowledge. People in this group may find lectures, structured case and class discussions, and clearly structured assignments helpful in learning. A score of 20 or below indicates the opposite: you prefer an independent, less structured course where you explore, investigate, and learn at your pace. In this instance, you have considerable self-awareness and self-discipline to achieve results without the need for an external judge to monitor your performance. People in this group are more comfortable with leaderless discussions, programmed learning techniques, and assignments without clear problem definitions where the student is encouraged to find the problem first before attempting to resolve it. Scores between 20 and 40 indicate that you are comfortable with either mode and can adjust your behaviour to suit the needs of the situation.

- desired program content;
- the available training facilities;
- trainee preferences and capabilities;
- trainer preferences and capabilities; and
- learning principles.

The importance of these six trade-offs depends upon the situation. Consider the following situations.

Cost effectiveness may be a minor factor compared to learning when training an airline pilot in emergency manoeuvres. The training objective of maintaining high safety standards override cost considerations, at least in most instances. However, when training an office clerk in a new filing procedure, the hours spent by the trainer and the trainee and the cost of disruption to office work become more important.

This means that one training method is not universally the best for all occasions. The particular method chosen for an occasion also depends on the type of learning to be imparted. For this purpose, learning is grouped under two broad categories: cognitive learning and behavioural learning.

Cognitive learning causes changes in the content, organization, and storage of information on the part of the trainee. The primary effect of these methods is a change in the trainee's mental representation of objects and events, their characteristics, and their relationships to other objects and events.

In contrast, several other training methods primarily affect the behaviours of the trainee. In **behavioural learning**, relatively permanent changes in a trainee's behaviours occur. By comparing the behaviours of the trainee before and after training, the overall impact of the training program can be assessed.

Several training programs can be carried out at the workplace itself.[12] On the job training, job rotation, and so on fall into this category. In contrast, some other training programs like case studies and lectures are done away from the actual workplace. Figure 7-13 lists some of the more popular on the job and off-the job training programs. The same figure classifies these methods on the basis of the primary learning achieved. It should be emphasized that most training methods aim to achieve both types of learning, although to different degrees. The classification used in the figure only highlights the primary learning emphasis of each method. Given the number of training methods available, it is virtually impossible to discuss all of them here. What is attempted below is a brief look at the more popular training methods.

On-the-Job Training Methods

Four popular training methods, namely job instruction training, job rotation, apprenticeship, and coaching are discussed below.

Job Instruction Training

Job instruction training (JIT), imparted directly on the job by a supervisor, coworker, or other trainer, focuses on teaching the employee how to do his or her present job effectively. Almost all employees receive some sort of training in the beginning of their career, although there are significant differences in the depth of training. For some, it may be simply orienting to the equipment and coworkers, while in more progressive organizations, meticulous attention is paid to all job details that can have an impact on the job performance.[13] This method, when

Sidebar definitions:

Cognitive learning causes changes in the content, organization, and storage of information and results in a change in the trainee's mental representation of objects and events, their characteristics, and their relationships to other objects and events.

Behavioural learning occurs when relatively permanent changes in a trainee's behaviour happen.

Job instruction training (JIT) focuses on teaching the employee how to do his or her present job effectively and is usually imparted directly on the job by a supervisor, coworker or other trainer.

FIGURE 7-13 Popular Training Methods

	Primary focus of the training is learning at:	
	Behavioural Level	*Cognitive Level*
On-the-Job Training	Job Instruction Training Job Rotation Apprenticeship	Coaching
Off-the-Job Training	Role Play Simulation	Lecture Case Study Programmed Learning

properly done, can take advantage of various learning principles like active participation by the trainee, repetition, relevance, transference, and feedback. To reap the full benefits, JIT requires a series of carefully planned steps listed below:

1. The organization should clearly identify the skills and competencies that are to be imparted through the training.

2. A carefully planned training schedule that lists the type of skills and order of imparting them is prepared based on 1 above.

3. When the training begins, the trainee first receives an overview of the job and its purpose and the desired performance outcomes.

4. The trainer should next demonstrate the job to provide the employee with a model to copy.

5. Next, the employee is allowed to mimic the trainer's example. Demonstrations by the trainer and practice by the trainee are repeated until the trainee masters the job. The learner is provided with feedback on what was done correctly and how to improve. Repeated demonstrations and practice provide the advantage of repetition. Since the employee is being shown the actions that the job actually requires, the training is transferable.

6. The trainee performs the job without continuous supervision, although the trainer may visit the employee periodically to see if there are any lingering questions.

7. The trainee's performance is assessed after a reasonable period. Skill gaps are identified and corrective actions taken.

In practice several of the above steps may be altogether ignored or only ineffectively carried out. Consequently, many on-the-job training programs do not work very well. Many training programs are not well planned and may miss key skill-building routines or steps. Often, the person chosen to "help Joe learn the job" is not qualified to train the new employee or motivated to do well (often, such a request is considered a distraction). In several instances, trainers may be chosen on the basis of their technical expertise or sheer availability rather on the basis of their training ability. There are certain jobs (e.g., flying an aircraft, fire fighting) that require learning complex job behaviours where safety concerns or high speed of production processes make JIT inappropriate. In such instances, mock work settings (e.g., vestibules or simulators) are used to teach primary job skills. Only after acquiring a certain degree of mastery, is a trainee allowed to work in a real-life job setting. Even then, the person typically starts as an apprentice and only after considerable on-the job experience is allowed to perform the job independently.

As the workplace becomes technically more sophisticated, **embedded training** is becoming a popular type of job instruction training. An example of embedded training is an office machine with graphic displays showing where a problem has occurred and listing the steps required to solve it. Many machines and software programs have built-in instructional systems and tutorials. The biggest advantage of embedded training is that it is available whenever the trainee needs it. This makes it extremely relevant and transference to a work setting is almost automatic. On the other hand, designing effective, easy to understand learning systems is no easy task. The training program designer must anticipate all potential problem areas and be able to respond to them effectively. Considerable expertise is, hence, needed to design such training programs.

Job Rotation Job rotation moves trainees from job to job, teaching them various required skills and helping them to recognize the interdependencies among the jobs. Job instruction training normally precedes each move from a job. In job rotation, the

Embedded training is a form of job training using built-in instructional systems like the machine that graphically displays where a problem has occurred and lists the steps required to solve it.

Job rotation moves trainees from job to job to teach various required skills and to enable recognition of the interdependencies among the jobs.

focus is on moving an employee among similar jobs (e.g., a clerk, assistant, and secretary). When an employee is rotated among totally different functions or operations, it is usually referred to as **cross-functional training** (e.g., sales, accounting).

Cross-functional training is the practice of rotating an employee through different functions or operations.

> Job rotation and cross-functional training are particularly popular in Japan. In many Japanese organizations, teams of three or four newly hired employees go through extended job rotation and cross-training programs (sometimes lasting as long as two years) that put them into all the organization's functional units (e.g., accounting, engineering, finance, human resource management, manufacturing, marketing, and sales). The system is also supported by the assignment of a mentor (called "godfather") to each new employee. After the job rotation, the godfather, the trainee, and the supervisors usually jointly decide which career the trainee should pursue. The result of such an extensive job rotation is that each employee is aware of the needs of other divisions and is able to make decisions that take into account the needs of various departments and functionaries.

Job rotation and cross training are beneficial in a variety of ways.

- Employees gain a broader perspective of the work that is done and this helps them relate their own work to the overall organizational purpose. This, in turn, increases task identity (see Chapter 3) and morale.

- The broader perspective on the part of the employees reduces the need for supervision.

- The cross-departmental and cross-functional ties that invariably emerge out of job rotation and cross training help collaborative problem solving across functions and faster response to problems.

- Workers are provided with variety in their jobs; for many repetitive jobs, where boredom can easily set in, job rotation provides a solution.

- Cross training and job rotation help the organization when vacations, absences, and resignations occur.

Learner participation and high job transferability are learning advantages to job rotation. To be valuable, as in the case of JIT, trainers have to be selected very carefully. A simple and effective way may be to ask for volunteers who are prepared to act as peer trainers to other employees and select the best among the volunteers. When selecting peer trainers—that is, high performing workers who double as internal, on-the-job trainers—both technical expertise and teaching ability have to be considered. Several firms offer training to the selected volunteers to become successful trainers.

> In one large retail chain, peer trainers receive five days of training before they are allowed to train coworkers. The training program for peer trainers focuses on adult learning theory, technical skills, analytical and facilitative skills, and supplementary technical skills.

Some organizations promote the peer trainer role as an honour and offer tangible rewards to peer trainers. Consider how Disney rewards its peer trainers.

> At Disney theme parks, peer trainers are paid extra while they are instructing. They also bear a "trainer" designation on their name badges-a sign of accomplishment.

Apprenticeships incorporate both classroom instruction and learning from an experienced employee or supervisor.

Apprenticeships Apprenticeships, most often used to teach various skilled trades, involve both classroom instruction and learning from watching more experienced employees or supervisors. Most tradespeople, such as plumbers, carpenters, bricklayers, and electricians are trained through formal apprenticeship programs. Internships are similar to apprenticeships. Just as apprenticeships are a route to skilled, blue-collar jobs, internships are a route to white-collar or managerial jobs. Often, high school and university students are hired as interns during summer vacation and are put on trainee positions. Recently, several universities have introduced programs where students can gain course credits for work done outside of the classroom.

Both apprenticeships and internships score high on several learning principles such as participation, feedback, and transference. A major advantage of apprenticeship is that trainees can earn while they learn. This is important because several trades require years of learning. Most learners start with very modest pay, but the salary goes up as their skills improve. To get the best results, as in the case of other training programs, clear definition of training objectives and incorporation of modelling, practice, feedback, and evaluation are necessary. This means that:

- the desired skills and the level of proficiency have to be defined in precise terms;
- the trainee's readiness to learn and current knowledge of relevant concepts should be assessed;
- the trainer must both be technically competent and possess training skills;
- the trainer can effectively demonstrate each step focusing on safety, quality, and speed;
- the trainee performs under supervision initially and is continuously monitored later to ensure accomplishment of all training objectives.

Coaching Coaching covers all activities on the part of a trainer (called a coach) intended to help an employee master skills and competencies, reach full potential, and facilitate life-long learning. Coaches in organizational settings, like sports coaches, exhibit a variety of successful styles and behaviours; however, almost all successful coaches provide a model for the trainee to copy and advice when they face problems. Most companies use some coaching, though the extent and quality of coaching varies considerably across organizations. In small organizations, coaching is almost always handled by the supervisor or manager and not the human resource department. In some other instances, a senior executive or employee may act as a coach. Someone who receives coaching by another person to assume that person's specific job is called an understudy. A senior executive may designate a replacement well before retirement so that person can serve as an understudy. Participation, feedback, and job transference are likely to be high in this form of learning. Coaching is discussed in greater detail in Chapter 8.

Coaching refers to a trainer's (coach's) activities that are intended to help employees master skills and competencies, to reach full work potential, and to facilitate life-long learning.

Knowledge Management: *www.cio.com/forums/ knowledge/*

Off-the-Job Training Methods
A variety of off-the-job training techniques currently exist. The more popular ones in the Canadian industry are discussed below.

Lectures A lecture involves a trainer verbally communicating what he or she wants the trainee to learn. The communication in a pure lecture format is typically one way—from the trainer to the trainees. Lecture is a popular approach because it offers relative economy and a meaningful organization of materials. A variety of different lecture formats are currently available (see Figure 7-14).

Lecture is the verbal communication of material from the trainer to the trainee.

A lecture is the least time consuming way to present a large amount of information. The lecture can also be used when large number of trainees are involved. Lectures to even 200 or 300 students are not uncommon in some universities and colleges. However, participation, feedback, transference, and repetition are often low. Feedback and participation can be improved when discussion is permitted after the lecture.

Television, films, slides, and filmstrip presentations are comparable to lectures. A meaningful organization of materials and initial audience interest are potential strengths of these approaches.

FIGURE 7-14   Variations of the Lecture Method

Lecture:

The trainer, with or without use of audio-visual aids, makes a presentation to convey concepts and practices to the trainees. In a traditional lecture format, the communication is mainly one way. Sometimes, videos, films, or guest lectures are used to supplement the key points in the lecture.

Team Presentation:

Two or more trainers make presentations on different dimensions of the topic or different topics forming part of a single main topic. Again, audio-visual tools may supplement the presentations. Team teaching can bring alternate viewpoints to the trainee, although it requires more time and resources to coordinate the work of different trainers. If not well planned, the teaching styles of trainers may not match each other, resulting in confusion in trainee's minds.

Panels:

Two or more speakers present information and debate with each other on important points thus providing alternate view points. However, trainees who are naive about a topic may not be able to understand the subtleties of the topic which emerge out of the debates.

Guest Lectures:

An expert on the topic makes a guest appearance and supplements the trainer's lecture. The guest is able to elaborate on specific points or show a concept's practical utility thus increasing relevance and transference. For guest lecturers to be effective, the expectations from them have to be clearly identified and communicated so that their material is well-integrated into the lecture topic.

Case studies describe how employees, teams, or organizations dealt with a challenge or problem and encourage trainees to analyze and learn by critiquing and synthesizing the described events and actions.

Case Study Case Studies describe how employees, teams, or organizations dealt with a challenge or decision problem and encourage trainees to analyze and learn by critiquing and synthesizing events and actions narrated in the case. By studying a case, trainees learn about real or hypothetical circumstances and the actions others took under those circumstances. A major assumption of the case study approach is that employees are most likely to recall and use principles that they learned through a process of self-discovery. Cases have been claimed to develop higher-order intellectual skills such as analysis, synthesis, and evaluation of information.[14] Besides learning from the content of the case, trainees can develop decision-making skills. Cases can help trainees develop risk-taking behaviours since they encourage the analysis of uncertain outcomes and the evaluation of alternate actions on the basis of limited information.

Developing good cases require considerable time and skill. It is not enough if the case-writer has access to all relevant information; the material must be presented in such a way that there is scope for further analysis and choice of varying actions under different assumptions. Good cases are also accompanied by searching questions that guide the trainee's analysis of the information. The cases should also be written in an interesting manner to maintain trainee interest. Unfortunately, many cases may not fit all the requirements so many firms seek out cases from publishers and universities. However, the pre-existing cases may not actually relate to the current work situation of the firm, thus limiting their relevance.

When cases are meaningful and similar to work related situations, there is some transference. There also is the advantage of participation through discussion of the case. Feedback and repetition are usually lacking. In general, cases are more effective for developing problem-solving skills rather than developing some other important skills (e.g., interpersonal skills).

Programmed Learning Programmed learning includes a variety of tools such as self-instructional materials, computer programs, pre-recorded audio or video tapes, automated teaching machines and programmed texts-all aiming to systematically present information to the trainee using the principles of reinforcement and encouraging the trainee to learn the material at own pace. These are particularly useful when employees are dispersed geographically or when learning requires little interaction with the trainer or other trainees.

> Pepsi-Cola Management Institute is responsible for training bottlers all over the world. To contend with this dispersion, it created a network of videotape recorders and supplied bottlers with videotaped materials.

The biggest advantage of programmed learning is that it offers an opportunity to learn at one's own pace rather than a pace determined by the trainer. Commonly, instructional materials contain key concepts followed by a series of questions and answers. After a question is answered, trainees check their answers against the correct ones and evaluate their own learning. If the trainee was right, he or she is encouraged to proceed with the next lesson. If not, the trainee is directed to review accompanying materials. For the organization, programmed learning requires fewer trainers, reduces the costs associated with travel and training facilities, and makes simultaneous multiple-site training practical.

> When the Four Seasons Hotel opened its new hotel in Indonesia, it needed to teach basic English skills to 580 of its new employees. Four Seasons created a self-directed learning centre enabling the employees to learn English by themselves. Video-recorders, training booklets, and teaching modules were prepared for the purpose.[15]

Programmed learning provides several of the learning principles such as participation, repetition, relevance, and feedback. Transference of the new knowledge to actual work settings may vary depending on the type of job and type of skills taught. In recent times, several companies have combined traditional classroom training with programmed learning especially using the Internet and computers (coined as "**e-learning**"). IBM is a good example in this context.

> With more than 300 new front-line managers to train each year and with less available training time each year, IBM Canada decided that it was time to take e-learning up a level. A program called Basic Blue for Managers retains a week of classroom workshops, but now surrounds that week with six months of e-learning. Basic Blue starts with a three to four month phase in which new managers follow weekly e-learning on human resources and leadership themes also working collaboratively on-line with management colleagues using case studies. What was a month in the classroom is now down to five days in addition to the e-learning. IBM notes that this approach delivers five times the program at one-third the cost. The out of pocket costs of training has also come down from $400 to $135 for each employee per day.[16]

In the future, e-learning may play an even more important role in many organizations (Figure 7-15). The biggest challenge, however, is the motivation and maturity required on the part of the trainee for effective programmed and e-learning modes. This type of learning requires motivation and self-discipline to learn on one's own. Developing good quality programmed learning materials costs considerable money and time, which may make it out of reach of several smaller firms. The cheaper packages that may be available in the market may not, often, meet the specific training needs of the firm.

Role-Playing Role-playing requires trainees to act out roles or identities assigned to them with the objective of bringing better understanding of the belief system and behaviours of the person(s) depicted in the role. For example, a male supervisor and

Programmed learning is the use of tools such as self-instructional materials, computer programs, pre-recorded audio or video tapes, automated teaching machines, and programmed texts to systematically present information to the trainee using the principles of reinforcement and to encourage learning at a comfortable pace.

E-learning is the combination of programmed learning and the use of the Internet.

Role-playing requires trainees to act out roles or identities assigned to them in order to develop a better understanding of the belief system and behaviours of the person depicted.

FIGURE 7-15   E-learning

E-learning combines the advantages of programmed learning with the openness and interactivity of the Internet. In many e-learning sessions, participants start by reading a primer, then play on-line simulations, and finally are assessed electronically on what they have learned. In between, should they desire additional assistance, they can go through programmed learning tutorials and "chat" sessions with other participants. In some more advanced e-learning situations, group cases may be offered which the participants have to resolve in a virtual team setting—often participants separated geographically and temporally. The advantages of e-learning include:

- the participant can choose the pace of learning
- the participants can choose the time for learning
- interactivity and connectivity of the Internet and company-wide intranet are utilized
- group assignments not typically seen in programmed learning can be used
- the combination of new material with a participant's real life work problems facilitate transference of learning
- compared to traditional in-class lectures and cases, it is less expensive to administer

E-learning is not a panacea for all training ills, however. Depending on the training objectives, several e-learning programs may be expensive to design initially. Designing effective e-learning programs also requires the presence of highly qualified trainers and program designers. E-learning is likely to be most beneficial when it is combined with other face-to-face training sessions especially when teaching process skills such as leadership and communication. The trainee's maturity and commitment to learning may determine the training. It may be unsuitable for individuals who do not have self-discipline.

---

a female worker may trade roles. The result? Usually participants exaggerate each other's behaviour. Ideally, they both get to see themselves as others see them. The experience may create greater empathy and tolerance of individual differences.

Role-plays differ from simulations in the level of details provided to trainees. Typically, unlike in simulations, limited information regarding the roles or the situation is provided. This requires the trainee to improvise often acting out stereotypes, assumptions, and perceptions that facilitate interpersonal communication and attitude change. Unlike simulations and vestibule training where physical responses are needed (e.g., pull a lever, switch on a meter), role-plays focus on interpersonal responses (e.g., seek information, counsel another). The outcomes in a simulation are also predetermined and totally dependent on the trainee's actions (e.g., if a trainee does not switch on a circuit, electricity will not flow). In the case of role-plays, emotions intervene making a range of (at times even unpredictable) outcomes possible.

Typically, role-plays aim to change attitudes of trainees, such as to improve racial understanding.

> In the past, the RCMP in British Columbia used role-playing exercises to reduce tensions between members of the force who are of Caucasian and Indian (mainly Sikh) origin.

Role-plays can also help develop interpersonal skills.[17] Many companies employ role-playing to train supervisors to give performance feedback, a crucial managerial skill in motivating employees. Although participation and feedback are present, the inclusion of other learning principles depends on the situation. To be effective, role-plays must be carefully designed. Some guidelines for improving the effectiveness of role-play are listed in Figure 7-16.

Closely related to role-playing is role or behaviour modelling. **Behaviour modelling** involves presenting trainees with a model who exhibits key behaviours that are

Behaviour modelling occurs when trainees copy key behaviours presented to them via a model.

FIGURE 7-16   How to Improve the Effectiveness of Role-plays

1. Before starting the role-play, explain its objectives clearly.

2. Specify the time available for the role-play.

3. Describe the situation and the role in general terms. Encourage the trainee to improvise other details.

4. If possible, videotape the role-play so that the participants can see their own behaviour. This is particularly important if the training focuses on improving nonverbal communication skills.

5. Closely monitor the role-play, making notes of each participant's reactions and arguments and intensity of feelings expressed. This information will be critical for providing feedback at the end of the role-play.

6. At the end of the role-play, request that each trainee discuss their new insights of each other, what they learned during the exercise, and how the experience relates to workplace behaviour

7. Provide feedback and guidance in a non-judgmental tone.

8. Supplement the role-play with other instructional aids and information sources.

---

later copied by the trainees. Employees may learn a new behaviour through modelling by observing a new behaviour and then imitating it. The recreation of the behaviour may be videotaped so that the trainer and trainee can review and criticize the behaviour. Often, when watching the ideal behaviour, the trainee also gets to see the negative consequences of not behaving in the ideal way. Observing both the positive and negative consequences of the taped behaviour gives the employee vicarious reinforcement to adopt the right behaviour. One area where this approach has been used successfully is in teaching supervisors the correct way to discipline employees.

> In the supervisory training of a large, unionized steel company, supervisors were put through a half-day disciplinary training session that used videotape-based behaviour modelling. After a short lecture on the principles of discipline, trainees were shown a brief tape of a supervisor conducting a disciplinary interview incorrectly and another where the discipline was handled properly. Then trainees were paired off and each one was told to "discipline" his or her partner using the correct method. These mock discipline sessions were filmed and played back, often to the horror of the participants. Each saw how they appeared when they conducted a disciplinary interview. After a brief and largely positive critique from the trainer, each supervisor conducted a second and a third "discipline session" that was followed by a critique. By the end of the morning, each trainee was able to conduct a disciplinary interview in the correct manner. Whether this training was actually transferred to their day-to-day behaviour on the job was not evaluated by the training department or the shop manager.[18]

Role modelling is discussed in greater detail in Chapter 8.

Simulation Simulations represent real life situations and permit trainees to see the impact of their decisions and behaviours in an artificial, risk-free environment. The essence of a good simulation is its ability to replicate the reality accurately and completely so that the trainee's actions and decisions result in outcomes that mirror the actual job outcomes. In several simulations, a mechanical simulator that replicates the major features of the work situation and provides almost instantaneous feedback is used. Driving simulators used in driver's education programs are an example. When simulators do not provide immediate feedback, they are sometimes called vestibules, although they still represent reality. The training facilities in some hotels provide a good example in this context.

Simulations represent real-life situations and permit trainees to see the impact of their decisions and behaviours in an artificial, risk-free environment.

At the corporate training facilities of Best Western Motels and Hotels, vestibules exist that duplicate a typical motel room, a typical front counter, and a typical restaurant kitchen. This allows trainees to practice housekeeping, front-counter service, and kitchen skills without disrupting the operations of any one property.

Many grocers and departmental stores use mock cash registers to train their employees. Almost all air pilot training institutes have some form of simulator where trainees "fly" planes in simulated settings controlling for different degrees of air turbulence and visibility. Simulations, however, need not always focus on imparting mechanical or other psycho-motor skills or behaviours. They are also helpful in developing several managerial and communication skills.[19]

For example, in one managerial simulation, trainees are assigned different roles in a fictitious firm. On the basis of memos and correspondence, each trainee interacts with other members of the management team over a six-hour training period. The trainee's responses to various decision problems are carefully recorded and assessed by the trainer. At the end of the exercise, the trainee is given performance feedback and ways to improve effectiveness are discussed.

Computer simulations are gaining in popularity. These are often employed in the form of games. Players (or trainees) make a decision and the computer determines the outcome of the decision, given the conditions under which it was programmed. This technique is used most commonly to train managers, who otherwise might have to use trial and error in decision-making.

The biggest advantage of simulations is that they offer real-life experience without disrupting normal operations. Separate simulators or vestibules can be set up with the same kind of equipment that will be used on the job. This arrangement allows transference, repetition, and participation. The meaningful organization of materials and feedback is also possible

The key success factor is how well the simulator replicates the reality. Even a minor difference between the simulated setting and the reality can have grave consequences in some instances as American Airlines found out.

In 1995, American Airlines Flight 965 crashed into the mountains in Colombia after one of the pilots entered the wrong code into a navigational computer. An investigation into the accident indicated that the pilots might have been fooled by a discrepancy between standard navigational charts and the navigation computer. Charts used by airlines list a radio beacon signal "R" to mean "Rozo"; however, the navigational computer interpreted it as "Romeo" and changed the plane's direction toward the mountains. Following this accident, airline simulators began to pay greater attention to navigational codes and potential errors.[20]

EVALUATING TRAINING EFFECTIVENESS

Training evaluation is used to determine if training is effective on specific criteria.

Training evaluation aims to determine if training is effective on specific criteria. Training serves as a transformation process. Untrained employees are transformed into capable workers, and present workers may be trained to assume new responsibilities. Despite the clearest training objectives or intentions, the training may not deliver the intended results. The evaluation process enables a firm to monitor its training success and take corrective actions to improve future outcomes. More specifically, training evaluation facilitates the following:

- To identify the program's success in meeting training objectives;
- To evaluate the degree of transference of learning to actual work;

Focus on Small Business:

How to Train Family?

While almost all the training principles discussed in this chapter are relevant to small businesses (with appropriate modification for situational, resource, or size constraints), family businesses face some unique challenges that make supplementary training programs necessary.[21] Some of these challenges include issues such as how to make smooth management transition from one generation to the next, how to smooth conflicts between family members who may hold different positions but equal family status and power, and how to motivate a family member who has access to all rewards regardless of their performance.

This means that training programs in family businesses should look at issues beyond simple job duties and performance requirements. Past studies indicate the following as some of the more important areas to focus on in such businesses.

- How to handle family issues which conflict with business issues.

- How to educate the older generation to adapt their past success in the light of emerging realities.

- How to educate the newer generation to work with the older generation and yet be able to infuse newer ideas.

- How to train the management to make a smooth transition from one generation to the next.

- How to help managers to learn from the experiences of other family firms.

- How to manage conflicts among family members over business decisions.

- How to motivate affluent, powerful family members to contribute their share of efforts.

- How to create a smooth relationship between hired, professional employees and family members who are in high positions.

Some of the issues that are unique to family businesses are also worth special attention:

- Managing the transition[22]: How to identify and implement a smooth transition of ownership from one generation to the next.

- Management continuity: How to prepare the next generation professionally and personally to participate in the business. What should they do now and five years from now?

- Establishing rules of entry: How to establish and communicate a set of consistent rules, standards of performance and compensation to family members, especially, non-nuclear family members.

Over the years, several universities have begun offering family business programs. These programs can assist family businesses by addressing issues that affect their long-term health and survival.

- To identify the profiles of trainees who benefit most and least from specific types of training programs;

- To plan future training programs;

- To help the firm to choose between alternate approaches to productivity improvement (e.g., training versus job re-design; training versus better selection of employees); and

- To identify the most cost-effective training approach.

Depending on the precise objective of evaluation, alternate training evaluation methods may be used. The steps involved in training evaluation are shown in Figure 7-17. As may be seen from the figure, it consists of four interrelated steps. These are discussed below.

IDENTIFY TRAINING OBJECTIVES

As already discussed, the objectives may be cognitive, attitudinal, or behavioural outcomes or a combination of these. Whatever they are, they have to be clearly identified including the desired level of proficiency.

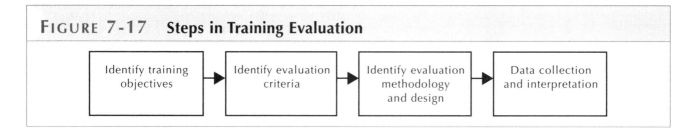

FIGURE 7-17   **Steps in Training Evaluation**

Identify training objectives → Identify evaluation criteria → Identify evaluation methodology and design → Data collection and interpretation

IDENTIFY EVALUATION CRITERIA

Almost all systematic evaluations should begin with a clear specification of desired training outcomes. These training outcomes, in turn, define the criteria to be used for assessing training effectiveness.[23] The more important criteria for training evaluation are shown in Figure 7-18.

Training objectives determine which of the criteria is best suited for evaluation purposes. If the objective were to increase the knowledge of the participants, the obvi-

FIGURE 7-18   **Criteria for Training Evaluation**

1. Reaction to the program. The most popular of the criteria employed, reaction simply measures the trainee's satisfaction with the program. Questions such as "how satisfied are you with the program?" "do you feel that you have learned necessary skills?" and "would you recommend this training to another?" are often employed. There is no real measure of the trainee's learning or change in attitudes or behaviours.

2. Knowledge of the material. This measures the trainee's acquisition of new knowledge and concepts. Typically, knowledge is measured through examinations and tests—thus, a person's newly acquired awareness of the safety rules or knowledge of inventory planning technique may be measured by a paper and pencil test. There are two problems here, however. Unless the trainee's knowledge was measured before and after training, it cannot be assumed that the learning was due to training. Also, knowledge need not always relate to behavioural changes or work outcomes.

3. Skills and behaviours. Measures of changes in trainee's technical or motor skills and behaviours are often used to gauge training effectiveness. Skills assessed may range from purely mechanical (e.g., properly use a lathe or milling machine) to interpersonal (e.g., coaching skills). The assessments may be made through observation (by neutral observers, peers, customers, or superiors), random testing, ratings by others, or an inspection of work sample. When supervisors who sent the trainee to the program rate their later behaviours, there is an inherent tendency to inflate post-training ratings to justify the decision to send them for training.

4. Attitudes. Often, trainee's attitudes toward other people and things are used as a measure of the training effectiveness. For example, attitudes toward minority workers may be used as a measure of effectiveness of a diversity training program. To be useful, pre- and post-training measures of attitudes have to be compared; but even here, there are limitations. Attitudes, which are typically assessed through self-reports, may be quite unreliable. Respondents often give a "socially desirable response," that is, they answer the way they think they should answer to save face. The validity of self-reports can be increased by assuring the respondent's anonymity.

5. Organizational results. Ideally, the impact of training on organizational results should be assessed to gauge training effectiveness. Here, the focus is on determining the training program's payoff for the larger organization. Examples include reduced number of accidents, employee turnover, errors, improvements in service quality, number of product innovations, and so on. However, determining the cause-effect relationship between training programs and organizational results is by no means, an easy task. The time difference between a training program and the availability of reports on organizational results can be many months. Who can, then, confidently assert that it was the training program and nothing else that caused the results?

ous choice would be the knowledge criterion; if it were behaviour change, then the behaviour criterion would be the most appropriate measure. As shown in Figure 7-18, no criterion is devoid of limitations. Often, by combining various criteria, the firm is able to gauge the effectiveness of a training program in a more valid fashion.

IDENTIFY EVALUATION METHODOLOGY AND DESIGNS

The training evaluation design determines the degree of confidence that can be placed on the results. A good training evaluation design must ensure two things: the results (or changes in the pre- and post-training results) are attributable, and only attributable, to the training and nothing else; the results must be generalizable to other similar training groups and training situations. In other words, the findings must be representative of the larger population from which this training program was chosen as a sample. In real life, a number of factors prevent achievement of these two objectives (see Figure 7-19) making the identification of an evaluation design a challenging task.[24] In the past, a number of alternate designs have been offered seeking to eliminate one or more of the threats to the validity shown in the figure. An elaborate discussion of all is beyond the scope of this book. What is attempted below is a brief look at five important designs in the context of training evaluation.

Post-test Only Design In this design, training outcomes such as knowledge and attitude are measured only at the end of the training. Though popular, there are several inherent problems with this approach. How do we know that the training caused a high score on knowledge or attitude? We can never be sure. Perhaps the participants were already experienced and did not need the training in the first place.

Pre-test, Post-test Design A slightly better approach would be to measure a trainee's attitude, knowledge, or behaviour before the training begins and again at the conclusion of the training. This provides a crude measure of the change caused by the training. However, even here, it is not at all certain that it was the training and not some other factor that caused the change. Many of the threats listed in Figure 7-19 are present, reducing the validity of the measure.

Pre-test, Post-test, Control Group Design In this design, trainees are randomly chosen from the work group and assigned to two groups: the training group and the control group. Each group is given a pre- and a post-test, but only the training group receives the instruction. The design looks like this:

Group 1 (Training group, randomly chosen)	Pre-test	Training given	Post-test
Group 2 (Control group, randomly chosen)	Pre-test	No training given	Post-test

Since factors like outside events, maturation and effects of pre-tests on post-tests should affect both groups equally, this design is able to produce more reliable measures of actual training effectiveness. However, this design cannot control for several other sources of invalidity (e.g., regression towards the mean score).

Four Group Design A more complex, four-group design avoids several of the threats to validity. The overall design looks like this:

Group 1 (Training group, randomly chosen)	Pre-test	Training given	Post-test
Group 2 (Control group, randomly chosen)	Pre-test	No training given	Post-test
Group 3 (Training group, randomly chosen)		Training given	Post-test
Group 4 (Control group, randomly chosen)		No training given	Post-test

By having two extra groups without pre-testing, this design permits the identification (and removal) of the effects of pre-testing on subsequent test performance. It also

FIGURE 7-19   Threats to Validity of Training Evaluation

1. Occurrence of external event(s). The occurrence of external events, other than training, may have an impact on the training. For example, the results of a training program to heighten safety consciousness in a mine may be significantly influenced if a large mine explosion occured elsewhere while the miners were undergoing the training.

2. Changes in the trainees. This phenomenon, which is also referred to as *maturation*, refers to the various biological and psychological changes in the trainees attributable to passage of time. Trainees become older (and sometimes wiser), fatigued, more or less interested in the training between the beginning of the program and its end. This means that the difference between pre- and post-training assessments of their knowledge is not solely attributable to training. This is particularly relevant when the training program is of long duration (e.g., a two-year management training program).

3. Loss of trainees. This, also referred to as *mortality*, denotes the departure of some of the trainees from the training program (for whatever reason). While the loss of any trainee is of concern, the persons who are most likely to leave are those who scored poorly on the pre-test (because they got discouraged) or very high (because they are the better employees who got called for another assignment or left the firm for a better job). The result could be that most of the trainees are of "average" capabilities or motivation, thus confounding the results of training evaluation.

4. Measurement error. Questionnaires used to gauge attitude change measures are particularly susceptible to this error if they do not have adequate reliability, but even the so-called "objective" and observational measures may be inaccurate. Grading standards can show substantial variation from one occasion to the next, the observer may miss important items and even mechanical instruments have random fluctuations.

5. Differential selection of participants. In an effort to weed out the influences of external events and trainee characteristics, *control groups* are often used. The control group does not undergo any training but its performance and/or attitude is measured at different time periods and compared to the training group to determine the impact of other, extraneous factors on learning outcomes. However, if the members of the control and training groups are not randomly chosen, the differences between them may be attributable to their innate differences rather than to training. In practice, random selection of participants in work situations may not be feasible on many occasions. Many organizations use one work group as the training group and another as the control group (e.g., day shift versus evening shift). However, there may be systematic differences between day and night shift workers which bias the findings.

6. Effects of pre-tests on post-test score. When the trainees have been pre-tested, this itself can influence their subsequent test scores. Not only do most individuals become "test-wise" thus improving their later scores, but a pre-test may also sensitize the trainee to key topics in the training program to which he or she pays additional attention, thus influencing the later outcomes.

7. Reaction to evaluation. The very fact that they are going to be evaluated at the end of the training program may cause a trainee to try harder in the training program, affecting his or her test scores. The higher test score, in this instance, is not attributable to the quality of the training, but the very fact of being evaluated or observed. For example, while they are being observed, the trainees may exhibit a set of behaviours that is not part of their normal, everyday behaviour.

---

helps remove other sources of invalidity. For example, a comparison of the post-test scores of Group 4 with the pre-test scores for Groups 1 and 2 permits the analysis of the combined effects of maturation and external events on training outcomes. While theoretically elegant, this design may prove to be impractical in several situations.

Time-Series Design In a time series design, training outcomes are collected at periodic intervals pre- and post-training. Unlike other designs where pre-measures are collected only once before the training and once after the training, this design necessitates multiple measurements before and after training. The design may look something like this:

Time Periods						
	1	2	3	4	5	6	7

	1	2	3	4	5	6	7
Training group	Pre-test 1	Pre-test 2	Pre-test 3	Training	Post-test 4	Post-test 5	Post-test 6
Control group	Pre-test 1	Pre-test 2	Pre-test 3	Pre-test 4	Pre-test 5	Pre-test 6	Pre-test 7

A comparison control group is also sometimes used in a time series design that is also continuously tested using the same instrument. The time series design permits the analysis of the stability of the training outcomes over time. This is particularly helpful when the intent is to measure observable outcomes such as absenteeism, accidents, or productivity.

How to Select a Design? As may be apparent by now, there is no single appropriate design for all occasions. An evaluation design has to be chosen in the light of training objectives, desired outcomes, and the situational contingencies facing the firm. Some of the factors to consider when choosing an evaluation design are briefly discussed below.

Training Objectives The specific objectives of the training program (learning, attitude change, behavioural change, etc) make certain evaluation designs and measurement criteria more relevant than others.

> If the objective is to improve trainee's communication skills, a pre-test-post-test control group design is needed. However, if the training aims to help the trainee achieve a pre-determined level of performance in a certain area (e.g., data analysis using a certain software), a pre-test may not be very necessary. In the latter situation, the focus is not on how much change has occurred, rather on whether the trainee, after training, is able to perform the job at a certain level.

Size of the Project If the project involves a large number of trainees with multiple classes a more complex design is necessary than when training a small team of employees.

Managerial Expertise If the managers and performance analysts do not have the requisite data analysis skills, then complex research designs are wasted since much of the available information may not be analyz and used.

Ongoing versus One-time If the philosophy of training is well-entrenched within the firm and training programs take place on an on-going basis affecting several employees, there is justification for complex research designs. A one-time, modest training program involving a few workers may not justify the costs of an elaborate design.

Urgency The time available for research, data collection, and analysis also plays a major role in determining the appropriateness of a design. If the firm desires to have the information urgently, some designs like the time series are simply out of the question.

Organization Culture Some organizations emphasize results and measurements, where others pay relatively less attention to these. Simpler, softer measures of learning are likely to be encountered in organizations that do not emphasize tangible results for every project or activity.

DATA COLLECTION AND INTERPRETATION

Whatever evaluation design is chosen, data has to be collected on a timely and accurate basis. The type of data collected will vary depending on the training objectives and the evaluation designs used. However, most evaluations collect attitudinal, performance, behavioural, or cognitive measures.

Attitudinal Measures Popular attitudinal measures include satisfaction and commitment measures, measures of beliefs on a variety of matters (e.g., need for safety, concern for environment), and changes in perceived importance of specific activities (e.g., gender-neutral communication style).

Performance Measures Performance test scores are possible when the training is focused on developing specific skills or competencies.

> A driving test after taking driving lessons and a computer-based test for a programmer's command over a specific programming language would seem logical measures for evaluating the respective training programs. However, even these have limitations. The outcomes may only partially reflect the person's proficiency (e.g., the student who took the driving test was nervous at that time resulting in a poor score). It may not accurately evaluate the trainer's effectiveness, nor does it evaluate the quality of training process itself. For example, the student may have done well in the driving test in spite of the trainer's instructional style.

Behavioural Measures Behavioural measures are particularly relevant to assess the impact of training programs in customer relations, supervisory behaviours, interpersonal communications, and interviewing proficiency. Some of the behaviours looked at include:

- use of specific words or phrases;
- voice modulation;
- order of presentation of information;
- eye contact;
- non-verbal behaviours; and
- hand, face, or leg movements.

However, as pointed out, there is no guarantee that the same behaviours will emerge when the trainee is not being observing.

Cognitive Measures Measures that assess the trainee's cognitive learning are very similar to performance tests except that these are mostly paper and pencil or computer-based tests.

> Most university and college courses (especially in lower level courses) have some written tests that assess the cognitive learning of the students. As in the case of performance measures, other extraneous factors may affect the outcome and not accurately reflect the trainee's learning.

Whatever the information collected, it has to be analyzed and summarized and patterns noted for future action. Often, it is desirable to categorize the findings by trainee's age, gender, years of work experience, level in the hierarchy, and so on to find out possible relationships among variables. Such a detailed analysis also helps to tailor-make the training program to meet the needs of specific trainee groups.

DETERMINING RETURN ON INVESTMENT

Return on investment (ROI) compares the monetary benefits of training with its costs.

Return on investment (ROI) compares the monetary benefits of training with its costs. A training investment should be treated like any other investment decision. No professional manager would invest a significant amount of money without an appropriate cost benefit analysis. Such an analysis assesses the cost effectiveness of a project or program.[25] It also assists a trainer or performance analyst in demonstrating the contribution the training or performance management department makes to the organization's profit.[26]

Training costs include direct and indirect costs.[27] Direct costs include salaries and benefits for all trainers and employees including all those undergoing training and involved in training program design, delivery, and evaluation. These costs also include costs of all program materials, office supplies, rent, and travel costs directly attributable to a specific program. Indirect costs are not related directly to the design and delivery of a specific training program, but reflect a training program's share of costs of general office supplies, support staff salaries, travel costs, and other overheads. Benefits refer to all the gains and benefits attributable to the training. All reductions in production, overtime costs, and wastage and increases in productivity, repeat business, and sales directly attributable to training form part of benefits. Figure 7-20 lists some of the items that go into cost-benefit analysis. Often, the costs avoided or prevented by the new training have to be included to get a clearer idea of the overall benefits.

> Assume that a firm that produces 2000 metal panels per day had, on average, 2% rejection of all its production. Assume that each panel costs $10. If after the training, the rejection rate comes down to 1%, it has saved $200 per day or about $5000 per month (assuming 25 working days per month on average). In the same way, if a safety training program could reduce preventable accidents by one-third, the benefits include not only saving of the obvious costs (e.g., costs of production disruption, loss of material, compensation to employees) but less obvious savings (e.g., difference in insurance premium for high and lower accident rates, revenues saved because of savings in time, etc).

Focus on Ethics

How to Train Employees to Act Ethically

Throughout this book, we have emphasized the need for ethical business conduct. Indeed, if our present system of free enterprise is to continue successfully, it is vital that every employee—from the highest CEO to the lowest level worker—act ethically and responsibly. But how can we ensure that employees are aware of their ethical responsibilities and that they choose the "right" behaviour?

There is no simple answer.[28] By definition, ethics deals with the grey area of moral responsibility, much beyond a person's and a firm's legal responsibility. Since "right" and "wrong" show great variation across individuals,[29] societies, and cultures, establishing a common set of codes that guide behaviour in all situations may be difficult. Yet, an Ethical Code of Conduct which details the minimum expected standards of behaviour may be an important weapon in a firm's arsenal against unethical behaviours.[30] Employees should also be formally exposed to the firm's ethical standards during orientation and subsequent training programs. While the contents of such training will show vast variation across firms, issues to consider may include the following.

- How can we ensure that the firm does not harm any person, other living thing, or the environment?

- How can we ensure integrity in all aspects of operations (including selling, production, accounting, treating its employees, etc)?

- How can we respect and respond to the legitimate demands of our customers, investors, employees, and all other stakeholders? If the stakeholder interests conflict, what rules should be employed to resolve them?

- How can we respect and protect the intellectual property of employees, competitors, and others?

- How can we ensure complete and fair disclosure of all data on operations that affect public safety, health, and welfare?

- How can we ensure that all major decisions by the firm automatically examine associated ethical issues?

Establishing a uniform code of ethical beliefs and behaviours is no simple task in today's global organization employing highly diverse workforces. Yet, it has to be done if the firm is to survive and prosper in the long term. Only a well-designed training program reinforced by other systems can accomplish this goal.

FIGURE 7-20   **Determining Costs and Benefits for a Cost-Benefit Analysis**

COSTS
Direct Costs

1. Training Needs Analysis
 Labour (analyst, clerical staff)
 Material
 Travel
 Telephone, postage, shipping
2. Program Development
 Labour (consultant, analyst, clerical; include salary and benefits)
 Material (office material; CD-ROMs, software, video films)
 Equipment rental
 Travel
 Accommodation
 Per diem expenses
 Postage, shipping, telephone
3. Training Delivery
 Audio-visual equipment, computer, projector rental
 Room rental
 Food and refreshments
 Trainers' salaries
 Trainees' salaries
 Clerical and administrative salaries directly attributable to training
 Lost production
4. Training Evaluation
 Evaluator's fee
 Travel and accommodation (if external evaluator)
 Data analyst's salary and benefits
 Clerical and support staff salary and benefits directly attributable to this phase
 Cost of office space

Indirect Costs
 Clerical and management salaries and benefits
 Postage and shipping
 Telephone, fax, Internet charges
 Pre- and post-training learning materials
 General organizational support; management time (%)

TOTAL COSTS
Number of trainees
Cost per trainee

BENEFITS (illustrative only; varies with industry and firm. The monetary benefits have to be assessed by comparing pre- and post-training performance and multiplying it by relevant dollar figures.)

Increase in production directly attributable to training
Increase in number of customers served
Reductions in:
 Product rejection
 Preventable Accidents
 Wastage
 Absenteeism
 Employee turnover
 Other employee errors

....
....

TOTAL BENEFITS

RETURN ON EACH TRAINING DOLLAR'S TOTAL BENEFITS divided by TOTAL COSTS

CREATING A LEARNING ORGANIZATION

Learning necessarily involves disorganizing what we already have in our memories in order to accommodate new knowledge. It creates a variety of responses and a number of exceptions in decision rules and practices. To organize, on the other hand, involves reducing variety in responses and choices. Thus, in a sense, organizing and learning are essentially antithetical processes, which makes organizational learning inherently contradictory.[31] Today's unpredictable environments make it imperative that organizations continually learn to survive.

> PCL Constructors Inc. in Edmonton is an organization that has recognized the importance of training for continued organizational success. PCL, Canada's largest construction company, requires every staffer to complete at least 35 hours of professional development annually. PCL, which has 1700 employees in Canada and the U.S., offers staff dozens of internally developed programs. The emphasis on training is part of the company's overall philosophy of offering careers rather than jobs to its employees. According to one senior executive in the firm, employee surveys indicate that training and professional development are two of the most valued items by PCL's employees, and in fact attract them to the company. It has also helped the firm to be chosen as one of the top 100 Canadian employers in 2001.[32]

How can an organization encourage its employees to continually learn? What are the characteristics of organizations that facilitate learning? Below, we try to briefly answer these questions.

In learning organizations, employees continually expand their capacity to create the results they truly desire, new thinking is actively encouraged, new behaviours and patterns are continuously explored and fostered and employees are continually learning how to work and learn together.[33] An organization and its managers can learn from several sources: the external world (competitors, customers, suppliers), the organization's past actions (its strategies, its responses to problem situations), the actions of its members (such as their behaviours, the existing culture), the existing processes (such as the rules governing various activities, the systems and procedures), and the collective consciousness (the experience of all of the above).[34] However, because of factors such as strong bureaucratic structures, high task specialization, and focus on short-term (financial) performance measures, only very rarely do organizations take full advantage of learning opportunities.

Learning can occur at two levels: adaptive or transformational.[35] An adaptive organization focuses on making incremental improvements to processes, strategies, structure, and products. In contrast, a transformational organization is interested in making quantum leaps in its processes, products, and technology and makes radical changes in its structure and strategies to accomplish them. The latter type of learning is akin to the re-engineering practices currently popular in a number of organizations. Re-engineering involves fundamental rethinking and radical re-design of products and processes to achieve dramatic improvements in performance. It is possible that a firm may reflect characteristics of both types of learning (depending on the context) and hence fall somewhere along a continuum.

Case studies on organizational change: *www.chrs.net*

Not withstanding the differences, all learning organizations share some common features (see Figure 7-21).[36] These are briefly discussed below.

TAKING A BROAD VIEW OF LEARNING

Prior to industrialization, people did not have "jobs" as we know them today rather, they worked in a number of activities that were determined by the needs of the day.

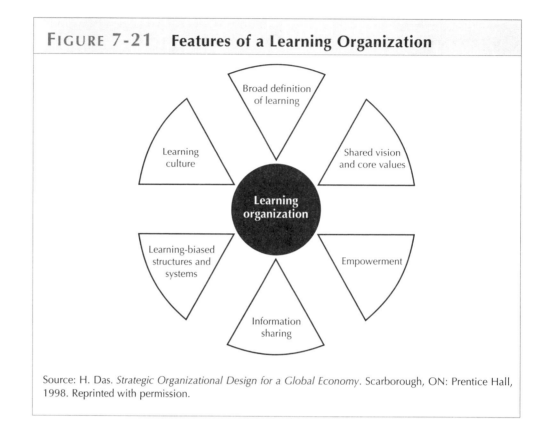

FIGURE 7-21   Features of a Learning Organization

Source: H. Das. *Strategic Organizational Design for a Global Economy*. Scarborough, ON: Prentice Hall, 1998. Reprinted with permission.

Our present conception of jobs limits our learning.[37] The emergence of unions and consequent rigid job classifications also restricted workers to single tasks. A learning organization encourages its employees to go beyond the requirements of their immediate jobs and look at the varied aspects of the products and/or services the organization offers to the public. The traditional function-based career plan is considered by many organizations as irrelevant to meeting needs in the 21st century, when a broader, organization-wide perspective will be critical for success. A learning organization recognizes that learning can take place in interactions with customers, suppliers, other employees, in new assignments and in task forces; and that formal training and development programs are not the only ways to learn. In a learning organization, everyone is engaged in identifying and resolving problems and experimenting in new ways of behaving to improve performance.

Learning is also defined to include more than simply accounting, marketing, or engineering principles. It means enhancing each employee's and the larger organization's capability to do things they were unable to do previously. Often, knowledge is not acquired from textbooks, training or past experience, but from actually engaging in independent action and experimentation.

> An example of such independent action would be a store clerk taking the initiative to use a newly learned computer program to track customer demands and change re-ordering procedures to better meet customer needs.

SHARED VISION AND CORE VALUES

The leaders in a learning organization take considerable efforts to create a shared vision of the organizational mission among all employees. If the vision is clear, employees can be left free to identify and solve problems on their own that help achieve this vision. The steps in establishing an organizational mission and conveying it to members were discussed in Chapter 2.

EMPOWERMENT

Learning organizations empower their employees to a much higher level than other firms. In some organizations, teams of employees make virtually all decisions.

> An example of extremely high empowerment was seen in one organization where employees were expected to behave and make decisions as if they were owners. Employees were given all relevant information and trusted to make appropriate decisions.[38] In another firm, there were no budgets set by top management. Teams of employees, after discussion, decided what is an appropriate and feasible budget for the next period. Sometimes, the decisions involved the purchase of equipment worth over $1 million.[39]

The various steps in empowering employees and getting increased employee involvement are discussed in Chapter 4.

INFORMATION SHARING

If employees are to make appropriate decisions, they must have valid information. In learning organizations, information sharing reaches extraordinary levels. Various techniques such as reports, meetings, financial statements, newsletters, e-mail, voice-mail, intranets, and broadcasts are used to facilitate information transmission.

> One firm routinely feeds the results of customer surveys to all employees, along with the company performance on 100 key operational dimensions.[40]

STRUCTURES AND SYSTEMS

If learning is to become a way of life, then the organization must reward the activity. Learning organizations recognize this fact and incorporate appropriate internal systems and procedures to encourage experimentation, ownership of actions, and learning. For example, "knowledge-based pay" and "skill-based pay" are becoming increasingly in vogue in organizations that give priority to learning.

> In organizations including General Foods and Mars, "pay for skill" has generally been accompanied by positive outcomes in the past.[41]

Simultaneously, existing disincentives to learning are removed from the system. Traditional notions of a superior conducting performance appraisals and deciding on pay raises are eliminated in many firms. Instead, employees are given a share in profits and stock ownerships.

> One organization pays all its employees a 10% bonus for meeting company goals. Employees also receive $500 for each new idea adopted. One employee received $7500 for generating creative solutions.[42]

ESTABLISHING A LEARNING CULTURE

Consistent with the above, these organizations attempt to establish a learning culture. To achieve this, they also encourage "unlearning." This needs to start with the top management and includes every single worker. First, top level executives and senior managers must unlearn some of their present practices and assumptions to foster a learning atmosphere in their organization.[43] Successful learning organizations also assume that everyone is capable of learning new things and will create a rewarding, supportive environment where employees are encouraged to experiment. Further, task assignments and promotions are also planned bearing the learning agenda in mind. When employees are hired, their ability to learn rather than their ability to do the present job is given a premium.

> A past president of Pepsi emphasized infusing the organization with learners. According to him, the best way to start is to hire a group of proven managers without having any particular jobs in mind for them. As job openings emerge, they can be fed into them; meanwhile the company has access to the skills of proficient managers who are not overly influenced by the internal culture and past ways of doing things.[44]

Information on creativity and learning (non-profit settings): *www.mapfornonprofits.org*

A number of factors, usually ignored, facilitate learning. Even encouraging a sense of humour may create a "sense of anarchy, a sense of chaos"[45] and hence an opportunity for new learning.[46] Requiring employees to improvise to meet the needs of the situation often triggers learning[47] as do the challenges of dealing with alien cultures. Using metaphors, symbols, and stories has been found effective in communicating a culture of learning,[48] as has encouragement of questioning by employees.[49] The ultimate goal in all instances is to help the employee grow and meet new and harder challenges.

Implications for Practice

1. To be successful, an organization must be effective at four levels: organizational, structural and system, process or task, and individual employee. If faced with a performance deficiency, performance gap analysis involving a careful examination of the firm's functioning at organizational, structural and system, process or task, and employee levels should be attempted.

2. While training can contribute to improve performance at all levels, its maximum impact is at the individual employee level. For this reason, employee training should be attempted when the performance deficiency is most likely attributable to inappropriate employee behaviours, skills, and attitudes. There are a number of organizational development tools that can enhance performance at organizational, system and process levels (see Chapters 2, 3, and 4 for some strategies to enhance performance at these other levels).

3. Training objectives, which are formulated after a thorough training needs analysis, specify the performance outcomes and changes in trainee behaviours and outcomes that are expected from the proposed training program. To be useful, these objectives should be specific in terms of performance outcomes or behaviours of the trainee, should be measurable using clear criteria, clear about the quality or level of performance, should define the time period within which they are to be accomplished, and specify the other conditions under which they would occur.

4. Learning principles are guidelines to the ways in which people learn most effectively. The more learning principles present in a training setting, the more effective the training is likely to be.

5. There is no best training method for all occasions. The particular method chosen for an occasion depends on a variety of factors including availability of time and resources, profile of trainees, subject matter, and the type of learning (e.g., cognitive versus behavioural learning) to be imparted. For this reason, careful attention should be paid before choosing from the various on the job and off-the job training methods currently available.

6. Irrespective of the type of training and method used, all training programs have to be evaluated using one or more criteria and designs discussed in this chapter. Despite the clearest training objectives or intentions, the training may not deliver the results it was intended to do. The evaluation process enables a firm to monitor its training success and take corrective actions to improve future outcomes.

7. Today's unpredictable environments make it imperative that organizations continually learn to survive. In learning organizations, employees continually expand their capacity to create the results they truly desire, new thinking is actively encouraged, new behaviours and patterns are continuously explored and fostered, and employees are continually learning how to work and learn together. An organization and its managers can learn from several sources: the external world (competitors, customers, suppliers), the organization's past actions (its strategies, its responses to problem situations), the actions of its members (such as their behaviours, the existing culture), the existing processes (such as the rules governing various activities, the systems and procedures), and the collective consciousness (the experience of all of the above).

Key Terms for Review

Discussion Questions

1. What are the various steps in performance gap assessment?

2. In assessing the training needs of a firm, which of the three levels of analysis is most important? Why?

3. What are learning principles? Why are they important in a training context?

4. Are lectures better than case studies and role-playing in a university or college classroom setting? Why?

5. What factors will you consider when selecting a training evaluation design?

6. What should an organization do to create a continuous learning culture?

Critical Thinking Questions

1. You recently joined a house construction firm in a managerial capacity. In going through the firm's records, you find a history of submitting quotes to customers that is inaccurate. The result is that either there are cost overruns or irate customers who feel that some important items have been missed (e.g., towel and screen rod in the bathroom, electrical dimmers). Performance deficiency at what level probably explains this? What should you do now?

2. How would you go about assessing the training needs of 45 managers in a large automotive products retail chain?

3. Assume you are a section manager in a firm with two supervisors and a secretary reporting to you. Assume further that your newly hired secretary does not have any prior exposure to important software that you use in your office. You also want to teach one of your junior supervisors how to manage the firm's diverse workforce. What training method might be appropriate in each case? What learning principles might be present in the methods you chose?

4. If you were asked to design a new training program for supervisors who have to manage employees from a wide variety of educational,

ethnic, national, and cultural backgrounds, what training would you suggest?

5. If you were the leader of a student team that is asked to evaluate the training program you just completed here, how would you go about it?

6. You have joined a traditional, family-controlled firm as the human resource manager. The relations between the firm's union and management are not very warm, nor do the employees trust the management. During your professional training, you studied the importance of creating a continuously

learning culture to meet today's economic challenges. What challenges might you face in this context? What actions are possibly appropriate now?

Web Research

Visit www.hrdc-drhc.gc.ca/common/home.html and go to the "learning opportunities" and "learning and training resources" pages. Identify four different training programs available across Canada and report to your class. What kind of financial assistance may be available from the federal government for each of these learning programs?

CASE INCIDENT

Ontario Electronics Company Limited

Ontario Electronics Company Limited (OECL) is a manufacturer of electronic, communication, aerospace, and audio equipment. The company currently employs over 500 workers, a large percentage of whom are professionals. The company's head office and major plant are located in Scarborough, Ontario, and its plants and sales offices are in four other Canadian provinces and in major U.S. cities.

In the recent past, the company has faired well financially but the top management was somewhat unhappy with the productivity levels seen in various plants. The management was particularly displeased with the performance of employees in its head office. The management decided to embark on an organization-wide training program to improve work procedures and productivity.

Recently, OECL entered the field of laser beam signalling and tracking equipment manufacturing. For the purpose of training its 320 skilled workers in the production and service of the new products, the company had a choice of two training methods: job instruction training, where a co-worker serves as the instructor, or in-class training using lectures, discussions, and video presentations. Before embarking on a full-scale training program, the company decided to carry out a pilot study that compared the benefits of the alternate methods of training in its Oshawa plant. It was a relatively new plant with ninety skilled workers who were generally younger than those in the other plants. OECL decided to conduct a pilot training for 40 workers in the plant. OECL management felt that the results of the pilot exercise would enable the company to fine-tune its training program, and make it applicable to other plants where the task could be even more complex. It also made a decision to train the remaining 50 workers in Oshawa plant on the basis of the results of the pilot study. By staggering the training, the company felt that it could avoid or reduce production delays.

The training program in the Oshawa plant lasted fourteen days. The first four days were spent in general skill-building training covering a number of areas the

management considered important (the same training was to be given in other plants in future to improve productivity levels). Twenty workers in the morning shift were trained using the Job Instruction Training Method (JI); another 20 from the late evening shift were selected for training using the in-class lectures and discussion method (LD). The results of the training were monitored and summarized. The key findings follow:

1. The cost of training per participant under the JI was $120, and the corresponding figure for LD was $185.

2. All trainees were asked to complete a written test on various aspects of the manufacture and use of the new product, along with questions relating to its maintenance. The LD group received an average score of 70 out of the maximum 100, while the JI group received an average of 63. The range of scores for the LD group was from 42 to 90; the corresponding range for the JI group was 60 to 78.

3. All trainees also completed a questionnaire at the end of the program to indicate their satisfaction with the training program and to evaluate the working conditions at OECL. For this purpose, a five-point scale was used: strongly agree (SA), mildly agree (MA), agree (A), disagree (D), and strongly disagree (SD). The tabulated results are shown in Figure A.

Questions

1. *What is your evaluation of the approach taken by the firm to improve employee performance?*

2. *Specifically, what comments do you have about the training-program design and evaluation approach used to measure training effectiveness at the Oshawa plant?*

3. *If you were asked to assist the company to improve performance what would be your approach? Why?*

(continued)

FIGURE A

Questionnaire Item		SA	MA	A	D	SD
		(% responses under each category)				
1. The objectives of the	JI	20	30	15	30	5
training were clear.	LD	25	35	25	15	–
2. This is one of the	JI	15	10	35	30	10
most enjoyable training	LD	40	20	15	5	20
programs I have experienced.						
3. The instructor was very	JI	40	20	25	10	5
knowledgeable.	LD	15	30	30	25	–
4. The instructor was very	JI	20	25	35	15	5
helpful.	LD	30	20	35	15	–
5. I am confident of my	JI	60	20	16	5	–
skills now.	LD	40	40	16	5	–
6. All relevant technical	JI	70	10	15	5	–
skills were imparted during	LD	60	15	18	7	–
the training program.						
7. The training method	JI	60	15	10	25	–
employed was appropriate.	LD	60	25	10	5	–
8. The objectives of the	JI	20	25	35	15	5
training were achieved.	LD	30	20	35	15	–
9. I believe that I	JI	50	40	10	–	–
have a bright future in	LD	30	20	50	–	–
this company.						

CASE

Metro Water Utility: Training to Enhance Performance

One of the outcomes of the tragedy that struck Meadow Brook Town (see the Case at the end of Chapter 3 for details) was the provincial government's decision to tighten and upgrade safety regulations in all its waterworks. Some of the smaller municipality waterworks were amalgamated to reap economies of scale and install uniform testing procedures. A new amalgamated water utility, Metro Water Utility, employing 50 operating personnel (including 3 middle level managers, 5 supervisors, 15 safety and quality inspectors, and 20 mechanics and plumbers) currently oversees water purification and distribution in the region. A set of new performance appraisal procedures was also instituted (see the Case at the end of Chapter 6).

To avoid future similar mishaps, the Utility decided to intensively train its personnel in all aspects of water safety management. To cause minimal disruption to day-to-day activities, the training will be conducted in two phases. In the first phase, one-half of the supervisors and one-third of safety inspectors and mechanical and electrical personnel will be trained. After successful completion of the training and evaluating its outcomes, the second phase of training (all remaining staff) will be trained. The government and Human Resource and Development Canada approved an initial grant of $18 000 for the first phase of training, expected to be completed within six months. If successful, additional budget would be granted for the second phase of the project. It was expected that clear, valid measures of training effectiveness would be provided by the Utility at that time in support of its request for additional funding.

The Utility's Human Resource Manager (HRM) was asked to prepare a detailed training proposal. The position of HRM was newly created after the amalgamation. Jeff Harwood, the Human Resource Manager, recognized the importance of training for Utility's future success. Many of the employees were in their mid to late forties (as a matter of fact, there were only four employees below 30 years of age, called "juniors" by the older employees) and had not undergone any training in the last fifteen years. None of the supervisors (all of whom were males) had any training in the past and had acquired their skills on the job. There were only 2 women, both in the mechanical and electrical division. Harwood heard through the grapevine that the female

(continued)

employees were unhappy in their new work setting although, in his mind, they were among the best performers. There were occasional conflicts between "juniors" and their older colleagues, especially when they had to work together in smaller teams, but generally, ther was camaraderie in the workforce. Looking through the employee records, he found that the younger employees had higher educational training than their senior colleagues.

Questions

1. *If you were Jeff Harwood, how would you go about identifying training needs for various employee groups?*

2. *What training methods might be appropriate here? Why?*

3. *What training evaluation criteria and approaches would you include in your proposal?*

8 Counselling and Discipline

What coaches do is to anchor people to their own internal strengths; they inspire organizations to dream beyond their plans. They apply emotional and intellectual intelligence to the long haul of life and work.[1]

Frederic Hudsong

Chapter Objectives

After studying this chapter, you should be able to:

- Describe the importance of counselling in organizations

- Discuss the key types of counselling for improving present and future performance

- Explain how progressive discipline can be implemented

- Outline the characteristics of an organization that encourages employee learning and growth

IBM Canada is one of the nation's largest suppliers of information technology products and services. IBM's products range from supercomputers and sophisticated enterprise servers to small laptops and printers. IBM is also a major software developer and offers consultancy services in various aspects of information technology. Founded over 80 years ago, IBM today employs nearly 300 000 worldwide. IBM Canada is a subsidiary of IBM Corporation of New Jersey and has an impressive history of leadership in computer and information technology.[2] While it is a hi-tech firm with vast resources, the company recognizes that a key-if not the most important-factor in its success is its people. To attract and keep the very best people in the industry, IBM gives its employees control over their careers and their career paths. IBM has created several worldwide "professions." Each career path is based on specific skill sets, goals, and employee accomplishments. The career paths are also flexible so that employees can build a portfolio of expertise and improve their skills.[3] Since each career path is as unique as each employee, IBM offers a number of programs to help individuals progress in their chosen direction. Mentors, career coaching, and continuous training are offered to help individuals achieve their career goals. All employees have access to CareerNet, an online career coaching system and are also encouraged to participate in the mentorship programs. Skill development and training are offered through a number of vehicles. Employees can participate in hands-on technical courses and classroom training through IBM Learning Services while the company intranet offers an on-line computer based training available most of the day. Each year, the firm invests over $60 million in employee education and training. IBM's "Lifeworks" offers a lifestyle assistance program to all its employees. The program offers practical advice, useful materials, and information on a variety of work-life balancing issues such as child care, elder care, and living with illness and injury.[4] All employees have access to a confidential counselling service that offers professional assistance on a variety of personal and work related issues.

IBM's concern for its employees has made it a highly desirable employer. It has also enabled the firm to attract top calibre technical employees in a highly competitive labour market and keep them for extended periods of time.

Such elaborate employee counselling and support systems do not exist in many Canadian firms. This chapter begins with a discussion of why counselling is important in most organizations-small or large, profit-oriented or non-profit. It then details the various approaches to counsel employees for improving their present and future performance. Despite counselling and training, there may be occasions when desired work behaviours do not emerge. Finally, there is a brief discussion of the key steps in disciplining employees who, despite all assistance, repeatedly perform below established benchmarks.

IMPORTANCE OF PERFORMANCE COUNSELLING

As discussed in Chapter 7, a performance gap may be attributable to a variety of factors. For example, poorly planned systems or methods often result in poor outcomes; even well qualified and motivated employees may not be able to overcome systemic deficiencies. Other uncontrollable factors may also result in the poor performance of organizations (Figure 8-1).

> The terrorist attack on the World Trade Center (WTC) on September 11, 2001, resulted in a general economic slump in the surrounding neighbourhood for several weeks. While the human cost was staggering, there were also significant economic costs, especially for several restaurants and retailers who depended on the businesses located in the WTC for their survival.

If after a thorough analysis of the causes of the performance gap (see Chapter 7), the cause is identified as employee skills/motivation-related, there are three possible actions: train the employee, counsel and energize the employee, and when no satisfactory outcomes are found, discipline the employee. Chapter 7 looked at the role of training. This chapter examines counselling to enhance the performance of marginally performing employees. Even in the case of superior employees, counselling may help bring out the best in the person. Some employers have recognized and taken advantage of this fact.

> CGI Group Inc. of Montreal, the largest full service information technology consulting company in Canada with annual revenues exceeding $740 million and employing nearly 8500 is one such firm. New employees at CGI receive an extensive orientation and

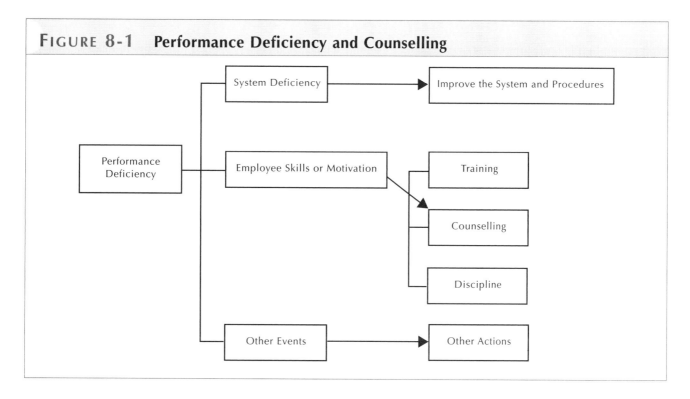

FIGURE 8-1   Performance Deficiency and Counselling

integration program. All employees also receive formal performance reviews. Employees and supervisors meet four times each year to discuss progress and career development. CGI also conducts an annual employee satisfaction survey that solicits feedback on a variety of work related issues. CGI strongly encourages continuous employee development through in-house training programs. The company also employs a formal mentor program to help employees assimilate and advance more quickly.[5]

In the context of performance management, **counselling** is the discussion of performance-related problems or matters with an employee in order to identify a specific action plan to overcome them or achieve specific objectives. Irrespective of whether the counsellors identify the solutions themselves or help the employee in this regard, the focus is on resolving a specific problem. While counselling in the context of a work organization has a slightly different connotation than psychological counselling and has less intensity and scope, the counsellor does have to display a number of attitudes and behaviours of a trained psychologist.

Performance counselling results in a number of benefits to the individual employee and the larger organization (Figure 8-2). Today, more than ever, counselling has become more critical. Four key reasons for the increased importance of counselling are discussed below.

COPE WITH CHANGE

As the popular saying goes, today the only certainty is continuing uncertainty. Irrespective of the nature and size of business, virtually all work organizations face considerable instability, uncertainty, and turbulence. In the new world of technologic and market discontinuity, employees who cannot manage change are unlikely to be high performers. Counsellors, as positive change agents, motivate others with new hope, purpose, and concrete action plans to cope with change.

Counselling is the discussion of performance-related problems or matters with the objective of identifying specific action plans to overcome them or achieve specific performance objectives.

Website describing the meanings and terms of counselling: *www.counsellingcharity. freeserve.co.uk/*

Website of the Counselling Foundation of Canada: *www.counselling.net/*

RESOLVE CONFLICTS

The diverse workforce, the ever changing organizational landscape (whether in terms of geographical boundaries or structures), the continuously changing technology, and the increasing use of teams and workgroups have increased the potential for misunderstandings, missed communication, and conflicts in organizations. The ever-increasing demands on most employees-from both work and personal life-have made it more challenging than ever before to identify a good work-family balance. Counsellors help the employee swim through the powerful currents of multiple demands and multiple priorities and retain a sense of balance and rhythm in work and personal lives. More specifically:

- Most people find emotional release when they discuss their problems with someone else.

- Discussion of a problem helps most individuals gain new insights into problems or new ways of coping with them.

- Counsellors who are not personally involved in the problem are able to give a more objective assessment of the situation and help the employee identify possible cause-effect relationships that may have escaped their attention.

- Counsellors can often provide employees with reassurance or the confidence that they are following a suitable course of action.

ESTABLISH CORPORATE CULTURE

The case studies of several successful organizations have shown that creating and sustaining value for all key constituencies—customers, employees, shareholders, etc.—is important for long-term success. However, sustaining value over a long period for all constituencies requires developing an appropriate corporate culture, management infrastructure, adequate systems, and maintaining a competent workforce. Of the above, the creation of an over-riding corporate culture that bonds employees together for a common ideal and purpose is facilitated through coaching and counselling. Often, a coach is able to re-orient the employee's own and work-related values and beliefs toward those that are more in line with the firm's mission and strategies. Counselling also encourages upward communication to the manage-

---

FIGURE 8-2   Benefits of Performance Counselling

- Provide greater direction and clarity of organizational goals
- Help build self-confidence
- Improve motivation and morale
- Develop specific skills and competencies
- Support personal and career development
- Improve alignment of corporate and employee goals
- Develop clear performance goals
- Facilitate human resource and succession planning
- Foster corporate culture

ment informing them of the necessary actions to build and strengthen a cohesive workforce. It, often, generates a more responsive management that recognizes employee needs and incorporates these into management strategies and tactical plans, which in turn, reinforce employee loyalty and identification with the firm.

TAP INTO THE WISDOM OF SENIOR EMPLOYEES

Typically, more experienced employees not only have well developed job skills but also knowledge of the firm's history, mission, and unique strengths and limitations. Through the many organizational stories, myths, and anecdotes drawn from past, they can illustrate how the firm survived amidst adversity, how it met past challenges by changing, and how its vision permeated and withstood tests of time. The more experienced workers, in their roles as mentors and coaches, can convey a sense of purpose and mission to their junior colleagues. They will not only be able to impart job skills but also convey the organization's spirit and act as role models to their junior colleagues.

Websites for information on counselling:
http://admin.acadiau.ca/ counsel/Edisorder/index.html
www.eapinc.com

RESPONSIBILITY FOR COUNSELLING

In one sense, the responsibility for counselling should lie with the immediate supervisor. After all, other than the employee, the immediate boss knows best about the working conditions and the challenges that the employee faces. However, in many of today's organizations, this may simply not be feasible. In the past, supervisors were typically in charge of only a few employees. Automation, computerization, de-layering, and globalization have changed this picture significantly. In today's flatter organizations, many managers and supervisors are not only in charge of dozens (sometimes, hundreds) of individuals but also responsible for geographically dispersed operations. Apart from their role as supervisors, these individuals are also often required to perform other activities, preventing them from playing the role of a coach effectively. In today's conditions, it would be more realistic to share the responsibility between the immediate supervisor and the counsellor in the performance management department. The immediate supervisor will still be the best person to advise the employee on the more technical or routine aspects of the job. The supervisor is also in the best position to show how the job contributes to the overall organizational mission and strategic success and what competencies are required for superior performance. The specialists in the performance management department should supplement this with individual counselling on a variety of topics including personal matters that prevent the individual from reaching full potential, growth areas, specific actions, strategies, and spiritual coaching (or coaching related to resilience, inner values, self esteem, and so on). Needless to say, the size, the constraints, and the unique character of the organization will determine the specific arrangements for counselling. What is most important is that employees have a source where they can receive insightful and well-considered advice from someone who has their best interests at heart. In all instances, the activities of different counsellors should be well integrated so that all relevant information is shared. This also avoids contradictory or confusing advice being provided to employees by different counsellors.

Irrespective of who is involved in counselling, it involves a number of steps. Depending on the nature of the problem, counselling can also be of different types. The next section deals with these.

STEPS IN COUNSELLING

Specific counselling style and actions during counselling are perhaps as varied as the employees. No two employees will respond the same way to the same style of counselling. To be effective, a counsellor must take several steps including:

1. Consider all facts of the situation. This includes not only looking at the employee's behaviours but also the context within which they occurred in an effort to identify the "why" and "how" more clearly.

2. Study all relevant employee records.

3. Be familiar with the organizational and human resource policies and guidelines.

4. Choose the appropriate counselling style.

5. Adapt behaviour to the situation.

6. Monitor the outcomes of the counselling and follow up where necessary.

The next section details the various counselling styles and the contexts when they are appropriate. The specific actions associated with each counselling style are detailed below.

Counselling, in a work situation, can vary on two dimensions: the focus and the style.

- The focus of counselling may be to improve present or future performance of the employee.

- Depending on the situation, the counsellor's style may be directive, interventionist, or passively reassuring. In a directive style, the counsellor takes active steps to bring about a change in the performance of the employee and intervenes with appropriate tactics or advice. When using an indirect or passive style, the counsellor listens to the concerns and, in many instances, tries to help the employee elicit solutions to the problem.

Combining the above dimensions, there are four major types of counselling formats (Figure 8-3). The role of the counsellor and the steps taken during counselling also show variation depending on the format.

TRAINER

Training is an active, interventionist counselling role to improve performance through providing additional skills, competencies, or information.

Training, in the context of counselling, refers to an active, interventionist role of the counsellor to improve performance through providing additional skills, competencies, or information to the employee. It is particularly relevant when poor performance is attributable to lack of adequate skills or information. However, even when poor performance is caused by inappropriate attitudes of employees, counsellors may be able to bring about improvements through informal training as the following example shows.

Antonio Lavetti worked as a section supervisor in an engineering assembly plant in Ontario for over ten years. Recently, he had occasion to supervise female employees. Historically, his firm hired women only for secretarial or other administrative positions. So, when two female employees were hired in his section, he was not quite sure how to deal with them. He had always maintained excellent relations with the 13 employees—all white and male—often going out to ball games and joking with them (often risqué humour). It was normal practice for male employees to hang posters and keep other

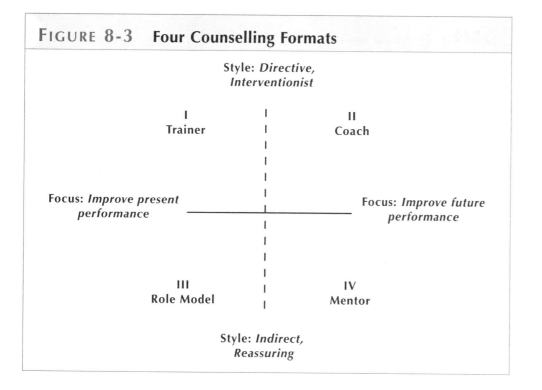

FIGURE 8-3 Four Counselling Formats

Style: *Directive, Interventionist*

| | I Trainer | | II Coach | |

Focus: *Improve present performance*   Focus: *Improve future performance*

III Role Model   IV Mentor

Style: *Indirect, Reassuring*

paraphernalia in their workplace that could be offensive to women and minorities. Antonio ignored this practice until now, but was not sure it should continue given the presence of the female employees. Antonio's supervisor, Tim Donovan, sensed Lavetti's dilemma. He spent an entire Saturday with Antonio training him in the new responsibilities of a supervisor of a more diverse workforce. Antonio was shown how the management style, communication, and even office decor had to be changed to recognize the new reality. He provided Antonio with a few case studies of supervisors who successfully handled diverse workforces. Soon after this informal training session, Antonio asked his employees to remove the offending posters and material. He also communicated that, henceforth, no potentially offensive jokes could be made at work. When the firm hired two Asian employees later that year, they experienced no difficulty as part of the group.

Job instruction training (see Chapter 7 for details) is most popular in this context, although other approaches such as lectures, role-plays, case studies, and coaching can be used depending on the demands of the situation. In all instances, the employee should perceive the training as job relevant and practically useful. Training should also be done in an atmosphere devoid of interruptions and tension. Some of the other guiding principles of training are shown in Figure 8-4. Most of the material discussed in Chapter 7 on training needs identification, training delivery, transfer of learning, and training evaluation with appropriate modifications are relevant in the counsellor's role as a trainer.

Website articles on training: *www.hr-guide.com*

COACH

Coaching covers all activities intended to help master skills and competencies or reach full work potential. It involves a variety of actions aimed to help a person identify and respond to corporate culture and priorities, improve performance in emerging scenarios, and facilitate life-long learning. Coaches in organizational settings, like sports coaches, exhibit a variety of successful styles and behaviours;

Coaching is the act of helping others to master skills and competencies and reach full work potential through a variety of actions that help identify and respond to corporate culture and priorities, improve performance in emerging scenarios, and facilitate life-long learning.

FIGURE 8-4   Training to Enhance Employee Performance

Objectives: Before starting the training session, the trainer should jointly identify the training objectives with the employee. Unless the employee perceives the training need, no learning may take place.

Location: The training should take place in a private location devoid of interruptions.

Contents: Only information that is meaningful and practical to the employee for the current position should be presented. Long-term, developmental training should be done through more formal, professionally-managed and delivered training programs.

Sequencing: Information and instructions should be presented one step at a time permitting the employee to apply the newly learned skills under realistic conditions.

Language: The language used by the trainer should be simple and easily understood by the employee.

Participation: As far as possible, the trainee should actively participate in the training by doing specific activities or making specific decisions. Often, simple lectures alone may not impart important practical skills to the trainee.

Reflection and evaluation: The training session should have a provision for reviewing and evaluating the material learned. The trainee should be given every opportunity to reflect on the newly learned concepts or skills.

Feedback: During and after the training, the trainee should be made aware of the improvements in skills, behaviours, or competencies.

Reinforcement: In the initial periods following the training, whenever the trainee exhibits appropriate behaviours, they should be reinforced. Use of rewards to reinforce newly learned skills or competencies should be employed where feasible.

Action plan: The trainer and the trainee should agree on an action plan that details steps to be taken to ensure that training transfers to the job.

however, there are a few characteristics that seem to be common to all successful coaches. These include:

- the adoption of the role of a teacher and colleague rather than that of a judge or superior;

- the effort to understand the true problem or real obstacles present in a situation;

- the use of alternate sources of data to verify the accuracy of interpretations before recommending any solution;

- the intent to help the other person to improve;

- a focus on the long-term success as well as short-term improvement;

- the reinforcement of desired behaviours through positive feedback; and

- recognition of the importance of regular meetings with the person whose performance they are attempting to improve.

Coaches require the ability to identify the heart of a problem and respond to it dispassionately and in a non-critical, yet explicit manner. Criticizing someone evokes defensive responses that, often, reduce willingness to change or even listen to the critic. However, problems have to be defined in specific terms so that corrective actions can be identified. Achieving this fine balance is often difficult. By stating the problem in specific, non-judgmental terms and focusing on needed future actions, a manager can reduce an employee's defensiveness. Vague, generalized accusations against

Website with articles on counselling and coaching: *www.work911.com/*

Self-test:

Are You a Good Counsellor?

This exercise tests your counselling skills. Please answer all questions frankly using the anchors *strongly agree (SA)*, *agree (A)*, *neither agree nor disagree (NAD)*, *disagree (D)*, or *strongly disagree (SD)*. Do NOT change your response to any statement once you have indicated it.

1. During one-on-one meetings, I tend to talk more than the other person.

2. When someone with a problem comes to me, I never mention what they should have done to avoid the problem in the first place.

3. I tend to offer solutions soon after someone approaches me with a problem.

4. When listening to someone I say "uh-huh" or repeat their statements periodically in a low voice.

5. I plan my time very carefully to ensure that I don't waste it listening to unimportant matters.

6. People who know me would probably say that I am a better listener than an interesting talker or narrator.

7. When listening to others, I frequently ask them questions to speed up their talk.

8. I practice the wise saying, "listen twice the volume than you speak because you have two ears and only one mouth."

9. When meeting someone whom I have not seen for a while, I am the first to offer news of events happening in my life.

10. I always have the time to listen to someone else who needs assistance.

Scoring

For statements 1, 3, 5, 7, and 9, assign scores of 1, 2, 3, 4, and 5 for SA, A, NAD, D, and SD respectively. For items 2, 4, 6, 8, and 10, assign scores of 5, 4, 3, 2, and 1 for SA, A, NAD, D, and SD respectively. Total your scores for items 1 through 10.

Interpretation

Your total score will range from 10 to 50. Listening is an important skill for a counsellor. This brief exercise measured how good a listener you are. If your score is 40 or above it indicates that you are a very good listener. A score of 20 or below indicates the opposite: you tend to talk more than listen to others. By carefully cultivating the habit of listening to others, you can significantly enhance your counselling skills. Scores between 20 and 40 indicate moderate ability in listening.

---

employees or their attitudes and blaming employees for events beyond their control undoubtedly generate ill will and poor response. The manager should show genuine concern for employee needs and display a willingness to help employees improve performance. Criticisms that focus only on the needs of the supervisor are self-centred and unlikely to be well received. Figure 8-5 shows some examples of giving feedback in non-threatening manners. Not all supervisors are trained to provide feedback in this manner, underscoring the importance of supervisory training before assigning the responsibility for counselling to supervisors.

Many effective coaches begin their meetings after considerable reflection and preparation. They have a rough script of what they want to say, in what order, and know when to wait for a reaction. Coaches take considerable care to ensure that the person being coached emerges from the meeting with his or her self-esteem intact, yet convinced that there is room to grow. Often a "sandwich model" of feedback—where you position negative feedback between two genuinely positive pieces of information—softens the blow. Effective coaches are also able to shift from narrative and

Website with information on what to avoid during appraisal: *www.work911.com/ performance/particles/ stupman.htm*

Website on coaching and spiritual support/healing: *homepages.ihug.co.nz/ ~greg.c/spirit.html*

FIGURE 8-5   Reformulating Criticisms to Make Them Less Threatening

Criticisms	Reformulation to make the statement less threatening
"You are lazy and always late for work."	"The record shows that you were late three days in the last week." (Avoid generalized statements evaluating attitudes or personality traits and focus on objective facts.)
"Your team is always overspending. What is so special about your team that it cannot meet the budgetary lines?"	"For our new strategy to work, it is important that all teams stay within budgets. Is there something that I can do to help your team meet the budget lines next quarter?" (Avoid blaming; focus on the future and offer support.)
"Your performance really embarrasses me. It makes me look like an ineffective supervisor."	"I would like to help you to meet your performance goals next quarter. What actions on my part will help you? How can we achieve this goal?" (Focus shifts from how the other's behaviour affects the supervisor to how the goals can be achieved in the future.)

descriptive to prescriptive modes depending on the personality of the person being coached. Those who need more directive instructions are given specific suggestions; those who are able to come up with their own answers are provided with a support-

FIGURE 8-6   Guidelines for Successful Coaching

1. Prepare. Before beginning the coaching relationship, identify all relevant pieces of information and verify them for their accuracy. Have a rough plan of how to proceed; however, make the plan sufficiently flexible to respond to emerging realities.

2. Listen. All successful coaches are good listeners. They frequently paraphrase what the other person says and ensure that there are no misunderstandings.

3. Begin with easy problems. Initial focus should be on easy to change behaviours or easy to implement systems. Successful implementation of the simple actions not only improves the overall confidence but also fosters the relationship.

4. Use several small goals. Dividing one large goal or objective into several smaller, microgoals[6] or action plans and helping the person successfully achieve them not only increases the probability of success but also improves overall confidence.

5. Use positive feedback. Wherever feasible and relevant, positive actions should be mentioned. Positive feedback on performance is welcomed by most North Americans. Cultural differences must be recognized when providing feedback to members of other cultures.

6. Express feelings. In some instances where objective data is either not available or not valued feelings have to be expressed. Use of "I feel..." helps the employees understand the impact of their behaviours on others.[7] But even here, the descriptions have to be nonjudgemental.

7. Act as a change agent. Good coaches question the status quo and encourage the employee to look at the situation or problem in novel ways. They encourage risk taking and convey that making mistakes is the first step in learning.

FIGURE 8-7   Alternate Approaches to Developing Employee Potential

On-the-job coaching

Job rotation

Job sharing

Cross-training of employees

Working for a voluntary organization

Attending conferences

Working for a community development group

Attending university/college programs

Attending other workshops or training programs

Membership in chamber of commerce, board of trade, manufacturer's association, etc.

Internships in other divisions of the firm or other firms

Membership in libraries and reading groups

Subscriptions to journals and professional magazines

Networking with other members in the industry

ive setting where, under the guidance of the coach, they are encouraged to find answers. Some guidelines for successful coaching are shown in Figure 8-6 on the previous page.

Finally, while most coaches provide direct advice and actively engage in skill training or attitude change interventions, there are several other training approaches and tools they can use to develop an employee's potential. Some of these are shown in Figure 8-7. Figure 8-8 shows a sample form used by an employer to gauge employee input on their development needs.

In summary, coaches plant the seeds of collaboration by emphasizing priorities, balance, connectedness, and vision. Through this, they enable the gain of new insights which may facilitate problem solving, conflict resolution, and consensus building.

FIGURE 8-8   A Sample Form Used by an Employer to Gauge Employee Development Needs

Metro Insurance Company

At Metro, we want all our employees to have a career and not a job. We also recognize that our employees have multiple roles and responsibilities. Indeed, we actively encourage all members of our organization to become involved in varied activities that help them grow as individuals and citizens.

Can you please take a few minutes to complete the form and return it to the human resource department? The information you provide here will help us to jointly identify a plan to optimize your developmental plans. Please note that "development" does not merely mean a promotion or job switch. Your developmental plans should help you grow further in a variety of areas and take up newer and broader responsibilities. The information you provide here will help your manager and the human resource department identify alternate plans and present them to you during a meeting that will be held later this month.

(continued)

Please frankly indicate below the level of your current proficiency or skills.

Skills/areas	Very strong	Adequate	Needs improvement
1. Mathematical skills including actuarial skills where relevant			
2. Data analysis skills using Lotus, Excel, & SPSS			
3. Report writing skills			
4. Oral presentation skills			
5. Team leadership and interpersonal skills			
6. Other _____(please feel free to add)			

In the next three years, which of the following best describes your aspirations?

❑ I would like to stay in my current department in the same position.
❑ I would like to stay in my current department in a different position.
❑ I would like to stay in my current department after getting a promotion.
❑ I would like to move to another department. Which?_____

In the long term (beyond three years), which of the following job categories best describes your career aspirations? Please note that you are not bound by this choice forever! This only helps us to identify goals for now. If at a later time—say, next year—you change your mind, you can indicate your new priorities at that time.

❑ Sales
❑ Administrative
❑ Accounting
❑ Finance
❑ Human resources
❑ Computer systems
❑ Actuarial
❑ Client relations and claims
❑ Other _____

Which of the following training programs that we currently offer do you prefer most? Identify any three and rank them as 1 (most preferred), 2, and 3 (least preferred).

❑ On-the-job training
❑ Job rotation
❑ Lectures
❑ Programmed learning
❑ Discussion and lunch-time sessions
❑ University/college courses
❑ Attend conferences
❑ Structured reading groups

Which of the following activities would you like to get involved in? Your feedback will help us contact relevant agencies and seek assistance in this regard.

❑ Volunteering (Please specify type of organization if you have a choice.)
❑ Joining a community group
❑ Networking with other professionals (Please specify_____)
❑ Other (Please specify_____)

Thank you. A representative from the human resource department will be contacting you in the next three weeks to set up an appointment to discuss this information.

Role models are individuals who impact the values, beliefs, and behaviours of others indirectly through a variety of means including their own behaviours, informal conversations, and responses to situations.

ROLE MODEL

By acting as a **role model**, a manager attempts to shape the values, beliefs, and behaviours of employees and enhance their performance. This style of counselling is:

Focus on Ethics

How Much Confidentiality Can You Offer?

Coaching and counselling often provide the coach with information that would normally be inaccessible. For the most part, the counsellor has a responsibility to protect the interests of the client, but there are situations when the counsellor's responsibility to the employer or the larger society may override the duty to protect the client.

You have been acting as a friend and counsellor to your employees. In return, they have been confiding in you about a number of things. Consider the following situations and indicate your responsibility in each situation.

1. Mark, who reports to you and with whom you have excellent work relations admitted last week to embezzling $80 four years ago. At that time, Mark was going through a very bad financial situation and had to temporarily "borrow" the money to take care of his family. He told you that he returned the money the next month. No one was aware of either the "loss" or later "repayment." But for the employee's admission, you would have never known about this event. You always considered Mark to be a very honest, hard worker-one of your best employees.

2. Through the grapevine, you learned that Todd and Mathew have been exchanging child pornography literature and pictures both at work and outside. Both are good workers and until now, you did not have any evidence to indicate such behaviour. Since your firm deals with toys and children's food, anything that is related to children is of particular interest to you. Recently, you were asked to nominate one of your employees for a special project, and you were about to nominate Todd. The special project is of considerable significance to your firm and a successful completion of the project can result in a substantial advancement opportunity for the employee. You also know that the project involves the nominee dealing with toddlers when no other adults are present.

3. You work in a very large financial institution. You have been practicing the coach and counsellor roles with your subordinates with highly satisfactory results until now. Last week, you had nominated Trevor to head a new section where he will be handling dozens of accounts of elderly, wealthy clients. Trevor, who had been with the firm for four years and had shown considerable promise, was your natural choice for the job, especially given his interpersonal skills. The clients, whose portfolios ran into millions of dollars, neither have the time nor the ability to monitor their finances. They trust your institution to take care of their interests and ensure safe, happy retired lives Indeed, it was the trustworthiness of your institution that made it grow so quickly. After formally accepting his new position, as he was leaving your office, Trevor blurted out, "Now, all that money would help me pay those debts." You took it as a joke and ignored the comment until later that evening when you accidentally ran into him in front of a Casino. When confronted, Trevor admitted having gambling debts to the tune of $200 000.

- more indirect and passive than training or coaching;

- focused on aligning employee behaviours with organizational goals and strategies; and

- composed of several actions. The manager may convey his or her beliefs, values, and ethical standards through a variety of means including informal conversations, messages, responses to situations and overall vision.

In many instances, the focus is on unlocking the subtle forces of change including the employee's intellectual, emotional, and spiritual abilities and understandings. Key dimensions of employee performance and attitudes that can be impacted by managerial behaviours and values include:

- Vision. The view of what the organization and its work is all about and the ultimate purpose toward which every employee should strive.

- Ethical standards. The notion of what is right and what is wrong; integrity, trust and honesty in dealings with others; clear definition of the stakeholder interests; and approaches to manage conflicts.

- Creative thinking. Importance given to independent thinking; support for thinking outside the box and generating novel responses to situations.

- Compassion. Importance given to caring, compassionate, and helping behaviour toward people within and outside the firm.

- Entrepreneurial behaviour. The courage to step outside traditional roles and boundaries; the willingness to leave the comfort zone and take risks, to lead and to be a non-conformist.

- Teamwork. The willingness and ability to work in teams for the larger benefit of the organization.

- Compliance. Obedience to organizational goals, policies and rules; exhibiting good organizational citizenship behaviours.

Website about self-improvement through on-line courses: *www.higherawareness.com/*

For effective role modelling to occur, the manager should have credibility with the employees, formulate visions and philosophy, and make these easily communicable. The manager's actions should be visible to the employees and proclamations heard by them if change is to occur. Some specific actions that can be taken in this context are listed in Figure 8-9.

Most major changes in employee behaviours and beliefs require managerial actions in three phases: unfreezing, changing, and re-freezing.

Phase 1: Unfreezing This phase focuses on actions that are aimed at convincing the employee for the need for change. Through communications or actions, the manager needs to convince the employee that the work situation has changed profoundly, requiring new actions, strategies, or behaviours.

FIGURE 8-9   Guidelines for Being an Effective Role Model

1. Focus on actions. Remember the old adage: "Actions speak louder than words." Build credibility in specific values by demonstration, not simply through words.

2. Cross-validate. Always cross-check and validate your assumptions, perceptions, and understanding about events and people before espousing them.

3. Seek help. Work with partners who can help you see how your behaviours may be communicating messages of which you are unaware.[8]

4. Focus on learning. As role models, successful leaders embody commitment to change through demonstrating willingness to learn, change, and adapt.[9] They emphasize continual learning and keep an open mind to new ideas and ways of doing things. They lead through their acceptance of the new and willingness to change rather than simply attempting to convince others that they need to change.

5. Understand motivations. The factors that motivate different individuals vary. This is particularly important in the context of the new diverse workforce. People with different backgrounds and allegiance to different ethnic, cultural, demographic, or racial groups exhibit considerable differences in their motivations, perceptions, and behaviours. Role models must understand the people around them and be responsive to their needs.

6. Communicate using multiple tools. Your values, beliefs, and attitudes should be communicated through a variety of methods including informal and formal communications, behaviours, office lay out, symbols and artifacts, and the day-to-day dealings with others. Often the tone of communication is as important as the content; similarly, how a manager treats employees with a problem may send a more important message than the several formal communications the person may routinely send.

In the earlier example, Tim Donovan can attempt to influence and change Antonio's prevailing beliefs and attitudes by providing information on the new workforce and the need for new workplace ethics. He can also cite laws or court cases relating to workplace discrimination and harassment to bolster his arguments and change Antonio's attitudes.

Phase 2: Changing The desired changes in an employee may be achieved through a variety of methods such as changing the person's ability and motivation (through training), role perceptions, and work environments (including physical settings, budget, time and other resources). Of particular relevance here are the role perceptions which can be altered by a manager's behaviours and expressed attitudes and beliefs.

A manager who wants his subordinates to reduce waste and recycle garbage may not only change the work environments by providing recycling bins but also act as a role model in this regard. Behaviours such as using washable coffee mugs and cloth towels, using both sides of paper, saving paper clips, and reusing envelopes are likely to be noticed by others and slowly impact their behaviours, especially when combined with frequent exhortations by the manager or posters at the workplace.

Phase 3: Re-freezing After unfreezing and changing the behaviours, it is important to refreeze them so that the employee does not slip back into previous patterns. To ensure that the desired changes continue, the manager should alter the systems and team dynamics where necessary. Reward systems must also be altered to reinforce new behaviours and attitudes.

Closely related to the concept of role model is the notion of transformational leadership. Transformational leaders manage and change the context within which people work-mission, shared values, and ideals-and engage their employees in the big picture that provides them with broad direction. The transformational leader acts as a teacher, a role model, and inspirational figure to create conditions under which subordinates enthusiastically perform.[10] Typically, transformational leaders pay great attention to non-routine aspects of an organization including its culture and vision.[11] In contrast, transactional leaders micro-manage the specific steps that lead to the successful execution of a task. For example, they may focus on financial incentives or task sequencing which will result in goal accomplishment. While both types of leaders are important for organizational success, there are occasions when an organization may have to engage in totally new activities or enter uncharted territories with no past guidelines to direct efforts. A value based, transformational leadership style may be the only option to break prevailing mental barriers and encourage employees to take unbeaten paths. An experiment using goldfish illustrates how traditional barriers, even when removed, may not be seen by the participants.

In an experiment with goldfish, a Plexiglas plate was placed in the middle of an aquarium, with goldfish on both sides. At first, the goldfish bumped their noses on the invisible plate, but over time, they learned to swim in circles without hitting the plate. After a few weeks, the plate was removed. Though the whole tank was now open to them, the fish did not change their patterns and stayed only on one side.[12]

In work organizations, simply introducing novel ideas or changing tactics such as employee empowerment, re-visioning, re-engineering, socio-technical systems, etc., may not have the desired results unless the management actions on a daily basis reflect the new philosophy. Herein lies the importance of role modelling in changing employee attitudes and behaviours.

MENTOR

A **mentor** is an experienced person who provides guidance and support in a variety of ways and acts as a guide, tutor, and confidante to an inexperienced person.

While different writers have varied definitions of a **mentor**, generally, the term connotes an experienced leader who provides guidance and support in a variety of ways and acts as a guide, tutor, and confidante to an inexperienced or novice person.[13] The crucial role that mentors play in career development of others—especially, women and minority employees—has been well documented in the past.[14] Mentors help their protégés, apprentices, or disciples by sharing their knowledge and understanding of the organization, how it works, and what it needs to succeed. The mentoring process consists of teaching, demonstration, feedback, and even personal counselling.[15] It encourages supervisors to share their experiences with subordinates, helping the latter gain additional insight and understanding that will be invaluable in their career development. A good mentor often becomes a model that the protégé can follow whenever he or she is unsure how to approach a problem.

To be effective, a mentor must possess a number of skills and knowledge and display certain behaviours and values. Good mentors are not only good at their own jobs but also have knowledge about the organizational requirements-what is needed to succeed in the firm, where it is headed, what will work, and what will not. An effective mentor also has high credibility and status—especially, his or her ethical standards are beyond reproach. A good mentor not only tells the protégé when he or she is doing a good job, but also points out deficiencies and performance gaps. Candour is essential, but tact is also equally important. Mentors create a supportive setting where protégés are encouraged to pursue their realistic dreams and experiment. This, in turn, requires a good understanding of the protégé's skills, strengths, and weaknesses. The mentor must know the protégé better than any one else (except for close family members). Figure 8-10 provides a partial list of the mentor attributes.

FIGURE 8-10   Desirable Mentor Characteristics

To be successful, a mentor must possess several attributes. Here is a sample:[16]

SKILLS, COMPETENCIES, AND VALUES

Counselling and communication skills

Ability to bypass red tape, offer inside information, and point out short cuts

Ability to provide moral support when the protégé is under stress or confused

Commitment to high ethical standards

A degree of charisma

High credibility as a supervisor

KNOWLEDGE

Knowledge of organizational mission, long-range goals, strategy, and culture

Knowledge of critical factors to succeed within the firm

Technical competence to help the protégé overcome skill deficiencies

Communication links with key individuals giving them access to important information

Knowledge of the protégé's motivations, values, skills, competencies, and career aspirations

BEHAVIOURS

Behaviours supportive of the protégé and reflecting faith in the person's dreams

Behaviours aimed at providing honest feedback to the protégé about his or her performance

Behaviours such as alternate job assignments, training, or counselling to improve the protégé's skill and knowledge repertoire

Behaviours indicating sponsorship of the protégé and helping to improve his or her visibility

It has been suggested that the mentor relationship has four major phases, each of which should be carefully planned for successful outcome.[17]

Phase 1. Initiation.
This initial period lasts from 6 months to one year and focuses on establishing a mentor-protégé relationship. The mentor provides coaching, challenging work, and visibility; the protégé provides technical assistance and acknowledges respect to the mentor. The expectations of each party are slowly acknowledged and the protégé shows his or her willingness to be coached.

Phase 2. Cultivation.
This period of 2 to 5 years further strengthens the relationship between the mentor and the protégé. More frequent and meaningful interactions between the two occur at this stage, focusing on improving the protégé's career and psychosocial abilities. The protégé and mentor are emotionally tightly linked.

Phase 3. Separation.
This period lasts 6 months to 2 years and comes after a major change in the relationship caused by transfer, promotion, or other events that physically separate the mentor from the protégé. The protégé may no longer require coaching or may receive it only occasionally. The mentor may be physically or psychologically unable to provide advice because of physical distance or organizational role demands. The protégé may feel independent, anxious, rejuvenated, and tense after the separation. The mentor may feel emotionally lost, betrayed, and satisfied depending on the conditions under which the separation occurred.

Phase 4. Redefinition.
This is an indefinite period during which time the relationship ends or takes on a more peer-like, friendship character. The protégé may find a new mentor. Peer status is fostered by diminished resentment and anger and increased gratitude and appreciation on the part of the protégé.

Several studies have indicated the importance of mentoring for individual and organizational success. Firms where employees leave because of unclear career paths may be able to retain valuable employees through the institution of mentor programs.[18] Organizations may be able to preserve their culture and value system through their mentors. Mentoring also helps employees in a variety of ways: employees avoid costly mistakes that may damage their careers; employees adjust to the organization's culture faster and more effectively; protégés develop political savvy and awareness that enable them to be effective participants.[19] One research study indicated that employees who had mentors, by and large, earned higher salaries at an earlier age and were more likely to have firm career plans.[20] Mentoring may have a special role in improving the quality of work life for female employees.[21] Past writings indicate that mentoring relationships may help alleviate stress by increasing the protégé's self-confidence, forewarning of career challenges, and indicating alternate approaches to dealing with stress. Female mentors play a unique role in this regard since they can more easily relate to the challenges that young female employees face-discrimination, stereotyping, and family-work conflicts.[22]

Website with articles on work-family issues: *www.radcliffe.edu/pubpol/ publications/index.html*

Ernst & Young LLP, is a large, multinational company offering accounting, tax, legal, and other services. Its Canadian head office in Toronto employs 3300. It actively encourages development of mentor relationships with senior members of the firm who can provide both professional and personal guidance to its junior employees. The company also goes to great lengths to offer professional development opportunities to its employees. The company tries to keep abreast of issues and concerns through regular employee surveys and incorporates them into its human resource policies. Actions by senior managers often have the effect of communicating an important message of work-family balance to all employees-as in the case of Kent Kaufield, a senior manager in the firm, who took paternity leave to care for his son.[23] The results of these efforts is that Ernst & Young was rated as one of the top 100 employers in the country.[24]

Website on mentoring: *www.mentoringgroup.com/*

Website on mentoring at work: *www.workplacetoolbox.com*

Focus on Small Business

Good Coaching Starts with Changes in Your Behaviour!

Most small firms cannot afford to hire professional counsellors. Yet, coaching and counselling employees is as critical in a small firm as in a large firm. The owner not only has to act as a formal leader, but also as a friend, philosopher, and guide to the hired help if the owner is to inspire excellence and help employees grow as individuals-something that is critical for long term viability and success of the firm. What starts as performance coaching, if properly done, can lead to a trusting relationship where the leader might also do spiritual coaching[25] helping to improve self-esteem, courage, purpose, and crystallize values. Devoid of formal training in coaching, how is the small business owner to offer counsel to his or her employees? Here are some helpful guidelines.

1. Be a role model: As the saying goes, "actions speak louder than words." An employer who engages in specific behaviours not only is acting as a role model to his or her workforce but is also increasing credibility by showing that actions are consistent with the advice provided. Imagine how the employees are to view the constant nagging for cost control if the owner is always travelling first class, driving expensive cars, and eating in five-star restaurants. The perception that there are two sets of rules-one for the owner/manager and the other for the rest of the workforce-not only reduces the credibility of the counsellor but also creates a perception of "we" and "they" which may be hard to overcome in future.

2. Listen: One of the most important skills for a counsellor is the ability to listen to other person's concerns without passing value judgements. Cultivating this important skill is no easy task, yet critical if the small business manager is to keep the communication lines open.

3. Focus on the problem: When conflicts or problems emerge, it pays to focus on the specific issue or outcomes rather than on the inadequacies of the employee or commenting on the employee's attitudes. Statements that focus on "How this situation affects the customers" or "My feelings on this matter when I heard it" are less likely to provoke defensiveness on the part of the employee (compared to statements like "You should not have done it" or "Your attitude.")

4. Link short-term strategies with long-term plans: By focusing on the long-term viability of an action and linking short-term actions to them, the coach will not only create a sense of purpose but also indicate to the employee how his contributions are important.

5. Consider multiple roles: Almost all employees play multiple roles-they are not only employees but also parents, children, brothers or sisters, grandchildren, neighbours, friends, and ordinary citizens. This means that each person has multiple demands on his or her time. A coach should recognize and respond the need for work-family balance[26] when responding to problems.

6. Recognize the individual needs: Just as the different flowers in a garden require different levels of sunshine and moisture, different kinds of fertilizers and care, different individuals require varying levels of attention and care as well as somewhat differing motivators. While every effort at maintaining equity should be made, this should not be at the cost of impersonal treatment of the employees. This means that the coach should make a conscious effort to understand each employee, the unique personal circumstances the person faces, and respond to them individually.

7. Be available: Finally, it is important to be available for employee consultation and coaching on a predictable basis. Some successful managers allocate a portion of their weekly or daily time simply to listen to their subordinates and respond to their concerns. While this may appear "unproductive" at a cursory glance, the benefits of creating a long-term trusting relationship cannot be over emphasized.

Despite the above benefits, mentoring should not be instituted without careful planning and prior training for supervisors. Not every manager or supervisor is naturally equipped to act as a mentor. Training supervisors to act as mentors should be an organizational priority for firms that want to successfully use this approach. In cross-gender mentoring relationships, the parties must define the boundary between professional intimacy and romantic involvement. When a mentor and a protégé develop an emotionally and physically intimate relationship, they run the risk of seriously damaging their professional effectiveness as well as personal lives.[27] Finally, the performance evaluation and reward system within organizations should be modified to include mentoring responsibilities if a large number of supervisors are to take this role seriously. This is particularly true of organizations which want to encourage mentors for female and minority employees.

IMPLEMENTING DISCIPLINARY PRACTICES

Despite the existence of the best performance management and counselling systems, there are occasions when inappropriate, disruptive, or unacceptable performance occurs. Under these circumstances, disciplinary action is needed. **Disciplinary actions** aim to encourage compliance with organizational policies and performance standards. The objectives of disciplinary actions include:

- reforming the offender;

- preventing others from similar undesirable actions; and

- maintaining consistent, effective performance standards.

Ideally, the disciplinary action should be preventive-it should be taken to encourage employees to follow standards and rules so that infractions are prevented. To achieve this, the standards of performance should be clearly determined and widely understood. Employees usually want to know the reasons behind a policy or standard so that it makes sense to them. Standards which are stated positively instead of negatively are also likely to be better welcomed.

> Positive statements such as "a clean workplace is a safe workplace" or "safety first!" rather than "don't dirty your workplace" or "don't be careless" are likely to receive a better response from employees.

Website with information on occupational outlook: *http://jobfutures.ca/doc/jf/index. shtml*

Disciplinary actions are procedures that encourage compliance with organizational policies and performance standards.

Website for articles on disciplinary practices: *www.p-management.com/ articles/2008.htm*

ATTRIBUTES OF EFFECTIVE DISCIPLINARY PRACTICES

To be effective, a disciplinary system should have several attributes. Some of the more important features are discussed below.

Immediate and Consistent Disciplinary actions should be immediate and consistent. A useful guideline in this context is the hot-stove rule. Just as a person touching a hot stove (an undesirable action) receives immediate, consistent, and impersonal punishment, so should the violator of an organizational policy or standard. Irrespective of who the violator is, the punishment should be the same and immediate.

With Warning The offending employee should be warned in clear and unequivocal terms that failure to improve the behaviour will result in discipline (including possible discharge).

Progressive A policy of **progressive discipline**, where repeated offences are accompanied by stronger penalties has been found useful in many organizations. An example of a progressive discipline system is shown in Figure 8-11. As can be seen from the figure, repeated violations are accompanied by harsher punishments and finally discharge. It is important to clearly indicate in writing the nature of the problem and the impact of the offender's behaviour on organizational performance, success, or stature in the larger society.

Progressive discipline is a system of imposing stronger penalties for repeated offences.

FIGURE 8-11   Illustration of a Progressive Discipline System

First violation: Verbal reprimand and counselling by the supervisor
Second violation: Written reprimand, counselling, and a record in the file
Third violation: One or two day suspension from work (depending on the gravity of offence)
Fourth violation: Suspension for one week or longer
Fifth violation: Discharge for cause

Due Process Due process, or a system of consistent rules and procedures where employees are provided with an opportunity to respond to the charges against them, should be followed in all instances. Sufficient documentation must exist to support all charges against employees.

Dismissal for Just Cause Only The ultimate disciplinary action, namely dismissal, should be resorted to only for just cause and after all avenues for corrective action and change in employee behaviour have been explored. Past court decisions indicate that just cause may include:[28]

- violation of a fundamental term of the employment contract (e.g., not to steal) or making false statements or omitting essential facts in employment application;

- endangering health and safety of others;

- illegal conduct;

- insubordination;

- serious misconduct in the workplace or misconduct of a more minor nature that is persistent and uncorrected by the employee; and

- persistent and deliberate poor job performance despite warning, training, feedback, and provision of appropriate working conditions.

Website with articles on handling difficult employees: *www.hr-guide.com*

It is the employer's responsibility to show that adequate warnings have been given to the erring employee and appropriate training, time, and feedback have been provided to improve the person's performance.[29] In the case of long-term employees, a one-time behaviour, even a refusal to attend to work, may not constitute "just cause" for dismissal as the following case showed.

> Timothy Minott had worked for O'Shanter Development Company for 11 years. Until his dismissal, the employer did not have any complaints about Minott or his performance. Due to his refusal to show up for work one day, Minott was given a 2-day disciplinary suspension without pay. A misunderstanding of the date on which the suspension was to be served led to a heated exchange between Minott and his supervisor at the end of which Minott was terminated. The judge who looked at the case concluded that Minott was honestly confused about the dates on which his suspension was to have been served and his failure to return to work on the date his employer expected him was not just cause for termination. In a later decision, an appeal court judge decided that given the long record of loyal service by the employee and the fact that he was not given any warning by the employer that his job was in jeopardy, even a wilful refusal to attend work for one day did not constitute just cause.[30]

Discharge of an employee without just cause or reasonable notice is considered as **wrongful dismissal** by courts. Dismissal of unionized employees should conform to the provisions of the collective agreement signed between the management and the union. Some employee behaviours that may qualify for dismissal are listed in Figure

Wrongful dismissal is the discharge of an employee without just cause or reasonable notice.

FIGURE 8-12 Situations for Which Dismissal May Be Appropriate

Theft of company property

Vandalism of company property

Falsification of employment application

Consumption of illegal drugs or alcohol at work

Fraud, stealing, and falsification of company records

Unauthorized release of confidential information

Receipt of bribes, gifts, or rewards for offering a service that undermines the organization's interests and solely focuses on personal gain

Abandoning the job or not showing up for work for an extended period (usually, a week) without an explanation or receipt of leave of absence from management

Endangering health and safety of themselves or others

Other illegal conduct such as drug trafficking

8-12. If just cause does not exist, an employer is expected to give reasonable notice to the employee whose services are being terminated. All Canadian provinces have employment standards legislation that requires minimum periods of notice (usually termed "reasonable notice") to employees terminated without cause. Past court decisions indicate that "reasonable notice" should reflect employee's age, length of service, salary, occupational status, and labour market conditions, among other things.

Termination Procedures Termination of employee services should be approved by the human resource department and conform to organizational policies. A termination meeting with the employee in the presence of another manager (preferably the human resource manager) as a witness is to be held in a private and neutral location. The termination meeting should cover all issues that must be dealt with before an employee leaves the location-it also offers an opportunity to return employee's back pay and benefits and other properties and provide him or her with information about his or her Record of Employment. The notice and severance pay offered to the employee should, at a minimum, meet the standards established by the provincial employment standards. For example, Ontario's Employment Standards Act establishes minimum notice and severance pay requirements in the province. All relevant security measures (e.g., invalidating employee passwords to accounts and phone, releasing office and parking space held by the employee) should be taken care of before the final meeting. If the employee's past history indicates potential for an emotional outburst or violence, precautionary security arrangements may be required. Some of the "do's and don'ts" in the context of terminating an employee are listed in Figure 8-13. A checklist of key items to consider in the wake of termination is shown in Figure 8-14. Figure 8-15 provides an illustration of the notice and severance policies for one large manufacturing organization.

In summary, the employer's employment rules must be reasonable and consistently employed. The criteria against which the "reasonableness" of employer's rules are measured include:[31]

- the rule must be clear and unequivocal;

- the rule must be brought to the attention of the employee affected before the company can act on it;

FIGURE 8-13   Do's and Don'ts when Terminating Employees

DO

Review the decision to terminate very carefully looking at all possible, including legal, repercussions.

Consult the human resource department and/or legal counsel before undertaking the decision.

Inform boss about the decision to terminate the employee (to avoid possible complications when the employee appeals to higher management).

Hold the termination meeting in the presence of a manager, preferably someone from the human resource department.

Invalidate the employee's passwords and access words to systems before termination meeting.

Make security arrangements if employee's past behaviours give reason to believe violent outburst.

Make detailed notes of the discussion either during or immediately following the meeting.

Clearly identify the reason for termination.

Provide the employee a copy of the termination letter and an opportunity to read it thoroughly.

Where feasible, identify positive aspects of the termination, highlighting how this will help the employee to get a fresh start or find a solution to his or her problems.

Ensure that employee has received the minimum notice and/or severance pay required by the provincial employment standards legislation.

Ensure that all company property and employee identification cards have been returned.

DON'T

Terminate the employee in public.

Terminate the employee on special days (important holidays, employee's birthday, or anniversary day).

Engage in a lengthy debate with the employee over the decision to terminate.

Respond to threats by the employee to go to a lawyer or to the union.

Get angry or threaten the employee even if the employee is angry. Anger is a natural response for people who receive a termination order.

- the employee concerned must have been notified that a breach of the rule could result in his or her discharge if the rule is used as a foundation for discharge;

- the rule should have been consistently enforced by the company since the time it was formulated; and

- the rule must be consistent with the provisions of the collective agreement between the firm and its union.

The last provision listed above is critical making it obligatory for a firm to be consistent in its treatment of employees. It also makes it necessary to keep clear records of each offence and how the management dealt with it. A past court case underscores the importance of consistent management action in the case of discipline.[32]

> MacMillan Bloedel dismissed an employee after the person was found to smoke a marijuana cigarette at work. The arbitrator recognized the employer's position that this was a very serious offence. The employee involved had also known about the employer's commitment to a drug-free work setting. However, in defence of the employee, the union pointed out that the employer's past practice in dealing with this offence was a 30-day suspension. The arbitrator held that the employer had an obligation to serve notice of an intention to change its approach to a workplace rule, including the punishment involved. The employee was reinstated and a 30-day suspension was substituted for the dismissal.

FIGURE 8-14   Checklist of Key Items to Focus on at Termination

Employee Name: _____
Job Title: _____
Employee Identification Number: _____
Last working day: _____
Reason for termination: _____

Were all the following items discussed with the employee?

Item		Comments if any (especially if box not checked)
Severance pay	❑	
Picking up last pay cheque	❑	
Pay in lieu of vacation	❑	
Company pension plan	❑	
Unemployment insurance	❑	
Group insurance	❑	
Other benefits/allowances	❑	
Stock ownership	❑	
Company life insurance	❑	
Profit sharing payouts/bonus	❑	
Patent obligations/trade secrets	❑	
Advances outstanding from employee	❑	
Mail pickup by the employee	❑	

Did the employee return all of the following items?

Item	Yes	No	Comments
Door keys or sensor cards	❑	❑	
ID cards/badges	❑	❑	
Car keys	❑	❑	
Computer/accessories	❑	❑	
Cellular phone	❑	❑	
Credit cards	❑	❑	
Uniforms (if applicable)	❑	❑	
Office records/files	❑	❑	
Locker keys	❑	❑	

Name of the person preparing this sheet: _____ Date: _____

FIGURE 8-15   Termination Notice and Severance Pay Policies of One Large Manufacturer

Length of service	Notice	Severance pay offered
Up to 3 months (probationary period)	1 day	None
3 months to 4 years	1 week's notice per year of service	None
5 years to 8 years	1 week's notice per year of service	1 week per year of service
Over 8 years	8 weeks	26 weeks

ENCOURAGING TO EMBRACE ERRORS

To be effective in today's continuously changing world, a firm should create a work environment that fosters teamwork, communication, trust, feedback, and participation. Systems that highlight top-down control, evaluation (without any focus on development), unilateral communication (from the superior to the subordinate), and a focus on punishment (rather than positive reinforcement) can often generate dysfunctional outcomes and can, in the end, be de-motivating.

Ideally, performance management systems should control yet provide freedom. Control systems in many effective organizations encourage employees to "embrace" errors rather than to totally avoid them.[33] In an **error-embracing organization**, errors are seen as unavoidable by-products of learning and change and are acknowledged as necessary ingredients of the learning process. The extent to which an organization can embrace a given error is, of course, dependent on the severity of the error or mistake. However, an error-embracing organization tends to use different criteria to determine how tolerable an error is:[34] In an error avoiding organization, all errors are bad, but mistakes in routine, unimportant matters are tolerable. In error embracing systems, errors resulting from risky decisions are probably more tolerable than (or at least as tolerable as) mistakes in routine matters.[35]

The key characteristics of an organization employing an error-embracing form of control are shown in Figure 8-16. As can be seen from the figure, an error-embracing system has different assumptions about individuals and their roles. For example, the work climate in an error-embracing organization is likely to be more open and trusting than in an organization that does not tolerate mistakes.

Error-embracing organizations are those that acknowledge errors committed by employees when making risky, entrepreneurial decisions as unavoidable by-products of learning and change and tolerate them more often than mistakes in routine matters.

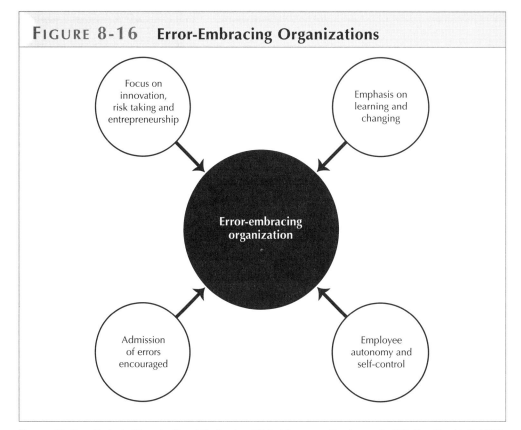

FIGURE 8-16   Error-Embracing Organizations

Focus on innovation, risk taking and entrepreneurship

Emphasis on learning and changing

Error-embracing organization

Admission of errors encouraged

Employee autonomy and self-control

Source: H. Das. *Strategic Organizational Design in a Global Economy*. Scarborough, ON: Prentice-Hall, 1998. Reprinted with permission.

Finally, the motivational power of even simple gestures by managers should not be underestimated.

> The bottle of champagne was sitting by Bert Bachmann's front door when he arrived home after running his marathon, a 42-kilometre slog through the streets of Vancouver. Tied to the bottle with a white ribbon was a card from his boss at B.C. Packers that read, "Congratulations on your achievement. Your willpower is something to be admired." The champagne is long gone, but two years later, Mr. Bachmann still cherishes the card. It is both a keepsake of his personal triumph and a lesson in how to reward employees in a memorable way.[36]

Praise, recognition of good work, and providing employees with opportunities to do a more fulfilling job often do not cost much money. However, in many organizations, it requires a fundamental shift in managerial attitudes away from the annual or semi-annual ritual of performance review where the superior dumps "on the table a gunny sack of all the mistakes an employee has made,"[37] and towards strategies that are more productive.

How are organizations built that are skilled enough, smart enough, and most of all enduring enough to survive in today's treacherously competitive world? The answer is by no means simple. It has been suggested that, in some instances, it may be useful for managers to draw lessons from the biological world.[38] The genius of nature, this theory says, is its capacity to create something from nothing and to build systems of enormous complexity without a master plan. Part of the new logic may thus be achieving complexity by creating multiple layers of simplicity, and building control from the bottom up rather than from the top down. Encouraging diversity, eccentricity, and instability may, ultimately, provide the greatest control in a turbulent world.

Implications for Practice

1. Performance counselling benefits individual employees and the larger organization. Hence, most organizations should attempt to install an employee counselling system. Depending on the size of the firm and resources available, the responsibility for counselling may be shared between the immediate supervisor and performance management specialists.

2. Different situations require different counselling styles. To meet the needs of the situation, a manager may have to play the role of a trainer, a coach, a role model, or a mentor. Before choosing the specific action, a counsellor has to recognize the nature of the situation and adapt behaviours and steps to the needs of the occasion.

3. Whatever the manager's role as a counsellor, to be effective, he or she must possess a number of skills and knowledge and display certain behaviours and values. Not all supervisors naturally possess these skills and competencies. This means that organizations focusing on employee counselling and development have to first look at the issue of supervisory training.

4. Despite the existence of the best performance management and counselling systems, there are occasions when inappropriate, disruptive, or unacceptable performance occurs. The disciplinary procedures used in such instances must be consistent, fair, and after fair warning. Existence of a due process is vital in all instances.

5. Progressive discipline where successive infractions are accompanied by higher penalties may be useful in most settings.

6. The ultimate disciplinary action of dismissal should be for just cause and after all other avenues for corrective action have been explored.

Key Terms for Review

Coaching, p. 249

Counselling, p. 242

Disciplinary actions, p. 261

Error-embracing organization, p. 266

Mentor, p. 258

Progressive discipline, p. 261

Role models, p. 255

Training, p. 248

Wrongful dismissal, p. 262

Discussion Questions

1. Why is counselling important today? Can all organizations benefit from counselling systems?

2. What is the role of a manager in counselling employees? Would this role change with the nature of the organization and situation? How?

3. What is meant by progressive discipline? What are the duties of a supervisor under this system?

4. What is an error embracing organization? Is this idea relevant only for hi-tech firms which have to exist amidst continuous change?

Critical Thinking Questions

1. Is counselling relevant in a small, owner operated unit with nine employees?

2. If an organization that had employed 210 white male employees in its light appliance assembly line newly hires 25 female and minority employees, what problems are likely to be faced by the workforce and the supervisors? Which of the counselling tools discussed in the chapter would seem relevant in this context?

3. If an employee refuses to abide by a supervisor's instruction to pick up garbage, would this constitute valid ground for dismissal? Why?

4. Assume you are a work supervisor. If you want your employees to be innovators and risk takers, what actions are necessary on your part?

Web Research

Visit the websites of three large, multinational organizations. Now take three firms operating in a traditional industry like mining, fishing, or forestry. Compare the employee policies listed on their websites. Do you see any patterns in regard to their support and career development systems for employees?

CASE INCIDENT

Office Products Limited

Office Products Limited is a medium-sized distributor of a number of office machines and equipment. It has a policy of on-site service for all the equipment it sells. Aggressive marketing and introduction of a performance-based compensation system resulted in the fast sales growth of the firm. In just two years, the company's sales increased by 220%. However, the customers were beginning to note delays in service and maintenance of equipment. About one-third of the customers noted that they had to make a second call to Office Products before the service personnel arrived at the site.

Steve Plummer, the manager of the Winnipeg branch employing 28 (including 4 supervisors) in sales, service, technical, packaging and delivery, had a problem: he was getting very concerned about the absenteeism and late arrival of a number of employees. Generally, service personnel checked each morning with the firm's daily "router" and directly attended to customer service calls. Several of those who were on outside service calls were said to start their work late or take unofficial "coffee breaks" or "mini-rest periods" between two service calls. He looked through the attendance records of the firm for the past week and found these entries in the log:

- Jack Hutton, a senior technician was late. He lives on a farm located 40 kilometres away from the city. Jack is 58 years old and is planning to retire in two years. Steve recollected that the firm had helped Jack with a small loan to buy this country property. The road to his farm was often badly maintained resulting in frequent delays for the persons who live there. On the days when Jack is late, two other junior technicians wait idly for instructions.

- Ann Gatton was late again—by 25 minutes this time. Steve felt sorry for Ann; she had three small children and an ailing mother to take care of. Ann was a very conscientious worker and consistently performed her duties at a high quality level. However, this was the third time she was late in a week, although on the other two occasions, she was late only by five or six minutes. On the days when one of the children or her mother was sick, Ann had to rush them to the nearby clinic. As a single mother, she had no one else to provide help.

- Jim McCaulay, 28, was late for the first time this month. His wife had just given birth to his first baby the morning that he was late. Finding that his wife and daughter were fine, Jim had rushed to work, but was late by ten minutes.

- Tim Reittman, 34, was late for the third time in a week. Each time he was late by only one or two minutes. No particular reasons were offered.

Steve looked at the overall attendance records for the past quarter. Here is a summary of his findings:

Through the grapevine, Steve had heard that Clyde Dougherty was on a fraudulent sick leave for the past 10 days. He was wondering whether it would be a good idea to fire Clyde and convey a firm message to the other employees. He was unsure about the correct action at this time.

(continued)

Segment of total workforce	Tardiness (# minutes last quarter)	Absenteeism (# days last quarter)
55%	0	0
25%	1-3	1
10%	4-7	2-3
5%	8-10	4
5%	11-45	5-6

Questions

1. Would you recommend firing Clyde? Why?

2. What actions are appropriate to improve the situation now?

CASE

Pay and Save Groceries: Developing Female and Minority Employees

Pay and Save Groceries (PSG) is a regional grocery chain with 45 supermarkets spread over Eastern Canada. The firm, which began as a mom and pop store in Halifax 25 years ago, grew to its present size of 480 full-time employees and approximately 2300 part-time employees with annual revenue of over $2.4 billion. Historically, the firm was proud of its informal, familial atmosphere with hardly any formal systems and procedures for most human resource matters. For example, the firm did not have any rigid job descriptions or specifications, or any systematic job evaluation schemes. Jane Werther, who joined the firm eight months ago as the Human Resource Manger has been incorporating various systems and procedures. More details on PSG are provided at the end of Chapter 1.

In a recent review of employee records, Werther was struck that there were very few female and minority employees at supervisory levels or higher. Figure A shows a summary of the human resources in the firm as of last month. Depending on the time of the year, the total number of employees shows some variation, but Werther noted that the proportions remained essentially the same during the whole year. She was also aware that part-time workers received only a small portion of the total compensation received by full-timers (when various benefits and pension contributions are taken into consideration). Hence, she felt that it was important that the workforce represented the larger communities within which the firm operated. She also realized that the local labour markets had the following composition: Male: 52%; Female: 47%; White: 80%; Black: 7%; Other minorities: 9% and Native Canadians: 4%.

Werther is keen on instituting a developmental program so that all employees can rise to their full potential. She was particularly concerned about the career prospects for women and minorities.

Questions

1. Do you think that Werther's concern for women and minorities is warranted? Why?

2. If your were Werther what steps would you take?

3. What systems and procedures are likely to be relevant in this context?

FIGURE A Workforce Composition in Pay and Save Groceries

Job classes	Male	Female	White	Black	Other minorities	Native People
Managers	60	8	63	1	4	0
Supervisors	140	16	143	2	10	1
Full-time cashiers	20	146	125	10	25	6
Part-time cashiers	117	1310	920	157	300	50
Other technical employees	210	28	200	12	24	2
Other non-technical employees	110	602	328	200	120	64
Total	**657**	**2110**	**1779**	**382**	**483**	**123**

PERFORMANCE MANAGEMENT SYSTEM REVIEW AND ENHANCEMENT

Like all other systems, a performance management system requires continuous review and change. Every change in corporate goals, strategies, or operational priorities requires changes in performance plans and assessment procedures, while changes in technology or workforce characteristics necessitate new ways of working. This part introduces the reader to the important task of reviewing the performance management system and details the steps to do so in this context.

9 REVIEW OF THE PERFORMANCE MANAGEMENT PROCESS

The new workforce, if it is to be energized at all, will more and more demand a genuine say in how the work is to be done. The prevailing mode of work has shifted to empowerment, collaboration, and teams. These changes mean that every manager will serve in a new role. It requires a shift from "managing" people to "helping" people to manage themselves and the business... Though well intended, appraisal uniformly imposes a single method for conveying feedback, managing performance, measuring competencies, developing employees and the like.[1]

Tom Coens and Mary Jenkins

CHAPTER OBJECTIVES

After studying this chapter, you should be able to:

- Discuss the importance of auditing a performance management system

- Outline the steps in a performance management audit

- Detail the various approaches to audit and the methods used for data collection

- Describe the contents of the performance management audit report

Fred is the manager of a fast food franchise that is located two blocks from an inner-city high school of predominantly disadvantaged youth. Sales to students are a large part of store sales. Fred's primary source of labour is also these students. Consequently, many of Fred's employees need confidence-building and extra training because they are young and from disadvantaged homes. The extra training time drives up his labour costs. The high-school customers come in throughout the day and litter the eating area and it is difficult to manage this without driving away his main source of business. Despite his best efforts, Fred gets marked down on "cleanliness" in every standardized appraisal of the franchise. At night, the roughness of the neighbourhood necessitates a security guard to monitor the premises. While this helps the business, it also increases overhead costs—another dimension on which Fred is being evaluated by the franchise. Fred invariably gets the lowest pay increase each year.[2]

Fred's dilemma is that, to get higher performance ratings, he has to keep the premises cleaner and overheads down but to accomplish that would cut into his overall performance and success. The very actions that help him score higher ratings on some performance dimensions may actually spell disaster in the long term.

It is not unusual to see such inconsistencies and contradictions even in well-designed performance management systems. Only continuous review and reassessment of the system can help reduce or eliminate such inconsistencies. This chapter introduces a variety of tools that can be used to review the performance management system. But first, we must look at some of the factors that make such a review essential.

WHY AUDIT THE PERFORMANCE MANAGEMENT SYSTEM?

Performance management system audits evaluate all human resource activities, systems, and procedures that form the performance management in an organization.

A **performance management system audit** evaluates all human resource activities, systems, and procedures forming part of performance management in an organization. It gives feedback about the performance management function to operating managers and performance specialists. It also provides feedback about how well managers are meeting their performance management duties. Research into HR practices may uncover better ways for the department to contribute to organizational and employee objectives. If the evaluation is done properly, it can also build support between the performance management department and operating managers. Consider the following scenario.

> Martha Gannon (Plant Manager): "I thought as a performance specialist you know the best way to plan and monitor performance. Why the audit, then?"
>
> Matteo Galetti (Performance Analyst): "We realize that there is always room for improvement. In fact, the reason we are doing this review is to check our methods and learn how we can better serve managers like yourself."
>
> Gannon: "What do you hope to discover? I thought with all those weekly and monthly reports about performance, you already have all the necessary information."
>
> Galetti: "First, we want to see if our present procedures are being followed. We need uniformity in our appraisal, coaching, compensation, and disciplinary activities. If there is no uniformity, employees may perceive inequity that can cause poor morale and performance. If there is inconsistency in the practices, we want to find out why. Maybe managers and employees don't understand our procedures. Or maybe our methods aren't practical and should be changed. Second, we are checking to ensure compliance with employee relations laws such as human rights, safety, and others. This audit is not a 'witch hunt.' We are simply trying to improve our performance."

As the above dialogue indicates, there are several benefits from a human resource audit. Figure 9-1 lists the major ones. An audit reminds managers like Gannon of the department's contribution. It also creates a more professional image of the department among managers and human resource specialists. Indeed, frequent review and modifications to performance management practices are necessitated by a number of internal and external factors. Four of these are discussed below.

FIGURE 9-1   Benefits of a Performance Management Audit

- Helps align performance management practices to the strategic success of the larger organization
- Provides specific, verifiable data on contributions of the performance management system
- Improves the professional image of the performance management department
- Clarifies the performance management department's duties and responsibilities
- Stimulates uniformity of performance management policies and practices
- Finds critical performance management problems
- Ensures timely compliance with legal requirements
- Reduces human resource costs through more effective procedures
- Helps redesign jobs to maximize efficiency and employee satisfaction

---

ENVIRONMENTAL CHANGES

All organizations and their parts are influenced by changes in their environment. The performance management department is no exception. Changes in technology, legal systems, economy, and society profoundly affect the various performance management practices.

> An organization's decision to install sophisticated computer systems or automate some activities has major implications for performance criteria and standards. The emergence of new safety or employment laws may necessitate modifications to performance criteria or workplace behaviours.

ORGANIZATIONAL ENTROPY

Almost all systems have entropic tendencies. **Entropy** is the tendency of a system to run down over time. In the absence of continuous vigilance and follow-up, communications break down, employees make mistakes, or systems and rules take on added importance. **Organizational atrophy** results when organizations lose "muscle tone" and experience a breakdown in their internal operating systems.[3] A principal cause of atrophy is the "success breeds failure syndrome." Past successes often make organizations feel invincible, and their approaches to customers, employees, and the public become inflexible. Thus, organizations may apply standard procedures and policies almost indiscriminately even when novel responses are called for, thus reducing their effectiveness. Unless systems are continuously monitored, ultimately they break down or wither away.

Entropy is the tendency of a system to run down over time.

Organizational atrophy results when organizations lose "muscle tone" and experience a breakdown in internal operating systems.

STRATEGIC, STRUCTURAL, OR TACTICAL CHANGES

To respond to economic turbulence, most organizations adapt by changing their strategic or tactical plans. In some other instances, re-organization of the firm or its activities is not uncommon. Whatever the response, any change in strategy, structure, or tactics affect the roles, required competencies, or behaviours of employees, in turn necessitating the identification of new performance criteria and standards.

A decision to change strategy from cost leadership to differentiation has profound implications for job incumbents. Under a cost leadership strategy, an employee may be required to possess only narrow range of skills compared to the broad range of skills required in a differentiation strategy. The focus of employee performance appraisal might also reflect a change away from control to employee development.

DEMOGRAPHIC CHANGES

The workforce composition in many organizations continually changes. The percentage of women, minorities, or physically challenged in the workforce is increasing in most organizations, requiring new employment practices and performance criteria. The education level of workers is also increasing and there is an associated increase in workplace expectations. Consider the following example.

> The arrival of large numbers of knowledge workers has necessitated changes in performance criteria for supervisory personnel. The old notion of leaders being directive, "take-charge" individuals is no longer valid for many modern settings. Indeed, today's leaders may have to inspire employees and act as catalysts to bring the best out of individual workers and teams. This means that performance criteria and behaviours for supervisors have to be reassessed for their relevance to the firm's current workforce.

Performance audits may also highlight areas where current human resource management functions excel and where gaps exist. Figure 9-2 summarizes the results of two large-scale research studies that measured human resource management effectiveness in Canadian organizations. Data such as this provide approximate benchmarks for individual firms to compare performance. This type of information also initiates new programs aimed at improving employee and organizational performance.

FIGURE 9-2   Indices of Human Resource Management Effectiveness in Canadian Organizations

Index	Organizations across Canada (Except Atlantic Canada) (n = 650)	Organizations in Four Atlantic Provinces (n = 1277)
Productivity	4.38	4.38
Employee satisfaction	4.02	4.21
Employee commitment	4.33	4.38
Grievance rate	2.02	1.90
Absenteeism	2.68	2.28
Turnover	1.99	2.11
Employee quality of life	4.15	4.16

Note: All items are measured on a scale of 1=very low and 6=very high.

Source: Terry Wagar. *Human Resource Management and Labour Relations: A Study of Canadian Organizations*. Department of Management, Saint Mary's University, Halifax, October 1993, 11-13.; Terry Wagar. *Human Resource Management and Labour Relations: Preliminary Results from Atlantic Canada*. Department of Management, Saint Mary's University, Halifax, October 1993, 10-13.

SELF-TEST:

Do You Focus on Continuous Performance Improvement?

This exercise assesses your focus on continuous performance improvement. Please rate each of the following items using the anchors *always* (A), *often* (O), *sometimes* (S), and *rarely or not at all* (R). Since your first reaction to a statement is critical, do NOT change your response once you have indicated it and do not omit any items.

1. I aim to get satisfactory or passing grades in courses rather than the maximum grade possible.

2. I often compare my performance with relevant others to see how I can improve.

3. Only when I perceive difficulty in successfully completing a course will I approach my instructor to seek guidance.

4. I look at how I spend my time and constantly attempt to reduce its wastage.

5. My philosophy is "if something works, don't break it."

6. I often take different routes to work or university to see which takes the least time or effort.

7. If someone in my work group tries to change things, I object it since it disrupts established routines.

8. I look at even routine problems in totally new ways to see whether any new approaches work.

9. I believe that change is what brings stress and unhappiness to our lives.

10. I constantly worry about ways to improve my performance.

Scoring

For statements 1, 3, 5, 7, and 9, assign scores of 1, 2, 3, and 4 for A, O, S, and R respectively. For items 2, 4, 6, 8, and 10, assign scores of 4, 3, 2, and 1 for A, O, S, and R respectively. Total your scores for items 1 through 10.

Interpretation

Your score will range from 10 to 40. If you scored 32 or above, you take continuous effort to improve your performance and find alternative ways to reduce efforts or improve your productivity. If you scored less than 16, you are satisfied with the status quo and consider change and improvement as stressful and undesirable. Scores in between 16 and 32 indicate that you are moderately focused on continuous improvement.

STEPS IN A PERFORMANCE MANAGEMENT AUDIT

Auditing performance management function involves four major steps:

1. Defining the scope of the audit.

2. Choosing the research approach.

3. Identifying data collection method.

4. Data analysis, evaluation, and report preparation.

Figure 9-3 shows these steps and they are discussed in detail below.

THE SCOPE OF THE PERFORMANCE MANAGEMENT AUDIT

The scope of an audit extends beyond just the performance management department's actions. The department does not operate in isolation. Its success depends on

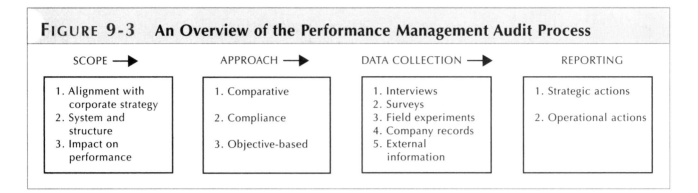

FIGURE 9-3   **An Overview of the Performance Management Audit Process**

SCOPE ➜	APPROACH ➜	DATA COLLECTION ➜	REPORTING
1. Alignment with corporate strategy 2. System and structure 3. Impact on performance	1. Comparative 2. Compliance 3. Objective-based	1. Interviews 2. Surveys 3. Field experiments 4. Company records 5. External information	1. Strategic actions 2. Operational actions

how well it performs and how well its programs are carried out by others in the organization. Consider how supervisors in a firm reduced the effectiveness of the performance appraisal process.

> To appraise performance, The Western Paper Company used a behaviourally-anchored rating scale that had high predictive validity. The supervisors were expected to allot at least an hour in rating and counselling employees on ways to improve performance in the future. To become a work supervisor, an employee needed a minimum of three years of performance improvement. However, in practice, this rarely occurred. Most supervisors spent less than twenty minutes in the activity with the result that employees received very little feedback on their performance. Employee performance showed no consistent improvement over years which disqualified many of them for a promotion. Many of the employees blamed the appraisal process for their lack of promotions.
>
> A performance audit uncovered this misuse of the program and led to additional training for supervisors in employee appraisal and counselling. If the audit had not uncovered this problem, employee dissatisfaction might have grown worse.

As the above example illustrates, "people problems" are seldom confined to just the performance department or even the larger, human resource department. Increasingly, performance audits recognize this fact and transcend the assessment beyond the concerns of the department and operating managers. In practice, the scope of the audit typically focuses on alignment with corporate strategy, performance management systems, and structure and performance outcomes.

Alignment with the Corporate Strategy While performance analysts do not set corporate strategy, they strongly determine its success. If the internal systems, processes, and member behaviours are not in alignment with corporate strategy, a firm's competitiveness is reduced. Whether the company stresses superior marketing (e.g., McCain Foods), service (e.g., IBM), innovation (e.g., Northern Telecom), low-cost operations (e.g., Canadian Tire), or some other approach, performance management is affected. More specifically, various aspects of performance management such as the following need to be examined in detail:

• Are the performance criteria consistent with corporate strategy?

• Are the performance standards in alignment with the firm's strategy and competitive advantage?

• Is the performance assessment system supportive of excellence?

• Are the superiors competent to counsel and inspire subordinates toward corporate goals?

• Is the firm's training program supportive of organizational strategy?

Although the department may lack both the expertise and resources to audit the corporate strategy and its fit with the external environment, the strategy and environmental fit cannot be ignored. Performance management professionals must audit the department's policies and practices against the firm's strategic plans.

> An organization that employed a low-cost strategy continued to employ students and other part-time workers often offering little more than minimum wages. Even after the firm changed its strategy in favour of growth through aggressive acquisitions, several managers continued the old practice of hiring low wage employees. However, the firm's new rapid growth strategy required highly skilled, longer-term employees. An audit revealed high turnover and low morale among employees who did not have adequate skills to meet the new work demands. Based on the audit results, a new training program was implemented to upgrade the skill levels of employees. The hiring policy was also revised in favour of finding permanent, highly skilled employees who could easily fit into a growing organization.

Website with articles on strategy, mission, and HR systems: *www.chrs.net*

Audit of Performance Management Systems and Structure

Audits should logically begin with a review of the performance management department's work. Figure 9-4 lists some of the questions that can be asked. As shown in the figure, an audit should focus on three areas: planning, execution, and control. These three areas of the audit integrate with and supplement each other. Therefore, no single area should be overemphasized in the audit. As may be seen, an audit touches on virtually every topic discussed in this book.

Admittedly, an audit of every activity is time-consuming. As a result, large organizations use sampling techniques to identify tasks and positions that are to be audited in each time period. Some larger organizations also have full-time audit teams

---

FIGURE 9-4   Sample Questions to Assess the Performance Management System and Structure

Planning

- What is sought by each activity? What are the objectives?
- How are the activities planned? How appropriate is the planning process given today's conditions?
- Who is responsible for its execution? What are the expected outcomes?
- How do these objectives reflect and support organizational strategies?

Execution

- What policies and procedures seem to support the execution of these plans?
- Are the systems and procedures internally consistent with one another? Are the logistics reasonable and attainable?
- Does everyone know what is expected of them? How is this ensured?

Control

- What kinds of systems exist to ensure that the plans are being executed properly?
- What records, information, and procedures are being used to monitor proper execution of the plans?
- Who is responsible for monitoring it? Does the person have enough authority, information, and resources to do the job well?
- What plan of action exists to monitor deviations and take corrective actions? How timely and effective is it?

Websites with articles on performance management systems:
www.p-management.com
www.hr-guide.com

similar to those who conduct financial audits. These teams are especially useful when the human resource department is decentralized into regional or field offices. Through the use of audits, the organization can maintain consistency in its practices even though there are several human resource offices in different locations.

Audit of Managerial Compliance

An audit also reviews how well managers comply with performance management policies and procedures. If managers ignore these policies or violate employee relations laws, the audit should uncover these errors so that timely corrective action can be taken.

> In a large, diversified firm, the manager of a section discharged an employee for poor performance. The employee filed a grievance with the management stating that adequate warning was not provided. Unless the decision was reversed, the employee threatened to sue the firm for damages. On investigation, it was found that the manager had tolerated the same level of performance for the last two periods. The performance management department decided that the manager did not meet his obligation to demonstrate that poor performance was identified and communicated to the employee in question. An out-of-court settlement with severance pay was initiated. The performance management department initiated a new training program for all managers educating them of their responsibility to show "just cause" and employ progressive disciplinary procedures. In the immediate future, all managers were also asked to seek the guidance of the performance department before they initiated a drastic disciplinary action such as dismissal.

Besides assuring compliance, the audit can improve the performance management department's image and contribution to the company. Operating managers may gain a higher respect for the department when an audit seeks their views. If the comments of managers are acted upon, the department will be seen as more responsive to their needs and effective in achieving organizational objectives. Consider the following example of how one performance department improved its image and effectiveness.

> After several interviews with the divisional managers of a large food-processing unit with three plants, the audit team discovered a pattern to their comments. Most managers believed that, although the information coming from the performance management department about employee turnover and absenteeism made them aware of the challenges facing them, it did not train the work supervisors and section managers to reduce the same. Day-to-day pressures in the plant caused supervisory training to be superficial and resulted in several employee relation problems, especially when dealing with minority employees. The managers felt an organization-wide training program should equip the supervisors and section managers with skills to manage a diverse workforce. In her next budget, the manager of the performance department sought funds for a two-day workshop on diversity management for all junior managers. Later feedback indicated that the divisional managers appreciated the department's responsiveness. What is more, within six months, the absenteeism and turnover figures in all three plants showed a marked improvement.

Audit of Performance

As mentioned in Chapter 1, an effective performance management department must help the firm achieve its mission and strategies by introducing methods and systems that attract and utilize valuable human capital. It should result in benefits to both employees and the larger organization (see Figure 1-2, page 5) and prepare the firm for the new global economy, rapidly changing technology, and diverse workforce.

At the individual employee or team level, a variety of performance indicators can be used (Chapter 6 lists some of these). Chapter 3 describes the approach to setting performance standards. At the organizational level, it is important not only to look at items such as profitability and productivity gain, but also less tangible outcomes (see Figure 2-2, page 30, for popular organizational goals and sample measures for each). The fact that all organizations are open social systems should be kept in mind (see Figure 3-1, page 56, for a view of a hamburger chain as an open social system). Sample measures to assess the performance of the hamburger chain mentioned in Figure 3-1 are shown in Figure 9-5 below.

RESEARCH APPROACHES TO AUDITS

Performance management audits may be done using a variety of research approaches. Sometimes the "research" is little more than an informal investigation or fact-finding effort. At other times, the approach may be advanced and may rely on sophisticated research designs and statistics.[4] Whether informal or rigorous, this research seeks to improve the contributions of the performance management department within an organization. The three most common research approaches are the comparative approach, compliance approach, and objective-based approach. The benchmarks used in each case are summarized in Figure 9-6 and are explained below.[5]

Comparative Approach
Perhaps the simplest form of research is the **comparative approach**. It uses another division or the performance department in another firm as a model. The audit team then compares its results or procedures with those

Comparative approach uses another division or the performance department in another firm as a model against which the audit team compares its results or procedures.

FIGURE 9-5   Sample Measures to Assess the Performance of a Fast Food Hamburger Chain

Inputs

- Quality of raw materials used
- Qualifications and competence levels of employees hired
- Selection ratio (i.e., number of applications for each job vacancy) for various jobs
- Sophistication of the kitchen equipment used
- Ease of raising capital when needed and the cost to do the same

Processes

- Productivity levels
- Number of hamburgers/other products that don't meet quality standards
- Employee absenteeism rates
- Employee turnover
- Input:output (or efficiency) ratio for various products and processes
- Time taken to produce various products

Outputs

- Profitability
- Market share
- Number of new products introduced
- Growth rate
- Number of new socially responsive initiatives
- Innovation; ability to adapt to new challenges

Focus on Small Business:

Continuous Review Is the Key to Success

Since small businesses do not have elaborate performance management systems, the day-to-day activities of managing and improving employee performance assume great importance. Review of performance management processes, consequently, must happen almost continuously to maintain employee productivity at high levels. The effectiveness of current performance management procedures has to be assessed by looking at concrete indicators as well as observing employee behaviours. Some questions to ask in this context include the following.

1. How is the employee turnover in our firm compared to similar firms? The industry in general?

2. How is our absenteeism rate compared to the industry and our own past records?

3. What are the employee attitudes towards their jobs, supervision, performance assessment procedures, and compensation? Are the results satisfactory? Are there improvements needed?

4. Do we offer rewards for superior performance by individuals and teams? How? Are there better ways?

5. What are our procedures to bring marginal performers to desired levels? Are our training systems adequate?

6. How many improvements in procedures or new products did the employees come up with in the recent past? Is this level satisfactory? Do we reward innovation and entrepreneurship? How do we encourage elimination of waste?

7. What systems do we have in place to ensure work-family balancing by employees?

8. What systems do we have to ensure high quality? How do our quality standards compare to key competitors? To the industry in general?

9. Do the employees have enough resources (including time) to achieve the goals?

10. Do the employees trust their supervisors and the management in general? What evidence do we have in this regard? What can be done to improve this?

Website with compensation data:
www.compensationlink. com

of the other organization. This approach commonly is used to compare the results of specific performance management activities or programs and their relation to absence, turnover, and salary data. This approach also makes sense when a new procedure is being tried for the first time.

FIGURE 9-6	Benchmarks Used in Various Performance Management Audits
Approach	**Typical Benchmarks Used**
Comparative Approach	1. Comparable firm's performance 2. General industry standards 3. Judgements of an expert 4. Company historical data 5. Other external standards like ISO 9000
Compliance Approach	1. Legal requirements 2. Company policies and rules 3. Company ethical code 4. Minimum regulations in the industry (e.g., safety)
Objectives-based Approach	1. System or unit objectives 2. Strategic goals

For example, when Alberta Gas Exploration Ltd. installed a drug rehabilitation program, it copied salient features of a long-running similar program at another local firm. Later the results of the two programs were compared, helping Alberta Gas to remove "bugs" in its program.

Sometimes, the opinions of an outside expert may be employed to evaluate the department or one of its programs. Standards set by a consultant or from published research findings serve as benchmarks for the audit team.

A well-respected professor in human resource management with considerable practical experience was invited by Nova Scotia Food Processors to evaluate its employee performance management systems and practices. After a detailed review, the professor concluded that the performance standards and job specifications for a number of jobs, especially in the firm's new, automated plant were outdated. A new performance evaluation form for the plant was also suggested. A comparison of employee and supervisory attitudes before and after the change showed that the firm benefited from these changes.

Another approach is to develop statistical measures of performance based on the company's existing information system. For example, research into the company's records reveals its absenteeism and turnover rates. These data indicate how well the performance management department and operating managers control these problem areas. This statistical approach is usually supplemented with comparisons to external information, which may be gathered from other firms and expressed as ratios.

In Nova Scotia Food Processors, which has an approximate workforce of 300, had 45 quit during a year. The firm recognized that its turnover rate of 15% was significantly higher than the industry average and decided to investigate the matter in detail.

Compliance Approach
The **compliance approach** reviews past practices to determine if those actions followed company policies and procedures. Often the audit team reviews a sample of job descriptions and specifications and employment interview, compensation, discipline, and employee appraisal forms. The purpose of the review is to ensure that field offices and operating managers comply with internal rules and legal regulations.

Compliance approach reviews past practices to determine if they followed company policies and procedures.

An internal audit of the performance appraisal process used at Nova Scotia Food Processors revealed that the work supervisors followed the correct procedures. But the audit team noticed that many appraisal forms had comments written in the margins referring to personal data that were not asked on the form, such as marital status, ages of children, and race-related matters. Some of the managers had also kept records of employee's family matters in the files to help them jog their memory and counsel individual candidates. But the performance management department was concerned about possible complaints of invasion into privacy. The supervisors were asked not to list personal and family details in office files.

For global organizations, the existence of uniform human resource policies and practices throughout their world operations may be desirable but hard to achieve. Different countries and cultures value different rewards. Geographical and cultural distance pose severe communication problems for expatriate managers in performance appraisal, job design, and employee relations. The legal frameworks in various countries show marked differences making the same practice acceptable and unacceptable in different cultural settings. Because of these variations, it is vital that the performance management practices are frequently checked for their compliance with local laws as well as the home office human resource policies and ethical codes.

Objectives-based Approach
In the **objectives-based approach**, specific objectives against which the activities and success of various performance manage-

Objectives-based approach identifies specific objectives or strategic needs against which the activities and success of various performance management programs and systems are compared and corrective actions identified.

ment programs and systems are identified and the actual performance compared against these previously set objectives in the light of strategic needs.[6]

> Supervisors may set a goal of reducing the absenteeism or improving employee productivity. These objectives can be compared against actual achievements. The audit would evaluate the trends in this area.

No single audit approach works for all situations. More commonly, audit teams use several of the strategies, depending on the specific performance management activities under evaluation. Whatever the approach used, it is desirable to involve managers in developing relevant criteria for evaluating performance management function.

RESEARCH DESIGN AND DATA COLLECTION METHOD

Regardless of the research approach used, data about the performance management system and activities have to be collected. Typically, a number of data collection tools or sources may be needed to gauge effectiveness of performance management systems since each tool or source may only provide partial insights into the effectiveness. Popular data collection tools and sources include interviews, surveys, experiments, use of company records, and use of external information.

Interviews Interviews, or face-to-face meetings with employees and managers to collect information usually based on a list of questions (usually called "interview schedule") are one key tool in the context of a performance management audit. The comments from respondents help the audit team find areas that need improvement. Suggestions by managers and feedback from employees may identify areas where improvements can be made. When their criticisms are valid, changes should be made. But when it is the human resource department who is right, it may have to educate others in the firm by explaining the procedures being questioned.

> Linda McDonald served as a member of the audit team at Canadian Electronics Limited, a medium-sized manufacturer and distributor of electronic, computer software, and telecommunications equipment that was fast expanding into foreign markets. She interviewed various managers, who complained that the frequent updating of job descriptions and specifications was a problem. They complained that frequent updating of these documents took away time from other important activities. Linda understood their concerns. She explained that the unique nature of the industry coupled with the fast growth of the firm necessitated frequent hiring and training of staff. Unless job duties and specifications were clearly identified, the training might not be properly carried out; wrong hiring might actually result in greater loss of time and inefficiency for various departments. Although many managers still disliked the situation, the audit interview helped them understand the need for the frequent review and updating of job descriptions and specifications.

Interviews are helpful in assessing a firm's internal culture. Such cultural audits aim to gauge the prevailing organizational culture and how it is revealed to members. While in-depth interviews can provide useful information, it should be emphasized that culture is often invisible even to close observers; and hence it must be assessed using a variety of tools and over a relatively long period of time and using a significant sample of organizational members.

Sometimes, instead of individual interviews, group or team interviews and focus groups are used. A **focus group** involves an unbiased discussion leader guiding

Interviews are face-to-face meetings with employees and managers to collect information from a list of questions (called "interview schedule").

Focus group is a panel of 8 to 12 employees, led by unbiased discussion leader, discussing various performance management related matters in an unstructured and free-flowing environment.

unstructured and free-flowing discussion on various performance management related matters by a panel of eight to twelve employees knowledgeable about the topic. After the initial warm-up period when members introduce themselves, the discussion leader (usually called "moderator") sets the ground rules for the discussion and introduces the topic. Usually, focus groups last from one to two hours.

A typical approach is to have the group talk about performance management activities in the company and the specific strategies or methods used by the department in achieving organizational goals. From this discussion, the discussion leader may direct the group to talk about how they feel about the performance management practices and then move on to a discussion of what changes and improvements they would like to see.

In most focus groups, the moderator intervenes in group discussion only to introduce topics of importance that may not come up spontaneously, to move on when a topic has been exhausted, or to bring the discussion back to the area of interest when it has wandered into irrelevant areas. The interviews are usually taped so that the moderator can concentrate on keeping the discussion on track without fear of losing important information. To be effective, moderators must blend into the group and be accepted as a member rather than as a director who asks questions that others are expected to answer.

Surveys In many instances, interviews are supplemented with surveys. In a survey, information is gathered from a sample of persons by use of a questionnaire. Surveys can be done through office mail, Canada Post, telephone, fax, or more recently, the Internet. Interviews are time-consuming, costly, and usually limited to only a few people. Through surveys of employees, a broader, more accurate picture of employee perceptions can be developed. Mail questionnaires can reach a geographically dispersed sample simultaneously and at a relatively low cost because interviewers are not required. This makes it particularly attractive to large organizations that operate across the country or nations. Mail and self-administered questionnaires can be filled out at the respondent's convenience thus increasing the probability of response. Also, the anonymity offered by questionnaires may result in more candid answers than face-to-face interviews, especially if the survey includes any sensitive or socially undesirable information. Telephone and Internet surveys can improve the speed of data collection significantly. They are also extremely less expensive than interviews.

Website with information on employee surveys: www.hr-guide.com

Surveys can be several pages long and gather information on a variety of performance management related topics and attitudes. However, to be effective, a survey need not be very long. Sometimes even a short survey using a 6-item questionnaire such as the one shown in Figure 9-7 may capture overall employee attitudes towards key performance management issues. Naturally, when more information is needed, questionnaires employing dozens (sometimes even hundreds) of questions are employed. When longer questionnaires are used, the answers are grouped into areas of analysis to find out where employee attitudes are high and where they are low. The survey results may be compared across departments, to similar firms, to past survey findings, or to corporate objectives. Further analysis may identify problems with specific supervisors, employee subgroups, jobs, or benefits.

Surveys give valuable feedback about required changes in performance management procedures and systems. Of particular importance are trends revealed through repeated, periodic administration of questionnaires. The discovery of research-based trends suggests whether specific challenges are becoming more or less important to those surveyed.

Experiments Experiment is yet another powerful tool available to an audit team. In an **experiment**, conditions are controlled so that one or more variables can be

Experiments control conditions of performance so that independent variables can be manipulated to test a hypothesis and see the impact on dependent variables.

FIGURE 9-7   **A Short Survey of Employee Attitudes Toward Performance Management Systems**

Please indicate the degree of your agreement or disagreement with each statement by checking the appropriate boxes. Do not omit any item. Do not write your name or other identifying information anywhere on this form. Please return the completed form to the Performance Management Department on or before June 30, 2003.

	Strongly Agree	Agree	Undecided	Disagree	Strongly Disagree
1. I get timely feedback about my performance.	❏	❏	❏	❏	❏
2. The feedback I get on my performance helps me improve my performance.	❏	❏	❏	❏	❏
3. I believe that the performance standards for my job are fair.	❏	❏	❏	❏	❏
4. The job description for my position is no longer accurate.	❏	❏	❏	❏	❏
5. I believe that the performance criteria used for evaluating my performance are no longer valid.	❏	❏	❏	❏	❏
6. Considering everything, I believe that the performance management procedures, as they relate to my job, are appropriate.	❏	❏	❏	❏	❏

The Department I work in: _____

Date: _____

---

manipulated to test a hypothesis. The ideal research design is a field experiment that allows the performance management department to compare an experimental and a control group under realistic conditions.

> The department may implement a diversity management program for half of a division's supervisors. This half is the experimental group. The control group is the other half of the supervisors who are not given training. The subsequent employee grievance records of both groups are compared after an adequate time period. If the experimental group has significantly lower grievance rates (or higher satisfaction with their supervision using other indicators including employee survey results), this is evidence that the diversity-training program was effective.

Experiments provide the maximum control over variables and help the performance management department separate the effects of various factors on a particular outcome (e.g., length of training, pedagogy used (lecture versus case approach) can be manipulated to identify the ideal training procedure)). However, experimentation does have several drawbacks. Many managers are reluctant to experiment with only some workers because of morale problems and potential dissatisfaction among those who were not selected. Those involved may feel manipulated and the experiment may be confounded by changes in the work environment or simply by the two groups talking with each other about the experiment. Experiments that require control over several variables may require the presence of a highly qualified researcher and can also be expensive. Chapter 7 elaborated these and other sources of invalidity in experiments. Not withstanding the above, experiments perhaps provide the only cause-effect test in several settings.

Use of Company Records Not all problems are revealed through interviews or surveys; nor does performance management use these more expensive forms of data collection when the data is already available within the organization. Use of company records involves systematic and in-depth analysis of the company records and operating results to identify patterns and possibilities for improving performance management practices. Sometimes problems can be found only by studying records. This is particularly important while investigating compliance with company procedures and laws. The records normally reviewed by an audit team are listed in Figure 9-8 and discussed in the following paragraphs.

Use of company records involves systematic and in-depth analysis of records and operating results to identify patterns and possibilities for improving performance management practices.

Productivity Records An analysis of production records, absenteeism patterns, scrap rates and wastage, etc., provides clues to the performance management department about prevailing productivity levels and trends. Statistics on absenteeism patterns and turnover figures may provide the human resource department with important clues about underlying, more serious problems.[7]

Employee Files and Records An analysis of employee files can provide information on turnover and absenteeism patterns, career progression for various employee groups, and valuable information on the effectiveness of disciplinary, counselling, and training programs.

Performance Evaluation Records A look at the performance evaluation records may provide, among other things, valuable insight into the relative effectiveness of internal and external recruits and of specific employee training programs.

Safety Records An analysis of safety and health records may reveal violations of the Canada Labour Code or provincial safety and health regulations. Numbers of employees who have made claims on workmen's compensation plans classified by job, employee category, and time periods, number of safety violations observed, and number of complaints from employees about workplace safety are among popular indices looked at in this context.[8]

Legal Compliance Records Although several large companies employ one or more people to monitor the company's compliance with various laws, the audit can

Focus on Ethics

How Much Control Should You Exercise on Your Employee Performance?

Work and family lives are intertwined. What happens at the work affects our family, just as our family events affect our behaviour at work. This means that some of our outside work behaviours are relevant in understanding and predicting our work behaviour. It also raises an interesting question: how much control can an employer exercise on our non-work behaviour? Consider the following behaviours. Do you think that an employer is ethically justified in controlling them?

1. The frequency with which an employee swears and uses profane language at work and outside.

2. Whether an employee uses drugs outside work.

3. The amount of alcohol a person consumes in the evenings (when not working).

4. Whether the employee is openly philandering and being unfaithful to a spouse.

5. Whether the person is a member of a hate group that meets every weekend.

6. Whether the person's spouse works for a competing firm, if the employee has access to trade secrets.

7. Whether the employee criticises your firm in the public, which is later published by a newspaper.

FIGURE 9-8   Sample Company Records Used for a Performance Management Audit

1. Productivity Records

- Cost of production of different products, components, or processes
- Wastage, scrap rates for various processes and plants
- Absenteeism figures categorized by plant, section, time periods, and employee groups
- Employee turnover figures categorized by plant, section, time periods, and employee groups

2. Employee Files and Records

- Turnover and absenteeism records classified by age, gender, department, etc.
- Comparison of the above across time, departments, and industry data on file
- Career progression patterns of specific groups of employees (e.g., visible minorities, women)
- Accuracy, completeness, and currency of information contained in random inspections
- Number, type, and patterns in disciplinary and interpersonal problems

3. Performance Evaluation Records

- Performance of employees before and after specific training programs
- Performance evaluation of internally promoted candidates by their supervisors
- Performance of new hires classified by source of recruits

4. Safety Records

- Statistics on accidents classified by plant, section, process, etc., Comparisons of these with previous years and similar plants in the industry to see patterns
- Statistics on accidents before and after specific safety training programs
- Number of employees who have made claims on worker's compensation plans classified by job, employee category, and time periods
- Number of complaints from employees or unions about working conditions and workplace safety

5. Legal Compliance Records

- Firm's compliance with all labour laws as evidenced by contents of performance appraisal forms, job specifications, disciplinary procedures, etc.
- Number and patterns of sexual or other harassment charges
- Employment equity goals of the firm versus actual achievements
- Patterns in grievances (e.g., arising from specific contract clauses or supervisors)

6. Compensation Records

- Statistics examining external and internal wage equity
- Statistics on benefits offered along with trends in the firm; comparisons with industry data on file

---

act as a further check on compliance of various performance management practices. The team usually concentrates its attention on appraisal, discipline, counselling, and career progression patterns for minority employees. If patterns are detected, the underlying causes have to be identified and corrective actions initiated immediately.

Compensation Records A careful review of the level of wages, benefits, and services that are provided in the firm and comparison with industry benchmarks can provide useful insights into the effectiveness of current reward systems. Benefits and services are also studied to learn if they are competitive with those of other employers and in compliance with government regulations.

External Information Research into internal attitudes and records may uncover unfavourable trends. But outside comparisons also give the performance department a perspective against which the firm's activities can be judged. Some needed information is available readily, while other data may be difficult to find. Most of the external information is available from the publications of Statistics Canada, Industry Canada, and Human Resource Development Canada.

Statistics Canada website:
www.statcan.ca

HRDC website:
www.hrdc-drhc.gc.ca

> It is possible to benchmark workplace absenteeism using Statistics Canada figures (available since 1977). Two types of absenteeism are particularly important to track: those due to illnesses or disability and those resulting from personal or family responsibilities. It is possible to compare past figures and compare them to industry, occupational, provincial, and demographic patterns (e.g., age, gender).

These agencies regularly publish information about employee turnover rates, area wage and salary surveys, and severity and frequency rates of accidents.[9] Industry associations and boards of trade usually make specialized data such as turnover rates, absenteeism rates, standard wage rates, growth rates, standardized job descriptions, accident rates, and benefit costs available to members.

Website of the Society for Human Resource Management:
www.shrm.org

Website of the Canadian Council of HR Associations:
www.chrpcanada.com

McMaster University HR website:
www.hr.mcmaster.ca

Consultants and university research bureaus may be able to provide other needed information through research. Published reports of surveys on topics such as absenteeism can often provide important insights to the audit team.[10]

THE AUDIT REPORT

The **audit report** is a comprehensive description of performance management activities and includes both recommendations for effective practices and for improving practices that are ineffective. Recognition of both good and bad practices is more balanced and encourages acceptance of the report.

The audit report should look at both strategic and operational improvements in performance.

An **audit report** is a comprehensive description of performance management activities including both recommendations for effective practices and for improving ineffective practices.

- Strategic actions often require fundamental changes in the way the firm defines effective performance, hires and trains employees, and assesses their performance. For example, as shown in Chapter 1, an organization's strategic shift requires fundamental changes in the way it defines, measures, and rewards performance.

- On other occasions, such fundamental changes may not be called for. But even here, operational improvements involving fine-tuning of performance management systems and procedures may be required.

The audit report should highlight these necessary changes, classifying them into two types of actions: those necessary on the part of line managers and those to be carried out by the performance management department. For line managers, the report summarizes their performance management objectives, responsibilities, and duties. Examples of duties include evaluating performance, motivating workers, and counselling employees. The report also identifies "people problems." Violations of policies and employee relations laws are highlighted. Poor management practices are revealed in the report along with recommendations.

The performance management department should review the results of the audit paying particular attention to:

- attitudes of managers and employees toward the performance management department services;

- a review of the department's objectives and organization to achieve them;

- problems in the context of performance management and their implications; and

- strategies for making needed changes including identification of a clear, time-bound action plan.

With the information contained in the audit report, the performance management department can take a broad view of the function. Instead of solving problems in a random manner, the manager now can focus on those areas that have the greatest potential for improving the department's contribution to the firm. Emerging trends can be studied and corrective action taken while the problems are still minor. Prompt response to the problems of operating managers may earn added support among them.

Perhaps most important, the audit serves as a map for future efforts and a reference point for future audits. With knowledge of the department's present performance, the manager can make long-range plans to upgrade crucial activities. These plans identify new goals for the department.[11] These goals serve as standards that future audit teams will use to evaluate the firm's performance management activities. Ultimately, it is how effectively the organization prepares itself for the future that spells its success or even survival.

Implications for Practice

1. It is important to conduct audits of performance management function periodically to assess overall usefulness and value-adding function and to provide feedback about how well managers are meeting their performance management duties.

2. More frequent review and modifications to performance management practices are necessitated by a number of internal and external factors. Organizations that operate in turbulent environments, facing growth or restructuring challenges, or undergoing other major strategic initiatives are likely to need periodic audits of their performance management systems and structures.

3. The scope of a performance management audit should go beyond the function or department and focus on alignment with corporate strategy, performance management systems, and structure and performance outcomes.

4. The research approach used should recognize the goals and resources of the firm and may range from an informal investigation or fact-finding effort to rigorous designs that test one or more hypotheses. Depending on the objectives and resource constraints, a comparative, compliance, or objective-based audit (or a combination of these) should be adopted.

5. Regardless of the research approach used, a number of data collection tools should be used to gauge the effectiveness of performance management systems since each tool may only provide partial insights into the performance management activities. Popular data collection tools and sources include interviews, surveys, experiments, use of company records, and use of external information.

6. To make the audit information useful and directive, it should be compiled into a comprehensive report with recommendations for effective practices and for improving practices that are ineffective. Recognition of both good and bad practices is more balanced and encourages acceptance of the report. The audit report should also look at both strategic and operational improvements in performance.

Key Terms for Review

Audit report, p. 287

Comparative approach, p. 287

Compliance approach, p. 281

Entropy, p. 273

Experiments, p. 283

Focus group, p. 282

Interviews, p. 282

Objectives-based approach, p. 281

Organizational atrophy, p. 273

Performance management system audits, p. 272

Use of company records, p. 285

Discussion Questions

1. Do you think that performance management audits are important for all types of firms? Are larger organizations more likely to need the audit?

2. If you were asked to evaluate the performance appraisal system of an organization, what steps would you take?

3. Are surveys a better tool in a performance management audit than interviews and company records? Why?

4. What are the typical areas on which a performance audit report should focus?

Critical Thinking Questions

1. The institution where you are currently enrolled as a student has hired you to look into the appraisal procedures for its support staff. What criteria would you employ? What questions would you ask?

2. You have been hired as a consultant to evaluate and improve the performance of an assembly unit in a garment factory that employs mostly immigrant workers who only speak Chinese or Punjabi. How do you go about setting performance standards and assessing performance?

3. "Interviews make the respondents shy, surveys make them lie," noted a manager who was disillusioned with the lack of candour by respondents. Do you agree? What steps can you take to ensure that the data you collect represents the reality?

4. If you were to write an audit report for the garment factory in question 2 above, what sections should the report have?

Web Research

Collect absenteeism and employee turnover rates in any two industries over the last eight years. What patterns do you see? What are the implications for individual organizations operating in this industry? Are your recommendations for improvement likely to be different for smaller and larger firms operating in the same industry?

CASE INCIDENT

Kanata Electronics Limited

Kanata Electronics Limited is a medium-sized distributor of a number of office machines, computer and graphic systems, and other electronics products. From a single shop in the 1980s, it has grown today to a national chain with 67 retail store outlets. For larger, commercial customers, the firm also directly supplies from one of its four large regional warehouses.

The present incident relates to the firm's Calgary branch that currently employs eleven sales and service staff, nine of whom are men. The firm has a base-salary plus merit bonus dependent on the appraisal ratings received by individual employee.

Steve Smith, who joined the firm about a year ago, manages the office. Within the year, Steve has gained a reputation as a friendly, considerate boss. Often, he can be seen at the bowling alley, in the pub, or at the swimming pool with his employees. He is always available for advice and help. He encourages the employees to call him at home even in late evenings or the weekends if they needed any assistance. If one of the assistants needs a small loan, Steve always obliges by giving it out of his own pocket. Often, he pitches in to help an employee who has to leave work for a personal errand. During the entire year, he did not dock the pay of anyone, even though several had been absent (beyond their normal leave) from work on several occasions.

This week Steve faced an unusual dilemma. It involved Harry Callahan.

Harry is one of the most senior, although not a very effective, salespeople in the branch. He has a large family—four children and an ailing wife. Harry's 88-year-old mother-in-law has been living with the family for the last two years. Steve knows that Harry is going through a particularly bad phase in life. His eldest daughter just recovered from a drug problem; his second son recently had a bad accident that required him to be hospitalized for an extended period of time in a hospital about 18 kilometres from where Harry lives. Given her ailments, Harry's wife cannot drive, meaning that Harry had to personally drive the family around to meet his son at the hospital besides taking care of all household errands. Harry's father in Sydney, Nova Scotia is dying and Harry wants to see his father at least once more.

When it was time for Harry's half-yearly performance appraisal, Steve did not know quite what to do. Kanata Electronics employed a rating scale where each employee's performance was to be rated on a 5-point scale (1 - need to improve; 2 - fair; 3 - good; 4 - very good; and 5 - excellent). Usually, an employee had to receive a rating of at least 3 on 12 out of 15 dimensions before he or she qualified for a merit bonus for the year. In the last three years, Harry received average ratings of 3.1, 3.2, and 3.0, qualifying him for the bonus.

Steve's current dilemma is this: on the one hand, Harry's performance in the last period was worse than ever in the past. He probably deserved only a rating of 2.5 to 3.0 on most dimensions, depriving him of any bonus. On the other hand, Harry's need for money was greater than ever before. Even a few hundred dollars now meant a fortune to him. Even a decimal point increase in the average rating would mean another hundred or hundred and fifty dollars.

(continued)

A rating of 4 or 4.5 would provide a considerable sum of money to Harry that will help him tide over the difficulties.

After considerable thought, Steve gave Harry a rating of 4 to 4.5 on 6 of the dimensions and a rating of 5 on seven other dimensions. On the two remaining dimensions referring to attendance and other factors that could be verified against company records, Steve gave him a rating of 2.8. Steve did not want to do anything illegal like falsifying the attendance records.

Steve called Harry and informed him of his decision to help. He told Harry that he was sticking his neck out for him. Harry acknowledged his gratitude.

Questions

1. What is your assessment of the situation? Do Steve's actions create any difficulties? Why?

2. What improvements, if any, can you recommend to the appraisal system in Kanata Electronics?

CASE

Pay and Save Groceries: Views on the Performance Management System

Pay and Save Groceries (PSG) is a regional grocery chain with 45 supermarkets spread over Eastern Canada. The firm, which began as a mom and pop store in Halifax 25 years ago, grew to employ 480 full-time employees and approximately 2300 part-time employees with annual revenue of over $2.4 billion. Historically, the firm prided itself on an informal, familial atmosphere with hardly any formal systems and procedures for most human resource matters. For example, the firm did not have any rigid job descriptions or specifications, or any systematic job evaluation schemes.

Jane Werther, who joined the firm eight months ago as its Human Resource Manager has been incorporating various systems and procedures. More details on PSG are provided at the end of Chapter 1.

In an effort to gauge the views of managers, supervisors, and staff, the human resource department identified 60 of the full time and 100 of the part-time employees for interviews. The details of the sample are shown in Table 1. Werther and three others (her full-time assistant in the department and two graduate students from a local

TABLE 1   Sample Used for Interviews

	Total number	Number interviewed
Cashiers		
Full-time		
Men	20	10
Women	146	16
Part-time		
Men	117	11
Women	1310	17
Other employees		
Full-time		
Men	50	2
Women	40	2
Part-time		
Men	330	32
Women	530	40
Supervisors		
Men	140	20
Women	16	3
Managers		
Men	60	5
Women	8	2
Total		
Full time	480	60
Part-time	2287	100
GRAND TOTAL	**2767**	**160**

(continued)

university—one specializing in biology and the other in business—hired for this purpose on a part-time basis) conducted the interviews over a month. An interview schedule was prepared for the purpose. The questions used for the survey and the average responses for each question by different groups of employees are shown in Table 2.

TABLE 2 Interview Questions and Average Scores for Various Groups of Employees

(Note: The respondents were asked to respond to each question using a five point scale. For all questions, the higher the score, the more positive the response. Some of the questions were considered irrelevant for the management group and hence not used.)

	Cashiers				Other				Supervisors		Managers	
	Full-time		Part-time		Full-time		Part-time		M	F	M	F
	M	F	M	F	M	F	M	F				
Performance Standards												
1. Did you have enough input into setting the performance standards?	3.7	3.1	3.1	2.8	3.8	3.2	3.4	2.9	4.1	3.9	4.5	4.3
2. Do you believe that performance standards are fair?	3.8	3.2	3.2	3.0	3.8	3.3	3.4	3.0	4.2	4.0	4.5	4.2
Performance Criteria												
3. Are the performance appraisal criteria appropriate?	3.9	3.7	3.8	3.6	3.9	3.4	3.5	3.2	4.3	4.0	4.6	4.0
4. Are the criteria within your control?	3.9	3.6	3.5	3.3	3.8	3.3	3.2	3.0	4.2	3.8	4.2	3.9
Rewards												
5. Are the rewards appropriate for the efforts required?	4.2	3.8	4.0	3.4	3.2	3.0	2.8	2.6	3.5	3.2	4.4	3.8
6. Is the reward system fair and equitable?	4.0	3.6	3.8	3.2	3.0	2.8	2.7	2.5	3.4	3.1	4.2	3.6
Counseling												
7. Do your supervisors show genuine concern for you as individuals?	4.1	3.7	3.8	3.4	3.2	3.2	3.2	3.1	3.2	3.0	n.a	n.a
8.Do your supervisors provide useful advice?	3.5	3.3	3.2	3.1	3.0	2.9	2.9	2.7	3.7	3.4	n.a	n.a
Overall												
9. Overall, do you feel that you have a future in this firm?	3.9	3.8	3.5	3.4	3.3	3.3	3.0	2.8	3.9	3.5	4.6	4.4
10. Overall, is the HR department effective?	4.4	4.3	4.3	4.2	4.2	4.1	4.2	4.4	4.3	4.4	4.6	4.3

Questions

1. What is your overall evaluation of the audit? What improvements, if any, would you recommend for future audits?

2. Based on the current findings, what conclusions can you form? What recommendations would you make to the human resource department? To the top management?

ENDNOTES

Chapter 1

1. Dana Gaines Robinson and James C. Robinson, *Performance Consulting: Moving beyond Training,* San Francisco: Berrett-Koehler Publishers, 1996.

2. Michael Hammer and Steven Stanton, "The Power of Reflection," *Fortune,* 24 November 1997, 291-296.

3. Andrew Templer and Julian Cattaneo, "A Model of Human Resources Management Effectiveness," *Canadian Journal of Administrative Sciences,* 12, no.1, 1995, 77-88.

4. D'Arcy Jenish and Berton Woodward, "Canada's Top 100 Employers," *MacLean's,* 5 November 2001, 51.

5. Ken Mark, "No More Pink Slips," *Human Resources Professional,* November 1996, 21-23.

6. Shona McKay, "The Best 35 Companies to Work for in Canada," *Report on Business* Magazine, February 2001, 61.

7. "Canada: A Special Report," *Time,* 28 June 1999, 41.

8. Bruce Little and Marian Stinson, "Canada Reports String of Trade Records," *The Globe and Mail,* 22 February 2001, B-1, B-10.

9. Bredrup, H. Background for performance management. In A. Rolstadas (ed). *Performance Management: A Business Process Benchmarking Approach.* London: Chapman and Hall, 1995, 61.

10. Bruce Little, "U.S. Pulls ahead in Productivity," *The Globe and Mail,* 15 February 2001, B-3.

11. Report by Canadian Manufacturers and Exporters quoted in "Canada rates last in survey of G7 Countries," *The Globe and Mail,* 1 August 2001, B-1.

12. A study by Roger Martin, Dean of the Rotman School of Management at the University of Toronto, and Michael Porter, a competitiveness expert at Harvard Business School, cited by David Crane, 2001. "Corporate leaders failing to keep up globally," *The Mail Star,* May 4, B-3.

13. John McCallum, "Will Canada Matter in 2020?" *Royal Bank Current Analysis,* Royal Bank of Canada Economics Department, May 2000, 5.

14. Brian Orr, "Will the 21st Century Belong to Canada?" *Canadian HR Reporter,* 29 December 1997, 18-19.

15. "The path to unlocking employee knowledge" *The Globe and Mail,* 25 October 1999, M-1.

16. "Employment Trends in the Information Economy," *Applied Research Bulletin,* 3, no.2, 1997; HRDC website: www.hrdc-drhc.gc.ca

17. "The Industries that Will Define the Decade," *The Globe and Mail,* 21 April 1997, A-6.

18. Results of International Adult Literacy Survey reported on www.nald.ca/nts/ials/ialsreps/high2.htm, 10 February 1998. Also see: Morton Ritts, "What if Johnny Still Can't Read," *Canadian Business,* May 1986, 54-57, 124.

19. Statistics Canada, *Population 15 years and over by highest degree,* Ottawa.

20. "Canada's ranking slips in ability to innovate," *The Globe and Mail,* 12 March 1999, B-3.

21. Fred Nickols, Senior Consultant with the Distance Learning Company quoted by Susan Heathfield, "Performance Management is not an annual appraisal," www.humanresources.about.com accessed from 22 February 2001.

22. *Employability Skills Profile,* prepared by Corporate Council on Education, a program of the National Business and Education Centre, The Conference Board of Canada, 255 Smyth Road, Ottawa, Ont. K1H 8M7, Undated.

23. *Workplace Education-PEI: Creating Partnerships with Business and Industry,* April 2000, Charlottetown, PEI, C1A 8W5.

24. Simon Tuck, "Internet milestone set as 50% connected in Canada," *The Globe and Mail,* 1 May 1999, B-1.

25. "Working from Home Cuts Employee Stress, Study Finds," *The Globe and Mail,* 16 November 1994, B-19.

26. Shari Caudron, "Working at Home Pays Off," *Personnel Journal,* 71, no.11, November 1992, 40-49.

27. Virginia Galt, "Executives warm up to telecommuting," *The Globe and Mail,* 23 February 2001, B-10.

28. Ross Laver, "Kids, Bosses and Work," *Maclean's,* 24 February 1997, 38.

29. John Porter, *The Vertical Mosaic: An Analysis of Social Class and Power in Canada,* Toronto: University of Toronto Press, 1965. See also V.V. Murray, "Canadian Cultural Values and Personnel Administration," in Harish Jain, ed., *Contemporary Issues in Canadian Personnel Administration,* Scarborough, ON: Prentice Hall, 1974.

30. "Face of Canada Changes," *The Globe and Mail,* 5 November 1997, A-1.

31. "No longer a two-language nation," *The Mail Star,* 3 December 1997, A-19.

32. Jane Armstrong. "Canada is 30 million, but will that last?" *The Globe and Mail,* 15 March 2002, A-1.

33. Statistics Canada, *Fertility in Canada - From Baby Boom to Baby Bust,* Ottawa, Catalogue 91-524E.

34. For a good exposition of the differences between two age groups, please see, Claire Raines and Jim Hunt. *The X-ers and the Boomers.* Berkeley, CA: Crisp Publications, 2000, 32-39.

35. Professor Richard Woodward of University of Calgary quoted by D. McMurdy, "Falling Expectations," *Maclean's,* 4 January 1993 36.

36. Frank Vallee and Donald Whyte, "Canadian Society: Trends and Perspectives," in Harish Jain (ed). *Contemporary Issues in Canadian Personnel Administration,* Scarborough, ON: Prentice Hall, 1974, 31.

37. Stephen Jackson, "All of HR reaps benefits from performance based job descriptions," *Canadian HR Reporter,* 7 September 1998, 12.

38. E. Falkenberg, T.H. Stone and N.M. Meltz, *Human Resource Management in Canada,* 4th edition, Toronto: Harcourt Brace & Company, 1999, 282.

39. For example, see A.J. Templer, R.J. Catteneo, D.A. DeCenzo and S.P. Robbins, *Human Resource Management,* Toronto: John Wiley & Sons, 1999.

40. www.royalbank.com accessed 22 February 2001.

41. Joe Chidley and Andrew Wahl, "The New Worker's Paradise," *Canadian Business*, 12 March 1999, 37-38.

42. For example, see James Chrisman, Alan Bauerschmidt and Charles Hofer. The determinants of New Venture Performance: An Extended Model, *Entrepreneurship Theory and Practice*, 23(1), 1998, 5-29. D.A. Duchesneau & W.B. Gartner. A profile of new venture success and failure in an emerging industry. *Journal of Business Venturing*, 5, 1990, 297-312. J.G. Covin & T.J. Covin. Competitive aggressiveness, environmental context, and small firm performance. *Entrepreneurship Theory and Practice* 14, 1990, no. 4, 35-50.

43. D'Arcy Jenish. "Ten that made the grade," *Maclean's*, 5 November 2001, 49. Also see, Richard Yerema. *Canada's Top 100 Employers*, Mediacorp Canada Inc, Toronto, 2000, 286-288. More company information is available at the website: www.zenonenv.com.

44. Hari Das, *Strategic Organizational Design for a Global Economy*. Scarborough, ON: Prentice Hall, 1998, 204.

45. Adapted and summarized from Randall Schuler and Susan Jackson, "Linking competitive strategies with Human Resource Management Practices," *Academy of Management Executive*, 1987, Vol.1, No. 3, 207-219; also see, Susan Jackson and Randall Schuler, "Understanding Human Resource Management in the context of organizations and their environments," *Annual Review of Psychology*, 1995, Vol.46, 237-264; Randall Schuler, Steven Galante, and Susan Jackson, "Matching Effective HR Practices with Competitive Strategy," *Personnel*, September 1987.

46. Mark Maremont, "Blind Ambition" *Business Week*, 23 October 1995, 78-92.

47. Institute of Personnel Management survey quoted by Richard Williams. *Performance Management: Perspectives on Employee Performance*, London: International Thompson Business Press, 1998, 31.

48. Arthur Young, Wayne Brockbank, and Dave Ulrich, "Lower cost, higher value: human resource function in transformation," *Human resource planning* 17, no. 3, 1994, 10-12.

49. Diana Winstanley and Kate Stuart-Smith, "Policing Performance: the ethics of performance management," *Personnel Review* 25, no. 6, 1996, 66-84.

50. R.E. Miles, and C.C. Snow, "Designing strategic human resource systems," *Organizational Dynamics* 13, 1, 1984, 36-52.

51. D'Arcy Jenish. "Ten that made the grade," *Maclean's*, 5 November 2001, 50. Also see, Richard Yerema. *Canada's Top 100 Employers*, Mediacorp Canada Inc, Toronto, 2000, 244-246.

52. Alan Barratt and Dimitri Georgides, "The synolic approach to human resource development," *Executive Development* 8 no. 2, 1995, 29-32.

Chapter 2

1. John Donovan, Richard Tully, and Brent Wortman. *The Value Enterprise*. Toronto: McGraw-Hill Ryerson, 1998, 1.

2. Daniel Stoffman. *Masters of Change*. Toronto: McGraw-Hill Ryerson, 1997, 56-67.

3. Arthur Thompson, Jr., and A. Strickland, III. *Strategy Formulation and Implementation*. 4th ed. Homewood, IL: Irwin, 1989, 23.

4. "How Coke Recaptured its Fizz," *The Globe and Mail*, 24 August 1995, A-12; ABC World News, 14 March 2001.

5. James G. March and Herbert A. Simon. *Organizations*. New York: Wiley, 1958; Richard M. Cyert and James G. March. *A Behavioural Theory of the Firm*. Englewood Cliffs, NJ: Prentice Hall, 1963; James D. Thompson. *Organizations in Action*. New York: McGraw-Hill, 1967, 83-105.

6. H. A. Simon, "On the Concept of Organizational Goal," *Administrative Science Quarterly*, 1964, vol. 2, 1-22.

7. A. Etzioni. *Modern Organizations*. Englewood Cliffs, NJ: Prentice Hall, 1964, 13-15.

8. Adapted from Robert Kaplan and David Norton, "The Balanced Scorecard: Measures that Drive Performance," *Harvard Business Review*, January-February, 1992.

9. Milton Friedman, "A Friedman Doctrine: The Social Responsibility of Business," *The New York Times*, 13 September 1970.

10. W. Evan and R. Freeman, "A Stakeholder Theory of the Modern Corporation: Kantian Capitalism," in *Ethical Theory and Business*, 4th ed., eds. T. Beauchamp and N. Bowie. Englewood Cliffs, NJ: Prentice Hall, 1993.

11. Dennis Barnhart, "Balanced Scorecard Collaborative," *Nova Scotia Power Case Study*; Dennis Barnhart, Enterprise Risk Consultant, Nova Scotia Power, pers. comm., 29 September 2000; Robert Kaplan and David Norton, "Putting the Balanced Scorecard to Work," *Harvard Business Review*, September-October, 1993.

12. H.F. Schwind, H. Das, and T. Wagar, *Canadian Human Resource Management*. Toronto: McGraw-Hill Ryerson, 2002, 415-416.

13. R. M. Cyert and J. G. March, "Organizational Factors in the Theory of Oligopoly," *Quarterly Journal of Economics* LXX, 1956, 44-64.

14. Henry Mintzberg, "Organizational Power and Goals," in *Strategic Management*, eds. D. Schendel and C. Hofer. Boston: Little Brown, 1979, 64-80; also see Max D. Richards. *Setting Strategic Goals and Objectives*, 2nd ed., St. Paul: West Publishing, 1986, 50-59.

15. W. Chan Kim and Renee Mauborgne, "Value Innovation: The Strategic Logic of High Growth," *Harvard Business Review*, January-February, 1997, 103-112.

16. Ibid., 106.

17. Henry Mintzberg. *Power In and Around Organizations*. Englewood Cliffs, NJ: Prentice Hall, 1983, 176-179.

18. Robert Kaplan and David Norton, "Using the Balanced Score Card as a Strategic Management System," *Harvard Business Review*, January-February, 1996.

19. For example, see D. Whetten, K. Cameron, and M. Woods. *Developing Management Skills for Europe*. London: Harper Collins, 1994.

20. "Sears: The Turnaround Is Ending: The Revolution Has Begun," *Fortune*, 28 April 1997, 106-118; also see, "Strategic Planning," *Business Week*, 26 August 1996, 49.

21. H. James Harrison. *The Complete Benchmarking Implementation Guide*. New York: McGraw-Hill, 1996.

22. Mohamed Zairi, "Benchmarking: The Best Tool for Measuring Competitiveness," *Benchmarking for Quality Management & Technology* 1, no. 1, 1994, 11-24.

23. Jeffrey F. Rayport and John J. Sviokla, "Exploiting the Virtual Value Chain, in *Creating Value in the New Economy*, ed. Don Tapscott. Boston: Harvard University Press, 1999, 35-51.

24. Nicholas Zacchea, "The Use of Computer Modelling and Simulation in the Audit Process," *Managerial Audit Journal* 10, no. 1, 1995, 25-30.

25. Galen Britz, Donald Emerling, Lynne Hare, Roger Hoerl, Stuart Janis, and Janice Shade. *Improving Performance Through Statistical Thinking*. Milwaukee, WI: ASQ Quality Press, 2000.

26. Richard Allen and John Thatcher, "Achieving Cultural Change: A Practical Case Study," *Leadership & Organization Development Journal* 16, no. 2, 1995, 16-23.

27. Nancy Papalexandris and Irene Nikandrou, "Benchmarking Employee Skills: Results from Best Practice Firms in Greece," *Journal of European Industrial Training* 24, no. 7, 2000, 391-402.

28. H. James Harrison. *The Complete Benchmarking Implementation Guide*. New York: McGraw-Hill, 1996, 277.

29. John Rodwell, Jeremy Lam, and Maureen Fastenau, "Benchmarking HRM and the Benchmarking of Benchmarking," *Employee Relations* 22, no. 4, 2000, 356-374.

Chapter 3

1. Jerry W. Gilley, Nathaniel W. Boughton and Ann Maycunich. *The Performance Challenge* (42). Cambridge, MA: Perseus Books, 1999.

2. Dave Ulrich. *Human Resource Champions* (55-56). Boston, MA: Harvard Business School Press, 1997.

3. C. L. Hulin and M. Roznowski, "Organizational Technologies: Effects on Organizations' Characteristics and Individuals," in *Research in Organizational Behaviour* vol. 7, eds. L. L. Cummings and B. M. Staw. Greenwich, CN: Jai Press, 1985, 39-86.

4. For example, see Langdon Winner, *Autonomous Technology: Technics-Out-of-Control as a Theme in Political Thought*. Cambridge, MA: MIT Press, 1977; Stephen Barley, "The Alignment of Technology and Structure through Roles and Networks," *Administrative Science Quarterly* 35, 1990, 61-103.

5. Joan Woodward. *Industrial Organization: Theory and Practice*. London: Oxford University Press, 1965.

6. Some of these terms were originally used by D. J. Hickson, D. S. Pugh, and D. C. Pheysey, "Operations Technology and Organization Structure-An Empirical Reappraisal," *Administrative Science Quarterly* 14, 1969, 378. The terms, in this context, cover broader concepts than used by the authors.

7. John Huey, "Wal-Mart: Will It Take Over the World?" *Fortune*, 30 January 1989, 52.

8. David Hickson, Derek Pugh, and Diana Pheysey, "Operations Technology and Organization Structure: An Empirical Re-appraisal," *Administrative Science Quarterly* 14, 1969, 378-397.

9. James D. Thompson. *Organizations in Action*. New York: McGraw-Hill, 1967.

10. G.D. Sandefur, "Efficiency in Social Science Organizations," *Administration and Society* 14, 1983, 449-468; Hari Das. *Strategic Organizational Design*. Scarborough, ON: Prentice Hall, 1998.

11. R.D. Pritchard, "Organizational Productivity," in *Handbook of Industrial/Organizational Psychology*, eds. M.D. Dunnette and L. M. Hough. Palo Alto, CA: Consulting Psychologists Press, 1992, 447-450.

12. David Crane, "Experts Confirm IT Revolution Is Good for Us, Sort of," *The Mail Star*, 1 June 2001, B6.

13. Based on a report by Professor Michael Porter of Harvard University and Dean Roger Martin of University of Toronto. Cited in "All Together Now: Innovate We Must," *The Globe and Mail*, 13 February 2002, A16.

14. "All Together Now: Innovate We Must," *The Globe and Mail*, 13 February 2002, A16.

15. John Campbell, Richard Campbell, and Associates. *Productivity in Organizations*. San Francisco: Jossey-Bass, 1988, 19.

16. C.I Barnard. *The Functions of the Executive*. Cambridge: Harvard University Press, 1938, 19.

17. A. G. Bedeian. *Organizations: Theory and Analysis*, 2nd ed. Chicago: The Dryden Press, 1984, 143.

18. David Braybooke. *Ethics in the World of Business*. Totowa, NJ: Rowman & Allanheld, 1983, 379.

19. Ibid., 353.

20. Richard Swanson. *Analysis for Improving Performance*. San Francisco: Berrett-Koehler Publishers, 1996, 205.

21. P.R. Scholtes, B. Streibel, B.L. Joiner. *The Team Handbook* 2nd ed. Madison, WI: Oriel Inc., 1996.

22. L. Ramsay, "No Business Too Small for ISO 9000 Certification," *Financial Post*, 23 August 1995, 18-19.

23. Additional information on ISO is available through Global Info Centre Canada, 240 Catherine Street, Suite 305, Ottawa, Ontario K2P 2G8. Also see, Rob Murakami, "How to Implement ISO 9000," *CMA Magazine*, March 1994, 18.

24. Mary Anderson and Amrik Sohal, "A Study of the Relationship Between Quality Management Practices and Performance in Small Businesses," *International Journal of Quality and Reliability Management* 16, no. 9, 1999, 859-877.

25. Tord Haversjo, "The Financial Effects of ISO 9000 Registration for Danish Companies," *Managerial Accounting Journal* 15, no. 1/2, 2000, 47-52.

26. Bjorn Andersen and Tom Fagerhaug. *Root Cause Analysis: Simplified Tools and Techniques*. Milwaukee, WI: ASQ Quality Press, 2000, 118-121.

27. For a detailed discussion of various techniques, see Bjorn Andersen and Tom Fagerhaug. *Root Cause Analysis: Simplified Tools and Techniques*. Milwaukee, WI: ASQ Quality Press, 2000.

28. H.F. Schwind, H. Das, and T. Wagar. *Canadian Human Resource Management* 6th ed. Toronto: McGraw-Hill Ryerson, 2002.

29. For example, see Susan Greenberg and Raymond Bello, "Re-Write Job Descriptions: Focus on Functions," *HR Focus* 69, July 1992, 10.; Michael Brannick, Joan Brannick, and Edward Levine, "Job Analysis, Personnel Selection and the ADA," *Human Resource Management Review* 2, no. 3, 1992, 171-182.

30. William Wooten "Using Knowledge, Skill and Ability (KSA) Data to Identify Career Planning Opportunities: An Application of Job Analysis to Internal Manpower Planning," *Public Personnel Administrator* 22, no. 4, 1993, 551-563.

31. Sidney Fine, *Functional Job Analysis Scales: A Desk Aid*. Kalamazoo, MI: Upjohn Institute for Employment Research, 1973.

32. Howard Olson, Sidney Fine, David Myers, and Margarette Jennings, "The Use of Functional Analysis in Establishing Performance for Heavy Equipment Operators," *Personnel Psychology*, Summer 1981, 354.

33. Purdue Research Foundation. *Position Analysis Questionnaire*. West Lafayette, IN 47907, 1989.

34. Wayne Cascio. *Applied Psychology in Personnel Management* 4th ed. Englewood Cliffs, NJ: Prentice Hall, 1991, 207

35. Paul Sparks, "Job Analysis," in *Personnel Management*, eds. K. Rowland and G. Ferris. Boston: Allyn and Bacon, 1982; Edward

L. Levine, Ronald A. Ash, H. Hall, and Frank Sistrunk, "Evaluation of Job Analysis Methods by Experienced Job Analysts," *Academy of Management Journal* 26, no. 2, 1983, 339-348; E.J. McCormick. *Job Analysis: Methods and Applications*. New York: AMACOM, 1979; Luis R. Gomez-Mejia, Ronald C. Page, and Walter W. Tormow, "A Comparison of the Practical Utility of Traditional, Statistical and Hybrid Job Evaluation Approaches," *Academy of Management Journal* 25, no. 4, 1982, 790-809; Ronald A. Ash and Edward Levine, "A Framework for Evaluating Job Analysis Methods," *Personnel*, November-December 1980, 53-59.

36. Hari Das, Peter J. Frost, and J. Thad Barnowe, "Behaviourally Anchored Scales for Assessing Behavioural Science Teaching," *Canadian Journal of Behavioural Science* 11, no. 1, January 1979, 79-88; Tom Janz, "Estimating the Standard Deviation of Job Performance: A Behavioural Approach," *Administrative Sciences Association of Canada (Organizational Behaviour Division) Meeting Proceedings* 2, Part 5, 1981, 70-78.

37. Richard Swanson. *Analysis for Improving Performance*. San Francisco: Berrett-Koehler Publishers, 1996, 100.

38. Brian Orr, "The Challenge of Benchmarking HR Performance," *Canadian HR Reporter*, 21 April 1997, 6.

39. Richard Mirabile, "Everything You Wanted to Know About Competency Modeling," *Training and Development*, August 1997, 73-77.

40. Patricia A. McLagan, "Competencies: The Next Generation," *Training and Development*, May 1997, 41.

41. Jean-Pascal Souque, *Focus on Competencies*, Report No. 177-96, The Conference Board of Canada, 1996, 18.

42. Based on a real life incident; most names and some facts have been changed to protect the identities of the persons and agencies involved.

43. Danylo Hawaleshka, "A Matter of Trust," *Macleans*, 12 June 2000, 22-23.

44. Ibid., 23.

45. Andrew Nikiforuk, "When Water Kills," *Macleans*, 12 June 2000, 18-21.

46. Gary Gallon, "Death on Tap," *The Globe and Mail*, 26 May 2000, A15.

47. Andrew Nikiforuk, "When Water Kills," *Macleans*, 12 June 2000, 19.

48. Ibid., 21.

49. Andrew Nikiforuk, "Health Canada Saw Danger to the District," *The Globe and Mail*, 31 May 2000, A8.

50. Gary Gallon, "Death on Tap," *The Globe and Mail*, 26 May 2000, A15.

51. Andrew Nikiforuk, "When Water Kills," *Macleans*, 12 June 2000, 20.

52. Martin Mittelstaedt, "Water Crisis Is National, Experts Say," *The Globe and Mail*, 5 May 2001, A1.

53. Lisa Priest, "Municipalities Want Ottawa to Get Tough," *The Globe and Mail*, 5 May 2001, A9.

54. Martin Mittelstaedt, "World Water Use to Soar to Crisis Levels: Study," *The Globe and Mail*, 14 March 2000, A8.

Chapter 4

1. Thomas B. Wilson. *Innovative Reward Systems for the Changing Work Place*. New York: McGraw-Hill, 1995, xiv.

2. Andrew Willis, "Sky Chefs mid managers become millionaires," *The Globe and Mail*, 6 June 2001, B-1, 6.

3. Bonnie Flatt, a principal in William M. Mercer Ltd. in Toronto, quoted by Andrew Willis, "Sky Chefs mid managers become millionaires," *The Globe and Mail*, 6 June 2001, B-1, 6.

4. D'Arcy Jenish, "The Ten that Made the Grade," *MacLean's*, 5 November 2001, 52.; also see, Richard Yerema. *Canada's Top 100 Employers*, 2001 ed., Toronto: Mediacorp Canada Inc, 2000, 78-80.

5. James Baron and David Kreps. *Strategic Human Resources*. New York: John Wiley & Sons, 1999, 96.

6. D'Arcy Jenish, "The Ten that Made the Grade," *MacLean's*, 5 November 2001, 49; also see, Richard Yerema. *Canada's Top 100 Employers*, 2001 ed., Toronto: Mediacorp Canada Inc, 2000, 96-98. For more information on the company, visit the website: http://www.gwl.ca

7. B. Nelson. *1001 ways to reward employees*. New York: Workman Publishing, 1994.; B. Parus, "Designing a Total Rewards Program to Retain Critical Talent in the Millennium," *ACA News*, February 1999, 20-23.

8. J.B. Barney and P.M. Wright, "Organization Culture: Can It Be a Source of Sustained Competitive Advantage?" *Academy of Management Review* 11, 1986, 656-665.

9. Robert Heneman, Judity Tansky, and Michael Camp, "Human Resource Management Practices in Small and Medium Sized Enterprises: Unanswered Questions and Future Research Perspectives," *Entrepreneurship Theory and Practice*, Fall 2000, 11-26.

10. www.windriver.com/press/html/acq_audesi.html; Richard Yerema. *Canada's Top 100 Employers*, 2001 ed., Toronto: Mediacorp Canada Inc, 2000, 25-27.

11. Source: www.windriver.com/press/html/acq_audesi.html

12. R.L. Opsahl and M.D. Dunnette, "The Role of Financial Compensation in Industrial Motivation," *Psychological Bulletin* 66, 1966, 100-121.

13. W.L. Seidman and S.L. Skancke. *Competitiveness: The Executive's Guide to Success*. New York: M.E. Sharpe, 1989, 41.

14. E.E. Anderson, "The Externalization of Drive: Theoretical Considerations," *Psychological Review* 48, 1941, 204-224.

15. D. Rapaport, "On the Psycho-Analytic Theory of Motivation," in *Nebraska Symposium on Motivation-1960*. ed. M. R. Jones. Lincoln: University of Nebraska Press, 1960.

16. C. L. Hull. *Essentials of Behavior*, New Haven, CN: Yale, 1951.

17. V. H. Vroom. *Work and Motivation*. NY: Wiley, 1964.

18. A.F. Earle, *Determination of the Compensation of Chief Executive Officers in Canadian Corporations*. Working Paper NC 88-15, School of Business, University of Western Ontario, 1988.

19. E.E. Lawler III. *Pay and Organizational Effectiveness*. NY: McGraw-Hill, 1971.

20. D.M. Cable and T.A. Judge, Pay Preferences and Job Search Decisions: A Person-Organization Fit Perspective," *Personnel Psychology* 47, 1994, 317-348.; T.A. Judge and R.D. Bretz, "Effects of Work Values on Job Choice Decisions," *Journal of Applied Psychology* 77, 1992, 261-271.

21. A. Furnham, "Many Sides of the Coin: The Psychology of Money Usage," *Personality and Individual Differences* 5, 1984, 501-509.; B. Kirkcaldy and A. Furnham, "Predictors of Beliefs about Money," *Psychological Reports* 73, 1993, 1079-1082.; T.L.P. Tang, "The Meaning of Money: Extension and

Exploration of the Money Ethic Scale in a Sample of University Students in Taiwan," *Journal of Organizational Behavior* 14, 1993, 93-99.

22. T.R. Mitchell and Amy E. Mickel, "The Meaning of Money: An Individual-Difference Perspective," *Academy of Management Review*, July 1999, 43-56.

23. For example, see, Paul Milgrom and D. John Roberts. *Economics, Organization and Management*. Englewood Cliffs, NJ: Prentice Hall, 1992, Chapters 6, 7, 12 and 13.; Oliver E. Williamson. *The Economic Institutions of Captialism*. New York: Free Press, 1985.

24. V. Vroom. *Work and Motivation*, New York: John Wiley, 1964.; Also see, L.W. Porter and E.E. Lawler. *Managerial Attitudes and Performance*. Homewood, IL: Irwin, 1968.

25. L.W. Porter and E.E. Lawler. *Managerial Attitudes and Performance*. Homewood, IL: Irwin, 1968.; also see, E.E. Lawler. *Rewarding Excellence: Pay strategies for the New Economy*. San Francisco: Jossey Bass, 2000.

26. See, for example, J. Stacey Adams, "Toward an Understanding of Inequity," *Journal of Abnormal and Social Psychology* 67, 1963, 422-436; George Homans. *Social Behaviour: Its Elementary Forms*. New York: Harcourt Brace Jovanovich, 1961.

27. J. S. Adams, "Inequity in Social Exchange," in *Advances in experimental social psychology*, vol. 2, ed. L. Berkowitz. New York: Academic Press, 1965, 267-269.

28. Craig Pinder. *Work Motivation*. Glenview, IL: Scott, Foresman and Company, 1984, 115-121.

29. H. F. Schwind, H. Das, and T. Wagar. *Canadian Human Resource Management: A Strategic Approach*. Scarborough, ON: McGraw-Hill Ryerson, 2002, 405.

30. L.W. Lehr, "The Care and Flourishing of Entrepreneurs at 3M," *Directors and Boards*, Winter 1986, 18-20.

31. M. G. Wolf, "Theories, Approaches and Practices of Salary Administration," in *The Compensation Handbook*, eds. M.L. Rock and L. A. Berger. New York: McGraw-Hill, 1991.

32. M. Deutsch, "Equity, Equality and Need: What Determines which Values Will Be Used as the Basis of Distributive Justice?" *Journal of Social Issues* 31, 1975, 46-57.

33. J. S. Adams, "Inequity in Social Exchange," in *Advances in experimental social psychology*, vol. 2, ed. L. Berkowitz. New York: Academic Press, 1965.

34. Karl Marx, "Critique of the Gotha Program-Marginal Notes to the Program of the German Worker's Party," in *Karl Marx on Revolution*, vol. 1, ed. S.K. Padovov. New York: McGraw-Hill, 1875.

35. Howard Risher (ed.). *Aligning Pay and Results*. New York: AMACOM, 1999, 8.

36. W. Edward Deming. *Out of Crises*. Cambridge, MA: MIT Center for Advanced Engineering Studies, 1982, Chapter 3.

37. H. F. Schwind, H. Das, and T. Wagar. *Canadian Human Resource Management: A Strategic Approach*. Scarborough, ON: McGraw-Hill Ryerson, 2002, 416.

38. Ibid., 415-416.

39. Ibid., 416.

40. Ibid., 416-417.

41. "Stock options are not a free lunch," *Forbes*, 18 May 1998, 213.

42. Bill Saporito, "Speak No Evil," *Time* (Canadian edition), 18 February 2002, 22.

43. ABC World News, 28 February 2002.

44. Howard Risher (ed.). *Aligning Pay and Results*. New York: AMACOM, 1999, 11.

45. Ibid., 13.

46. "50 Best Paid Executives," *Report on Business Magazine*, July 2001, 123.

47. H.G. Barkema and L.R. Gomez-Mejia, "Managerial Compensation and Firm Performance: A General Framework," *Academy of Management Journal* 41, no. 2, 1998, 135-145. Quote taken from page 135.

48. A. Mitra, J.D.J. Jenkins, N. Gupta, and J.D. Shaw, "*Financial Incentive and Performance: A Meta-Analytic Review*," Paper presented at the annual meeting of the Society for Industrial and Organizational Psychology, St. Louis, 1998.

49. "50 Best Paid Executives," *Report on Business Magazine*, July 2001, 123 and 128.

50. J. Daly, "Paying the Boss," *Macleans*, 21 June 1993, 34-35.

51. H.L. Tosi, S. Werner, J. Katz, and L.R. Gomez-Mejia. *A Meta-Analysis of Executive Compensation Studies*. Unpublished Manuscript, University of Florida, Gainesville, 1998.

52. Patrick Brethour, "CN's Stock Option Plan a Textbook for New Economy Companies," *The Globe and Mail*, 25 June 2001, B-1.

53. Wm. Gerard Sanders, "Behavioural Responses of CEOs to Stock ownership and Stock Option Pay," *Academy of Management Journal* 44, no. 3, 2001, 477-492.

54. Lisa Slipp, leader of Canadian compensation practice at William M. Mercer quoted by Patrick Brethour, "CN's Stock Option Plan a Textbook for New Economy Companies," *The Globe and Mail*, 25 June 2001, B-1.

55. Patrick Brethour, "CN's Stock Option Plan a Textbook for New Economy Companies," *The Globe and Mail*, 25 June 2001, B-1.

56. Wm. Gerard Sanders, "Behavioural Responses of CEOs to Stock ownership and Stock Option Pay," *Academy of Management Journal* 44, no. 3, 2001, 487.

57. Patrick Brethour, "CN's Stock Option Plan a Textbook for New Economy Companies," *The Globe and Mail*, 25 June 2001, B-1.

58. Hari Das, "The Four Faces of Managerial Pay," *International Journal of Commerce and Management*, vol. 12, no. 1, 2002, 16-40.

59. Craig Pinder. *Work Motivation*. Glenview, IL: Scott, Foresman and Company, 1984, 115-121.

60. E.E. Lawler III. *Pay and Organizational Effectiveness*. NY: McGraw-Hill, 1971, 262.

61. E.E. Lawler III. *Strategic Pay*. San Francisco: Jossey-Bass, 1990.

62. For a good discussion on the inconsistency in reward systems, see S. Kerr, "On the Folly of Rewarding A, while Hoping for B," *Academy of Management Executive* 9, no. 1, 1995, 7-14.

Chapter 5

1. D'Arcy Jenish and Berton Woodward, "Canada's Top 100 Employers," *Maclean's*, 5 November 2001, 46.

2. Dave Ulrich. *Human Resource Champions*. Boston: Harvard Business School Press, 1997, 139-140.

3. Peter Cappelli. *The New Deal at Work*. Boston: Harvard Business School Press, 1999, 2-3.

4. C. Motherwell, "Pancanadian Uncaps the Enthusiasm of Guys Like Ed," *The Globe and Mail*, 25 August 1992, B-20.

5. For example, see T. Amabile, R. Contri, H. Coon, J. Lazenby, and M. Herron, "Assessing the Work Environment for Creativity,"

Academy of Management Journal 39, no. 5, 1996, 1154-1184.;
R.W. Woodman, J.E. Sawyer, and R.W. Griffin, "Toward a Theory
of Organizational Creativity," *Academy of Management Journal*
18, no. 2, 1993, 293-321; Gaylen Chandler, Chalon Keller, and
Douglas Lyon, "Unraveling the Determinants and Consequences of
an Innovation-Supportive Organizational Culture,"
Entrepreneurship Theory and Practice, Fall 2000, 59-76.

6. "Technomania," *Newsweek*, 27 February 1995, 26.

7. Michael Losey, "HR Comes of Age," *HR Magazine*, 50th
anniversary issue, 1998, 40-53.

8. Robert Inman, "Workflow," *Transactions* 28, no. 7, July 1996,
555-556.

9. E. Joy Mighty and Judy Ann Roy, "Re-designing Job Design," in
Global Business Trends: Contemporary Readings. Cumberland,
MD: Academy of Business Administration, 1997, 261-269.

10. E. Grandjean. *Fitting the Task to the Man*, 4th ed. Bristol, PA:
Taylor and Francis, 1990.; also see, Chris Knight, "Office
Workers Frustrated with their Workspace," *Canadian HR
Reporter*, 1 December 1997, 21.

11. Monica Belcourt, Arthur Sherman, George Bohlander, and Scott
Snell. *Managing Human Resources*, 2nd ed. Toronto: Nelson
Canada, 1999, 112-113.

12. W.F. Dowling, "Job Redesign on the Assembly Line: Farewell to
the Blue Collar Blues? *Organizational Dynamics*, Autumn 1973,
51-67.

13. R. Kanungo. *Work Alienation: An Integrative Approach*. New
York: Praeger, 1982.

14. Frederick Herzberg, Bernard Mausner, and Barbara Snyderman.
The Motivation to Work. New York: Wiley, 1959. See also E.F.
Stone and L.W. Porter, "Job Characteristics and Job Attitudes: A
Multivariate Study," *Journal of Applied Psychology* 59, 1975,
57-64.; Kae H. Chung and Monica F. Ross, "Differences in
Motivational Properties Between Job Enlargement and Job
Enrichment," *Academy of Management Review*, January 1977,
113-121.; J. Richard Hackman, June L. Pearce, and Jane
Caminis Wolfe, "Effects of Changes in Job Characteristics on
Work Attitudes and Behaviours: A Naturally Occurring Quasi-
Experiment," *Organizational Behaviour and Human
Performance* 21, no. 2, 1978, 289-304.

15. Ian Gellatly and Gregory Irving, "The Moderating Role of
Perceived Autonomy on Personality-Performance Relations
Within a Public Sector Organization," *ASAC 1999 Proceedings
(Human Resources)* 20, no. 9, University of New Brunswick,
Saint John, NB, 1999.

16. J.R. Hackman and E.E. Lawler III, "Employee Reactions to Job
Characteristics," in *Readings in Organizational Behaviour and
Human Performance*, eds. W.E. Scott and L.L. Cummings.
Homewood, IL: Richard D. Irwin, 1973, 231. For a detailed
summary of research on job design, see C.L. Hulin and M.R.
Blood, "Job Enlargement, Individual Differences, and Worker
Responses," *Psychological Bulletin*, 1968, 41-55. Jon L. Pierce
and Randall B. Dunham, "Task Design: A Literature Review,"
Academy of Management Review, October 1976, 83-97.

17. Richard W. Woodward and John J. Sherwood, "A
Comprehensive Look at Job Design," *Personnel Journal*, August
1977, 386.

18. Patricia Chiholm, "Redesigning Work," *Maclean's*, 5 March 2001,
36.

19. D'Arcy Jenish and Berton Woodward, "Canada's Top 100
Employers," *Maclean's*, 5 November 2001, 51.

20. "Moving Beyond Assembly Lines," *Business Week*, 27 July
1981, 87-90. See also Eric Cousineau, "Job Satisfaction: Impact

of Work and Non-work Related Factors," paper presented at the
ASAC 1991 Conference, Niagara Falls, ON, 1991.; Mitchell W.
Fields and James W. Thacker, "Job Related Attitudes of Part-time
and Full-time Workers," *Journal of Managerial Psychology* 6,
no. 2, 1991, 17-20.

21. Terry Wagar. *Employee Involvement, Strategic Management and
Human Resources: Exploring the Linkages*. Waterloo, ON:
Wilfrid Laurier University, 1997.

22. D. Jones, "Robo-shop," *Report on Business Magazine*, March
1997, 54-62.; L. Gutri, "Pratt & Whitney Employees Don't
Want to Be Managed: Teams Demand Leadership," *Canadian
HR Reporter*, 2 May 1988, 8.

23. Chris Argyris, "Empowerment: The Emperor's New Clothes,"
Harvard Business Review, May-June 1998, 34-40; R.E. Quinn
and G.M. Spreitzer, "The Road to Empowerment: Seven
Questions Every Leader Should Consider," *Organizational
Dynamics*, Autumn 1997, 41; R.C. Ford and M.D. Fottler,
"Empowerment: A Matter of Degree," *Academy of Management
Executive* 9, 1995, 21-31.

24. R.E. Quinn and G.M. Spreitzer, "The Road to Empowerment:
Seven Questions Every Leader Should Consider," *Organizational
Dynamics*, Autumn 1997, 41.

25. Pierre Pelletier, "Semi-Autonomous and Autonomous Production
Groups," *Quality of Working Life: The Canadian Scene* 3, no. 1,
22-25.; Toby D. Wall, Nigel J. Kemp, Pauly R. Jackson, and
Chris W. Clegg, "Outcomes of Autonomous Workgroups: A
Long-term Field Experiment," *Academy of Management Journal*
29, no. 2, 1986, 280-281.

26. Paul Roddick, "Work Improvement Plan at Air Canada,"
Quality of Working Life: The Canadian Scene 1, Autumn 1978,
2. See also Dale Yeatts, "Self-Managed Work Teams: Innovation
in Progress," *Business and Economic Quarterly*, Fall/Winter
1991/92, 2-6.

27. William Fox, "Socio-technical System Principles and Guidelines:
Past and Present," *Journal of Applied Behavioural Science* 31,
no.1, March 1995, 91-105.

28. "Moving Beyond Assembly Lines," *Business Week*, 27 July
1981, 87-90.; John Butman, "Quality Comes Full Circle,"
Management Review, February 1992, 49-51.

29. Hari Das, *Strategic Organizational Design for a Global
Economy*, Scarborough, ON: Prentice Hall, 1998, 140.

30. James Baron and David Kreps. *Strategic Human Resources*. New
York: John Wiley, 1999, 121.

31. Ibid., 136.

32. Jon Katzenback. *Peak Performance*. Boston: Harvard Business
School Press, 2000, 119-122.

33. Ibid., 93-95

34. P. Booth. *Challenge and Change: Embracing the Team Concept*.
Ottawa: Conference Board of Canada, 1994.

35. For example, see Donna Deeprose. *The Team Coach: Vital New
Skills for Supervisors and Managers in a Team Environment*.
New York: American Management Association, 1995.

36. William B. Werther, Jr., "Quality Circles: Key Executive Issues,"
Journal of Contemporary Business 11, no. 2, 17-26.

37. Brent King, "Quality Circles Have Achieved Acceptance," *The
Financial Post*, 18 January 1986, 15. See also John Loring, "Dr.
Deming's Traveling Quality Show," *Canadian Business*,
September 1990, 38-42.; Frederick R. Reichfield and Earl W.
Sasser, Jr., "Zero Defections: Quality Comes to Services,"
Harvard Business Review, September/October 1990, 105-111.;
Don Well. *Soft Sell: Quality of Working Life Programs and the*

Productivity Race. Ottawa: Canadian Centre for Policy Alternatives, 1986.

38. "Two Lessons in Failure from the Silicon Valley," *Business Week*, 10 September 1984, 78-83.

39. K. Ishikawa. *QC Circle Activities*. Tokyo: Union of Japanese Scientists and Engineers, 1968.

40. W. L. French, C. H. Bell, and R. A. Zawacki, eds. *Organization Development*. Plano, TX: Business Publications, 1983, 201.; E. E. Lawler and S. A. Mohrman, "Quality Circles After the Fad," *Harvard Business Review*, January/February 1985, 65-71.

41. S. G. Goldstein, "Organizational Dualism and Quality Circles," *Academy of Management Review* 10, 1985, 504-517.; D. Hutchins, "Quality Circles in Context," *Industrial Commercial Training* 15, 1983, 80-83.; S. A. Mohrman and G. E. Ledford, "The Design and Use of Effective Employee Participation Groups: Implications for Human Resource Management," *Human Resource Management* 24, 1985, 413-428.

42. M. W. Pczak, "Quality Circles Come Home," *Quality Progress* 21, no. 12, 1988, 37-39.

43. T. L. Tang, P. S. Tollison, and H. D. Whiteside, "Quality Circle Productivity as Related to Upper-Management Attendance, Circle Initiation, and Collar Color," *Journal of Management* 15, 1989, 101-113.

44. Robert P. Steel and Kenneth R. Jennings, "Quality Improvement Technologies for the 90s," *Research in Organizational Change and Development* 6, 1992, 1-36.

45. Nealia Bruning and Patrick Liverpool, "Membership in Quality Circles and Participation in Decision Making," *The Journal of Applied Behavioural Sciences* 29, no. 1, 1993, 76-95.

46. Frank Shipper, "Quality Circles Using Small Group Formation," *Training and Development Journal*, May 1983, 82. See also Kathleen D. Ryan and Daniel K. Oestreich. *Driving Fear Out of the Workplace: How to Overcome Barriers to Quality, Productivity and Innovation*. San Francisco: Jossey-Bass, 1991.

47. Ira Levin and Jonathan Gottlieb, "Quality Management: Practice Risks and Value Added Roles for Organization Development Practitioners," *The Journal of Applied Behavioural Sciences* 29, no. 3, 1993, 296-310.

48. J. Juran. *Juran on Leadership for Quality: An Executive Handbook*. New York: The Free Press, 1989.

49. D. N. Burt, "Managing Product Quality through Strategic Purchasing," *Sloan Management Review* 30, no. 3, 1989, 39-48.; H. Noori, "The Taguchi Methods: Achieving Design and Output Quality," *Academy of Management Executive* 3, 1989, 322-326.

50. G. Keenan, "Lego: The Toy as Training Tool," *The Globe and Mail*, 7 May 1999, B-2, 5

51. W. E. Deming. *Out of the Crisis*. Cambridge, MA: Center for Advanced Engineering Study, MIT Press, 1986, 21.

52. Harry Costin, "Exploring the Concepts Underlying Total Quality Management," in *Total Quality Management*, ed. H. I. Costin. Fort Worth, TX: The Dryden Press, 1994, 7-26.

53. C. Pavsidis, "Total Quality Control: An Overview of Current Efforts," *Quality Progress* 17, no. 9, 1984, 28-29.

54. D. T. Kearns, "Leadership through Quality," *Academy of Management Executive* 4, no. 2, 1990, 86-89.

55. R. C. Camp. *Benchmarking: The Search for Industry Best Practices that Lead to Superior Performance*. Milwaukee, WI: Quality Press, 1990.

56. James Donnelly. *The Quality of People at Motorola*. Schaumberg, IL: Motorola, 1992.

57. Richard Blackburn and Benson Rosen, "Total Quality and Human Resource Management: Lessons Learned from Balridge Award Winning Companies," *Academy of Management Executive* 7, no. 3, 1993, 49-66.

58. William Sandy. *Forging the Productivity Partnership*. New York: McGraw-Hill, 1990.; Edgard Schein. *Organizational Culture and Leadership*. San Francisco: Jossey-Bass, 1991.

59. Gordon Arnaut, "The Tax Payer as the Customer," *Total Quality Imperative*, an insert to *Report on Business*, January 1995.

60. Alex Appleby and Cynthia Jackson, "The Impact of Lip on TQM and Staff Motivation in General Practice," *International Journal of Health Care Quality Assurance* 13, no. 2, 2000, 53-64.

61. Dotun Adebanjo and Dennis Kehoe, "An Evaluation of Quality Culture Problems in UK Companies," *International Journal of Quality Science* 3, no. 3, 1998, 275-286.

62. Survey results quoted by Robert Schaffer and Harvey A. Thompson, "Successful Change Programs Begin With Results," *Harvard Business Review*, January-February 1992, 80-89.

63. J. Richard Hackman and Ruth Wageman, "Total Quality Management: Empirical, Conceptual and Practical Issues," *Administrative Science Quarterly* 40, June 1995, 309-342.

64. Ageeth Balkema and Eric Molleman, "Barriers to the Development of Self-organizing Teams," *Journal of Managerial Psychology* 14, no. 2, 1999, 134-150.

65. Gillian Shapiro, "Employee Involvement: Opening the Diversity Pandora's Box?" *Personnel Review* 29, no. 3, 2000, 304-323.

Chapter 6

1. Dick Richards. *Artful Work*. San Francisco: Berrett-Koehler, 1995, 65.

2. Richard Yerema. *Canada's Top 100 Employers*. Toronto: Mediacorp Canada Inc., 2001, 232-234.

3. Timothy Schellhardt, "It's Time to Evaluate your Work, and All Involved Are Groaning," *Wall Street Journal*, 19 November 1994, A-1.

4. John Bernardin, Christine Hagan, Jeffrey Kane, and Peter Villanova, "Effective Performance Management," in *Performance Appraisal*, ed. James W. Smither. San Francisco: Jossey-Bass, 1998, 3.

5. Quoted in Alain Gosselin, John Werner, and Nicole Halle, "Ratee Preferences Concerning Performance Management and Appraisal," *Human Resource Development Quarterly* 8, 1997, 315-333.

6. Tom Coens and Mary Jenkins. *Abolishing Performance Appraisals*. San Francisco: Berrett-Koehler Publishers, Inc., 2000, 18.

7. Jeffry Timmons. *New Venture Creation: Entrepreneurship for the 21st Century*. Burr Ridge, IL: Irwin, 1994, 185.

8. J.S. Kane and E.E. Lawler, "Performance Appraisal Effectiveness: Its Assessments and Determinants," *Research in Organizational Behaviour* 1, 1980, 425-478.

9. Tom Coens and Mary Jenkins. *Abolishing Performance Appraisals*. San Francisco: Berrett-Koehler Publishers, Inc., 2000.

10. Wayne Cascio. *Applied Psychology in Human Resource Management*. Englewood, NJ: Prentice Hall, 1998, 69.

11. Luis Gomez-Mejia, David Balkin, Robert Cardy, and David Dimick. *Managing Human Resources*. Scarborough, ON: Prentice Hall, 2000, 209.

12. "Air Transat Hit by Fine, Lawsuit," *The Globe and Mail*, 7 September 2001, A1, A4; also see "Jet Leaked Fuel After Engine Change," *The Globe and Mail*, 29 August 2001, A1, A14.

13. M.M. Harris and J. Schaubroeck, "A Meta Analysis of Self-supervisor, Self-peer and Peer-supervisor ratings," *Personnel Psychology* 41, 1988, 43-62.

14. C.C. Hoffman, B.R. Nathan, and L.M. Holden, "A Comparison of Validation Criteria: Objective versus Subjective Performance Measures and Self versus Supervisory Ratings. *Personnel Psychology*, Vol. 44, 1991, 601-619.

15. G.H. Dobbins, J.L. Farh, and T.R. Lin. *Rating Anchors and Self Assessments of Ability: A Field Study*. Paper presented at the Annual Meeting of the Society for Industrial and Organizational Psychology, Montreal, Canada, 1992.

16. J. Peter Graves, "Let's Put Appraisal Back in Performance Appraisal II," *Personnel Journal*, December 1982, 918.

17. Kenneth Bettenhausen and Donald Fedor, "Peer and Upward Appraisals," *Group and Organization Management* 22, no. 2, June 1997, 236-263.

18. Sabrina Salam, Jonathan Cox, and Henry Sims Jr., "In the Eye of the Beholder: How Leadership Relates to 360-degree Performance Ratings," *Group and Organization Management* 22, no. 2, June 1997, 185-209.

19. Christopher Meyer, "How the Right Measures Help Teams Excel," in *Harvard Business Review on Measuring Performance*. Boston: HBS Publishing, 1998, 99-122.

20. K.N. Wexley and R. Klimoski, "Performance Appraisal: An Update," in *Research in Personnel and Human Resource Management, Volume 2*. eds. K.M. Rowland and G.R. Ferris. Greenwich, CN: Jai Press, 1984.

21. Alan Mohrman, Jr., Susan Resnick-West, and Bruce Prince. *Designing Performance Appraisal Systems*. San Francisco: Jossey Bass, 1989, 111.

22. J.W. Gilley and J. Davidson. *Quality Leadership*. New York: William M. Mercer, 1993.

23. Eric Auchard, "Big Brother Really Is Watching You," *The Vancouver Sun*, 2 June 2001, F-2.

24. J.S. Kane, "Performance Dstribution Assessment: A New Breed of Appraisal Methodology," in *Performance Appraisal: Assessing Human Behavior at Work*, eds. H.J. Bernardin and R.W. Beatty. Boston: Kent, 1984, 325-341.

25. For more details of the PDA methodology, see J.S. Kane, "Performance Distribution Assessment," in *Performance Assessment: Methods and Applications*, ed. R.A. Berk. Baltimore: Johns Hopkins University Press, 1986, 237-273.

26. Michael McGill and John Slocum. *The Smarter Organization*. New York: John Wiley, 1994, 159.

27. A.E. Pearson, "Muscle-build the Organization," *Harvard Business Review,* July-August 1987, 49-55.

Chapter 7

1. Dana Robinson and James Robinson (eds.). *Moving from Training to Performance*. San Francisco: Berrett-Koehler Publishers Inc., 1998, 5.

2. Virginia Galt, "Training Falls Short: Study," *The Globe and Mail*, 9 July 2001, M1.

3. Richard Swanson. *Analysis for Improving Performance*. San Francisco: Berrett-Koehler Publishers. 1996, 252.

4. Bernard Bass and James Vaughan. *Training in Industry: The Management of Learning*. Belmont, CA: Brooks/Cole Publishing, 1966, 78-79.

5. Irwin Goldstein. *Training Program Development and Evaluation*. Monterey, CA: Brooks/Cole Publishing, 1974, 45.

6. George Odiorne. *Training by Objectives*. NY: MacMillan Publishing Co. Inc., 1970, 102-103.

7. Ibid., 103.

8. Irwin Goldstein. *Training in Organizations*. Pacific Grove, CA: Brooks/Cole Publishing, 1993, 80.

9. Charles Perrow, "A Framework for the Comparative Analysis of Organizations," *American Sociological Review* 32, 1967, 194-208.

10. Michael E. Porter. *Competitive Strategy: Techniques for Analyzing Industries and Competitors*. New York: Free Press, 1980.

11. Michael Treacy and Fred Wiersema, "Customer Intimacy and Other Value Disciplines," *Harvard Business Review,* January-February 1993, 84-93.

12. For a more complete discussion of various training methods, see R.L. Craig (ed.). *The ASTD Training and Development Handbook* 2nd ed., New York: McGraw-Hill, 1996.

13. L. Gold, "Job Instruction: Four Steps to Success," *Training and Development Journal*, September 1981, 28-32.

14. Raymond Noe. *Employee Training and Development*. Irwin-McGraw-Hill, 1999, 173-174.

15. C.M. Solomon, "When Training Does Not Translate," *Workforce*, March 1997, 40-44.

16. "Businesses Find a New Class of E-learning," *The Globe and Mail*, 18 June 2001, R-12.

17. P.N. Blanchard and J.W. Thacker. *Effective Training*. NJ: Prentice Hall, 1999, 297-299.

18. H.F. Schwind, H. Das, and T. Wagar. *Canadian Human Resource Management* 5th ed., Toronto: McGraw-Hill Ryerson, 1999, 269.

19. Raymond Noe. *Employee Training and Development*. Irwin-McGraw-Hill, 1999, 172-173.

20. S. McCartney, "Colombia Says Pilot Error Was Cause of 1995 Crash of American Airlines Plane," *Wall Street Journal*, 30 September 1996, B-5.

21. K. Gersick, J. Davis, M. Hampton, and I. Lansberg. *Generation to Generation*. Boston, MA: Harvard Business School Press, 1997.; Thomas Kaplan, Gerard George, and George Rimler, "University Sponsored Family Business Programs: Program Characteristics, Perceived Quality and Member Satisfaction," *Entrepreneurship Theory and Practice*, Spring 2000, 65-75.

22. Aron Pervin, "Remember, Family Before Business," *The Globe and Mail*, 4 February 1999, B-10.

23. D.L. Kirkpatrick, "Techniques for Evaluating Training Programs," *Training and Development Journal* 33, no. 6, 1979, 78-92.

24. D.T. Campbell and J.C. Stanley. *Experimental and Quasi-experimental Designs for Research*. Chicago: Rand-McNally, 1963.

25. B. Geber, "Does your Training Make a Difference? Prove it!" *Training*, March 1995, 27-34.

26. J.J. Philips (1996). ROI: The search for best practices. *Training and Development*, February, 42-47.

27. J. Hassett, "Simplifying ROI," *Training*, September 1992, 53-57.

28. For an interesting discussion, see Andrew Stark, "What's the Matter with Business Ethics?" *Harvard Business Review*, May-June 1993, 43-48.

29. L. Kohlberg, "Moral Stages and Moralization, the Cognitive Developmental Approach," in *Moral Development and Behaviour*. T. Lickona, ed. New York: Holt, Rinehart and Winston, 1976.

30. Lavern Urlacher. *Small Business Entrepreneurship: An Ethics and Human Relations Perspective*. NJ: Prentice Hall, 1999, 66-68.

31. Karl Weick and Frances Westley, "Organizational Learning: Affirming an Oxymoron," in *Handbook of Organization Studies*. Stewart Clegg, Cynthia Hardy, and Walter Nord, eds. London: Sage, 1996, 440.

32. D'Arcy Jenish and Berton Woodward, "Canada's Top 100 Employers," *Maclean's*, 5 November 2001, 53. Also see Richard Yerema. *Canada's Top 100 Employers*. Toronto: Mediacorp Canada Inc, 2000, 200-202.

33. Peter M. Senge. *The Fifth Discipline: The Art and Practices of the Learning Organization*. New York: Doubleday, 1990.

34. Michael McGill, John Slocum and David Lei, "Management" Practices in Learning Organizations," *Organizational Dynamics*, Summer 1992, 5-17.

35. Ibid., 6-8

36. Ibid., 14.

37. Michael McGill and John Slocum. *The Smarter Organization*. NY: John Wiley, 1994, 159.

38. Jack Stack, "The Great Game of Business," *Inc*, June 1992, 53-66.

39. John Case, "The Change Masters", *Inc*, March 1992, 58-70.

40. Ibid.

41. Michael McGill and John Slocum. *The Smarter Organization*. NY: John Wiley, 1994, 175-176.

42. L. Rhodes and P. Amend, "The Turnaround," *Inc*, August 1986, 42-48.

43. Michael McGill and John Slocum. *The Smarter Organization*. NY: John Wiley, 1994, 171.

44. A. E. Pearson, "Muscle-Build the Organization," *Harvard Business Review*, July-August 1987, 49-55.

45. Robertson Davies. *A Mixture of Frailities*. London: MacMillan, 1958.

46. Weick and Westley, "Organizational Learning: Affirming an Oxymoron," 451.

47. Ibid., 452-454.

48. Ikujiro Nonaka, "The Knowledge-Creating Company," in *The Learning Imperative*. Robert Howard, ed. Boston: Harvard Business Review, 1993, 41-56.

49. Gareth Morgan. *Riding the Waves of Change*. San Francisco: Jossey-Bass, 1988, 72-74.

Chapter 8

1. Frederic Hudson. *The Handbook of Coaching*. San Francisco: Jossey-Bass, 1999, 14.

2. www.can.ibm.com

3. www.can.ibm.com/hr.career.html

4. Richard Yerema. *Canada's Top 100 Employers*. Toronto: Mediacorp Canada, 2000, 110.

5. D'Arcy Jenish, "Ten that Made the Grade," *Maclean's*, 5 November 2001, 54.; Richard Yerema. *Canada's Top 100 Employers*. Toronto: Mediacorp Canada, 2000, 48-49.

6. James Waldroop and Timothy Butler, "The Executive as a Coach," *Harvard Business Review*, Nov.-Dec. 1996, 112-117.

7. J.W. Gilley and N.W. Boughton. *Stop Managing, Start Coaching: How Performance Coaching Can Enhance Commitment and Improve Productivity*. New York: McGraw-Hill, 1996.

8. Peter Senge and Katrin Kaufer, "Communities of Leaders or No Leaders at All," in *Management 21C*. Subhir Chowdhury. London: Pearson Education Limited, 2000, 195.

9. Peter Senge, "Leading Learning Communities: The Bold, the Powerful, and the Invisible," in *The Leader of the Future*. F. Hesselbein, et al. (eds.). San Francisco: Jossey-Bass, 1996.

10. B. Bass. *Leadership and Performance Beyond Expectations*. New York: The Free Press, 1985.

11. J. Kotter. *A Force for Change: How Leadership Differs from Management*. New York: The Free Press, 1990.

12. Joseph Bailey quoted by Tom Coens and Mary Jenkins. *Abolishing Performance Appraisals*. San Francisco: Berrett-Koehler Publishers Inc., 2000, 100.

13. E.B. Bolton, "A Conceptual Analysis of the Mentor Relationship in Career Development of Women," *Adult Education* 30, 1980, 195-207.

14. A. Morrison, R. White, and Van Velsor. *Breaking the Glass Ceiling*. Reading, MA: Addison-Wesley, 1987.; G.R. Roche, "Much Ado about Mentors," *Harvard Business Review* 57, 1979, 14-28.

15. H. Levinson. *Mentoring: Socialization for Leadership*. Paper presented at the 1979 Academy of Management Meeting, Atlanta, Georgia.

16. Based on a number of past writings including H. Levinson. *Mentoring: Socialization for Leadership*. Paper presented at the 1979 Academy of Management Meeting, Atlanta, Georgia.; K.E. Kram, "Improving the Mentoring Process," *Training and Development Journal* 37, 1983, 40-43.; also see, K.E. Kram, "Mentoring in the Workplace," in *Career Development in Organizations*. D.T. Hall and Associates (eds.). San Francisco: Jossey Bass, 1986, 160-201.; S. Merriam, "Mentors and Protégés: A Critical Review of the Literature," *Adult Education Quarterly* 33, 1983, 161-173.; G.R. Roche, "Much Ado about Mentors," *Harvard Business Review* 57, 1979, 14-28.; R.J. Burke and C.A. Mckeen, "Developing Formal Mentoring Programs in Organizations," *Business Quarterly*, Winter 1989, 69-76.

17. K.E. Kram, "Improving the Mentoring Process," *Training and Development Journal* 37, 1983, 40-43.; also see, K.E. Kram, "Mentoring in the Workplace," in *Career Development in Organizations*. D.T. Hall and Associates (eds.). San Francisco: Jossey Bass, 1986, 160-201.

18. R.J. Burke and C.A. Mckeen, "Developing Formal Mentoring Programs in Organizations," *Business Quarterly*, Winter 1989, 69-76.

19. Jerry Gilley, Nathaniel Boughton, and Ann Maycunich. *The Performance Challenge*. MA: Perseus Books, 1999, 86.

20. G.R. Roche, "Much Ado about Mentors," *Harvard Business Review* 57, 1979, 14-28.

21. R.A. Noe, "Women and Mentoring: A Review and Research Agenda," *Academy of Management Review* 13, 1988, 65-78.

22. D.L. Nelson and J.D. Quick, "Professional Women: Are Distress and Disease Inevitable?," *Academy of Management Review* 10, 1985, 206-218.

23. Kira Vermond, "Men Join Struggle for Work-Life Balance," *The Globe and Mail*, 1 March 2002, C-1.

24. D'Arcy Jenish, "Ten that Made the Grade," *Maclean's*, 5 November 2001, 53.

25. Fredric Hudson. *The Handbook of Coaching*. San Francisco: Jossey-Bass Publishers, 1999, 20.

26. Fredric Hudson. *The Handbook of Coaching*. San Francisco: Jossey-Bass Publishers, 1999, 19.

27. J.G. Clawson and K.E. Kram, "Managing Cross-Gender Mentoring," *Business Horizons* 17, 1984, 22-32.

28. For example, see, H.F. Schwind, H. Das, and T. Wagar. *Canadian Human Resource Management*. Toronto: McGraw-Hill Ryerson, 2002, 516-519.; Rights Management Consultants. *Best Practices: Termination*. Scarborough, ON: Carswell, 1999, 4-4.

29. *Canadian Employment Law Today*. Toronto: MPL Communications Inc., 26 June 1999, 685-686.; Howard Levitt. *The Law of Dismissal in Canada*, 2nd ed., Aurora, ON: Canada Law Book, 1992.

30. Ontario Court of Appeal decision on 9 January 1999.; 168 D.L.R. (4th) 270.

31. *Lumber & Sawmill Workers' Union, Local 2537 and KVP Co.*, 1965, 16 L.A.C., 73, Ontario-Robinson, 85.

32. *Macmillan Bloedel Ltd and C.E.P. Local 76*, 1997, 65 L.A.C., 4th 240 (B.C.).

33. L. G. Hrebiniak. *Complex Organizations*. St. Paul, MN: West, 1978, 230-240.

34. Ibid.

35. A.S. Tannenbaum. *Control in Organizations*. New York: McGraw-Hill, 1968, 3.

36 Robert Williamson, "How to Say Thank You Without Breaking the Bank," *The Globe and Mail*, 14 November 1995, B-13.

37. Ibid.

38. Kevin Kelly. *Out of Control: The Rise of Neo-Biological Civilization*. Reading, MA: Addison-Wesley, 1994.

Chapter 9

1. Tom Coens and Mary Jenkins. *Abolishing Performance Appraisals*. San Francisco: Berrett-Koehler Publishers, 2000, 5-6.

2. Ibid., 49.

3. D. A. Whetten, "Sources, Responses and Effects of Organizational Decline," in *The Organizational Life Cycle*. J.R. Kimberly, et al. (eds.). San Francisco: Jossey-Bass, 1980, 355.

4. Fred Luthans and Terry L. Maris, "Evaluating Personnel Programs through the Reversal Technique," *Personnel Journal*, October 1979, 692-697.

5. George Odiorne, "Evaluating the Personnel Program," in *Handbook of Modern Personnel Administration*. Joseph Famularo (ed.). New York: McGraw-Hill, 1972, Chapter 8; See also Vytenis P. Kuraitis, "The Personnel Audit," *Personnel Administrator*, November 1981, 29-34.

6. George Odiorne, "Evaluating the Personnel Program," in *Handbook of Modern Personnel Administration*. Joseph Famularo (ed.). New York: McGraw-Hill, 1972.

7. Nora Spinks, "The Absence of Absence in the Changing Workplace," *Canadian HR Reporter*, 24 March 1997, 19-20.

8 For example see, Russ Kisby, "The ROI of Healthy Workplaces," *Canadian HR Reporter*, 20 October 1997, 31.

9. Brian Orr, "The Challenge of Benchmarking HR Performance," *Canadian HR Reporter*, 21 April 1997, 6.

10. For example, see Ian Cunningham and Philip James, "Absence and Return to Work: Towards a Research Agenda," *Personnel Review* 29, no. 1, 2000, 33-47.

11. For example, see Linda Alker and David McHugh, "Human Resource Maintenance?" *Journal of Managerial Psychology* 15, no. 4, 2000, 303-323.

INDEX